The Christian Life And The History of Israel

Discovering how Israel's journey Parallels the Christian's spiritual walk today

Volume I

By Dr. Paul L. Dunteman, Th. D.

The Christian Life And The History of Israel:
Discovering how Israel's journey
Parallels the Christian's spiritual walk today
Volume I
by Dr. Paul L. Dunteman, Th. D.

Printed in the United States of America

ISBN 978-1-60791-274-3

The author is available for conferences and
may be contacted at the following address:
paulldunteman@yahoo.com

www.xulonpress.com

Acknowledgements

To my wife, Carmen Leticia, whose prayers, suggestions, and occasional prodding helped motivate me to finish this book.

To my children, John, Sandra, David, Joshua, Daniel, and Steven, who were there to encourage me and to believe in the value of this book for others.

To the prayer and fellowship group of pastors and other Christian leaders, who have encouraged me and held me up in prayer constantly as this book was being written, thank you all, and may God bless you.

To the people of the Nation of Israel. Throughout the ages, beginning with the call of your father Abraham, you have held the revelation of the One True God for all of mankind. You did this while enduring the hatred of those same nations, who also benefited from your unique revelation from the One True God. May the One True God bless you! It is my hope that the reader might see the light of your history shed on the internal walk and pilgrimage of the New Testament believer in Jesus.

To the faculty of Trinity Evangelical Divinity School. I thank you for all your patience and highest scholarship. I am especially indebted to Dr. Kenneth Kantzer for the basic ideas on revelation in chapter 2.

To the faculty of Jacksonville Theological Seminary. I thank you for all of your special insights into the text of Scripture. I am especially indebted to Dr. Craig P. Lokken in his course, The Old Testament, for the basic explanation of the Old Testament sacrifices in chapter 7.

Writing about the events of Israel's history in the Old Testament period, the Apostle Paul says (I Corinthians 10:11):

"Now these things happened to them as an example, and they were written for our instruction, upon whom the ends of the ages have come."

Contents

Volume I:
Prolegomena, The Infant, the Natural Man, and the Carnal Man

Preface

In the mountains of East Central Turkey the rainwater runs into a valley and collects to form the beginnings of the Euphrates River. A bit farther east is the origin of the Tigris River. These two rivers meander slowly south and eastward across the plains of Iraq, emptying into the Persian Gulf. On their journey, they pass by Babylon, the cradle of all civilization, from whence our ancestors were scattered to the ends of the world. Babylon represents the last place that the human race was together as one with one language and government.

It is not surprising that the Tigris-Euphrates valley is the dividing point between East and West in civilization, thought, and culture. To the East the emphasis has been on escaping the ravages of the individual ego. Hinduism, Buddhism and other religions try to attain peace by the death of one's individual consciousness and unity with the universe, however it is perceived. The unity of all of existence was emphasized to the point of pantheism-the belief that the universe was god. Man's individuality was seen as an illusion that needed enlightenment to overcome.

For those who were especially tied to their individuality, there was the continuous repetition of reincarnations, through which they returned time after time in various forms until they became fit for union with the cosmic consciousness in order to remain there in peace. Thus, a sort of living death was sought in order to enter into Nirvana-a state of spiritual union with the universe. This death included the end of one's selfish goals-especially where the individual mind and will were concerned, and resulted in a feeling of peace.

To the West of these great river systems, the emphasis was the opposite. Here the human being was valued as an individual. Western civilization has begun by affirming the value of individual consciousness as the beginning point of culture, truth, and understanding. Though people differ among themselves, individual thought and effort are valued in the West. It has been my privilege throughout my Western education to read the great works of Plato, Aristotle, Caesar, Cicero, and others in the Greek and Latin, respectively, and to appreciate the premium that is placed on philosophical learning by the Greeks and technical learning by the Romans. Other nations in the West have followed in this background, forming what is called in general Western Civilization.

Today one can stand back and see the limitations of these two perspectives on existence-the Eastern and the Western. People throughout the world have noticed these limitations and have sought to learn from the others. The West has long been deluged with gurus, and much of the psychotherapy in the West has consciously adopted Eastern thought into its methodology. The highly prized individualists of the West cannot handle the pressures and tensions of facing a world in which they are in constant struggle with others to survive, and the accumulation of riches is a hopeless, never ending, self-inflicted burden which can never bring peace because one never has enough.

In addition to the dissatisfaction with materialism and other practical exercises of the will, Western philosophy has fallen in shambles at the beginning of the 21st century. The optimism of Descartes who began all philosophy with man's independent human reasoning through the statement, "I think, therefore I am," has given way to modern nihilism and cynicism. Time and time again the optimistic philosophers have thought that they had a good line of reasoning starting from themselves and working outward, only to be shot down. Starting with himself, man has not been able to reason his way up to God, Ultimate knowledge, Cosmic Consciousness or any other thing transcendent. Thus the West is bankrupt in itself and dabbling in Eastern mysticism through various leaps of faith, seeking fulfillment in the spiritual dimension.

Meanwhile, those of the East have been discovering that man's individuality is not so bad, after all. The colonial era, followed by independence, has left these nations seeking fulfillment in the material sphere. The postwar development of the Asian countries is the greatest illustration of this revolution. It is not enough for these people to revere their ancestors and seek unity with the Cosmos, they want to live better here now.

Yes, those on both sides of these rivers are dissatisfied with their limited viewpoints, and now have imported and adapted many elements from the other side of the rivers. Are they now satisfied? No. Modern man still holds two separate compartments in his mind, and cannot reconcile them: the material and the spiritual. They both lead different directions and tend to pull him apart. The science of his workaday world cannot coordinate with his weekend binges of alcohol, drugs, Eastern Religion, or whatever spiritual fulfillment he seeks. His individual consciousness-so important for his 8 to 5 job Monday through Friday-is left behind as he "blows his mind" on the weekend.

What is the answer that can unify all of existence for man? Where is the Spirit that can sustain the law of gravity and fill us with peace and joy at the same time? How can my individuality be important without overcoming me with neuroses and psychoses?

What is the answer that can put together all of the pieces?

When all of mankind scattered from the Tower of Babel to go East or West, the God of the Bible called one man named Abraham and set him aside to restore what had been lost to the ends of the earth. Abraham and his people Israel represent neither Eastern thought, Western thought, nor a human synthesis of the two. The truth that is given to us through the Old Testament and the New Testament is fully truth--whether in the material sphere or in the spiritual sphere.

How can this be? The God that chose Abraham and his descendants and gave to them the Old and New Testaments has two basic names: Jehovah and Elohim. In the character of his name Elohim God created and sustains the universe. The Old Testament begins:

"In the beginning God (Elohim) created the heavens and the earth (Genesis 1:1)." In the character of this name God is the all-powerful Creator.

Everyone has to deal with God as Creator because they are creatures. In the nineteenth century among the liberals there was a movement towards natural religion. The idea was to worship God through one's experience of nature. This sometimes took the form of pantheism, the belief that all nature is God, as in Eastern mysticism. Other times it took the form of a worship of God as Creator and separate from the creation. The old line liberal preachers from the last century spoke thus of natural religion. Many in the West in the nineteenth and early part of the twentieth century thought that this was the only way to follow or understand God.

Others were not satisfied. They related to God as Creator in one compartment of their mind, often confused with the theory of evolution. On the other hand, they began to prepare for a "leap of faith" into some existential spiritual personal experience with God, thus forming the more recent neo-orthodox movement. But to what spirit would they leap? Is one's existential experience sufficient criterion to judge religion as valid? Should Christianity be cut from historic and scientific ties to become another Gentile religion?

No! The personal experience of a relation with the God of Abraham, Isaac, and Jacob requires is in a sense a "leap of faith," but the leap is into the arms of the Creator. God's other principal name, Jehovah, describes Him as He reveals Himself to people. In Isaiah 6: 1-5 God reveals Himself to Isaiah personally as "Jehovah of Hosts." In this name God can be known personally, and man can have fellowship with him. He acts personally just as we can, but without limits. When Jesus walked on the water, God as Elohim sustained the law of gravity and the other laws of Creation, and as Jehovah He exerted a contrary force to hold Him up, just like a person could choose to do of his own free will if he could.

One time I was talking with a Rabbi friend and he asked me my opinion about Barth, Teilhard de Chardin, and Kierkegaard. I told him I thought that they were all very clever pagans, along with Buber among the Jewish people. He was very surprised and asked why I thought that. I recalled the story of Elijah and the 450 prophets of Baal on Mt. Carmel in I Kings 18. To show He was the real God, Jehovah sent real fire and burned up the sacrifice of Elijah, while the other gods could not do it. "The key to the difference between a true Jew or Christian on the one side, and a pagan on the other," I concluded, "is the confession of the Jewish people after the fire fell (verse 39): 'Jehovah, He is Elohim! Jehovah, He is Elohim.'"

The personal local God that the Hebrew prophets converse with was none other than the Creator God Himself. The pagans had spirits, as well, and could communicate with them. They had prophecies and revelations and experiences in their personal relation with their gods, but the spirits behind the Gentile religions were only themselves created spirits who were in rebellion against the Creator. In Psalm 96:5 we read: "For all the gods of the nations are idols (weaklings), but Jehovah made the heavens." Hebrew monotheism does not deny the existence of other gods, but rather recognizes them as created spirits that are in rebellion against the God of Israel Who is the Creator, and the only one worthy of any recognition at all.

To disassociate the spirit of one's religious experience from the Creator is to be a pagan. To follow the God of Israel is to accept His revelation on the material, historical, and scientific level as being absolutely true, as well as His religious revelation. To follow modern science, accepting the theory of evolution, higher criticism of the Bible (thus to deny the character of God as Elohim), is to be left "leaping in faith" to find a Jehovah who is a different Jehovah, and not the Creator. Thus, these neo-orthodox do not transcend the dilemma of pagans: i.e. that their internal existential experience and vision of the world are out of harmony with the external historical and scientific reality.

When I was still in seminary, Karl Barth visited and was asked if he could have gotten a splinter if he had rubbed his hand on the cross of Jesus. Barth refused to answer that question. For him those two spheres remain separated in his mind, and in my mind he remains a pagan still in this. Like the ancient Israelites I would think that the God of Israel was no better than the gods of the Canaanites if He had not sent real fire from heaven to consume Elijah's sacrifice on Mt. Carmel. But He did send real fire. What if, as the neo-orthodox claim, my experience of the death, burial, and resurrection of Jesus is only a fantasy to help me get by in this life? Like the Apostle Paul, I must conclude (I Cor. 15:19): "If we have hoped in Christ in this life only, we are of all men most to be pitied." Paul could not contemplate a fantasy resurrection to help him get by in this world-only a real historical resurrection that is the model of Paul's own future resurrection. When we die, we don't need a fantasy resurrection-we need the real thing.

What can we say to modern man in this book? You are probably tired of studies in the material sphere of existence, and materialism itself probably alternately bores you and consumes your time and energies. You may be tired of "leaping in faith" to experiences with one spirit after another which do not satisfy, and you ask, "Is this all there is?" The East is trying to achieve a death of the human ego, but they have no resurrection-nothing left to do in the material world. On the other hand, the West is trying to actualize or resurrect something that has not died. They cannot escape the neuroses and psychoses and phobias of the "human condition." What is the answer here? In the God of Israel we have both the death of self that the Eastern peoples are seeking with its peace and deliverance from neuroses and psychoses, but we also have a resurrection of Christ in us-a Christ who loves other people through us and is concerned about all of life, including the material sphere.

We have good news for you! There is a True God out there! If you are accustomed to the "leap of faith" approach, then go ahead and leap into his arms, and believe His Scripture. You will then find that the Spirit you leaped to is also the True Creator God and works in history and rules over science. If you are given over to reason, then call upon the Creator and investigate His creation. However, I ask you to come into a real personal relationship with that Spirit who set up and sustains the laws behind our scientific endeavor. Starting either place, you may come into a full relation with the God of Israel. Don't seek after New Age spirits (demons), drugs, alcohol, or other false spirits, and don't feed on the empty husks of materialism without spiritual fulfillment. Seek the True God of Israel, for in Him you have everything fulfilled and resolved. This is the God that called out Abraham in Genesis 12:1-3 and sent him and his descendants to take his message to all mankind so that in him "all the families of the earth would find their blessing.

The history of the nation of Israel has always held a fascination for me from the time of my youth, even before I sensed the calling of God to dedicate myself to teach the Bible at the tender young age of seven. As I grew up, so did my understanding of the Scriptures, including the Old Testament. After learning Hebrew, I have become fascinated with the relationship of the history of Israel to the Christian life. In many ways the Christian life is an internalization of the history of Israel. I don't believe that this is due to the action of internalization by the individual Christian, but rather due to the design of God. In human flesh, culture, language, history, geography, and in many other ways He led in the history of Israel to sculpture it into the model of the World to Come, into which we enter upon believing in Jesus.

If the history of Israel is the perceptual model, or Gestalt, of our life in the Olam Habba (World to Come), how can we make the applications to our lives from there? In my many years of study of the Old Testament, I have found a consistent principle of using the roots of the words in Hebrew to make the applications for personal guidance. It is my hope that the reader will be drawn to understand and love the God of Israel through these pages dedicated to His glory, and find guidance for his life now and hope for eternity.

Above all, I want the reader to find the God whose Truth is True in all dimensions—physical and spiritual—and Whose presence alone can fill the void in one's life with true love, true meaning, and a true glorious future. Also, He alone can give one a fully unified worldview with His Absolute Truth that is True for all dimensions of existence.

Dr. Paul L. Dunteman
Miami, Florida

Introduction

As a youth I had a fascination with history and geography, which has not left me today. Even at a young age, I saw in the history of Israel a sort of pattern that suggested the different stages of human life. I was fascinated as I read how God talked about raising the nation of Israel as a son who later rebelled against Him (Hosea 12:1), or a daughter who later became a harlot (Ezekiel 16). While not seeking to condemn Israel in particular for these problems, I sought to see the problem in universal terms. Each one of us as an individual has this tendency to rebel against God. I was interested in the stages of Israel's history and the parallel stages in my life. How can these two be connected?

As my understanding grew, I developed the counseling technique of identifying myself or someone else with a certain stage in Israel's history and counseling them according to the Scriptures that were about that stage. I compared infants and young children with the patriarchal period, when these men had a relationship with God apart from law. The next stage was the captivity in Egypt, which corresponded to the natural man in the New Testament. The crossing of the Red Sea (actually the Reed Sea) corresponded to Christian baptism. The third stage of Israel was the wilderness wanderings, which correspond to the carnal period of a new believer. The crossing of the Jordan River corresponded to a special transition between the carnal and spiritual phase of a Christian's life. Finally, the conquest and possession of Canaan corresponds to the spiritual man, or mature believer in Jesus. The captivities and restorations were an unnecessary detour because of Israel's rebellion during their time in Canaan, and they correspond to a possible detour in the life of a Christian for the same reason.

However good these comparisons were, a real depth of discovery lay just below the surface. As I began to read the Old Testament in the original Hebrew and Aramaic (a few parts of the Old Testament are written in Aramaic, but most is in Hebrew), I found a whole new depth of learning. In addition to the stages of life that corresponded to the stages in human life, I found that there were many items corresponding to the Christian's pilgrimage which were made through the roots of the words in Hebrew. For example, the enemies of Israel all have spiritual problems referred to in the root of their names in Hebrew.

The word "Amorites" comes from the root from which the verb "to talk" comes. Thus, they refer to sins of speaking wrong. When the 10 spies gave a bad report about Canaan when Israel was about to enter, God decreed that Israel would wander in the desert another 38 years. At this announcement, some decided to enter anyway, and were defeated by the Amorites (Deuteronomy 1:44). As they talked bad about God, they lost to the "talkers." After those 38 more years were over, the Israelites entered the Promised Land from the east and had to defeat the Amorites on the east side of the Jordan River. This king was Sihon (complaint), King of Heshbon (accounting). When we take account of what God gave to others and compare it to what He gave to us, we usually complain as a result. This is another sin of the tongue. Israel could not get into the land from either direction without defeating Amorites; and in the same way, the believer in Jesus cannot become a spiritual believer without winning some victory over the use of his tongue. Since the word Canaan refers to humility, according to its root, the believer cannot begin to make progress toward humility without learning some control over his speech.

Since Canaan means humility, we see that the spiritual stage of a believer's life is to conquer our humility. This apparent paradox is understood in the light of II Corinthians 10: 4-5 where we are told to wage war to control our minds and "bring into captivity every thought to the obedience of Christ." This war for humility is won by conquering certain spiritual problems, just as the war for the possession of Canaan consisted in the defeat and annihilation of certain peoples. It is not the purpose of this introduction to tell everything at this point, but rather to explain the technique and to whet the reader's appetite for the upcoming chapters. The Old Testament stories are easy to understand, but not always easy to interpret and apply in the context of the Christian life.

I must confess that I have enjoyed the preaching of many Black and Hispanic preachers and their ability to make the Old Testament stories live in their applications to the believer's life. However, they did not always have a consistent method of explaining the comparisons. They were lacking a hermeneutic that would give them consistency in their applications to persons and events of the Old Testament in the Christian life. I have taught this material as a part of Bible geography in Mexico for a number of years, as well as submitting it in papers at Jacksonville Theological Seminary, where there are many African-Americans on the faculty, and these people have become interested in using the material.

I warn the reader that the style of writing here is not linear logic. I often repeat myself on material from chapter to chapter, and I do not apologize for this repetition. The Lord made me left-handed, and the right side of my brain is more highly developed. This means that I tend to think in pictures. Like a painter, I am painting pictures with words about the different topics in this book. If a particular teaching is related to several topics, I will repeat the teaching in different chapters. I do not apologize for the repetition, and I do not consider the repetition to be an error on my part. The reader is asked to apply the material to a different topic every time it is presented, and should benefit from seeing it from different angles.

This book can also explain to a modern Jewish person the character of Biblical Christianity, as well as explaining similarities and differences between us. Without denying the absolute historical truth of the Old Testament, we can see applications and lessons for the church today from that history. I hope that any Jewish person that may read this book will see that the one True God sent multidimensional messages for all generations from his nation's history. The struggles of the nation of Israel are also the struggles of the Christian as one dead, buried, and resurrected to the Olam Habba

(World to Come), even while he is still walking this planet. I hope also to convey my hope and joy as I contemplate the victory of an Israel ruling over all nations at the end of history, comparing it to the victory of the Christian over the powers of darkness in his life.

Our method for deriving the comparisons between Israel and the modern Christian's life will consist of the following steps:

1. Remember that we are comparing real historical events, persons, geography, culture, language, and other items from This World to a whole different dimension: the internal life of the Christian in the World to Come. There will not be exact equivalences, but the overall perceptual model will be similar. The correspondence will be like a to a', b to b', etc.
2. We will first identify the Hebrew word—usually a noun, which refers to something or some people in the history of Israel.
3. Next we will identify the Hebrew root of this word. The root in Hebrew usually consists of three consonants.
4. When we find this root in the Hebrew lexicon, we will then analyze every word under that root and their basic meanings.
5. From this list of different meanings, we will then seek for a single basic meaning that would underlie all of the meanings.
6. We would compare that underlying meaning to try to find a connection between the original Hebrew context and the sphere of the Christian life, taking into consideration the stage of development where it is.
7. From this connection, we will then try to come up with a single word that would reflect the same concept for the Christian's internal pilgrimage that the original Hebrew word meant in the context of the Old Testament narrative.
8. Finally, we will tell the composite story of Israel and the New Testament believer at that stage in the two narratives in such a way that the correspondence may be seen, especially in terms of the practical applications for our own lives. Where we teach concerning a doctrine, it will be made very

clear in the light of the story so that anyone can understand it and apply it much more easily than otherwise.

While these steps are not always shown in detail, the author follows them almost automatically after many years of using them.

As the book was organized, the parallel stories of Israel and the New Testament believer are interwoven and compared in such a way that the average person can follow them for their own reading enjoyment and edification. However, for the more scholarly who understand the Biblical languages of Hebrew, Aramaic, and Greek, the footnotes will give sources and help for understanding the above steps better. Indeed, as one seeks to go deeper, he can begin to apply these steps to many more Hebrew roots than this book contains, and, thus, go beyond this modest beginning.

If this book has a unique contribution, it is a systematic approach with replicable results extended over the whole history of Israel and comparing it to the whole internal walk of the Christian. It is a systematic approach, rather than isolated sparks of enlightenment that have been found in a few works. We are comparing the whole history of Israel in the Biblical period to the whole internal spiritual pilgrimage of the believer from new birth to heaven. Wherever there are periods that are missed or skipped deliberately, the reader who knows the Hebrew may develop this running comparison through the Hebrew roots and a discernment of their application to the New Testament Christian walk.

At the end it is hoped that the Christian might locate himself somewhere in the narrative and look out for the next steps along the way. He may see the way out of a trap into which he has fallen or a trap to avoid. He may see the light at the end of a tunnel that has him discouraged, or simply find the determination to continue from a glimpse of the victory at the end of the pilgrimage.

If the reader is helped in any way at all from this humble attempt to shed light on the Christian walk from Old Testament Israel's history, the efforts of this author will have served their purpose. It is possible that the reader may disagree with the author in the development of ideas from Hebrew roots on occasion. However, it will be clearly seen that the evidence is overwhelming that the Hebrew roots with their comprehensive reference actually bridge the gap between the material and spiritual worlds and provide the background for the application of the Old Testament historical truths to the lives of modern Christians. Let us now begin with by setting the stage for the walk by considering who is God, how God reveals Himself to man, and who man is. After that we will begin the narrative together. May God bless you in your pilgrimage on this earth. May you come to know and love the God named Jehovah and Elohim as you understand Him in both the spiritual and material spheres of existence.

Dr. Paul L. Dunteman
Miami, Florida

Chapter 1

Come to the Waters: An Inquiry into God's Characteristics As They Satisfy Man's Greatest Longings and Needs

People have long sought to relate to a Supreme Being by working up to Him or seeking to appease Him in some way through a religion, but few are satisfied. People sense that there is a God out there somewhere, and they recognize their need for contact with Him. In most cases, where people have not come into a relation with a Higher Being, Whom they may call God, they sense that something is missing in their lives, and they are not satisfied with the substitutes that they have found instead.

In the light of many failures of people to find God on their own, many in modern times have come to the conclusion that there is no God at all—no Supreme Being Who can meet their needs. They see man himself as a miniature god, who is trying to create his own meaning in life. For them, religion is an individual self-created fantasy to help one get by in this world. It is also evident that man is dissatisfied with this approach to God. Where can a modern man go for spiritual fulfillment?

There are two spiritual options open to modern man. The first is to seek contact with whatever spirit he might encounter. The New Age movement encourages its followers to get their own spirit-guide without thinking that there might be different sides and a conflict in the spirit world. Other people contact spirits through the use of drugs and alcohol. The Apostle John in Revelation warned of sorcery in the last days (Rev. 9:21 & 18:23), using the word *pharmakia* (*φαρμακια*), from which we get our word pharmacy. This sorcery involves demonic possession through the use of drugs. Also, some try to obtain spiritual fulfillment by witchcraft, through which a person becomes a medium for a spirit to communicate with people.

The final option open to modern man is the option for which man was created: to be filled with the Spirit of the Creator God directly. In this special relation with God all of man's deepest needs are met because this is the purpose and the relation for which we are all created. Jesus says in John 7:37: "If anyone is thirsty, let him come to Me and drink." Jesus promised to provide cold waters for every thirsty soul that would come to Him. Jesus did not reproach people for their spiritual thirst, but rather for the many false ways they have for fulfilling it.

In his book *Inside Out*, Dr. Larry Crabbe quotes Jeremiah 2:13, and then comments on it. "My people have committed two sins: They have forsaken Me the spring of living water, and have dug their own cisterns, broken cisterns that cannot hold water."[1] ... Observe carefully that in our text, God assumes that His people are thirsty but He never condemns them for that thirst. Thirst is not the problem. Neither of the two sins that He rebukes them for involves the fact that people are thirsty."[1]

God expects people to be thirsty for spiritual fulfillment that only He can give. Their sin is involved in the fact that they want to run their own lives and look for that fulfillment in their own way. The specific sins that they commit are really the variety of false ways that they try to find their fulfillment without God. As Crabbe continues: "The Scriptures consistently expose people as both thirsty and foolish. We long for the satisfaction we were built to enjoy, but we all move away from God to find it. An inside look, then, can be expected to uncover two elements imbedded deeply in our heart: (1) thirst or *deep longings* for what we do not have; and (2) stubborn independence reflected in *wrong strategies* for finding the life we desire" (Emphasis by the author).[2]

If the other options represent our foolish strategies to find fulfillment, what is the real fulfillment that God intended for us? In this chapter it will be our purpose to explore the nature of God, to the extent of what we can know about Him, and to show how we are designed to find fulfillment in a loving relationship with Him. Later on, we will see how we need to be in that relationship with God so that we receive His guidance and provision for our human journey on this earth.

In this chapter we will look at each of the three elements of human experience: being, perceiving, and doing. Under each one of these we will look first at the human condition with respect to it, including especially where we as human beings suffer and are thirsty for fulfillment. We will especially want to see where the hurts and needs are. Next, we will examine the attribute or attributes of God that relate to that topic and need. Finally, we will seek to see how man can find his fulfillment in that area of his life through a personal relationship with the God of the Bible.

Next, we will give a summary of the human experience apart from any relation with God and contrast it to the human experience in a full relationship with God. Lastly, we will consider some suggestions as to how to enjoy deeper spiritual fulfillment as a human being through our relationship with God. In pursuing a discussion of God's attributes through an understanding of our human experience of the world, it will not be with the desire of limiting or judging God by our experience of Him, but rather to show the value of knowing God to people who have neither a desire nor an inclination to know Him, for God alone can satisfy man's thirst for fulfillment and meaning.

I. Being (Ontology).

The most basic problem of our human condition is that we experience ourselves as infinite beings trapped in a finite condition. For example, we have a feeling that we will live forever, yet we experience death around us constantly. We are hungry for absolute truth, but find ourselves in a morass of pious subjectivism while groping to find the key to transcendent truth during a very limited lifetime. Our drive to know all things crashes continually against the limitations of the "finiteness" of our five senses, short life, and limited reasoning and fails as death knocks on our door. Thus, limited knowledge with a thirst for infinite knowledge leaves us humans unfulfilled and frustrated. We set out to do wonderful deeds and build a better world, but experience alienation, crime, and warfare as each of us sets out to build his one-man kingdom at the expense of others. What can we do to find relief from the suffering of the human condition?

In the logical order of being, perceiving, and acting, being must come first, for existence is implied in the process of perceiving and knowing, as well as in doing. In our quest for authenticity, we must invariably begin with the ontological questions. Who am I? Where did I come from? Where am I going? These questions knock first and loudest at the door of our conscious reflection and demand an answer in order that we may build our reasoning on an adequate foundation.

Descartes begins his philosophy with man and attempts to reason out to find truth. His famous starting point was the statement, "*cogito, ergo sum*," which means, "I think, therefore I exist." He defends his starting point, as compared to walking as proving existence in the following way, "For example, you have no right to make the inference: *I walk, hence I exist,* except in so far as our awareness of walking is a thought; it is of this alone that the inference holds good, not of the motion of the body, which sometimes does not exist, as in dreams, when, nevertheless, I appear to walk. Hence from that fact that I think that I walk I can very well infer the existence of the mind which so thinks, but not that of the body which walks. So it is also in all other cases."[3]

Here Descartes establishes that the activity of the mind proves existence, but what kind of existence? In the absence of standard, unified human knowledge of our purpose, many people have gravitated to many religious and philosophical systems, consciously or unconsciously. Since we cannot live in an ideological vacuum, many of us set out to construct a belief to help him get by in the world. The varied systems either clash as ideologies or merge into a syncretistic philosophy. In the final analysis, these different systems do not give us satisfactory meaning because they do not transcend the human experience and limitations.

For man in this situation, it is a good start to say that being does not come from non-being, nor life from an inanimate origin, hence the ontological argument for the existence of God. Thus, we need to realize that we are in need of a Superior Being that could give us life. At the same time, we have no contact with that Superior Being through our five senses. In order to have meaning, most of us adhere to a religious or philosophical system through a faith that goes beyond the reach of his senses. Others, however, choose to restrict themselves to just what comes through the senses and what they know about their mental makeup. The latter are natural philosophers.

There are some who are trying to interact with spiritual power as they experience it intuitively within themselves. Christina Grof, in a book about recovering from addiction, puts it this way: "We discussed the pitfall of assuming that spirituality is separate from ordinary life, that it has to do with an unreachable, external God who transcends the world. During our recovery, many of us recognize the immanent divine, the Higher Power in and around us. We have a new lease on life, as well as a new strength to live it."[4]

These people see the importance of tapping into a spiritual power that is greater than them, but Grof specifically rejects the exclusivist claims of the Christianity in which she was raised in favor of an inclusive eastern orientation. She treats as valid whatever spiritual contact anyone experiences or whatever they call it.

Grof is right that we need spiritual input. She even talks of being thirsty for fulfillment and that it is by union with the divine, but she envisions it as something available to all people through a process of progressive 12-step enlightenment. She says, "As we become freer and more accepting, we awaken to our own wholeness. The word *whole* means healthy, free from wound or injury, healed. Wholeness is also defined as the unity or totality of complex components. This is what we have been thirsting for—and it is possible to find it in our everyday world. As we experience the spiritual awakening that the twelfth step promises, we unite with the divine, we retrieve that core of wholeness within."[5]

The problem that Grof and all mystics leave is this: How can we know if that ultimate reality is personal or not? Mysticism tends to do away with individual personality as one's identity is seen as being merged with the oneness of the universe. Does this answer satisfactorily the ontological questions? The mystic sees our particular personality as a problem to be overcome—not a beautiful reflection of a Personal God. Since the mystics' god is not personal, there is no personal I-thou relationship possible.

What is God like in His very Being that satisfies man in his deepest ontological needs? I believe that they are four: personality, self-existence, immutability, and eternity. We will consider these ontological characteristics of God as they relate to man's ontological quest.

God is Personal. As was mentioned above, one may conceive of the Ultimate Being as either personal or non-personal. The mystics think of Him as non-personal, while Christians think of Him as existing eternally in three persons: Father, Son, and Holy Spirit—the quintessence of personhood. The mystic goes through exercises to awaken his perception to his oneness with an impersonal universe, as he sees it, but there is no personal relationship.

In our human experience, we note that the privation of personal relationships has negative effects on people, and they are more satisfied when they are again in the company of others. Though most often our greatest pain comes from interpersonal relationships, so also does our greatest joy. Our experience of marriage shows how a union of two persons produces something better than the sum of the two individuals comprising it. Why should the Ultimate Reality be impersonal?

In the human experience of the world, we observe that the existence of complex objects implies the presence of intelligence, which is an element of personality. The teleological argument for the existence of the traditional God goes beyond mere cause and effect. The argument has been presented in philosophy the following way. A man walking on a deserted beach finds a watch. He is most likely to conclude that that watch is evidence of an intelligent watchmaker. In addition to being true as an evidence of the existence of God in the traditional sense, the teleological argument is also evidence that He is a Personal Being.

It is difficult for this author to imagine how someone can believe that the universe with all of its intricacies and details just happened by chance, as materialistic evolution asserts. The intricacies of each human cell, let alone the organs, such as the eye defy the greatest faith of the materialists to produce a sufficient cause through an impersonal process. For example, human speech consists of five different abilities, located on five different genes, and all five must be present for language to occur. Then it must occur in two persons at once—one male and one female—in order for it to yield greater adaptability to the environment for natural selection to favor it.

In the same way, we human beings are made to experience the highest level of fulfillment in personal relationships. If the One True God that Exists is Personal, then our very highest fulfillment would lie in a personal relationship with this Being, not a mystic loss of our personhood through merging it with an impersonal universe.

God is also Self-existent. At this point, the mystical pantheistic may agree substantially. However, we must also ask if an impersonal god that is a self-existing and self-sustaining universe would tend toward more disorder, or randomness. If nature = god = substance, as Spinoza declared, then how is it that any closed system of matter and energy will tend toward more disorder? Our understanding of whatever the Supreme Being was should include self-existence in a somewhat steady state—not an ever-increasing chaos.

The God of the Bible is separate from the universe He created, but nevertheless sustains it. In Psalm 102:25-28 we can see how God can be Self-existent and eternal, but create a temporary universe that is wearing out: "Of old You founded the earth, and the heavens are the work of Your hands. Even they will perish, but You endure; and all of them shall wear out like a garment; like clothing You will change them and they will be changed. But You are the same, and Your years will not come to an end. The children of Your servants will continue, and their descendants will be established before You."

It is the fact that this world is wearing out that shows that mysticism, with its affirmation that the universe is an impersonal god, is wrong. The Ground of Being does not itself consist of something that is wearing out, or tending to more disorder. In fact, if we take the universe as a whole, including all matter and energy, it is a closed system for the mystic and the materialist, for they admit of nothing beyond. Our experience with this universe is that in closed systems disorder increases. Therefore, we must come to one of two conclusions: that there was outside input, that was neither matter nor energy, when it came into being all ordered, from which order it is gradually degenerating now, or that there is a continual input of that which is neither matter nor energy to produce a continual positive evolution of greater order. In either case that input can be neither matter nor energy. The only other thing that could be considered here that is neither matter nor energy we may call spirit.

God is that Spirit Who gives creative input and life itself into the universe. In the same way that the Psalmist saw God as the Self-existent One Who sustains a dying and crumbling universe, so Jesus presents Himself in John 5:26: "For just as the Father has life in Himself; even so He gave to the Son also to have life in Himself." God is Self-existent, but we are not. We as human beings have come into existence, and we need an understanding of who we are. We are also heading toward death, followed by the unknown. Nothing can be more important than to know personally the Self-existent God Who gave us our existence, rules over the universe we live in, and ushers us unto His eternity. Only in Him can we satisfy our thirst for a purpose that transcends our existence and gives meaning to it.

God is immutable. For the mystic, the universe is a god that is undergoing changes continually, though it is eternal. In some schemes, such as Hinduism, the universe collapses into chaos and is reborn in order. Thus it undergoes an infinite series of cycles. The Bible teaches in contrast to the mystical view that God is transcendent from the universe, such that the universe is changing, but God is not changing. The Psalmist says, "Even they will perish, but You endure." In all of the change that we are continuously experiencing, it is fulfilling to relate to a God that does not change. We may encounter ourselves changing, sinning, confessing the sin, maturing, growing, and finally, dying; but what fulfills our thirst in all of this change is a relation to a Personal Being that does not change, sin, mature, grow, and finally, die. He is.

Also, we could not define progress or maturity unless we perceived ourselves in continual comparison to the Immutable God. Maturity is becoming more like Him; evil is the opposite of His character; and good is defined by His character. We cannot discern good and evil unless we have some understanding of a Totally Good being. Living in a constant world of good and evil combined leaves us unable to separate between what is good and what is evil from our own viewpoint. We can only create our own subjective good and evil, which are not applicable to others. Those that have this viewpoint cannot even say that Hitler was wrong because they cannot define a right and wrong that would be applicable for all people, whether they believed it or not.

When God revealed His name to Moses at the burning bush (Ex. 3:14), He said: "I AM WHO I AM… Thus shall you say to the sons of Israel, I am has sent me to you." This name in Hebrew is *Eheyéh*, which He uses to refer to Himself. In the next verse God tells the children to use the name *YHWH* (יהוה, often rendered as Jehovah) to refer to Him. Why the difference? When He uses it of Himself, it is in the first person, meaning, "I am." Jesus uses it of himself in John 8:58 and the people tried to kill him for blasphemy: "Before Abraham was born, I am." The word we are to use for God is in the third person. Jehovah means "He Is." God is constant and always the same. If we were to encounter God varying in His attributes as we encountered Him multiple times, we would have no way to relate to Him.

In this changing world we live in, only God can satisfy our thirst for a personal relationship with One Who is ever constant. We need a fixed standard of right in order to define and judge what is wrong and measure our progress toward what is right. We also need to know a Self-existent One in order to value our own existence.

God is eternal. The name "I AM" also refers to His eternity. God is not only eternal, as though existing along a time line that extends infinitely to the past, as well as the future, He stands outside of time itself. In I Timothy 6:16 Paul describes God "Who alone possesses immortality and dwells in unapproachable light." Einstein's theory of relativity indicates to us that, as one approaches the speed of light, time slows down for him. Thus, if one went in a spaceship near the speed of light for five years and then returned to earth, he would have aged five years, but the earth could have aged 500 years. This illustration gives us an idea how the "God Who dwells in unapproachable light" can be present in all epochs of history at once, and have no limits of time.

Only an Eternal God can give fulfillment to our existence in time. To the human eye there is ultimately no difference between the baby aborted in a clinic and the richest, most satisfied man that ever lived. Both die, are buried, and their bodies rot in the grave. If all ends for them there in the grave, then everything that could humanly be called "fulfilling" or something to be sought after in this life was ultimately meaningless. If man's existence is limited to his time here in this life, then all of man's striving is in vain and his existence is more like a sick joke played on him than a blessing.

In the Book of Ecclesiastes, Solomon tries one of these fulfilling things after another: wine (2:3), building projects (2:4-6), servants and cattle (2:7), silver, gold and material things (2:8), and music (2:8). Solomon saw that he was wise and wealthy, and that wisdom was more desirable than folly, but that death leveled everything out (2:14): "The wise man's eyes are in his head; but the fool walks in darkness. And yet I perceived that one fate befalls them both." In the next verse he asks himself, "'As is the fate of the fool, it will also befall me. Why then have I been extremely wise?' So I said to myself, 'This too is vanity.'" Solomon sees that man's existence is meaningless, in and of itself, apart from a reference to something beyond it.

In chapter 3, verse 11, Solomon goes further to explain his "futility and striving after wind." He says, "He (God) hath made everything appropriate in its time. He has also set <u>eternity</u> in their heart yet so that man will not find out the work that God has done from the beginning even to the end." In this verse the translation "eternity" (NASB) rather than "world" (AV) is to be preferred for the Hebrew *olam* (עוֹלָם). Both translations are possible because the word includes both the notion of a long time, as well as the world. Franz Delitzsch in his commentary on Ecclesiastes also rejects the AV reading "the world," which follows Jerome and Luther, for *olam* here. He explains it this way: "In itself the thought that God has placed the whole world in man's heart is not untrue: man indeed is a *microcosmos* in which the *macrocosmos* mirrors itself (Elster), but the connection does not favor it; for the discussion does not proceed from this that man is only a member in the great universe, and that God has given to each being his appointed place, but that in all his experience he is conditioned by time, and that in the course of history, all that comes to him, according to God's world-plan happens at its appointed time. But the idea by which that of time (*eth-zemán*) is surpassed is not the world, but eternity, to which time is related as part is to the whole."[6]

As Delitzsch indicates, the emphasis is temporal, not material here, and therefore the word with both potential meanings should be translated in its temporal sense. Delitzsch then goes on to capture the implications of taking the temporal sense. "The author means to say that God has not only assigned to each individually his appointed place in history, thereby bringing to the consciousness of man the fact of his being conditioned, but that He has also established in man an impulse leading him beyond that which is temporal toward the eternal: it lies in his nature not to be contented with the temporal, but to break through the limits which it draws around him, to escape from the bondage and the disquietude within which he is held, and amid the ceaseless changes of time to console himself by directing his thoughts to eternity."[6]

Mankind is conscious of eternity, but unable to grasp it or contain it in his finite mind. What can he do about the tension that results? Solomon's conclusion is chapter 12 of Ecclesiastes. In verse 1 he gives his exhortation in the light of the human condition here "under the sun:" "Remember also your Creator in the days of your youth, before the evil days come, and the years draw near when you will say, 'I have no delight in them.'"

Solomon's wisdom leads him to advise fellow men to seek and cultivate a personal relationship with the Creator. His resolution of the problem is to live one's life in reference to the Being Who is Eternal, obey Him in everything, and prepare to face Him in judgment after this life is over. The eternity in his heart would not let him conclude that this life is all that man has. The final conclusion of all of Solomon's wisdom is (12:13-14): "The conclusion, when all has been heard, is: fear God and keep His commandments, because this applies to every person. For God will bring every act to judgment, everything which is hidden, whether it is good or evil."

As much as man feels uncomfortable at the thought of giving an account of everything he has done to an Omniscient God Who is his judge, the eternity in his heart leaves him more uncomfortable with the prospect of ceasing to exist at death. Often young people try to escape accountability by denying that they will live beyond death, but the elderly usually prefer to accept their accountability before God, rather than to face the prospect that death ends their existence.

Each man has a certain existence here on earth, limited to the time between birth and death, but has a consciousness of being eternal. We are indebted to the authors of the philosophy of the absurd, such as Jean Paul Sartre for their many insights into the meaninglessness of life lived in the purely materialistic context. Sartre describes this consciousness well in his short story "The Wall." In this story the main character, who was to be executed the next day, spends the night trying to imagine himself dead. In the end, he cannot imagine himself dead because he is doing the imagining. Man cannot conceive of himself as dying, though he can see and conceive of other people dying. The frustration created by the unnatural invasion of death into the human experience leaves many people uneasy beneath the surface of their daily lives. Man thus lives as a consciously eternal being in a temporary existence, thirsting for eternal significance while encountering numerous reminders of his impending death, followed by the unknown.

Added to this uneasiness are the questions of origin. Where did we come from? The average person, without knowing how he got here, is also hard-pressed to understand who he is and where he will go after his life here ends. The sum total of the ontological questions leaves man (in his natural state) in a great deal of Angst about his life, being, and identity. With a bad start in this area, it won't be hard to predict failure in the other two areas of thought and action.

For the believer in God, his thirst for eternity is partially satisfied through his personal relationship with the Eternal Creator God. He can also see his value in the fact that he is in the image of the True God Who is of value; and the more he celebrates the value of that God, the more he understands the value of every person created in the image of that God. Thus, man finds affirmation of his worth as he resolves his thirst for eternity. Man is given eternal life by the Eternal God Who loves him. The Christian, in particular, has the evidence of the resurrection of Jesus Christ from the dead, and Jesus' promise that we will be resurrected and live forever with Him in heaven. Though he lives with a certain tension in the face of death, he answers that tension with the faith in the truth of what God has revealed in Jesus.

My favorite expression of this tension of knowing and believing in the Creator God and my natural human fear of death is Mahler's second symphony. This symphony is written so that each movement represents a point or stage in life: birth, childhood, early adulthood, mature adulthood, and death. From beginning to end, there is a pair of notes, sol-do, which is inserted in the melody as a mystery. In the last movement, the choir sings the meaning of these notes: *sterben* (to die). From birth onwards man's impending death hangs over him, threatening to cut off his life here in any stage of his life. In the end it finally gets him and takes him out of his life in this world. But to where?

Mahler answers this mystery in the final movement: *"Sterben werd' ich um zu leben!"* (I shall die in order to live again!). But where will he live again—here on earth without his body? No! He finishes the symphony in a flash of glory: *"Aufersteh'n, ja aufersteh'n wirst du, Mein Herz in einem Nu! Was do geschlagen, Zu Gott wird es dich tragen!"* (You will rise again, yes, rise again, My heart, in a moment, Though stricken, Borne aloft—to God!).[7] The Self-existent One who gives existence to us within this limited world will resurrect us and give us eternal life. We **will** live forever—either with that God in heaven or apart from Him in the Lake of Fire. The

Christian seeks to reconcile with that God now so that he will spend eternity in heaven. Either way, though, we all will live forever.

That brings us to the second element of human experience: perceiving.

II. Perceiving (Epistemology).

In addition to the three ontological questions, there is the problem of how to discover and verify truth. Without truth, man is as a wanderer in a wilderness—without a beginning point, without a destination, and without a map. People are also thirsty to have truth—especially about the ultimate nature of reality.

For modern man, beginning with Descartes' *cogito ergo sum* (I think, therefore I exist), philosophers have been trying to work outward towards all knowledge, each man beginning with himself and his own rational processes, and reasoning out to discover all truth. The problem was that man was starting from a point in which man himself was seen as the ultimate fact in the universe, and God and the universe were seen as dependent on man to be accepted as authentic. This made man the ultimate reality in the universe, not God. By starting from himself, man could reason a completely ideal system that was consistent with itself and logically perfect. However, he could not prove that that system had any relation with the real world that he was trying to discover. The system was only in his head.

Next came the empiricists, Locke, Berkeley, and Hume. They held that all that man can know must come from their experience through their five senses. The final development of this thought came from David Hume as summarized by Tal Brooke: "All that man can know, they (Locke, Berkeley, and Hume) proposed, must originate in experience. All "abstract ideas" such as God or truth must derive from some sense impression in order to be noetically valid. Of the three philosophers, only David Hume explored the implications of a pure empiricism with unremitting vigor. All that man can legitimately know from experience, Hume concluded, is a succession of sensations. Therefore, since things like God, one's personal identity, and the events of life are not immediate sense impressions like pain, or color, or size, we cannot know that they exist (because of this observation by Hume, the philosophical category of metaphysics was effectively shut down and abandoned)."[8]

The problem with Hume's reasoning was that he limited man's input to his five senses, and then declared that what was not perceived by those senses was not there. This was no more than circular reasoning. If God is a Spirit, then He is indeed invisible to man's five senses, as a spirit can be neither seen, heard, tasted, touched, nor smelled. To say, however, that God does not exist because He is not perceived with our senses is to affirm that our senses perceive all that exists, or all that exists is matter and energy, interchangeable according to the equation of Einstein, e = m x c squared. This is a faith assertion that says nothing about the existence of things that are non-matter in the world. It simply chooses to ignore them, *a priori*. The empiricists could perceive things from the outside universe, but they could not perceive causal links or tell if any data existed beyond what their senses could perceive. They also failed to find truth.

Thus, by starting from himself, man could neither reason to find real truth that fit the external world, nor could he perceive things as they really were and discover cause and effect, as science was claiming to do. How could this impasse be breached without denying the starting point of man's reasoning, which almost nobody disputed anymore?

Immanuel Kant made the next step. Brooke summarizes Kant's move this way: "Kant's revolutionary move was this: In order to rescue science and philosophy from skepticism while at the same time preserving humanistic assumptions, Kant removed the form and structure of reality from their precarious place in a problematic external world and established them within the mind of man. The patterns that science studies, the dynamic orderliness of nature that rewards the efforts of science, are not the result of habit and custom, as David Hume had proposed. Instead, Kant now argued, this order originates in the mind of the observer ...All of a sudden the mind contained the creative power which produces what we know as 'reality.'"[9]

Not only was the way opened for knowledge apart from God, but also now the mind became susceptible to mysticism and the occult because the question was not addressed as to what was moving and organizing each person's mind to understand the perception. Man himself was given credit for doing it.

The expectation throughout Kant's work was that, since we all have human minds, we would all come to an agreement. Kant believed that science is successful in its generalizations about the normal causality because it is established a priori by the forms and categories of human experience, or the categorical imperatives, which allow objective experience to occur. In other words, the world necessarily corresponds to our perception of it. Brooke summarizes Kant's knowledge this way: "What reality is, what "things in themselves" are, cannot therefore be known. What we "know" is not made possible by God, not by the mind's penetration of a real world, but by the mind's projections of what we can know upon an essentially unknowable world. Kant placed God, the soul, moral freedom, and the like in the realm of the unknowable 'things in themselves.'"[10]

The result of this mentality was to effectively remove God from any relationship to existence. He is not knowable within this framework that seems so real to the individual. At the most, God could only be for a post-Kantian thinker a projection of one's own fantasy onto a nebulous body of stimuli in order to create a meaning to help him get by in an unknowable universe. For post-Kantians, even if God were to exist in the way presented in the Bible, men cannot know Him. Their faith is just a "leap in the dark," rather than a rational inquiry. To them the universe is inside their heads—outside are only nebulous stimuli interpreted differently by different people who weave their perception out of their own nature.

What are the results for a twenty-first century post-modern man who is thirsting for truth? A subjective truth for every man—truth with a small "t." Today we find a multiplication of different ideas of reality. Religions, philosophies, etc. abound to the point that one thing is sure: there is no truth that all people can agree on, except the idea that "whatever you think is right is right for you," or "if believing that helps you, that is good for you." Statements like these abound today, and I wonder if the people actually think through the implications of them. Would they say this to a person with a gun who is ready to shoot and rob them? Are wars just as good as peace?

Are terrorists who hijack planes and crash them into buildings right for themselves?

Does the mind really create the truth? Let us consider two men who are standing on top of a tall skyscraper. Both intend to jump off. However, the first man thinks he is Superman and will begin to fly as soon as he jumps. The second is tired of living and wants to commit suicide. What will happen if they both jump? The Post-Kantian should expect that the man that thinks he is Superman will actually fly and the other will splat on the sidewalk and die. If the mind creates the truth, then the truth must be different for each mind. I submit that in this case both would splat on the sidewalk and die because the reality is the sidewalk, not the perceptual truth model that is in man's head. The true reality is outside of our mind, and our model of it may or may not be right.

The model *could* be right, according to reality, but it could also be wrong, as in the case of the man who thought he was Superman. The flaw in Kant's categorical imperatives, which are supposed to make objective truth possible, is that no person's experience is inherently better than another's. How, then, can the categorical imperatives be established? Kant's categorical imperatives are therefore no better than Descartes' innate knowledge, which was excluded by the nature of the empiricists' assumptions. Kant's categorical imperatives only have the appearance of validity while the "normative" group is carefully selected. Kant did not foresee the extreme fragmentation of society into a multitude of highly different subjective viewpoints that we have today.

Kant thought that he would be able to unite the human viewpoints, but he has done the opposite. He has loosed man from an objective inquiry into a knowable universe to project his own meaning onto a nebulous void. In his own mind, man passed from being an important creature of a Transcendent God to a miniature god who was trying to discover or invent his own meaning to project onto a meaningless universe. The modernist with this viewpoint thus develops an antipathy to all religion that affirms that its beliefs are objective truth to the point of denying the validity of other religions. He thinks that evangelism is an attempt of arrogant people to force their own subjective meaning system or collective fantasy on someone else, as though it were objective fact, when they think that all truth is created in the mind of man and only is true for that man. Since they assume that transcendent truth is non-existent, then the proselytism of other people appears ludicrous.

The survival of modern secular humanism, especially as a positive and optimistic position, is due, chiefly, to the inability of modern man to see the implications of his position. If one were honest, he would be mixing with the nihilists and those of the Theater of the Absurd. Instead of this, modern man has sought meaning in the irrational—mysticism, drugs, alcohol, New Age spirit guides, and many other things that alter the consciousness of the person. They are trying to find or create a universal truth consciousness that will lead them to a consensus understanding of the meaning of originating from the faceless void that is the universe.

As background to our strategy, we have to understand God better. God has two most basic names: *Jehovah* (יהוה) and *Elohim* (אֱלֹהִים). The name *Jehovah* refers to God in His religious and existential relationship with His people. *Jehovah* does miracles, answers prayer, and is involved in the lives of His people. God appeared to Moses at the burning bush as *Jehovah*, and in the character of this name He frees His people from bondage in Egypt.

The other principle name of God is *Elohim*. In the character of this name God creates and sustains the universe. In Genesis 1:1 we read, "In the beginning God (*Elohim*) created the heavens and the earth." He sustains the universe as *Elohim*, as well. The word *Elohim* comes from a root referring to strength. There are four passages in which the word el (אֵל) refers to power: Genesis 31:29, Deuteronomy 28:32, Micah 2:1, Proverbs 3:27, and Nehemiah 5:5. In all these references, the word is connected to the word "hand" to mean "in the power of your hand," or "in the ability of your hand." God, as *Elohim*, is the One Who is supremely able, in creative power, intelligence, design, and sustaining force.

The immediate effect of Kant's thought was to relegate God as Creator of a knowable universe to the category of the unknowable "things in themselves," thus removing Him from the picture. The effect on theology was to develop a mystical, romantic, occult, pantheistic, "god-in-nature" emphasis on religion. Instead of worshipping God as *Elohim*, the modernists sought to transform the universe by bypassing their rational faculties and seeking intuitive understanding of the world. As Brooke summarizes it: "Mysticism attached itself to the Romantic quest. To penetrate the secret world of "things in themselves" required an occult approach. Many adopted the attitude that since by definition the rational, causal structure of the world is an aspect of man's consciousness, the rational faculties were merely an obstacle to true knowledge. Penetration to the true essence of things required deep intuition, mystical mind states, or some meditative epiphany. Ecstatic self-absorption into a mystical oneness with or through nature—most obvious in Wordsworth, Shelley, and Whitman—had become an almost conventional form of religious experience. Nature began to be regarded as somehow divine. It was a tabloid for the sacred experience. Pantheism crept in."[11]

At this point, we see that people are looking for an experience to alter their consciousness in order to bypass their intellectual abilities to arrive at an understanding of "things in themselves." This did not have to require a rejection of the Bible or Christianity if they knew what God was like. Even if one does not understand or accept God as *Elohim* and the universe as knowable, he could still, through a leap of faith, seek God as *Jehovah*. However, if he really finds the true *Jehovah*, he will understand later that Kant was wrong and the universe is knowable in two ways: through our rational faculties and scientific endeavor, and through our intuitive personal relationship with God through the Holy Spirit.

We can deal with the *phenomena* through our five senses and by the scientific process because God as *Elohim* made a knowable universe. We can also have some insight into the *noumena*, or "things in themselves" as we understand God as *Jehovah* better. The same Holy Spirit that was hovering over creation and supervising it in Genesis 1:2 also gave to mankind the Scriptures. As *Elohim* He gave the law of gravity, and as *Jehovah* He gave us the Ten Commandments. He is the Spirit that sustained all of creation in Genesis as *Ruach Elohim* (אֱלֹהִים), and He is the *Ruach Jehovah* (Spirit of *Jehovah*, רוּחַ יהוה) as He reveals His message to the prophets, as in Ezekiel 11:5.

If people can contact any spirit with no discernment at all, as to which one it is, then the Spirit of God is as legitimate an option as any other spirit. We just have to make sure that we don't try to "turn on" with the Holy Spirit in isolation from His other characteristics. Man needs both intuitive truth, which cannot come from his senses, as well as objective empirical truth, which comes from his senses.

By following Kant, modern man has denied objective empirical truth in favor of an intuitive truth. However, because we human beings are not being transformed by the same spirit, the intuitive approach has only fragmented us into many individual viewpoints and further alienated us from each other. Here we may note the uniqueness of following the God of the Bible: the same Spirit that created and sustains the world we can discover with our five senses (as the Spirit of Elohim) is the One that we can know intuitively and personally (as the Spirit of Jehovah). This is the same Holy Spirit that is transforming the believer and giving him a deeper and deeper understanding of the universe.

It is interesting to note here that the Hebrew word for "evangelism" and the verb "to evangelize" come from the same root as the word "flesh." In effect, in the Old Testament the believer is ordered to "flesh out" the good news. This is an all-encompassing expression that includes announcing the message, living the message—literally, "expressing the message in the flesh." In addition, this spiritual relationship has given us an understanding of the world that is external to us, as well. The moral laws, which the Holy Spirit transforms us to accept, turn out to be those that make society function best for all concerned. They are not categorical imperatives of man's experience, as Kant postulated, but rather decrees from the same God that ordered the universe into existence. The commandment, "Thou shalt not kill," came from the same mouth as the commandment to sustain the law of gravity.

As we look at our epistemology as believers in Jesus here in the twenty-first century, there are four contrasts between our truth and the truth of other people. The first is in the source of the spiritual dynamic of alteration, or transformation. For the modernist, any spirit, religion, spiritual technique, or activity that leads one to a spiritual understanding of the world is good for that person. There is no Truth, such that to deny it is to be wrong. Everyone is seen as right for himself, and all spirits that can transform, or alter a person are seen as equally valid.

For the Christian, this mindset is extremely dangerous. While it should always be our goal to understand the truth, we must reject all influences of false spirits. It is not enough to be spiritual, one must have the Right Spirit transforming him, or the transformation will be bad, rather than good. Into this spiritual darkness we need to preach the Word of God, for (Rom. 10:17): "Faith comes from hearing, and hearing by the word of Christ." It is only through the Holy Scriptures of the Old and New Testaments that man can be sure that the Right Spirit is altering his consciousness, and can thus avoid false spirits. It is not just the alteration process that is important, but also the Source of the alteration. We need the Right Spirit to transform us.

Only if the Right Spirit is transforming everyone will universal spirituality result in a unification of all mankind. That is why Jesus prayed concerning His followers (John 17:21): "That they may all be one; even as You, Father, are in me, and I in You, that they also may be in Us: so that the world may believe that You sent Me." As the church shows more and more unity, it is obvious to the world that there is One Supreme Spirit that can unify mankind by altering everyone the same way.

The second contrast between the believers and modernists on epistemology is the use of Scriptures. For the modernist, anything that brings a spiritual contact or alteration is good for that person, and everyone is right for himself. The idea is to bypass one's own intellectual faculties in order to discover "things as they are in themselves," as mentioned above. Thus, the Christian Scriptures, a ouija board, the Hindu Scriptures, Buddhist writings, the Koran, and any of the teachings of the popular modern gurus are all on the same plain. They all represent spiritual "channelings" from the beyond. A modernist would use them to see how different people achieved great intuitive understandings through spiritual contact.

For the believer in Jesus Christ, the Scriptures—both Old and New Testaments—are the authentic Truth of God because only they have been "channeled" from the Right Spirit. In II Peter, chapter one, Peter mentions the greatness of his experience on the Mount of Transfiguration (vv. 16-18): "For we did not follow cleverly devised tales when we made known to you the power and coming of our Lord Jesus Christ, but we were eyewitnesses of His majesty. For when He received honor and glory from God the Father, such an utterance as this was made to Him from the Majestic Glory, 'This is My beloved Son with Whom I am well-pleased'—and we ourselves heard this utterance made from heaven when we were with Him on the holy mountain."

Peter had great experiences while living with Jesus, and the greatest of them was probably this experience on the Mountain of Transfiguration. However, in order that Scriptures be not seen as just a collection of human experiences to initiate us to discover our own truth, he adds (vv. 19-21): "So we have the prophetic word made more sure, to which you do well to pay attention as to a lamp shining in a dark place, until the day dawns and the morning star arises in your hearts. But we know this first of all, that no prophecy of Scripture is a matter of one's own interpretation, for no prophecy was ever made by an act of human will, but men moved by the Holy Spirit spoke from God."

What makes the canon of Scripture certain is not that it contains the personal insights of people as reflections of their spiritual contacts, but that the One True Spirit provided the experience, and then the interpretation of that experience, down to the very words uttered or written. Peter is certain of the Scriptures because God gave both the events and the words to interpret them. The whole work of inspiration was the spiritual—intuitive work of the Holy Spirit through dedicated people who surrendered their own rational faculties to God's Spirit's alteration in order to "channel" His Truth to mankind. Therefore, if people surrender to these Scriptures, they will be altered by (i.e. transformed by) this Spirit, rather than another spirit. We will see more of this topic in the next chapter in greater detail.

The key to epistemology then is tied into one's choice of spirit, as well as the rational use of one's senses in a believable world made by the True God. However, when our human reasoning and senses tell us to do one thing and the Holy Spirit (directly or through the Scriptures) tells us to do another, we are to show our faith by following the Spirit and the Scriptures, realizing we are prone to error.

The third contrast between Bible believers and modernists with respect to epistemology is that for Bible believers, Jesus is personally the Truth. Jesus says (John 14:6): "I am the way, and the truth, and the life; no one comes to the Father, but through Me." Christianity is not primarily a set of doctrines to be recited as a creed, but rather a person.

The Apostle Paul was much known for his deep doctrine. The doctrine was not his primary aim, however, but rather a means to his greatest end. In Galatians 4:19 he mentions his frustration that the Galatian believers were not progressing in the faith, and says, "My little children, with whom I am again in labor until Christ is formed in you." His goal was not intellectual knowledge of God's word, though that was a means toward his end, but rather the working of the Holy Spirit in the lives of his disciples to the point of forming Christ in them—that it would actually be Jesus living through them. In Biblical Christianity, Jesus is actually living in the believer and transforming him through His Holy Spirit. The altered consciousness is actually the Creator God channeling His Life through the believer. What could be more exciting?

In contrast, though the modernist is also looking for personal intuitive truth, he is not looking for a particular truth or a particular spirit. Some modernists feel fulfilled by a particular personal spirit guide that they know, such as those of the New Age faith or any of the particular Bhakti groups of Hindus. These people seek their fulfillment in a personal relation with a particular known spirit. Others, such as western pantheists, Buddhists, and others seek their fulfillment through merging their identity with that of the universe and losing consciousness of being a particular human being. Thus, for some, the truth is a personal being with which they have contact, while for others; there is one collective cosmic consciousness into which they seek to merge their identity.

No matter which of the two options a modernist chooses, he does not exercise any discernment as to which personal reality is the right one. In fact, to ask such a question would violate the Kantian notion that each man's mind creates his own truth. The fallacy of this approach is that it doesn't judge the spirit that slips into the back door of a man's consciousness and organizes his perception of the world. By pragmatic considerations, if the person feels good and the perception of the world is arrived at by bypassing one's reasoning faculties, then it must be right for him. There is no idea of looking for or expecting anything to be right for everybody. The only error in this scheme is that of being intolerant of other people's viewpoints because that violates the Kantian starting point of every man's mind creating his own truth.

The fourth contrast between the Biblical believer and the modernist is that, while both are being progressively altered by the spirits in them, the Christian is being altered into conformity with the historical and scientific dimension of reality, while the modernist is progressively altered away from realities of the historical and scientific dimension of reality. Only of New Testament believers can it be said, as in I John 2:20 (AV): "But ye have an anointing from the Holy One, and ye know all things."

Let us take just one issue—our attitude toward work. For the majority of modernists, unless their work is related to furthering their religious fulfillment, they feel unfulfilled in the Monday through Friday work world. They have as their goal to escape from these pursuits in order to get their fulfillment. On the other hand, the Christian is just as fulfilled laboring in the material world as he is singing in a church service. In the former, he enjoys doing creative labor in which he resembles on a micro scale his Creator-God in the name *Elohim.* When he is in a church service, he relates to the same God, but in the name *Jehovah.* There is no separation between the physical and metaphysical spheres because the God of the Bible is the God over both. The same God that gives ecstatic experiences also says in II Thessalonians 3: 10: "If anyone is not willing to work, then he is not to eat, either."

In relating to the modern man about the existence of truth, it is important for the Biblical Christian that his testimony ring true and clear at all times. Non-Christians will not be very interested in our idea of truth initially; as to them it only represents our own particular understanding of reality. They think that everyone creates his own reality, and so are not looking to change systems, so much as to find a few good ideas from us that they can redact into their own understanding of the world. They may not be initially impressed when we tell them about how great the Lord is, as they probably have a spirit that helps them out, too.

Other people need to see that the truth that Christians have is true in all applications: religious, historical, scientific, psychological, etc. Also, all of our truth is unified, and there are no contradictions. Then they will thirst for the truth that we have. Truth, however, may be a little bit hard to communicate. Our actions, however, are more visible. Next we want to discuss just that: the Christian and his actions.

III. Doing (Ethics).

From the beginning man has sought out ethical systems to follow in the absence of God. The same is true in each person after they rebel against God and find themselves on their own. Considering the turmoil in the world, and the many unfavorable things that happen to people, there almost immediately presents itself the problem of evil. Though people vary somewhat in their understanding of what is right and what is wrong, man is inescapably a moral being. For a moral being, a look at this world immediately creates a tension between what he sees and what he perceives to be right.

Those of us who deal with ethics have a thirst for right actions to prevail. Jesus blessed this type of person when he said (Matthew 5:6): "Blessed are they which do hunger and thirst after righteousness: for they shall be filled." There are many moral people in the world. There are some ethics that many have in common, but no ethics are common to all. Therefore, most moral people have defined those who have similar standards as moral, while others are seen as immoral or amoral people.

Without God, modern man is only able to construct a subjective morality, especially if he is basing his system on Kantian principles, i.e. that each person's mind creates truth for him. On this philosophical base, many have sought to find a basis for morality that is applicable to all men. For example, in an article entitled "Ten Myths About Secular Humanism" by Matt Cherry and Moleen Matsumura, there is a defense of the position of secular humanism. Concerning the issue of morals, the authors defend their position that secular humanism does have morals: "If you believe the myth that you cannot have morality without religion and God, then you are forced to one of two conclusions. Either you can say that humanists have no morals, or you can concede that they have a moral code but insist that they must have gotten it from religion."[12]

These authors are missing the third alternative. We can concede that humanists have morals, and that they may have gotten them without reference to religion. However, we must assert that their morals are worthless *as morals*. Without a Transcendent God Who is the embodiment of true actions, and without accountability to Him, morals are not morals at all. They are personal ideals that are disconnected from the actions of others. Thus, Mother Teresa is right for Mother Teresa and Hitler is right for Hitler. The former's ethics involve helping widows and orphans and the latter's ethics involve genocide. There is nothing to make them right and the alternative wrong. In fact, there can be nothing wrong within the philosophical framework that Kant set up, since it is the person's own mind that creates the truth. Just as Kant's categorical imperatives do not work in the realm of truth, neither can they in the realm of ethics.

In the article by the secular humanists, they try to establish a basis for morality from the human viewpoint. "Humanist and religious morality share many basic principles because in fact both are underpinned by the fundamental human moral sense summarized in the Golden Rule: treat others with the same consideration as you would have them treat you. Humanists recognize that the common moral decencies—for example, people should not lie, steal, or kill; and they should be honest, generous, and cooperative—really are conducive to human welfare… Humanists also emphasize the importance of self-determination—the right of individuals to control their own lives, so long as they do not harm others. Secular humanists, therefore, often promote causes where traditional religion obstructs the right to self-determination, for example, freedom of choice regarding sexual relationships, reproduction, and voluntary euthanasia."[12]

The basis for morality cited above is full of contradictions and the subjectivity in its application can lead one to wonder whether it represents ethics at all. For example, the right to control one's own life "so long as they do not harm others" conflicts with the legalization of abortion, and sexual licentiousness (which passes sexually transmitted diseases in epidemic proportions). It also harms others that the people who are doing these things are demanding vast sums of public money for medical research to overcome the consequences, such as AIDS. People who are not involved in these activities are then expected to pay higher taxes to cover the expense.

As far as not harming others, Communists believe that whatever helps the revolution in the long run is right. Therefore they murder millions upon millions of people in order to impose their moral criteria on others, thinking that things will be much better when they succeed in their revolution. Does the end justify the means? If the humanist claims that "not harming others, etc." is the true morality, aren't they trying to impose it others? Are they different from the Communists and the Nazis? As they defend the "reproductive rights" of the pregnant lady to have an abortion, aren't they overlooking the harm caused to the baby by murdering it?

Thus, the secular humanist turns his back on the harm in the abortion clinics in order to win the mother to his cause. When one pursues a "higher good," it is easy then to justify harming many people that get in one's way, and depersonalizing them as fetuses, or Jews, or bourgeois. Friedrich Nietzsche first emphasized the logical result of this viewpoint. He enjoyed clubbing fellow modernists over the heads with the implications of their beliefs. He proudly declared to all of the world that God is dead, and then went about advocating that mankind "set themselves the task of rearing a ruling race, the future "lords of the earth"—a new, vast aristocracy based upon the most severe self-discipline, in which the will of philosophical men of power artist-tyrants will be stamped upon thousands of years... taking the fate of the earth into their own hands, and working as artists upon man himself."[13]

In the light of these mega-goals for the human race, it is not surprising that the value of the individual would suffer. Nietzsche says, "to this end, a host of transitional and deceptive measures must be discovered, and that the life of a single individual stands for almost nothing compared to the accomplishment of such lengthy tasks and aims."[14] Thus, for Nietzsche, "Not "mankind," but superman is the goal."[15] But we need to ask, "How can you define the characteristics of superman? And who decides how he is brought about?

Modern man only has two options if he will not let go of the modernistic system. First of all, he may say that every man is right for himself. This leads to total anarchy, but it is consistent with Kant's idea that each person's mind forms his own truth. The second option is to declare one person's or small group of people's idea the right one and force everyone to follow it. There is no middle ground between anarchy and dictatorship for the modern man. To espouse a morality such as the secular humanists do it and to hold it in contradiction to their post-Kantian notion that the human mind is the creator of truth is to be a hypocrite. To be consistent, they must drop one position or the other. They cannot logically hold both.

Into this moral void Christians can speak—and must speak. As a matter of fact, the stage is set for coming great destruction in the world (which many call Great Tribulation), as each group claims their leaders to be the infallible superman and tried to force everyone to accept him. At first the Bible indicates that it will be the European leader, and then groups will break off and fight for supremacy of a world in which God has been excluded. The sad summary on that coming epoch of history is Jesus' pronouncement (Matthew 24:22): "Unless those days had been cut short, no life would have been saved."

What are we to say about ethics to a world where all moral pronouncements appear to be a form of bigotry and intolerance? We have God Who has given right moral decrees to go with His decrees that form the "natural laws." Therefore, we have true actions. It is interesting that secular humanists claim to have a core morality in common with us. As we have read from them earlier: "Humanists recognize that the common moral decencies—for example, people should not lie, steal, or kill; and they should be honest, generous, and cooperative—really are conducive to human welfare..."[16]

It is a fact that every one of the Ten Commandments is conducive to human welfare, but we cannot leave people to apply them in a partial way for their own benefits to condemn others, while ducking the implications for themselves. This is true in the case of abortion already mentioned.

To have a true morality is to have a standard of what is right or wrong that is above all people in authority. To have this we must have somebody in authority that is imposing his moral viewpoint on others. This enforcement might appear bigoted, and will certainly be intolerant of variant actions, but it is an essential element of morality. This gets back to the two alternatives left to modern men: anarchy or totalitarianism.

Anarchy is proceeding full course today, as secular humanists promote the spirit of lawlessness by declaring every man god for himself. This will probably continue until people demand an end to it at any price. There must be order for society to exist. Then their "superman" will be waiting in the wings to take over.

But what about totalitarianism? Are we safe with just anyone running the world according to his own whim without any safeguards? Who is fit to run the world? Only God. People are thirsting for God; and in His perceived absence, they are appointing inferior human substitutes for Him. What is it about God's attributes that man is thirsting for in ethics? I believe that there are three things: 1. God is Holy, Just, and Good, 2. God is judge, and 3. God is merciful.

To say that God is Holy, Just, and Good, is to make Him the standard for defining our own ethics. If man accepts God as the standard for right, and treats all contrary as wrong, he can understand where he is morally, he can see need for improvement, he can see his value in that the standard protects him, as well. This, however, requires surrendering moral sovereignty to God. One would think in the light of this, that it would be better to surrender moral sovereignty to God than to a mere human (Nietzsche's superman), or face anarchy. To do this, however, forces man to rethink the starting point of all modern philosophy. Man cannot start with Descartes' "I think, therefore I am," for God must be the "I am" (as the name Jehovah means in the first person) in the moral system that man needs.

For God to be Holy, Just, and Good would not be important for man, except for the fact that He is also immutable. God does not change in His moral character, and so His character, as revealed in

Scriptures is a fixed point of reference. Though people always fall short of acting like God, we can perceive people as more moral or less moral by comparing them to God's revealed character, since it never changes.

To say that God is judge is to admit that there cannot be law without accountability. Modern man is running away from accountability for himself, while demanding it of others. We need to live our lives in the light of the fact that every person that ever lived will have to stand before the judgment seat of God and answer for everything he has ever done. We of the church especially need to live in the light of the Rapture of the Church and the judgment at the Bema Seat of Christ (I Cor. 3:11-15). Even though unbelievers may mock the fact that we have well-defined moral principles, they must admit that society would be better off if everyone lived as the Bible advocates. If Christian teaching about the judgment of every man were not true, the world would still be a better place to live if people lived as though they would have to answer to an Omniscient Judge for everything they ever did.

It is not enough for God to be a just judge. That would condemn everyone to death from the start. God is also merciful. Some people just throw themselves on God's mercy and "do the best they can," thinking that they will turn out all right. God's mercy does not contradict His justice, however, and people need God's Gospel of salvation. Without mercy there is no point in repenting, since every man has already committed enough sin to guarantee his eternal damnation.

Thus, we see modern man in a dilemma about ethics. He wants to make every man a god for himself, but that results in anarchy and great suffering. The alternative, to erect an arbitrary totalitarian regime for a government is little better, as it tends to limit freedoms too greatly. Nietzsche advocated assembling the best people and creating the new super race, while playing down the value of the individual. However, the Nazis and Communists, who were directly influenced by his vision, have produced worse alternatives in their totalitarian regimes. Modern man is thirsty to have safety stepping out of his house, and admits that he needs limits on his actions; but he doesn't want his freedom taken away, either. What is the answer? God.

God's Word is the best moral standard for man. God is the best judge of man, and provides accountability at a final judgment at the end of history. God Himself in Jesus Christ is the best "superman" for the strategy of Nietzsche. Who has better qualifications? Jesus in His glorified state knows all things (Col. 2:3), and has all power in heaven and earth given unto Him (Mat. 28:18).; yet He wants man to repent and submit to Him so that he can be changed. So we see that man's need for and thirst for ethics can only be met by a Holy, Just, and Merciful God.

The reasoning I have just given is called the moral argument for the existence of God. It demonstrates—not only the existence of God—but something about the character of God as well. Just as man is incurably moral, though with varying personal ethics, so there must be a Supreme Being Who is moral, and Whose character is the unchanging standard of that morality. That Supreme Being must also hold us accountable, as well, or the morality is meaningless. Finally, that Supreme Being must make mercy available on His terms so that one who wishes to repent and be saved from condemnation has a genuine option to do so.

Conclusion:

In the course of this chapter we have looked at God as the only One Who can fulfill the needs of man in the areas of being (or ontology), truth (epistemology), and ethics (morality). By seeing man's needs and how they are met by a relation with God, one is moved to want to share the good news of Jesus Christ with modern men. However, modern men have a stereotyped idea of Christianity that is not accurate, and this idea leaves them closed to the message.

While the needs of each generation are really the same, their perception of those needs changes. Therefore, it is incumbent on the believers to present God in Jesus in a different way in different generations, though the message is ever the same. The present generation is looking for a quick spiritual transformation that will alter them to bring about peace. Jesus Christ can do this through the Holy Spirit. Later they need to see that the spirit they have received is also the Creator of the Universe, and they can rely on science and history, as well.

Man is ever thirsty spiritually and foolish in his attempts to satisfy that thirst. For modern man, beginning with Descartes' *cogito ergo sum*, philosophers have been trying to work outward towards all knowledge, each man beginning with himself and his own rational processes, and reasoning out to discover all truth. The problem was that man was starting from a point in which man himself was seen as the ultimate fact in the universe, and God and the universe were seen as dependent on man's reasoning to be accepted as authentic. This made man the ultimate reality in the universe, not God. By the time Kant passed off the scene, man was bracing himself and preparing to channel whatever spirit had him at the moment.

Man is not the ultimate fact in the universe, and man is not a god. The order of being is opposite the order of perceiving, and God is the center of the universe, though man is the center of his own perception. When Descartes made each man the "I am" for himself ("I think, therefore *I am*"), he blasphemously gave to everyone the Divine name: "I am." From this beginning no good could come, and no good did come. Man became like a picture trying to paint itself and define its content, but without being a picture of anything.

Modern man must reject Descartes' beginning point and seek God as the center of the universe. Man is a finite being with a thirst for infinity in his heart. As such, he will not be satisfied with the discoveries of his finite mind, his limited senses, and his limited time here on earth. There has to be more, and God is the Answer. Let us see how.

God is the only True Infinite Being. As Berkhof explains: "The infinity of God is that perfection of God by which He is free from all limitations. In ascribing it to God we deny that there are or can be any limitations to the divine Being or attributes. It implies that He is in no way limited by the universe, by this time-space world, or confined to the universe."[17] This is the only Being that can satisfy a man in the three areas of existence: being, thinking, and doing. He alone can satisfy His human creatures that are finite, but have a thirst for the infinite. Let us summarize these three areas.

Considering being itself, God is self-existent but man is created. Man receives his existence from elsewhere, and cannot even sustain himself. God is eternal, but man is mortal. He knows that his existence here is temporary and longs for eternal life. God offers man eternal life now through the Gospel, but man is trying to get it the wrong way. To answer the ontological questions, man came into being by the creative act of a Loving God. Man's purpose is to glorify God and come to know Him better and be more like Him, as well as representing Him before the rest of creation. Man's end is a glorious eternity in fellowship with God if he accepts forgiveness on God's terms, or an eternity in the Lake of Fire if he insists in running his own life. All of man's ontological needs are met in a relation with God in which man has a dependent role, but man cannot be the master and god for himself. He cannot give himself life, meaning in life, or a future beyond the grave.

After centuries of the best philosophy, man has come to recognize this need to be a channel for a spirit beyond himself. After rejecting the God of the Bible, though, he has ended up channeling other spirits. Man has thrown the God of the Bible out the front door of his presuppositions because He is not perceivable with his five senses; but he has invited all sorts of other spirits in the back door of his psychic quests, and these spirits are not perceivable with man's five senses, either. We ask the question, "Why not invite the God of the Universe in the back door?" He can satisfy one's need for spiritual filling, and He can give meaning to the universe that we perceive with our 5 senses, as well.

Considering knowledge of the truth, man has always sought to know more and more, ever since Eve took of the fruit of the forbidden tree to "become as gods knowing good and evil." Man has limited sensory input, limited reasoning abilities, and limited time to find out truth. Since our experience is very diverse, we humans come to different conclusions about the true nature of things, and therefore our finite attempts to discover truth only serve to divide us into disagreeing factions. We need absolute Truth revealed to us apart from human abilities or through Divine inspiration of certain people. Only God can give us Truth that is true in every dimension.

We are constantly using inductive observations and deductive theories and modifying our understanding of both spiritual and material spheres. God, however, conceives all of reality, creates all of reality, and can hold all of reality in His mind at once. He has full inductive knowledge, as well as full deductive knowledge because He created the universe. Thus, God's truth is absolutely true in every way, and as dependable as the very laws of the universe. Finite man can and should program the Bible into his thinking as absolute truth, and then work out from there. It is totally and perfectly true. Man must depend on the Holy Spirit to transform him to understand the Word better, as he submits. We cannot create Truth on our own. Again, in questions of epistemology, we can only be fulfilled in submission to God's Holy Scriptures and God's Holy Spirit. Everything else is a morass of pious subjectivism.

Concerning ethics, things are no different. Because of man's limited experience, limited reasoning, and limited time, his efforts to develop ethics meet with the same fragmented diversity, as does his search for truth. Factions, wars, crime, and other disasters are encountered daily. We cannot agree on what is right, and we cannot even obey what we think is right. We must depend on the Holy Scriptures to know what is right and depend on the Holy Spirit to produce in us "both to will and to work for to His good pleasure (Phil. 2:13)." Thus, the key for man to find fulfillment in his actions is dependency on God.

God, however, is very remote in the heavens—or is He? In Jesus of Nazareth lies all of the fullness of the Godhead bodily. Jesus says to mankind (John 7:37-38): "If anyone is thirsty, let him come to Me and drink. He who believes in Me, as the Scripture said, from his innermost being will flow rivers of living water." Jesus claimed to be that One that man was made to depend on.

Jesus also says (John 14:6): "I am the way, and the truth, and the life; no one comes to the Father, but through Me." As the Way, Jesus transforms us in our ethics and with the power to do what is right. As the Truth, Jesus is revealed as Living Truth to us through His Spirit and Scriptures—both material and spiritual Truth. As the Life, Jesus created us in the first place, offers to make us a new creature at conversion, and resurrects us with life for all eternity—whether for heaven or for the Lake of Fire. Jesus is personally the fulfillment for man in all of these three areas.

Nietzsche was looking for his superman among the philosophers, humanitarians, and scientists. He believed that the common man should be sacrificed to make way for the superman. He said, "Not mankind, but Superman is the goal."[18] We as believers can say the same thing, realizing that Jesus is the only Superman. Our old Adam is being crucified to make room for the superman in us (i.e. Jesus), and He alone should be the object of all of our endeavors. Jesus alone can satisfy our moral, epistemological, and ontological needs because only Jesus is the Way, the Truth, and the Life. Let us live His life before a world of desperately thirsty and foolish men. Jesus is the True God's only provision for man to experience satisfaction for his greatest longings and needs.

Chapter 2

God's Revelations to Mankind: How Can We Get to Know God?

In order to understand how things are in the universe, we have first begun with a consideration of God in the last chapter. The sad history of modern philosophy shows us how that man, starting from man, has been able to arrive at nothing. From the lofty optimism of Descartes and his *cogito ergo sum* ("I think, therefore I am") as a beginning place, man has been reduced in the most recent times to a mere haggling over linguistics, without any hope that those terms can actually be linked to anything external to man. It appears that, as a result, all transcendent knowledge and ethics are evaporating, being replaced by a subjective, self-serving and self-constructed "truth" and a private set of ethics, similarly constructed; and each person's ethics are considered equally "valid" for each person, regardless of the content. It is clear that theology, as well as any approach to Truth, must begin with God, not man. For Transcendent Truth to exist, it must exist in a Transcendent Being—God.

After one considers what God is like, in contrast to man, one must then consider God's revelations of Himself and His Truth to man. The Biblical doctrine of man (Biblical anthropology) yields us no confidence in man's ability to transcend his personal limits by intuition or intellectual analysis of incoming sensory data. As shown in the previous chapter in modern philosophy, the focus on man for the answers to the great existential questions only results in a mire of subjective opinions that are in contradiction with one another, but all seen as equally correct.

What can one do to seek transcendent truth when he is limited? He must have revelation from a Being that is transcendent, and he must rely completely upon the truth of that revelation. To the degree that he doubts that revelation or tries to pick and choose what part of that revelation to accept and what part to reject, he has fallen back again into subjective uncertainty.

The real question behind the problem of revelation is the following: How can a finite man, who is limited in his perspective and unreliable in his judgment, come to have reliable truth about the universe, God, and himself? This truth has to be equally true for all people, totally true as it touches all fields of endeavor (both physical and metaphysical), replicable (true from all viewpoints), beyond human wisdom, constant (unchanging from one moment to another), practical, and trustworthy as a basis for our daily living, as well as for times of special crisis. It may be something we think is wrong at first, but later find out that our false thinking was the problem.

There are three sources of revelation from God to man: the natural revelation, the written revelation, and Jesus Christ, and all of them are important to us in order to have Truth.

I. Natural Revelation.

There are two sources for natural revelation: innate knowledge (*cognitio insita*) and acquired knowledge (*cognitio aquisita*). The former comes to man through his birth makeup and the latter comes through his sensory experience. Descartes, the father of modern philosophy asserts that there is inborn knowledge, as he states in his Meditation V: "That God Necessarily Exists." He draws a contrast between false suppositions "and the true ideas that were born with me, the first and chief of which is the idea of God."[1]

Descartes continues with four reasons why the idea of God is inborn and cannot be simply a false supposition of his: "In the first place because I can conceive no other being, except God, to whose essence existence necessarily pertains; in the second because it is impossible to conceive two or more gods of this kind; and it being supposed that one such God exists, I clearly see that He must have existed from all eternity; and finally, because I apprehend many other properties in God, none of which I can either diminish or change."[1]

Here Descartes claims that knowledge of God's existence, as well as some of His attributes, is inborn in every man. Descartes depends on this inborn knowledge of God as the basis on which every other knowledge depends, and says, "that the certitude of all other truths is so absolutely dependent on it, that without this knowledge it is impossible to know anything perfectly."[1] Other philosophers did not heed this final warning of Descartes and have rejected the whole idea of innate knowledge. As a result, they have been unable to arrive at any other truth, and their "knowledge" of anything else is more an indication of what they are like than what the thing is in itself.

The subsequent denial of innate knowledge has sunk modern philosophers into a mire of subjectivism and pluralism, in which everyone is starting at his own subjective viewpoint, *cogito ergo sum,* but cannot reason out to any truth at all. The result is an agreement to disagree, with tolerance as the highest virtue. Each person then becomes his own little god, creating his own "truth," which is valid only for him.

Using the starting point "I think, therefore I am," a person is really claiming for himself that self-existence which is only true of God. It is implied in God's great name of self-revelation *Jehovah* (He who is). Later philosophers then use this starting point without Descartes belief in the inborn knowledge of God. If we can show how there can be inborn knowledge of God, then we can avoid the subjectivism that has put us in a moral freefall, and logically will end in chaos through the denial of all ethics.

What can we use to approach the notion of inborn knowledge in man? In the Biblical theology of man there is a controversy between the creationists and the traducianists. The former believe that God creates man's soul individually at conception, and the latter believe that all souls were created in Adam and passed on, along with our biological inheritance. Because he is so convinced a dualist, Berkouwer accurately explains the two viewpoints, with their strengths and weaknesses, but finds no resolution to the difference. Near the end of 31 pages of explanation, all he can conclude is the following: "In both theoretical views, the starting point was a description of the "essence" or "being" of man as soul and body, a description in which the relationship to God was not yet regarded as essential. This appears to be more clearly evident in traducianism, since creationism placed so strong an accent on a separate creative act. But in the final analysis, creationism also followed the same path, and viewed man as originating in the union between the created soul and the generated body. Thus man was a composite; both the view of man and question of his origin showed a dualism in relation to the whole man, similar to that which appeared within traducianism within generation."[2]

Having assumed dualism, both traducianists and creationists could only conclude dualism, without going beyond semantics or a slight difference of emphasis. If, however, we place the controversy within the context of trichotomy, I believe that we can arrive at a satisfactory resolution of the problem that will take into account the best of the two positions.[3]

The dilemma that the Catholic Church and the Calvinists, on the one hand, find themselves with respect to the origin of man is that they wish to hold onto the doctrine of original sin, which would imply that sin is inherited from Adam; but they also want to see each person's soul as a special creative act of God. If, however, the soul were created anew for each person, then it would be without sin. But how, then, could sin be transmitted through a mechanical biological mechanism of reproduction if the soul is not part of that transmission, but rather is directly created by God for each person?

For the traducianists, including Lutherans and other Protestants, the problem was the same, but seen from the other side. They emphasized that God created every man's soul and placed it in Adam, as well as the biological material of his body. Therefore we inherited the soul tainted with the sin of Adam because it was in him when he passed it on to us. The question is then, how did the sin taint a soul being transmitted, and how can there be a medium between the soul and God—especially a biological medium, which is seen as inferior to the spiritual contact?

Thus immediacy favors creationism and original sin favors traducianism. How can we resolve this apparent contradiction without retreating into mystery as Berkouwer does? I believe that the resolution lies in a trichotomy. I believe that man is body, soul, and spirit, and therein lies the basis for resolving the problem.

It is obvious that the body comes to us by biological inheritance from Adam through our parents. The question is what comes with that. Leviticus 17:11a shows that the *nephesh* (נֶפֶשׁ) is linked to the blood: "For the *nefesh* (rendered life in NASB) of the flesh is in the blood." We know that *nefesh* is mostly rendered as *psuché* (ψυχή) in the Greek of the Septuagint. This would give us a basis for believing that the soul of a man is also inherited along with the body, as the traducianists assert. Thus we may say that, in addition to the body, the human soul comes to man *per traducem* all the way from Adam. In this way we can cover the problem of original sin, for it is the soul in man that sins, as God says in Ezekiel 18:4: "Behold, all souls (*nefesh*, pl.) are Mine; the soul (*nefesh*) of the father as well as the soul (*nefesh*) of the son is Mine. The soul (*nefesh*) who sins will die."

So we can confirm the truth that the traducianists want most to preserve: original sin. Somehow the *nefesh*, or soul, of a man is present in the blood, and the blood is inherited biologically from a person's father, and so sin is transmitted from our father in the form of a soul that is self-exalting and seeking independence from God. This is the whole orientation of the soul. It is ready to respond to any temptation involving the lust of the flesh, the lust of the eyes, and the pride of life. This is our inheritance *per traducem* from Adam: body and soul.

At this point we ask what else there is in man that can satisfy the observations of the creationists. What does God create special in each man if both body and soul are transmitted from our parents? The answer is the human spirit. This can be expressed by some combination of the Hebrew words *neshamah* (נְשָׁמָה) and *ruach* (רוּחַ). It is interesting to note that Jewish mystics consider the *neshamah* to be the "Divine spark" that is in everyone, and this does correspond with the "God-consciousness" in Adam and Eve. However, we do not need to consider this to be a denial of original sin, though that doctrine is a total anathema to Jewish people—whether liberals, mystics, orthodox, or otherwise. They emphasize immediate creation only.

We see in Genesis 2:7 that God's *neshamah* was breathed into man, and man became a *nefesh hayyah.* The animals are also described as *nefesh hayyah* in Genesis 1:20, 21, & 23, but man is not considered in the same category as the animals. That the implantation of God's *neshamah* in man alone is a very direct act in the creation of Adam is clear in Genesis 2:7, but is it true of every person at conception? This appears to be the case, according to Ecclesiastes 12:7, referring to a person who has died, "Then the dust will return to the earth as it was, and the spirit will return to God who gave it." Even though the word translated here *spirit* is *ruach* (רוּחַ), they are used almost synonymously in the Hebrew Old Testament.

It is obvious that the body is the "dust that returns to dust," and it is important to remember that the soul (*nefesh*, or *psuché*) went down to *sheol* at death before Jesus, as was shown in Psalm 16:10, and that of believers goes to heaven since Jesus, according to Rev. 6:9. Thus, the reference to the spirit returning to God, instead of *sheol*, shows that the spirit is distinct from the soul, and that it returns to God Who gave it. I believe that the implication is that God gives the spirit individually to each person at conception, and takes it back at death.

If this is true, then we have the final point in the resolution of the controversy between the creationists and the traducianists. While the soul comes to us *per traducem*, along with our bodies, the spirit of each man comes to us *per creationem*, as a direct act of God. This is also suggested by God in Zechariah 12:1, where He says that He "forms the spirit of man within him." This maintains the sacredness and uniqueness of our contact with God and places us way above the animals in importance and relation to God—the very thing that creationists are eager to preserve. So we see that a tripartite division of man preserves the best of both positions: of traducianism through preserving original sin through natural propagation in the soul, and of creationism through preserving each man as unique and a special creative act of God through the creation of the human spirit as a special act of God.

Having established the elements of man and their source, we may now continue with what happens within man after birth. We have seen that the human spirit is created as a special act of God. It is obvious that the spirit was created without sin. The sin nature that we inherit comes from our parents through the soul, not the spirit. Since the spirit is created as a special act of God, and it is without sin at the beginning, it must be concluded that man begins in contact with God. This is what the Apostle Paul affirms of his case, and by extrapolation, to all men in Romans 7:9: "I was once alive apart from the law; but when the commandment came, sin became alive and I died."

Let us go through the sequence of events for Paul. He is born with a body and soul that came from his parents and inherited a sin nature in the soul. He also possessed at birth a perfect spirit without sin that was a special and direct creative act of God. Now the human spirit is the part of us that has God—consciousness. Since it begins without sin, we are alive in a relation with God spiritually at birth. Therefore, Paul stated that at that time he was alive without the law.

This spiritual relation with God lasts from conception until the child comes into an understanding of the law and inevitably rebels against it. It was the sin he inherited in his soul that rose up against the commandment of God, and he chose to rebel against the commandment. At that point during his childhood, Paul then died spiritually.

Paul was not born separated from God, and likewise, neither is any other person. He had a perfect spirit and was alive in some relation with God. Paul also states in Romans 5:13: "For until the Law sin was in the world, but sin is not imputed where there is no law." In the same way, sin is not imputed to a child before the Law comes to his attention and knowledge. Then, when he rebels, he dies, i.e. his spiritual relation with and perception of God ends. He then becomes dead in his sins without God's presence to guide him.

It appears that each one of us goes through the same willful rebellion against God that Adam himself experienced, except that we begin with a sinful soul that leads us into rebellion when the understanding of the Law is present later in life. In this way, we are fully responsible for our rebellion against God, even though we have inherited a sinful nature from Adam.

If we can establish that the human spirit is created specially with each person's conception, we have the original contact with God that Descartes claimed. As we review his claims about the knowledge of God, they seem almost empirical: his assertion that he can conceive of no other being who has existence necessarily pertaining to Him. How would a person conceive of such a Being without the spiritual contact at conception? Even atheists know what type of God they are denying. This is a real background for the ontological argument for God's existence. We may not inherit the knowledge of God in our mind directly, but we start with a specially created spirit that can perceive Him spiritually, and our knowledge comes from that internal perception. Descartes' second claim that he cannot conceive of two or more gods of this kind does appear to be purely logical, but it is based on a clear understanding of what God is like.

The third assertion, that Descartes clearly sees that God must have existed from all eternity, not only is based on "spiritual perception," but concurs with the teaching of the Apostle Paul in Romans about all men (Romans 1:19—20): "Because that which is known about God is evident **within them**; for God made it evident to them. For since the creation of the world His invisible attributes (*ta aorata, τὰ ἀόρατα*), His eternal power and divine nature, having been clearly seen, being understood (n*ooúmena,, νοούμενα*) by that which has been made (*tois poiémasi, τοῖς ποιήμασι*), so that they are without excuse."

Here Paul first refers to the knowledge of God that is "evident within them." This is similar to the "inborn knowledge" that Descartes refers to, though it is not strictly inborn. It comes, though, as a result God's creation of our spirit individually. When Paul says that God "made it evident to them," he implies an internal revelation in them. How can this be possible? Paul states in Romans 7::9: "I was once alive apart from the law; but when the commandment came, sin became alive, and I died." If one is alive in his spirit, which is created individually when one is conceived, there is the expectation of God's giving direct revelation of Himself to the person before he reaches the age of accountability and rebels. This covers the first part of Paul's explanation in Romans: "For since the creation of the world His invisible attributes… having been clearly seen. "They are seen on the inside through spiritual revelation.

They are not only seen internally through this spiritual revelation though, they are understood through natural revelation as the sensory information comes in "being understood by that which has been made." Because of this spiritual life with which one is born, the things that are made are naturally ascribed to God, and are seen as evidences of His eternal power and divine nature. The result is that people are without excuse. If we factor this knowledge of God into Descartes' formula for conducting philosophy, we can avoid the subjectivism to which it has fallen in our times; but if we insist on rejecting all revelation both direct and through the things that are made, as well as in Jesus, there is no way to come to any knowledge at all, as Descartes warned: "Without this knowledge it is impossible to know anything perfectly."[1]

Descartes' fourth assertion is even more direct: "I apprehend many other properties in God, none of which I can either diminish or change."[1] This is pure internal revelation from God, which shows him many other properties of God, besides His existence. This can only come from a special revelation of God. If it can be shown that these other properties of God include also the basis for human morality, it would support the moral argument for God's existence, in addition to the ontological.

Having opened the topic of natural revelation direct and internal in each person, we now turn to the topic of what God has revealed to us in the creation. In Romans 1:20, Paul continues: "For since the creation of the world His invisible attributes (*ta aorata, τὰ ἀόρατα*), His eternal power and divine nature, having been clearly seen, being understood (*nooúmena, νοούμενα*) by that which has been made (*tois poiémasi, τοῖς ποιήμασι*)." The internal revelation leads to a proper understanding of the external revelation in creation.

The "things that are made" also illustrate God's eternal power and Godhead separate from the Creation. The first and second laws of thermodynamics illustrate why there must exist that which is neither matter nor energy. If we first consider that matter and energy are interchangeable, according to Einstein's formula e=mc squared, then we may treat the whole known universe as one system. According to the laws of thermodynamics, in a closed system randomness, or disorder, increases.

I can only see two possibilities, with respect to the theory of evolution: either everything started out very complex and is evolving downward, or everything started random and disordered and is constantly evolving into something more complex.

In order for this system to come into being as highly ordered, there must have been order-producing ("creative") input from somewhere outside the system at the beginning. This input cannot be either matter or energy, as that is defined as the system, and therefore would have been from within the system. Therefore there necessarily exists that which is neither matter nor energy, and it gave input into the system that resulted in the original order.

If everything started out as disordered and is constantly evolving into something more ordered, then there must be constant order-producing ("creative") input in order to produce greater order, i.e. to reduce the randomness. This order must also come from something that is neither matter nor energy. Either way, there must be some "creative" input into the system for it to exist ordered in the first place or for it to develop greater order. This is the teleological argument for the existence of God.

This is the conclusion in Hebrews 11:3: "Through faith we understand that the worlds were framed by the Word of God, so that things which are seen (consisting of matter and energy) were not made of things which do appear (other matter and energy)." Where did they get the creative input? From something that is neither matter nor energy. I believe that this source of the creative input is spirit, and God is a Spirit (John 4:24). If we add to this our initial spiritual perception of God when we were "alive without the Law once," then we have the final element of this knowledge: our understanding of spirit, and God as a Creative All-powerful, Eternal Spirit. This is what Paul refers to when he says that in nature we perceive "God's eternal Power and Godhead (Romans 1:20)." The result is that no man is without excuse for rejecting God, even on the basis of natural revelation alone.

The main problem for modern philosophers is that they are doing their philosophy from a point of view of death. At the age they are doing philosophy, they have already rebelled against God and have been cut off from Him. They are after the point that the Apostle Paul said, "When the commandment came, sin revived and I died." At this point in the life of a person, he needs for God to reveal Himself in order to discover Him in a personal way. Because philosophers limit themselves exclusively to data from their five senses, plus their reasoning, they cannot reason their way up to God, Who is a Spirit. The five senses perceive input from the material world, not the spiritual, and this brings us to the next type of revelation of God: the Bible as Special Revelation.

II. The Bible as Special Revelation.

Given the extreme limitations of natural revelation, due to our rebellion against God, a greater revelation was needed for man to come to know God personally. In the beginning God walked with Adam and Eve in the Garden of Eden and talked with them around the cool of the evening. It was easy for them to ask God questions and hear His wise answers. However, with their expulsion from the garden, their communication with God was cut off.

From the day of their expulsion, sacrifices were begun when God made them coats of skins to cover their nakedness. God did have some contact with man after the expulsion from the garden by showing that He received Abel's sacrifice and rejected Cain's. God's revelation to man was very limited before Moses. He confused man's language at the Tower of Babylon, and dispersed people over all the earth. Beginning Genesis 12, God revealed Himself to Abraham, then Isaac, then Jacob, leading them into Canaan, and then into Egypt, where their descendants spent 400 years as slaves.

At the end of the 400 years of slavery, God raised up Moses and led the Israelites out of slavery. Moses was the first person to receive a written revelation from God, and he wrote the first 5 books of the Bible, as well as Psalm 90. In order that Moses would understand the nature of revelation, God explained to him how revelation would be given in Exodus 4:15-16: "You are to speak to him and put the words in his mouth; and I, even I, will be with your mouth and his mouth, and I will teach you what you are to do. Moreover he shall speak for you to the people; and he will be as a mouth for you and you will be as God to him."

Here we have an excellent illustration, given directly by God to Moses, of what God's idea of special revelation is. In this passage, Moses has complained that he was not eloquent in speech in order to go and tell Pharaoh to let the Israelites go. God answered that Aaron was on his way to meet him, and that Aaron was eloquent in speech. Then God explained how He was going to use Moses and Aaron to give His revelation to Pharaoh.

First of all, God says that He will be with Moses' mouth and Aaron's mouth, and will teach (*vehoreythi*, וְהוֹרֵיתִי) them what they shall do. This is the role of God. He is the initiator. Even as He appeared to Moses in the burning bush and spoke with him, using actual words, so God's revelation goes down to the very spoken words. The word translated "and I will teach" is the verbal form of the word Torah, which is the Jewish name for the Pentateuch. It is elsewhere rendered in the Greek as *voμos* (νόμος), which is the rough equivalent. However, the word law, as used in the English, limits the scope of the teachings too much.

Verse 16 gives us a graphic understanding of revelation. Moses was to put words in the mouth of Aaron, and the result would be that "he will be as a mouth for you and you will be as God to him." Here Moses, in the place of God for Aaron, is to speak to him all the words that God gave him. Here we have a high view of revelation, in that even the words were given to Aaron, who was like the prophet before the people. Aaron did not contribute—intellectually or in any other way—to the content of the revelation. He simply passed on, word for word, what he received from Moses. This was Aaron's activity as a spokesman, or prophet. Moses, in the place of God for Aaron, was responsible that all of the words of the revelation got to Aaron. This shows how some of the Scripture was given by direct dictation from God.

Another Old Testament example of Divine inspiration is II Samuel 23:2, where David says: "The Spirit of the Lord spoke by me, and His word was on my tongue." By the time the word is on David's tongue being spoken, it has already gone through his brain.

Here the emphasis is on the fact that every word in Scripture is inspired. God takes the responsibility for every word of the final product, but very little was given by dictation. As the Spirit of God moved in David, He used the vocabulary, literary style, and experience of David to blend together what He wanted to produce for the situation in David's life, which He brought about in which to express this revelation.

I believe that God brought about a perfect revelation through at least four means. First of all, God guided the Biblical author's development. He guided Paul to study under the Pharisee Gamaliel, and Peter to be a fisherman. He guided David to be a shepherd, and Matthew to be a tax collector. He guided each person to have the background so that his perspective was developed to express God's viewpoint within his viewpoint for the specific Biblical material they wrote.

The second way God guided the inspiration of the Scriptures was by preparing the events. These include the historic context, culture, type of opposition against God toward which the passage is directed, as well as many other events. For example, we would not know how to handle church discipline unless there arose the case in Corinth of a man living in sin with his stepmother. In that situation, the Holy Spirit spoke through Paul on how to discipline a brother, and then how to restore him after he has repented. Because believers were going to court against believers, the occasion arose for the Holy Spirit through Paul to forbid it in I Corinthians 6. In fact, with the exception of Romans, which appears more of a doctrinal manifesto, most letters in Scripture seem to be more a reaction to a situation that God brought about in order to communicate His truth concerning it.

The third way that God guided the inspiration of the Scriptures was in the preparation of the language in which it was given. This preparation includes the language itself and its development throughout the various generations, including that particular generation. As time progresses, the meanings of words change, and those for that generation that received the revelation are the meanings that we should accept for the words.

For example, most of the Bible is written in Hebrew. The Israelite people began with Abraham, who spoke Aramaic. The three patriarchs learned the Canaanite language, now called Ugaritic, from the Canaanites with whom they dwelled from the time Abraham arrived in Canaan until Jacob and sons departed for Egypt. The Aramaic of Rebekah, Rachel, and Leah reinforced the original Aramaic during this time, and so the language of the patriarchs already showed itself somewhat of a mixture of Aramaic and the Canaanite language.

The next stage of development of the language of Israel was their stay in Egypt. Egypt at this time spoke a Semitic language called Coptic, and influenced the developing Hebrew over the 400-year period they lived there. The word Sinai is probably from the Egyptian root "imt", meaning clay, of which *sin* is the transliteration."[4] The pronominal suffix is a first person possessive suffix, which is added to the plural construct form of the noun. The meaning is "my clays." At Sinai God, as the Divine Potter is molding His people, and He calls them individually "My clays." Through the commandments, then, God is molding "His clays," who were first saved by the blood of the lamb in Egypt, baptized in the crossing of the Red Sea, and who committed themselves to obey Him in Exodus 19:8.

I believe that God's revelation included the guiding of the formation of the Egyptian language so that the word, which would be transliterated into Hebrew as *sin*, with the meaning "clay," would be there, as well as would be the name of that mountain. This naming of Mt. Sinai was as much a part of God's revelation as was the giving of the Law there. For Semitic peoples, the name of the place usually tells what is going on there; but in the cases where it doesn't, a new name is often given, as in Exodus 17, where Rephidim ("Protected Places") is renamed Massah ("Testing (God)") and Meribah ("Striving"). Since it is important for revelation to give the right name to a place, God also supervises the naming of the places, and their use in the right form in the Biblical languages.

Finally, the Holy Spirit guided in the selection of the very words that were used to express His revelation. Sometimes a culturally refined word is used, and sometimes a more common word is used to refer to something. For example, Mark uses the rather coarse word *krábatton* (*κράβαττον*) for the cot that four men used to bring a sick man to Jesus in Mark 2:4. According to Bauer, this is a rather late word and specifically refers to the type of bed a poor person would have.[5] In the parallel account in Matthew 9, the word *klíne* (κλίνη) is used in verses 2 and 6. This means bed, but was a more refined term, which could be used for a couch one reclined to eat, as well as a bed, where one reclined to sleep.[6] Our word "recline" is probably related to it. Finally, Luke, in chapter 5 begins with the word *klíne* in verse 18. In verse 19, when he is being let down through the roof to Jesus, the diminutive *klinídion* (κλινίδιον) is used. It is also used in verse 24 when Jesus tells the man, "Get up, and pick up your stretcher (*klinídion*), and go home."

The difference in selection of words is very important in God's supervision of the revelation process. It is prepared in the human author through his upbringing and education, as well as the types of people that he associates with. Mark, in addition to Peter, who is thought to have assisted him with his Gospel, was apparently from the classes of common people. He is writing from that viewpoint and using that type of vocabulary. His Gospel would naturally be more readily accepted and better understood among those people. The common people who had this cheap type of cot as their only bed would better understand his choice of *krábatton*. Matthew was a wealthy tax collector who associated with the upper classes. These people would have considered *krábatton* to be a coarse, lower class or colloquial word, and unsuitable for their tastes. Matthew uses the refined general word *klíne* and lets the reader supply the type of *klíne* from the context. Luke, the doctor, begins with this general term, but later switches to the more medically precise diminutive *klinídion*, which was probably also used as a stretcher for medical purposes.[6]

The selection of the different words reflect both the upbringing and social status of the Gospel writer, and it also makes their Gospels particularly suited to the audience that they are from. There is no issue of truth or falsity about the selection of these 3 words, but they come from the different backgrounds of the 3 authors and they make their works more adaptable to different audiences so that the Word of God can better reach all people. Thus, we see that God's revelation includes the preparation of the author in his social context, as well as his selection of words as he writes. The result is a product that is 100% the work of the human author and 100% the product of God's work in everything.

Given the lost state of man, how could revelation be anything else? God must take the whole initiative. He must be with His prophet and guide him in everything through to the very words themselves. Jesus goes even beyond this when He says in Matthew 5:18: "For truly I say unto you, until heaven and earth pass away, not the smallest letter or stroke shall pass from the Law, until all is accomplished." This statement of Jesus assures us that the smallest letter in the Hebrew alphabet, the yod (written like a raised comma), and the smallest stroke that makes a difference between letters, the tittle, carries the full inspiration of God, and is totally reliable. The tittle makes a difference between the beth and the caph, the zayin and vav, and the dalet and resh, being present in the former but absent in the latter of each pair. Jesus did not mention any vowels, some of which are smaller, because these were not invented until the end of the first century. Hebrew was written with consonants only in Jesus' day.

By asserting that the written revelation of God was more secure than heaven and earth, Jesus may have been alluding to the fact that in the original creation everything came into being through the commands of God, which were issued in words proceeding from His mouth. I believe that there were angels obeying His words to labor in the creation of this world, rather than thinking that the words themselves magically created the universe. Since, however, the universe came into being as a result of the words of God, it necessarily follows that the word of God is surer and more certain of being true than the universe or whatever appears to our senses as an experience of this world.

Since the written revelation of God is absolutely sure and secure in its revelation to the Bible writers, the liberal view and the neo-orthodox view are excluded. The liberal view is that the Bible contains the Word of God, but that man must discover a certain criteria "X" that allows him to separate human error from the revelation. This view allows man to sit in judgment over the revelation of God, rather than sitting under its authority. It is reminiscent of the first temptation of the Serpent in the Garden of Eden, when he cast doubt on God's threat of death for eating from the forbidden tree. If man sits in judgment on the Bible, then he is a judge, rather than a student of God's "instruction," as the word *Torah* means.

The neo-orthodox position is no closer to the truth. Its adherents say that the Bible becomes the Word of God in the experience of the believer, but that the written word has human errors. Baillie summarizes a number of these authors, including Barth, Brunner, Bultmann, and Tillich and then says about them: "Each of the recent writers whom we have cited has been concerned to warn us against any simple identification of the Christian revelation with the contents of the Bible, and each has been well aware that in this respect he was breaking with the long-established tradition."[7]

The insistence of the neo-orthodox is that revelation is not revelation at all if we do not understand it. As we experience it, then, it becomes revelation to us. Baillie then concludes: "But there is no Christian who hears God through every passage in the Bible, so that for each of us there are some passages that are not revelatory at all."[8] While it would be admitted in terms of our Christian discipleship, that we come to understand the Bible more and more as we continue in our Christian walk, to insist that the unknown portions of the Bible are not revelatory for one until understood by him is to make its truth dependent on our experience of it, and to make that truth subjective. The result is that one person could get one meaning out of a passage and another person could get the opposite meaning out of the same passage and that the contradictory ideas would be revelatory for both of them. Why then, does the Bible warn about false teaching? There could be no false teaching, according to this way of approaching revelation. Everyone would think that he was right because his ideas are formed by his experience and his experience judges for him what is revelation from God and what is not.

It is none other than Karl Barth who says that the Bible does not claim authority for itself. "Why and wherein does the Biblical witness possess authority? Precisely in this, that it claims no authority at all for itself, that its witness consists in allowing that Other Thing to be itself and through itself the authority. Hence we do the Bible a misdirected honor, and one unwelcome to itself, if we directly identify it with this Other Thing, the revelation itself. This can happen in the form of a doctrine of the general and uniform inspiration of the Bible" (emphasis mine).[9]

Once one separates Divine revelation from the Bible, human experience becomes the judge of what is truly from God and what is just human content present in the same vehicle as God's revelation. If human experience is made the judge of the truth of the Bible, then it is just the criteria "X" that the liberals are looking for. In II Peter 1:16-19 Peter mentions his experience on the Mount of Transfiguration: "For we did not follow cleverly devised tales, when we made known to you the power and coming of our Lord Jesus Christ, but we were eyewitnesses of his majesty. For when He received honor and glory from God the Father, such an utterance as this was made to Him by the Majestic Glory, 'This is my beloved Son, with whom I am well-pleased'—and we ourselves heard this utterance made from heaven when we were with him in the holy mountain. <u>So we have the prophetic word made more sure</u>, to which you do well to pay attention."

If there was ever a glorious religious experience, that was it! However, what is Peter's conclusion about this? The written word of prophecy was "made more sure" to Peter than his personal experience. How could this be? Personal experiences are by nature highly subjective, and the person would be left to interpret the meaning. In fact Peter misinterpreted this event at the time, and wanted to celebrate the Jewish Feast of Tabernacles, which was associated with the Messianic Kingdom (also called the Millennial Kingdom) because he saw Jesus glorified. Peter still expected or hoped that Jesus would enter into his glory without suffering, and Peter was wrong. The experience was not enough because the interpretation would be left to the person. The written Word of God was "made more sure" specifically because it contained both the personal experiences of the Biblical writers <u>and</u> God's interpretation of what those experiences meant. Nothing is left to the creativity or imagination of the human instrument, and therefore no error is possible.

Peter returns to the importance of God's Word over man's experience again in verses 20 and 21: "But know this first of all, that no prophecy of Scripture is a matter of one's own interpretation, for no prophecy was ever made by an act of human will, but men moved by the Holy Spirit spoke from God."

First of all here, Peter is saying that the Scripture is not men's private interpretation of Salvation events that they are observing. The view of the Roman Catholic Church that this means that the church has to interpret Scripture to the people, who are not allowed their "private interpretations" is disallowed by the context here. The assertion by Peter is that Bible writers did not make their own interpretations of what God revealed to them, but rather depended on the Holy Spirit to explain the interpretation of the events and experiences to them down to the very words of the revelation.

In verse 21 we see that Bible writers spoke (and wrote) as they were moved by the Holy Spirit. I believe that the Holy Spirit took over and guided the writers as they were writing so that there were no errors in the original manuscript. The work can be said to be both the work of the human author and the work of the Holy Spirit because the Holy Spirit supervised everything, from the development of the language in which it would be written to the preparation of the author and the circumstances under which it was written. The inspiration reaches the very words, and even further, according to Jesus Himself, as mentioned above in Matthew 5:18: "For truly I say unto you, until heaven and earth pass away, not the smallest letter or stroke shall pass from the Law, until all is accomplished." There can be no higher view of the inspiration of the Scriptures than this affirmation of the smallest letter and the smallest stroke that makes a distinction between letters.

III. Jesus as Special Revelation.

It is clear what the Bible claims for its own inspiration. The universe's existence depends upon the word of God, as also does its maintenance. In Hebrews 1:1-3 we read what the Bible claims about the coming of Jesus Christ: "God, after He spoke long ago to the fathers in the prophets in many portions and in many ways, <u>in these last days has spoken to us in His Son</u>, whom He appointed heir of all things, <u>through whom also He made the world</u>. And He is the radiance of His glory and the exact representation of His nature, and <u>upholds all things by the word of His power</u>. When he had made purification of sins, He sat down at the right hand of the Majesty on high."

After a quick reference to the prior revelation of God in the Old Testament through the prophets, the author of Hebrews focuses on Jesus as the highest revelation of God to mankind. There are three special claims made about Jesus that are highlighted here. The first claim made here is that God spoke to humanity through His Son, Jesus Christ. This means that every word that Jesus spoke was a direct word from God. Unlike the dictation model revelation in Exodus 3, in which Moses was as God to Aaron and Aaron was as his prophet, Jesus was both God and the prophet together in the same person. There was no passing of information twice—once was enough. Jesus spoke God's words directly.

The verbal revelation in Jesus is superior to the verbal revelation of the prophets and apostles in that there is no question that every word that came out of Jesus' mouth was fully to be trusted in every way. For the prophets and apostles, we can be sure only of their canonical writings. In I Corinthians 7, for example, the Apostle Paul tries to separate what the Holy Spirit is giving to the church as authoritative truth from his own opinion, which is not binding on the church and is not necessarily true.

In I Corinthians 7:7-9 Paul first gives suggestions from his own perspective which are not binding. Then in verses 10-11 he switches from his own personal perspective to the authoritative command from the Holy Spirit for married people: "But to the married I give instructions, *not I, but the Lord*, that the wife should not leave her husband (but if she does leave, she must remain unmarried, or else be reconciled to her husband), and that the husband should not divorce his wife."

Here Paul is stating directly that some of the things he is saying are just suggestions, most notably his recommendation of the single life, and other things he is saying are direct commands from the Holy Spirit. Paul then finishes the chapter in verse 40 with his last advice that it would be better for widows to remain single: "But in my opinion she is happier if she remains as she is; and I think that I also have the Spirit of God." Paul thinks that he has the Spirit of God on that point, but he is not sure. There is a great difference between

Paul and Jesus. Everything that Jesus said *was the word of God.* In fact, The Apostle John reverses this emphasis by describing God's incarnation in Jesus in John 1:14 by saying "And the Word became flesh and dwelt among us." This statement declared Jesus to be a living, breathing statement of God's Word, and thus, infallible in every word he uttered.

The second way in which Jesus' words were superior to those of the apostles and prophets is that the latter said and wrote things which were not canonical, and these things may have contained errors. Jesus, on the other hand, was perfect in every word that He uttered in His whole life. Though the Gospel writers had much more material about Jesus than are written in their Gospels (John 21:25), all of the sayings of Jesus that they had were perfect. There was no need for the Holy Spirit to sort out which ones may have contained errors and which were "from Him." On the other hand we may freely admit that the Holy Spirit selected writings of the apostles and prophets to eliminate things they said that may have contained errors, as well as selecting them according to His purposes of content.

In Colossians 4:16 the Apostle Paul requests that the Colossians exchange epistles with the Laodiceans so that they could read that one also. However, Paul's epistle to the Laodiceans has not been preserved. Had there existed something that Jesus wrote or that contained sayings of Jesus, these sources could be confidently placed on the same level, and indeed added to the canon of Scripture. I believe that God worked things out so that just what is canonical of the prophets and apostles is Divine Revelation, but that everything about Jesus was Divine Revelation.

The second expression of the author of the Epistle to the Hebrews about Jesus was "through Whom also He made the world." According to this passage, God created the worlds through Jesus. The original Greek has the plural here. This statement includes this world and the world to come, as well as any others that might exist and are not revealed to us. It is important to note that Genesis begins with the verse: "In the beginning God (Elohim) created the heavens and the earth." It is in the name of Elohim that God deals with what we call the natural world. We can come to understand God through our five senses as we study this world, which is made by Him. This was discussed above under natural revelation.

It is interesting to note here that the persons of the Godhead appear to be speaking among themselves in Genesis 1:26: "Let us make man in our image, according to our likeness." A Jewish interpretation of this passage is that God is discussing His creation with the angels. This interpretation puts the angels on the same level with God that they could have the same image. Elsewhere God is shown to be jealous of others receiving any glory that is due Him alone, and so this interpretation does not fit with the rest of the Old Testament revelation.

Genesis 1:26 does, however, leave open the possibility that Jesus—before being born into the human race—was discussing with God the Father and the Holy Spirit what the creation was to be like. In this light we find it interesting that the image of God in the next verse is defined as "male and female." In Genesis 2:24 God sees a man and his wife as "one flesh." This is the fuller image of God. The Hebrew expression for "one flesh" is *basar echad* (בָּשָׂר אֶחָד). The word *echad* is a pluralistic unity, and it also appears in Deuteronomy 6:4 which Jewish people often quote: "Hear, o Israel, the Lord our God, the Lord is One." In this verse the word for one is *echad,* which leaves open the possibility that God Himself is a pluralistic unity, consistent with the Christian doctrine of the three persons in the Godhead that are One. It is this understanding of the Tri-unity of God that gives us understanding of Jesus as both the One who did the actual creation of the universe, and the One who came to redeem mankind.

The third statement about Jesus in Hebrews 1:1-3 is that "he upholds all things by the word of His power." This refers to the fact that it is Jesus Who is maintaining this universe right now with the word of his power. This means that the angels that are sustaining the natural forces are under His control. That is why the rest of chapter 1 of Hebrews continues with other statements about how Jesus is superior to the angels.

In addition to the natural realm of creation, there is the relation that God has with man, and this relation is also carried out under the name Jehovah. In the character of this name, God deals directly with people. As Jehovah Elohim He creates man in Genesis 2:7 (we are both spiritual and material), He appears to Moses at the burning bush in Exodus 3 in the name Jehovah. Specifically here in verse 14 God gives this name Jehovah as the one by which He is to be invoked as He delivers the Israelites from Egypt. The name Jehovah, then, is God's name to be used in relation to His specific personal dealings with people.

It is especially in the Gospel of John that Jesus is presented as the great revelation of Jehovah Elohim. In chapter 6:1-13 Jesus feeds the 5000 by multiplying fish and loaves of bread. This accredits His claim to be God as Elohim by showing that He can create matter. In verses 32-51 Jesus is teaching publicly and claims to be the Bread of Life which comes down from heaven and gives life to the world (vv. 48-50): "I am the bread of life. Your fathers ate the manna in the wilderness, and they died. This is the bread which comes down out of heaven, so that one may eat of it and not die." This statement is a religious claim to be the only one that can satisfy every man's spiritual need. Jesus here is claiming to be Jehovah, as He claims to be man's "religious" fulfillment in a personal relationship, and He does it in the same context where he fed the 5000 physically.

There are several other interesting combinations Jesus' claims in John's Gospel that attest to Jesus' claims to be God, both as Elohim and as Jehovah together about the same topic. In John 8:12 Jesus claims: "I am the light of the world: he who follows me will not walk in the darkness, but will have the Light of life." This is a "religious" claim that Jesus makes to offer the true light, or spiritual sight, to everyone. This is a claim to be God in the character of the name Jehovah, by which He deals directly with men. Later in the same chapter Jesus claims directly to be Jehovah when he says in verse 58, "truly, truly I say to you, before Abraham was born, <u>I am</u>." The expression "I am," is not just a claim to have existed before Abraham. "I am" is the name Jehovah used at the burning bush to refer to Himself: "I AM WHO I AM." The people properly understood what he was claiming and tried to stone Him to death for blasphemy. Instead of denying their interpretation of His statement or trying to defend Himself, He slipped out of the place. This was the message He was trying to get across: that He is Jehovah.

Jesus next substantiates His claim to be God in the character of the name Elohim by healing a blind man in chapter 9 right after He escaped being stoned for blasphemy for claiming to be Jehovah as the light of the world. Here He substantiates His claim be showing that he is God the Creator (Elohim) by giving sight to a man blind from birth.

In chapter 10 of John's Gospel Jesus claims: "I am the good shepherd: the good shepherd lays down His life for the sheep." In the light of Psalm 23, it is probable that He was claiming to be Jehovah through this claim. Jesus directly associates this claim with His coming death for the sheep. Jesus continues beyond this, though. In response to a demand that He tell the Jewish leaders if He is the Messiah, Jesus says in verse 25: "I told you, and you do not believe; the works that I do in my Father's name, these testify of me." From that point, Jesus goes on to present His claims to be God (vv. 27-30): "My sheep hear My voice, and I know them and they follow Me; and I give eternal life to them, and they will never perish; and no one will snatch them out of my hand. My Father, who has given them to Me, is greater than all, and no one is able to snatch them out of my Father's hand. I and the Father are one."

At this point that crowd is again ready to stone Jesus for blasphemy (v.33) "because You, being a man, make Yourself out to be God." Jesus makes a dodge here by referring to the fact that all men are called gods (Heb. Elohim) unto whom the Word of God came. He still placed Himself above them as the one "whom the Father sanctified and sent into the world." They then sought to kill Him, but He escaped again.

As Jesus had said that He is the Good Shepherd that gives His life for the sheep, and that he gives eternal life to whomsoever he will, Jesus was making a claim to be Jehovah. In addition to this claim, however, Jesus also demonstrates that He is God as Elohim by raising Lazarus in the next chapter. In John 11:25-26, Jesus claims: "I am the resurrection and the life: he who believes in Me will live even if he dies, and everyone who lives and believes in Me will never die."

This claim is clearly that claim to be God in the character of His name Elohim. Only God can give life to people. Jesus substantiates this claim by raising Lazarus, a believer in Him, from the dead after he was dead four days. The Jewish people thought that the human soul hovered around the body during 3 days after death trying to re-enter. By the fourth day they knew for sure that Lazarus was dead.

This potent combination of Jesus' self-revelation as God—both in the character of the name Elohim and the name Jehovah—is also found in the Gospels. In all three Synoptic Gospels we find the combined accounts of Jesus calming the storm on the Sea of Galilee (Mat. 8:23-27, Mark 4:35-41, and Luke 8:22-25) followed by the story of His casting the legion of demons out of the Gadarene man (Mat. 8:28-34, Mark, 5:1-20, Luke 8:26-39). Jesus first demonstrates that He is God in the character of the name Elohim by calming the raging sea. In Psalm 89:9 we read that this is expected of God, not men: "You rule the swelling of the sea; when its waves rise, You still them.."

After Jesus landed in the Gadarene area, a man possessed by a legion of demons met him. This man came running to him, having his soul raging. For this man the storm was on the inside in his soul. By casting out the Legion of demons, Jesus brought peace on the inside to the man. In Mark 5:15 we read: "They came to Jesus and observed the man who had been demon-possessed sitting down, clothed, and in his right mind, the very man who had had the "legion"; and they became frightened." Here Jesus illustrates that He is God in the character of the name Jehovah, showing "religious" authority over evil spirits, to calm the raging in a man's soul. This is the exact parallel of His calming of the sea just before he came there. The calming of the sea showed that Jesus was Elohim, and the casting out of demons to calm a raging man showed that Jesus is Jehovah.

There is no greater special revelation of God than Jesus of Nazareth. In John 1:18 we read: "No one has seen God at any time; the only begotten God, who is in the bosom of the Father, He has explained Him." The King James Version reads, "the only begotten son," but many of the best ancient manuscripts read, as does the NASB, "the only begotten God, Which is in the bosom of the Father." This would say directly (what can be established in other places) that Jesus is God living before our very eyes. The final declaration that Jesus has "explained" the Father in Greek is *ekeinos exegésato* (ἐκεῖνος ἐξηγήσατο). From the latter word comes our word exegesis, which is literally the "leading out" of the meaning of a Biblical passage as accurately as is possible.

Jesus' life is a "leading out" of the Father for us in every detail, and is thus authoritative for us in every detail. His teaching is binding on us, His miracles are authoritative and perfect acts revealing the character of the Father, and what Jesus was doing on earth was in perfect parallel with what the Father was doing and willing in Heaven. In John 8:28-29 Jesus says: "When you lift up the Son of Man, then you will know that I am He, and I do nothing on my own initiative, but I speak these things as the Father taught Me. And he who sent Me is with Me; He has not left me alone, for I always do the things that are pleasing to Him."

If ever there was to be lived on the earth one life that pleased the Father, it was that of Jesus of Nazareth. That was the only one. Both at Jesus' baptism (Mat. 3:17) and at His Transfiguration (Mat. 17:5), there was heard the voice of the Father from Heaven saying, "This is My beloved Son, with whom I am well pleased; listen to him."

It is clear that Jesus is accepted as God's highest revelation to mankind. Therefore, in Scripture, we can always be sure that everything that Jesus says is absolute truth. There will be no comments; such as those of Paul that he thinks that he has the Spirit's will on a particular topic. Absolutely everything Jesus says and does was the will of the Father in every moment, whether or not it was ever recorded in Scriptures, and that which is in Scriptures is the example for the life of every believer.

There is one limitation of the life of Jesus, however. Though it was by far much greater than any other, all those of us who were not there in the first century where He was, would not ever have known much about him were it not for the Scriptures. We cannot know anything authoritative about Jesus except from the Bible. The Old Testament gives prophecies about Him, and the New Testament tells of His life and records actual teachings of His. The rest of the New Testament comments on Jesus are also reliable and from apostolic eyewitnesses. Jesus Himself promised that the Holy Spirit would supervise the process of writing the New Testament material so that the product would be without error in reporting about Him (John 14:26): "But the Helper, the Holy Spirit, whom the Father will send in My name, He will teach you all things, and bring to your remembrance all that I said to you." Thus, the Scriptures are again our only totally reliable revelation from God for today.

IV. Christ in Us, the Hope of Glory.

The life of Jesus is the only one that will ever be approved on this earth. Does that mean, however, that the individual Christian will never have a chance of hearing God say, "Well done, thou good and faithful servant"? The answer is no. There is a further revelation necessary. At this point, we may concede to the neo-orthodox their claim that if the revelation of God does not reach us it does us no good. We cannot, however, assert that it is not revelation, as Baillie does: "But there is no Christian who hears God speaking to him through every passage in the Bible, so that for each of us there are some passages that are not revelatory at all."[10]

The Bible is God's special revelation to mankind, and from God's point of view it is 100% revelatory. Due to our human limitations, not every passage speaks to us. To Baillie's credit he recognizes this fact as he continues: "Nevertheless it is always our duty to ask ourselves whether the defect may not be in ourselves rather than in the text, whether even here it is not we who are not willing to listen, rather than that nothing significant is being said."[10]

The first reason that the Scriptures are not "revelatory" to many people is that they are not born again. The Scriptures are saying something significant for all people, but they call man to repent of running his own life and exhort him to surrender his life to God. Those who refuse to do this will lack the Holy Spirit and will therefore fail to grasp the deeper meaning of Scripture because it needs to be revealed by the Holy Spirit. As Paul says in I Cor. 2:14-15: "But a natural man does not accept the things of the Spirit of God, for they are foolishness to him; and he cannot understand them, because they are spiritually appraised. But he who is spiritual appraises all things, yet he himself is appraised by no man."

We need to be born again to have the Holy Spirit in us. Then we will be able to understand the Scriptures better because the same

Holy Spirit that guided in the preparation of the Scriptures will be in us guiding our understanding. This is the greatest defect in the approach of Baillie and other neo-orthodox. They are still trying to judge between what is Scripture and what is an erring human vehicle of literature through which it is conveyed. He cites as an example the medieval scholars who, when something in Aristotle seemed untrue, where more prone to doubt their own thinking than that of Aristotle because they carried their reverence too far.

Baillie declares that man's challenge in understanding the Bible is "to distinguish what is essential from what is peripheral...to distinguish also between its essential message and its numerous imperfections—historical inaccuracies, inaccurate or conflicting reports, misquotations, or misapplied quotations from the Old Testament in the New, and such like."[11]

One can well ask today if it is possible to carry a reverence for God too far, though I would agree that one could carry a reverence for Aristotle too far. I would certainly trust an apostle or prophet who wrote as the Holy Spirit inspired him above my own sin-warped judgment. As Baillie mentioned earlier that the problem may be in us, he understated it. Man is totally incapable of understanding the revelation of God in Scripture without the new birth, as Paul says of the natural man.

How then can man understand the Bible? We need to look at the last step in revelation: the revelation of Jesus Christ in the believer. In Galatians 1:15-16, Paul refers to his conversion in the following way: "But when God, Who had set me apart even from my mother's womb and called me through His grace was pleased *to reveal His son in me* so that I might preach Him among the Gentiles..." For Paul, the Christian life was Christ in the believer, not the imitation of Christ from afar. It is the Christ in the believer that accurately understands the Written Revelation of the Holy Scriptures, and Christ must be revealed in the believer by an act of the Grace of God in response to saving faith.

As Paul mentioned concerning his own conversion, so he sought to reproduce in every believer. As he wrote to the Galatians, whom he saw straying from the faith, he wrote to them thus (Gal. 4:19): "My children, with whom am again in labor until Christ is formed in you." Paul's goal is that Christ be formed in the believer. How could the believer use his own discernment to separate from between the words of Paul what was God's revelation and what was erroneous, if he needed to be transformed totally?

As mentioned in I Corinthians 2 above, the spiritual man is being guided to have the mind of Christ, but that is not all. He is being transformed to have the will of Christ, as well. As we read in Philippians 2:13: "It is God who is at work in you, both to will and to work for His good pleasure." Thus, the will of Christ is being formed in us, and our own will is being replace by it, to the degree that we submit to the Holy Spirit.

Where the mind and will of Christ are mentioned, the emotions will not be far behind. As we allow the Spirit of God to transform us, we will react the same way to the situation as Jesus would in our shoes. That is why we are exhorted to "Rejoice with those who rejoice, and weep with those who weep (Rom. 12:15)."

As we allow Jesus to take over and live His life through us, we are transformed, being continually given over to the death of our own mind, will, and emotions, and being continually filled up with Jesus living through us. The key to this ongoing revelatory process of Christ in us is Galatians 2:20: "I have been crucified with Christ; and it is no longer I who live, but Christ lives in me; and the life which I now live in the flesh I live by faith in the Son of God, who loved me and gave Himself up for me."

By way of comparison and contrast, it is useful to look at the New Age perspective on this matter. The key experience for a New Ager is to be "initiated", an experience whereby the person receives a spirit guide residing in him or coming often to him. After the initiation, the person is able to channel the spirit through his body and mind. Before the person is initiated he does not really understand things, but afterwards, the Spirit enlightens them.

There are some similarities between the New Ager and the Christian. First of all, to be a believer in Jesus, one must be "born again." This is the necessary experience to begin a Christian life. Jesus says to Nicodemus (John 3:3), "Truly, truly I say to you, unless one is born again, he cannot see the kingdom of God." Being born again is the initiation into a relation with the God of the Bible through the presence of the Holy Spirit.

For both there is an initiation experience. However, this brings up a great difference: to which spirit is one being initiated. The New Ager, with his aversion for Biblical Christianity is obviously not channeling the same spirit as the Christian. He is spiritual, but with a different spirit. In his book *When the World will be as One*, Tal Brooke describes the spirit behind the New Age initiations: "The mystery of Lucifer will finally be unveiled—"They will worship the dragon." Foreshadowings of this have recently appeared. Blatantly, there has been the rapid appearance of the phenomenon of Satanism. On a subtler level, Alice Bailey pointed to a coming Luciferic New Age initiation, as has David Spangler, a major New Age leader. New Age events dotting our horizon form a rising aggregate of voices speaking of New Age initiations."[12]

It appears that the New Agers are promoting a similar experience as the Christian "born again" experience, only the spirit is different. We must check by right doctrine whether the spirit is of God or not. The human elements of the religious experience are similar, though. God's written revelation in the Bible shows us what the Holy Spirit will do, and what He responds to. Any other spirit should be avoided.

As we undergo our metamorphosis by the power of the Holy Spirit, we must be careful to keep in mind that this process, as well, is subjective. Therefore we must keep checking everything by the Scripture, God's Written Revelation, which is objective and constant. If we find a difference, we must suppose that the problem is in us and allow the Lord to show us our error. We are following the God of the Universe, not Aristotle, and God is infallible.

Conclusion:

At this point the revelation goes full circle. We have discussed how we were born alive unto God once; but when the commandment came, sin revived and we died. This death was spiritual, and our spirit, which was created perfect and in harmony with God, died, being cut off from God's presence and God's Spirit. Thereafter, there began a struggle to "get back into the Garden of Eden," figuratively speaking. For we all have rebelled against the direct spiritual knowledge of God that we had, and were thrust out of God's presence. As a result we all have a God-sized vacuum within us that can only be filled by God.

Meanwhile, God has revealed many things about Himself in his creation. Through the creation, as we grew up, we came to know many things about Him, namely His eternal power and Godhead, so that we are without excuse. At this stage our conscience bothered us, but it did not show us the way back.

One day, we who are Christians heard the written revelation of God, the Bible, either by reading it ourselves or by hearing it from someone else, and we believed. "So faith comes from hearing, and hearing by the Word of Christ" (Romans 10:17). At that time we were born again and our spirit was again in contact with the Holy Spirit of God. According to II Cor. 3:18, we have been contemplating the Lord Jesus in our spirit since then, and we are being changed into the likeness of Jesus. The Christian life is the gradual replacement of our life with that of Jesus.

The same Spirit that inspired the Holy Scriptures is developing the mind, will, and emotions of Christ in us. As we act in the world, it is not we who are acting, but Jesus. Thus the Heavenly Father, Who is looking down from heaven is pleased with us because He sees less and less of the life we inherited from Adam and more and more of the life of His Son being lived out through us. As we are being transformed through the revelation of Jesus Christ in us, we ourselves, as living epistles, are becoming a part of God's revelation to other people, who are lost in their trespasses and sins.

Thanks be to God for His Marvelous Revelations!

Chapter 3

Just Who Are We, Anyway? What is a Human Being?

It is appropriate at the beginning of this story of a human being to ask the question, who are we, anyway? If we do not know who we are, then we cannot answer any of the great questions that we are faced with, nor can we set goals and determine our purpose here. It is not the purpose of this chapter to prove that the Bible is true and inspired by a Benevolent, Omnipotent, Omniscient, and Eternal God, as we Christians believe. Nevertheless, it is hoped that the reader will come to that faith as he sees the marvelous working of that God in Israel's history as a pictorial model of the Christian's walk in the World to Come. No only that, but as a result of seeing that model, he will want to internalize the history of Israel by setting out on that pilgrimage himself.

In the first two chapters we have dealt with material that was introductory, describing God and His revelation to us. In this chapter are beginning this narrative with man himself as a transition to the narrative itself. This will prepare us to understand the history of Israel as the perceptual model for the Christian life. We individual human beings are the actors in history, as well as the individual Christian's life. Therefore, if we don't know what man himself is, we will understand neither the Israelites nor the modern Christian.

Two things that stand out clearly in the Biblical narrative of the creation of man are that man is to be understood primarily in terms of his relation to God, and that man was created to rule over God's creation, including the angels. These two assertions about man place him in relation to God, and in relation to the rest of creation. This two-fold description of man's place locates him in a chain of command in the middle between God and the rest of His creation. In Genesis 1:26 we read: "Then God said, "Let Us make man in Our image, according to our likeness; and let them rule over the fish of the sea and over the birds of the sky and over the cattle and over all the earth, and over every creeping thing that creeps on the earth."

As we will see in more detail later, man, as image of God, is in a sense God's representative as a subordinate ruler on His behalf over the rest of God's creation. Therefore any explanation of man's identity must be primarily concerned with his relation to his Creator God, and secondarily with his relation to other created beings, such as angels, animals, plants, and even non-living things.

In this chapter we will look at five names for a human being, as described in the Hebrew, along with the applications of how to live today. Where appropriate, we will consider the different parts of the human being, as well as other issues. As a conclusion, we will try to establish an understanding of human identity that will serve as a base for the presentation of Israel's Heilsgeschichte (Salvation-history) as the Gestalt (perceptual model) for the internal spiritual pilgrimage of the modern New Testament believer in Jesus. Thus we can begin the narrative of Abraham knowing who he is and why he was called by God. Through that understanding, we will also understand why all human beings are in a sense called by God.

We need to keep these descriptions of man in the back of our memory to make sure that we are not going off the track as we proceed further. In the tradition of the best Semitic writers of Biblical revelation, we need, like an artist, to sketch in the broad strokes of the picture of God's truth first. Then, as we return to fill in details of basic categories, we will not violate the carefully drawn lines of God's earlier revelation, since later revelation must be developed in the historical, social, cultural, and linguistic context already established by God in the earlier revelation of His Truth.

I. Man: the Image of God (IMAGO DEI).

The Bible gives us two narratives about the creation of man: Genesis 1:26-27, and Genesis 2:7, 21-23. These two narratives are not contradictory, but rather supplementary. The first covers the overall story of the whole creation, and the second focuses in on man and gives more details, in the Semitic style just mentioned.

The first and foremost description of a human being occurs in Genesis 1:26: "Then God said, 'Let Us make man in Our image." The verb used here in the Hebrew is *asáh* (עָשָׂה), which means "to build" or "to construct."[1] It is a very general term, which is further explained by two other verbs. In the next verse we read "God created man in His own image." The verb used here is *bará* (בָּרָא), which was also used in Genesis 1:1. This refers to creation *ex nihil,* or without any prior substance.[2]

In Genesis 2:7 we read, "Then the Lord God formed man of dust from the ground." This Hebrew verb *yatzár*(יָצַר) means "to form" or "to shape."[3] Even though God used dust to make man, it may be said that He still made man *ex nihil* because He also made the dust. At any rate, the Bible makes it very clear that the creation was the result of the purposeful design of an infinitely Intelligent Creator God. God does not purposefully create things of low value. We are valuable and precious, as far as God is concerned, whether or not we believe it or understand why.

The first woman was created out of a rib of man, and so Adam recognized that she was of the same species as he was. In Genesis 2:23 Adam says concerning Eve, "This is now bone of my bones, and flesh of my flesh; She shall be called woman (*isháh,* אִשָּׁה), Because she was taken out of man (*ish,* אִישׁ)."[4] In Hebrew the feminine gender is usually formed by adding a final <u>ah</u> to a word with a masculine ending. For example, a male horse is *sus* (סוּס) and a mare is a *susáh* (סוּסָה). The fact that this characteristic of Semitic languages is necessarily implied in the original language of Adam suggests that the original language was Semitic in style. It was most surely not Hebrew, as the originator of the Israelite people was Abraham, whose language was most likely Aramaic, since he came from Ur of the Chaldees, and later Haran. This Aramaic base, reinforced by Rebekah, Rachel, Leah, Bilhah, and Zilpah, was later supplemented by the Canaanite language of the people around him as well as certain Egyptian words that came during their sojourn there. Biblical Hebrew appears to be mainly a combination of these three.

In order to understand what the Bible means about man being created in the image of God, we need to understand what is an image. According to Gesenius, the word image, *tzélem* (צֶלֶם), comes from the root meaning "to cut" or "to cut out."[5] Pagan images were usually "cut out" of stone or wood to look like the spirit they represented. While man was "formed out of the dust of the ground" rather than "cut out," there is essentially the same meaning in man as the image of God. To say that man is the image of God is equivalent of saying that man is the idol of God. It is interesting that in Modern Hebrew the word for camera is *matzlemáh* (מַצְלֵמָה), from the causative stem, meaning literally "image-maker."

There are three basic relations between images and the one whose image it is: 1. *the image resembles the spirit whose image it is*, 2. *the image is a dwelling place for the spirit whose image it is.*, and 3. *as one treats the image, he is held as treating the spirit whose image it is.* Let us now look at each relation individually.

First of all, the image resembles the spirit whose image it is. In our modern context, we may compare a person with a picture of that person. Even though the picture is only an image made of paper and ink, it genuinely resembles the person to the point that, if a stranger walked into a room, we could recognize him as the person whose picture we were just looking at. The same is true of pagan idols. If God were to open our eyes to see the spirit that is related with a pagan idol, that spirit would look like the image made in stone or wood that our physical eyes see.

Concerning the relation of human beings to God, the relation is the same. It is common for theologians to say that the Bible writers describe God in human language when they refer to "the arm of the Lord," "the eyes of the Lord," etc. They call these expressions "anthropomorphic," which means they describe God in human terms.

I believe the opposite. What came first, the picture of a person or that person? The person has to be there first in order that the light will come off from him in such a way as to make the particular impression in the film that results in his picture. In the same way, I believe that God was here first in a particular form, and created man in such a way that it reflects God's form. In Micah 5:2 (5:1 in the Masoretic Hebrew text), we read about the baby that was to be born in Bethlehem "whose goings forth have been of old, from everlasting." This reference is to Jesus' appearances before he was born. They occurred during the Old Testament period, and probably before.

When Joshua saw a man (Heb. *ish*) with his sword drawn in Joshua 5:13-15, he thought this was a typical human soldier and asked what side he was on. He ended up falling on his face on the earth and worshipping this "man." The "man" gave orders for Joshua to take off his sandals, an act of recognizing the Deity, as was required of Moses in Exodus 3:5. It is interesting to note that Joshua did not think at first that this person was any different than any other man, and yet it was Jesus before his incarnation. This is evident from the fact that the "man" receives Joshua's worship and orders a further step that recognizes that he is God, instead of rejecting the worship, as God's angels always do (*e.g.* Rev. 22:8-9).

In chapter 6 of his book (v.3), Isaiah says that he saw the LORD (אֲדֹנָי), "sitting on a throne, lofty and exalted, with the train of His robe filling the Temple." Whom did he see? If God is only a Spirit and has no form, how could Isaiah see Him? I believe that the answer is in John 1:18: "No one has seen God at any time; the only begotten God who is in the bosom of the Father, He has explained Him." Isaiah saw Jesus, and Jesus was in some recognizable visible form. This appearance to Isaiah was another of the "goings forth" of Jesus before His birth in Bethlehem.

The resolution of this teaching about man as the image of God is that God was going around from eternity with the same type of form in which He revealed Himself to Joshua and Isaiah. This Being in whose image we are made must be there first. Then we, as His images, are made in such a way—whether cut out or formed—to look like Him.

This order of appearance indicates that God was here first and then man. God had hands before He designed a man with hands. God had feet before He designed a man with feet, etc. We should really refer to parts of man as *theomorphisms*, or forms of God, since what we have reflects what God had first. When we refer to "the arm of the Lord," we are referring to one of the original arms, of which ours are copies. Though God is a Spirit, the Spiritual body-form of Preincarnate Jesus is the real original archetype, of which we are made as images.

Most modern theologians say that these expressions are *anthropomorphisms*, or descriptions of God in human language. As we see, the evidence points the other way. Our bodies are images of the body that Jesus went forth in before He was born here. Then we were made copies of that body.

In the light of this truth, it is strange that there should be atheists at all. Most of us would believe in the existence of a person if we had even one image (picture) of him. However, God has over six billion images of Himself walking on this planet at this very moment. How much more proof does one need?

The **second** special relationship of an image to its spirit is that it is a dwelling place for the spirit whose image it is. In Psalm 106:37-38 God says the following about the Israelites: "They even sacrificed their sons and their daughters to the demons, and shed innocent blood, the blood of their sons and their daughters, whom they sacrificed unto the idols of Canaan; and the land was polluted with the blood."

In this passage, the Hebrew poetry balances and equates certain things. Here the demons are in parallel with the idols. This indicates that sacrificing to demons and sacrificing to idols mean the same thing. How can this be? The Israelites sacrificed their children in front of idols, but they were really honoring the demons, or evil spirits, that lived inside those idols.

In the New Testament it is the same. In I Corinthians 10:20 the Apostle Paul says, "No, but I say that the things which the Gentiles sacrifice, they sacrifice to demons and not to God; and I do not want you to become sharers in demons."

Here, as well, the assertion is made that the sacrifice, which was made before an idol, was really being made to the evil spirit that dwelled inside the idol. The idol is a dwelling place for a spirit. Is man then just a dwelling place for any spirit at all?

The answer is no. Man was not created as an image in general, even as one cannot make a picture of something in general. Man was created as the image of God. In this context, it means that man was made to be a dwelling place for the Spirit of God, and not any other spirit. It has been well said that every man has a God-sized vacuum within, and will never be satisfied unless God Himself is dwelling in him.

In the New Testament believer we have this true element of human identity restored, as the Apostle Paul writes (I Corinthians 6:19): "Or do you not know that your body is a temple of the Holy Spirit who is in you, whom you have from God, and that you are not your own? For you have been bought with a price: therefore glorify God in your body."

Here Paul emphasizes that the body of a believer is the temple of the Holy Spirit, which is in us. The temple of a spirit in any heathen religion is the place where that spirit is said to dwell. It has a large idol of that spirit, and people go to consult that spirit there. For Paul, the human body is the true temple for the Creator God—even more than the physical building called the Temple in Jerusalem—and this description of man comes from his being "in the image of God."

Because of man's first sin, it would not seem best to say that man, as image of God, was marred, as some describe it Man continued to be a dwelling place for the Spirit of the Creator God, but now he was an empty dwelling place. As nature abhors a vacuum in the material dimension, so it is in the spiritual. Man does not go around continually with his God-sized vacuum empty. He tries to fill it up with spiritual content. In this context, we can understand where the many human vices originate. The many addictions to drugs, alcohol, witchcraft, as well as many other things, are directly attributable to an evil spirit residing in the person. Being filled with a false spirit is an unnatural state, according to the way man was created, and no person will never be satisfied with any false spirit. He will always feel varying degrees of emptiness without the Holy Spirit dwelling in him.

The **third** special relationship of an image to its spirit is that as one treats the image, it is considered that he is treating the spirit. Let us imagine that a pagan religious procession is passing by with an idol of Artemis of Ephesus. Let us suppose that a person standing by decides that he does not like art and would like to take the statue of Artemis from the people in the parade and smash it to smithereens, stomp on it, and finally, spit on the pieces. What would happen to him if he did this? He would not live five minutes. Why? Because everyone loves art so much? Of course not! His treatment of the statue is seen as his treatment of the spirit named Artemis that dwells in that statue.

This is the true essence of pagan idolatry. It is practiced by people who sense that they are empty spiritually. Instead of seeking to be filled as images of the True God, they remain empty because of their ignorance or deliberate sin. Then they cut out a statue—remember that the word image means "cut out"—that resembles a spirit that revealed himself to a person. The spirit then inhabits that idol, taking up residence there, and the human worshippers of that spirit build a temple for that idol. People come from miles around to visit the idol in order to worship that spirit inside and ask that spirit to do favors for them. They may feel a tingling or some feeling of filling while they are there; but there is nothing lasting, and they feel even emptier afterward. This emptiness leads to more worship and a vicious cycle of deepening emptiness and devotion. All the time, however, they venerate, and even worship the idol in order to give veneration and worship to the spirit inside the idol.

There are, of course, two positive applications of this truth. First of all, God first gives us the commandment to love Him, the God in whose image all men are made. We will never appreciate or love ourselves beyond the degree that we love God. Man has value only because God has value. It is not in being an image that we have value, or our functions and abilities. What gives us value is that the Spirit in Whose image we are has value. He is the One True Creator God.

Suppose that a man is walking down the sidewalk and comes upon a few photographs blowing along in the wind. One is of a garbage can, another of a vacant lot, another of a junked car, and the last of his mother. Which one will he pick up and keep? They are all ink and paper, and they all cost the same amount of money to develop. However the value of the picture lies in the contents. Since the man values his mother, he will pick up her picture and leave the others.

In the same way, we need to understand that our own value is derived from the value of God, not our own makeup (though we are "fearfully and wonderfully made"), or our own abilities. We humans have infinite value because we are the images of a God that has infinite value. The more that God is pushed aside, ignored, and even denied in existence, the less man can perceive His own value. The humanistic search for human value and identity apart from God is futile, just as it is futile to conceive of a picture of nothing, whatsoever or something in general. They can talk about the "ink and paper"—*homo rationalis, et al.*—but these cannot give transcendent value. They only lead to nihilism if one is honest.

Berkouwer shows up this problem of modern existentialists in his refutation of Heidegger: "The procedure which Heidegger follows makes his whole view of man precarious, since he wants to deal with man as he actually is; and the way to self-knowledge is impossible to traverse with this kind of horizontal analysis, since the decisive dimension of man's nature, his relation to God, remains outside the analysis. The key to true self-knowledge is lacking, since man is seen and analyzed ***outside*** of this basic dimension. And that is the reason that man can judge the other, his fellow man; that a bitterly serious ***j'accuse*** can be hurled as part of a heroic "phenomenology" which admits the existence of evil and stresses the ***Fragwürdigheit***, the constant "being-threatened" of man's being; and that—despite all this—there is still, from a Biblical point of view, no true knowledge of man's nature, no real evaluation of the actual man"(Emphasis the author's).[6]

What folly to think that one can develop a morality without a fixed standard of goodness outside of man! This leaves one two options: to pretend that one's own morality is universal and criticize others by our standards, or to define morality by consensus and replace the notion of evil with a simple "deviation from the norm." This latter option leaves deviation from the norm as logically acceptable as the norm itself, since there is no fixed point of reference. This option leaves the road open to absolute moral chaos, and has been promoted in efforts to legalize hitherto illegal things, such as drugs, homosexuality, etc. It is a smokescreen to undermine moral awareness and bring in sins that God hates. It creates a mindless relativism that leaves each person as a meaningless and worthless self-worshipping god, left to create his own fantasy of his worth and meaning in a meaningless and worthless universe. This is the modern liberal humanistic understanding of what religion is.

Regarding existentialism in the context of this contradiction, Berdiaev says, "This terror before the abyss of not-being, the anxiety for the absurdity of the world, is a new form of godlessness, which one is nonetheless to take on heroically; it is Nietzsche's ***amor fati***, (acceptance of fate). Man will save himself the while he relies only on himself; he will create, and only therein find relief from the nausea inspired by not-being and emptiness."[7]

This is the helplessness and hopelessness of man apart from God. The Bible uses the expression that man is lost in his sins. That would be a good description of what Berdiaev and Nietzsche experienced. They are like pictures trying to define their content. They are the ink and paper trying to paint themselves into significance without anything or anyone to copy. Man without God has no basis for self-understanding or self-worth, but man with God can see his value as the image of the infinitely Valuable God and rest in the glory he has been given at creation. The more he praises and values God, then, the more he will understand his own value as the image of That God.

There is a second good application of the truth that as one treats the image, he is seen as treating the spirit whose image it is: we ought to treat and value others—even unbelievers—the way we treat God. This is another reason that the two great commandments in Scriptures are in the order that they are. First we are to love God with all of our heart, soul, and might (Deuteronomy 6:5), and then we are to love our neighbors as ourselves (Leviticus 19:18). If we were to disregard the First Commandment to Love God, even Hitler could be seen as fulfilling the Second Commandment. He hated others and murdered them, and then he hated himself and murdered himself. He treated himself and others equally.

Out of the nihilism of Nietzsche and others came the death camps of Hitler and the Gulag of Stalin and his followers—and also the American abortion clinics. If man has no intrinsic value, then he may be disposed of according to certain definitions and criteria invented by those in power with no need to justify themselves to anyone. If there is no God, as Berdiaev says, no criteria is intrinsically better than another because there is no objective external standard by which to measure ourselves—all standards are subjective.

In stark contrast to this existential emptiness, meaninglessness, and moral vacuum lie the teachings of Jesus on the treatment of one's neighbor. The Lord told the true story of a good Samaritan who helped a Jewish man who had fallen among thieves and was robbed, beaten, and left to die. Previously a priest and a Levite had passed by on the other side of the road, probably concerned not to be ritually defiled by touching a dead body. The Samaritan treated the wounds, brought him to an inn, and paid the innkeeper to continue treating him. Jesus then asked, "Which one of these three do you think proved to be a neighbor to the man who fell into the robbers' hands?" (Luke 10:36). The other person answered, "The one that showed mercy toward him." Jesus then said, "Go, and do the same."

Religious leaders had been manipulating the definition of one's neighbor, trying to restrict the inclusiveness of the second commandment to love one's neighbor as oneself. If they could reduce the number of people who were to be considered as neighbors, then they could struggle to keep this commandment, while taking out their frustrations on the unlucky ones who were outside of that circle. Jesus transforms the debate by changing the focus from the object to the actor in the situation. He was saying, in effect, "What kind of neighbor are you to others?" Since the word translated "neighbor" is also the Hebrew word for friend, companion, or associate, many Jewish leaders taught that this verse was limited to one's dealings to neighbors and others with whom one had dealings. Jesus focused on man as actor, or agent of love, and said, effect, "You be the right kind of neighbor in your heart. Let God decide what other people to bring into your life, and you treat them right, according to the love which you have for God in your heart."

In all of Jesus' teaching, the emphasis is to love all people, no matter who they are or what they do to you. In His Sermon on the Mount, Jesus tells his followers to turn the other cheek when someone smites them, and then goes even further in Matthew 5:44-45: "Love your enemies, and pray for those who persecute you; so that you may be sons of your Father who is in heaven."

The basis for such a radical ethic as this is the recognition that every man is created to be a dwelling place for the One True God, and as one treats each human being, he is said to be treating the God in Whose image he is. Being children of the Heavenly Father refers to acting like the Father because the word child means "builder," etymologically.[8] If we want to function as building up the Father's program, we must recognize that every person is an image of Him—regardless of how they treat us or into which evil vices they have fallen prey—and as we treat others, we are seen as treating God. In this context, if we treat some people good and others bad, we are accounted as treating God good sometimes and bad other times. Our Heavenly Father wants consistency, and the First Commandment is the basis of the Second Commandment.

There is one more interesting thought in relation to idolatry. In the Bible, God actually approves of idolatry, but not in the way that the heathen practice it. In idolatry there is the spirit, its idol as a dwelling place, and the worshipper, or idolater. For heathen idolatry a demon takes the part of the spirit, and it is dwelling in a stone idol (Heb. *pésel,* פֶּסֶל)[9] or metal idol (Heb. *massecháh,* מַסֵּכָה).[10] Human beings worship the spirit by showing reverence to the idol, which represents that spirit. The human beings that worship that spirit then hope that that spirit will do certain things for them, such as sending rain, empowering them sexually, giving an abundant harvest, etc. They also bring offerings to sustain the expenses of the temple dedicated to that spirit.

The idolatry that God approves of follows the same pattern, but there are different beings in the roles. We all know that God is a

Spirit, and He is the only Spirit that is to be worshipped. We have already established that man is the image, or idol of God. Thus, man is the dwelling place of the True God. This being so, man cannot at the same time be the idolater. Although many celebrities today are called idols, their worship by their fans is just another form of the false idolatry. The fans are really worshipping the false spirit that is energizing that idol.

Since man cannot be the idol and idolater at the same time, who or what is the true idolater, according to God? In Genesis 9:2, God is talking to Noah, as representative of the human race and says, "The fear of you and the terror of you will be upon every beast of the earth and upon every bird of the sky; with everything that creeps on the ground, and all the fish of the sea, into your hand they are given." The words fear and terror in the Hebrew represent both the good kind of fear, such as "fear of the Lord," and the bad kind of fear. The first is the reverential respect often used to describe one aspect of worship.

One may well ask the question whether animals are capable of a reverential fear of man and why. In Daniel 4 God changed the nature of Nebuchadnezzar into that of a beast to learn the fear of the Lord that an animal has, at least. After seven years, he gave the glory to God, and his reason and kingdom were restored. With the nature of an animal, he learned to fear God. Since the animals have fear of the Lord, and man is the image, or idol, of the Lord, then the result is that animals show fear of the Lord out of their fear of man, who represents God before the creation. In this light it is particularly interesting that attacks by wild beasts may be a judgment sent from God (see Rev. 6:8) because people show their rebellion against God to the point that the animals no longer associate them with God, and so do not fear them.

We shall now contrast the Old Testament sacrificial system with the Aztec sacrificial system about the time of the arrival of the Spaniards. In the Aztec system, demons were the spirits that were worshipped, and they inhabited in stone images that were manufactured by the people. These stone images were the idols. The people themselves were the idolaters that worshipped the demons, represented by and inhabiting the idols. The people showed their worship of the idols and the spirits dwelling in the idols by killing people (the idolaters) and using their blood for the supposed needs of the spirits.

The Old Testament sacrificial system was similar, but man was cast in a different role. God was the Spirit, and all people are His idols—or, at least, they were made for that purpose, whether or not He inhabited them. The idolaters were the animals, showing their reverential fear for God by their reverential fear of human beings, His idols. In the act of idolatrous worship of the Old Testament, the animals (the idolaters) were killed and their blood was used to cover (atone for, or expiate) the sins of the people. The blood was used to propitiate the just wrath of God against the sinning people, and so it was also applied Godward. The animals were the idolaters, and their blood was used for the idols and for the Spirit dwelling in the idols (or supposed to be dwelling in the idols). So we see by analogy with pagan idolatry a main application of the truth of man as the image of God. We must remember, though, that we are the idols, and must never allow ourselves to become the idolaters. That role is rightfully for the animals, not for us.

II. Man: the Likeness of God.

Closely connected with the teaching that man is created in the image of God is the teaching that he is created according to the likeness of God. Among theologians there are many conflicting ideas about the different meanings of the expressions "image of God" and "likeness of God." Berkhof has an excellent summary of the different positions in his systematic theology: "Irenaeus and Tertullian drew a distinction between the "image" and "likeness" of God, finding the former in bodily traits, and the latter in the spiritual nature of man. Clement of Alexandria and Origen, however, rejected the idea of any bodily analogy, and held that the word "image" denoted the characteristics of man as man, and the word "likeness" qualities which are not essential to man but may be cultivated or lost. This view is also found in Athanasius, Hilary, Ambrose, Augustine, and John of Damascus...."[11]

In the face of such widespread diversity of views and inability to agree on the meanings of the terms "image" and "likeness, many theologians think that the expressions "image of God" and "likeness of God" are used synonymously and interchangeably. Berkhof himself agrees: "The words 'image' and 'likeness' are used synonymously and interchangeably, and therefore do not refer to two different things."[12]

At this point in the discussion, having established the basic meaning for the expression "image of God" with reference to man, I shall attempt to show a slightly different meaning and application for the expression "likeness of God." The word "likeness" in the Hebrew is *demuth* (דְּמוּת),[13] and comes from the Hebrew root which includes the following meanings: "likeness," "to be like," "to resemble," and "blood." I believe that the meanings "to cease," "to cause to cease," "to cut off," "to destroy," "cessation," "quiet," and "rest," as listed under this root by Gesenius, are just cognate forms of the root *dmm* (דמם) and thus, should not be considered here.[14]

There are two basic meanings under the root from which *demuth* comes: likeness, and blood. It is specifically stated in Leviticus 17:11 that "the life (lit. soul, Heb. *nefesh* נֶפֶשׁ) of the flesh is in the blood." What would be different about a person if all the blood were drained from him? All the qualities of life: thinking, feeling, deciding, getting angry, loving, being happy or sad, etc. are elements of the life we have, which is in the blood.

While the term "image of God" refers to man as a dwelling place for the Spirit of God, the term "likeness of God" deals with man's function. We have the same elements of life as God does. The soul is generally considered to be a combination of mind, will, and emotions, and representing our self-awareness. However, since sin entered into the human race, we express them wrongly, that is, out of synchronization with God. We are angry at the wrong things, think self-exalting thoughts, feel the wrong way, love the wrong things, are sad when we should be happy or happy when we should be sad, etc. The Apostle Paul expressed it this way in Romans 7:15: "For what I am doing, I do not understand; for I am not practicing what I would like to do."

Because of man's sin, the Holy Spirit's presence has been lost, and therefore he has become an empty image of God, as we have seen. But also, man has lost the Holy Spirit's control, and thus has lost his function as the likeness of God. The Holy Spirit is no longer maintaining control and order in man because He is not there. As a result, man expresses the elements of God's character, but out of control.

This brings us to a discussion of the elements of man's makeup. The word translated "life" in Leviticus 17:11 is *nefesh*. Of 691 times that the word *psuché* (ψυχή) is used in the Septuagint, 657 times it appears for the Hebrew *nefesh*, 27 times for *lev* (לֵב, usually rendered "heart"), 5 times for *chaim* (חַיִּים, usually rendered "life"), and once each for *ish* (אִישׁ, usually rendered "man") and *ruach* (רוּחַ, usually rendered "spirit").[15] Here we have the Hebrew word referring to the soul of man being connected to his blood. This places it in a position to be transmitted from generation to generation, as the blood composition is tied to genes.

It is important to note in this light that the term *nefesh hayyah* (נֶפֶשׁ חַיָּה), translated *living creature* in Genesis 2:7 is also used to refer to animals in Genesis 1:24: "'Let the earth bring forth living creatures (Heb. *nefesh hayah*) after their kind: cattle and creeping things, and beasts of the earth after their kind'; and it was so." So the term "living creature," or "living soul" does not even separate human beings from animals.

Though the *nefesh*, or soul, apparently comes to a man through his genetic inheritance from Adam through his parents, it endures after death. The soul represents the essence of man, and goes to *Sheol* after death, as David mentions in Psalm 16:10: "For You will not abandon my soul to *Sheol*." In the New Testament the soul is also the part of the person mentioned as enduring after death. In Revelation 6:9 John saw in heaven "the souls of those who had been slain because of the word of God, and because of the testimony which they had maintained." In fact, both *nefesh* in the Hebrew and *psuché* in the Greek are used in a representative way to refer to the whole person. By way of contrast, angels are called spirits, not souls.

Though the possession of a *nefesh* does not distinguish man from the animals, the possession of a *neshamah* does. In Genesis 2:7 we read: "Then the LORD God formed man of dust from the ground, and breathed into his nostrils the breath of life (*nishmat-hayyim*, נִשְׁמַת־חַיִּים); and man became a living being" (*nefesh hayyah*).

Some dualists assert that their reason for rejecting the tripartite position is that there are only two parts of man mentioned at creation. However, in the actual creation process in this verse alone, we see all three parts of a man: the body (formed out of dust), the soul (*nefesh hayyah*), and the *neshamah*, which God breathed into man. The word *neshamah* occurs 24 times in the Old Testament. In no instance does it clearly refer to something other than man, God, or angels. It never refers to animals. It is what distinguishes us from animals. We could have been a self-perpetuating species of *nefesh hayyah* as the animals, except for the *neshamah*, or breath of God in us.

Besides *neshamah*, there is another word in Hebrew, which is more often associated with the word spirit, and that is *ruach*. This word is much more common than *neshamah*, and has a much broader range of meanings. While *neshamah* basically means breath, and is rendered by *pnoé* in Greek, *ruach* means breath, wind, or spirit, when used in reference to man, and seems to merge with the less common *neshamah*.

There seems to be a slight shift of emphasis in Scripture from the breath of God in each man, mentioned in Genesis 2:7, to the wind that the breath forms in and of itself, to its activity as the human spirit. After Genesis 2:7, the interest is no longer so much in God's actual breathing out this *neshamah*, or breath, into man, but rather, how it appears as wind, and how it functions as spirit. Of course, the word *ruach* also refers to a literal physical wind.

As spirit, though, the human spirit can be described in varying terms. People that are impatient have a "short spirit (Micah 2:7)." One may have a troubled spirit (Gen. 41:8), bitter spirit (Is. 53:6), jealous spirit (Num. 5:14), etc. Sometimes the impression is rather that a spirit from outside the person is coming to influence him, such as a spirit of judgment (Is. 28:6), a perverse spirit (Is. 19:14), or an evil spirit from the Lord (I Sam. 16:16,23), etc. In truth, it appears` that the human spirit is neutral in content, and "channels" the content of the spirit from outside that is influencing it. That is why Paul says in I Cor. 6:17: "But the one who joins himself to the Lord is one spirit with Him." The human spirit is one spirit with whatever outside spirit that person has submitted to.

The full view of man, then, is that the body is the vehicle of awareness of the world. Through it man experiences the world with his five senses. The soul (*nefesh*, or *psyché*) is the vehicle of one's self-awareness. Here the person operates with mind, will, and emotions. However, the soul is influenced both from the body, which has its own desires, and from the spirit. The human spirit *(neshamah* or *ruach*, or Greek *pneuma*) is the spirit-conscious part of man. The spirit has a will different from the will represented by the will of the soul. The will of the human spirit is to choose fellowship with one spirit from outside instead of another. It is then that chosen spirit that gives the content to the human spirit, which then illuminates the rest of the person.

The ruling spirit of a man guides his intellectual processes. In Modern Hebrew the word for an intellectual is *ish-ruach*, or "a man of a spirit" ("or man with a spirit"). In German the word for intellectual is *geistig*, which means "spiritual." A person can reason better by channeling a spirit from outside, but he has to open the door an invite that spirit in. The spirit from outside also affects that person's will and emotions, according to his spiritual content. This position explains how the Bible can refer to a person with a broken human spirit or a bitter spirit, but also with "an evil spirit from the Lord," as Saul had.

It is this tripartite view of man is also what allows us to resolve the apparent conflict between the positions of Creationists and Traducianists. Creationists believe that God creates the soul of the man special for each man at conception, and only the body is generated biologically. The Traducianists, on the other hand, believe that both the soul and body come to us through generation.

Berkouwer in his book, Man: the Image of God, has a chapter on the controversy between the creationists and the traducianists on what is conveyed from generation to generation and what God creates anew in each person as he is conceived. Because he is so convinced a dichotomist, Berkouwer accurately explains the two viewpoints, with their strengths and weaknesses, but finds no resolution to the difference. Near the end of 31 pages of explanation, all he can conclude is the following: "In both theoretical views, the starting point was a description of the "essence" or "being" of man as soul and body, a description in which the relationship to God was not yet regarded as essential. This appears to be more clearly evident in traducianism, since creationism placed so strong an accent on a separate creative act. But in the final analysis, creationism also followed the same path, and viewed man as originating in the union between the created soul and the generated body. Thus man was a composite; both the view of man and question of his origin showed a dualism in relation to the whole man, similar to that which appeared within traducianism within generation."[16]

Having assumed dualism, both traducianists and creationists could only conclude dualism, without going beyond semantics or a slight difference of emphasis. If, however, we place the controversy within the context of trichotomy, I believe that we can arrive at a satisfactory resolution of the problem that will take into account the best points of the two positions.

The dilemma, which the Catholic Church and the Calvinists, on the one hand, find themselves with respect to the origin of man, is that they wish to hold onto the doctrine of original sin, which would imply that sin is inherited from Adam; but they also want to see each person's soul as a special creative act of God. If, however, the soul were created anew for each person, then it would be without sin. But how, then, could sin be transmitted through a mechanical biological mechanism of reproduction if the soul is not part of that transmission, but rather is directly created by God for each person?

For the traducianists, including Lutherans and other Protestants, the problem was the same, but seen from the other side. They emphasized that God created every man's soul and placed it in Adam, as well as the biological material of his body. Therefore we inherited the soul tainted with the sin of Adam because it was in him when he passed it on to us. The question is then, how did the sin taint a soul being transmitted, and how can there be a medium between the soul and God—especially a biological medium, which is seen as inferior to the spiritual contact?

Thus immediacy favors creationism and original sin favors traducianism. How can we resolve this apparent contradiction without retreating into mystery as Berkouwer does? I believe that the resolution lies in a trichotomy. I believe that man is body, soul, and spirit, and therein lies the basis for resolving the problem.

It is obvious that the body comes to us by biological inheritance from Adam through our parents. The question is what comes with that. I have shown above that the *nefesh* is linked to the blood, and *nefesh* is mostly rendered as *psuché* in the Greek of the Septuagint. This would give us a basis for believing that the soul of a man is also inherited along with the body, as the traducianists assert. Thus we may say that, in addition to the body, the human soul comes to man *per traducem* all the way from Adam. In this way we can cover the problem of original sin, for it is the soul in man that sins, as God says in Ezekiel 18:4: "Behold, all souls (*nefesh*, pl.) are Mine; the soul (*nefesh*) of the father as well as the soul (*nefesh*) of the son is Mine. The soul (*nefesh*) that sins will die."

So we can confirm the truth that the traducianists want most to preserve: original sin. Somehow the *nefesh*, or soul, of a man is present in the blood, and the blood is inherited from a person's father, and so sin is transmitted from our father in the form of a soul that is self-exalting and seeking independence from God. This is the whole orientation of the soul. It is ready to respond to any temptation involving the lust of the flesh, the lust of the eyes, and the pride of life. This is our inheritance *per traducem* from Adam: body and soul.

At this point we ask what else there is in man that can satisfy the observations of the creationists. What does God create special in each man if both body and soul are transmitted from our parents? The answer is the human spirit. This can be expressed by some combination of the Hebrew words *neshamah* and *ruach*. It is interesting to note that Jewish mystics consider the *neshamah* to be the "Divine spark" that is in everyone, and this does correspond with the "God-consciousness" in Adam and Eve. However, we do not need to consider this to be a denial of original sin, though that doctrine is totally rejected by Jewish people—whether liberals, mystics, or orthodox. They emphasize immediate creation only.

We have noted that the *neshamah* was breathed into man, but is not considered a part of animals. We have seen how *neshamah*, as breath, and *ruach* as breath, wind, and spirit dovetail together to describe this third part of man in the Old Testament, and the Greek word *pneuma* covers them in the New Testament.

That the implantation of the *neshamah* is a very direct act in the creation of Adam is clear in Genesis 2:7, but is it true of every person? This appears to be the case, according to Ecclesiastes 12:7, referring to a person who has died, "Then the dust will return to the earth as it was, and the spirit (*ruach*) will return to God who gave it." It is obvious that the body is the "dust that returns to dust," and it is important to remember that the soul (*nefesh*, or *psuché*) went down to *Sheol* at death before Jesus, as was shown in Psalm 16:10. Since Jesus' resurrection, according to Rev. 6:9, the believer's soul goes to heaven and the unbeliever's soul goes down to *Sheol* (Rev. 20:11-15). Thus, the reference (before Jesus' time) to the human spirit returning to God, instead of *Sheol*, shows that the spirit is distinct from the soul, and that it returns to God who gave it.

I believe that the implication is that God gives the spirit individually to each person at conception, and takes it back at death. This is also as Elihu asserts in Job 33:4: "The Spirit (*ruach*) of God has made me, and the breath (*neshamah*) of the Almighty gives me life." Since *ruach* and *neshamah* are used in parallel verse here, they are seen as roughly the same thing, and here we see that it is a special act of God that gives life to the fertilized egg of the mother. This also has implications for the issue of abortion. Life begins at conception with the breath of the Almighty blown into the fertilized egg. Without the special act of the breath of the Almighty blown into the fertilized egg of the mother, the union of the sperm and egg would just remain dead. God in Zechariah 12:1 also suggests this, where He says that He "forms the spirit of man within him."

If this is true, then we have the final point in the resolution of the controversy between the creationists and the traducianists. While the soul comes to us *per traducem*, along with our bodies, the spirit of each man comes to us *per creationem*, as a direct act of God. This maintains the sacredness and specialness of our individual creation by God, and places us way above the animals in importance and relation to God—the very thing that creationists are eager to preserve. So we see that a tripartite division of man preserves the best of both positions: of traducianism through preserving original sin through natural propagation in the soul, and of creationism through preserving each man as unique and a special creative act of God through the creation of the human spirit as a special act of God.

Having established the elements of man and their source, we may now continue with what happens within man after birth. We have seen that the human spirit is created as a special act of God. It is obvious that the spirit was created without sin. The sin nature, which we inherit, comes from our parents through the soul, not the spirit. Since the spirit is created as a special act of God, and it is without sin at the beginning, it must be concluded that man begins in contact with God. This is what the Apostle Paul affirms of his case, and by extrapolation, of all men in Romans 7:9: "I was once alive apart from the Law; but when the commandment came, sin became alive and I died."

Let us go through the sequence of events for Paul. He is born with a body and soul that came from his parents and inherited a sin nature in the soul. He also possessed at birth a perfect spirit without sin, which was a special and direct creative act of God. Now the human spirit is the part of us that has God—consciousness. Since it begins without sin, we are alive in a relation with God spiritually beginning at conception. Therefore, Paul stated that at first he was alive without the law.

This spiritual relation with God lasts from conception until the child comes into an understanding of the law and inevitably rebels against it. It was the sin he inherited in his soul that rose up against the commandment of God, and he chose to rebel against the commandment. At that point during his childhood, Paul then died spiritually, or, in our terms, the spiritual contact with God was broken.

Paul was not born separated from God, and thus, neither is any other person. He had a perfect spirit and was alive in some relation with God. Paul also states in Romans 5:13: "for until the Law, sin was in the world, but sin is not imputed where there is no law." In the same way, sin is not imputed to a child before the Law comes to his attention and knowledge. Then, when he rebels, he dies, i.e. his spiritual relation with, or at least, perception of God ends. He then becomes dead in his sins without God's presence to guide him.

It appears that each one of us goes through the same willful rebellion against God that Adam himself experienced, except that we begin with a sinful soul that leads us into rebellion when the understanding of the Law is present later in life. In this way, we are fully responsible for our rebellion against God, even though we have inherited a sinful nature from Adam. We all inevitably experience the equivalent of "being expelled from the Garden of Eden."

At this point, we need to return to the discussion of the differences between man as the image of God and man as the likeness of God. We had seen that the image of God refers to the presence of the Spirit of God in man. In the light of the above discussion, we can see that each person begins with spiritual contact with God and goes through the process of losing it through rebellion. I believe that we know God from the beginning, and most of the adult struggle of people is to get back to know God again—the equivalent of getting back into the Garden of Eden—but this time with knowledge of Him and His Law. It is also interesting in this light that the Jewish equivalent of Christian heaven is called *Gan-Eden,* or "the Garden of Eden." The fact that man has had contact with God from conception until his rebellion makes the need even deeper. Jesus is the only one that will fill the need, as we see that Jesus "was the true Light which, coming into the world, enlightens every man" (John 1:9).

Man as the likeness of God was also affected by the first sin in Genesis, and each one experiences this in his own life. The likeness of God refers to the control of the Holy Spirit in his life. As it has been noted above, man has the elements of the life of God, but, due to his sin, the Holy Spirit is no longer in his spirit to keep order and these elements are expressed out of order with the will of God. In addition to becoming empty as the image of God, man becomes disorderly as the likeness of God through his own personal rebellion. The result is that he feels unfulfilled, alienated, frustrated, dissatisfied, and spiritually hungry. Man's function has become disorderly. It is interesting to note that in Genesis 1:2 God says that the earth was without form and void (*tohu va-vohu*).

We may say exactly the same thing about man after his rebellion in his life leaves him cut off from God. God says this about the people of Judah in Jeremiah 4:23: "I looked on the earth (or "land" of Judah), and behold, it was formless and void (*tohu va-vohu*). They are void because they are empty of the Holy Spirit, and they are without form because the spirit is not there to bring the elements of the character of God into proper expression in them. When we receive Jesus as our Savior, we receive the Holy Spirit, Who begins His work to restore us and "moves" in us to bring order out of our chaos, as He did in the original creation. He is both present and in control.

We can also see the Psalmist's condemnation of the pagans' idols in the light of the teaching on the likeness of man. In Psalm 115 the Psalmist is mocking the pagan idols. He compares them to human beings. The false idols have eyes, but do not see, mouths, but do not speak, ears, but do not hear, etc. Since the idols cannot do anything that they are supposed to do, the spirit that lives inside of them is weak and impotent. In verse 8 the Psalmist says, "Those who make them will become like them, everyone who trusts in them." As the heathen continue to follow spirits that cannot give power to their images, they become blinder, deafer, and more impotent just like the idols they serve—at least they become blind, deaf, and impotent spiritually.

In contrast to the impotent idols is the True God Who makes human beings as His images. He gives us power to see, hear, and do things, unlike the false gods. He even sustains unbelievers so that they can do basic things. It is interesting that at the end time, the false prophet will imitate this creative work of God (Rev. 13:15): "And it was given to him to give breath to the image of the beast, so that the image of the beast would even speak and cause as many as do not worship the image of the beast to be killed." Satan will finally give life to an image, instead of having people worship dumb images, but it will still be far short of the creative work of God. It is a disappointment to think that people will be so impressed with that act when they don't appreciate how special they are as the images and likenesses of God. They don't even notice how God's Spirit sustains them with physical life all the time.

III. Man as Male and Female.

In Genesis 1:26 we are introduced to man as the image of God and man as the likeness of God. In verse 27, we find out the next description of man: "God created man in His own image, in the image of God He created him; male and female He created them." Here the image of God is defined as "male and female". It is interesting that God says, "Let Us make man in Our image," in the previous verse, and this goes well with the image as defined as male and female. Verse 26 suggests a plurality in the Godhead, and verse 27 suggests a plurality in mankind.

It is the married couple that is a reflection of the Creator God, not the single person. In Deuteronomy 6:4 we read that God is one, or *echad* in Hebrew (אֶחָד). *Echad* usually refers to a pluralistic unity, rather than an absolute unity. In Numbers 13:23 we find that the spies that searched out the land of Canaan brought one cluster of grapes (*eshkol echad*—אֶשְׁכֹּל אֶחָד). They have a single cluster made up of many grapes. In Judges 20:8 we read that all the people of Israel rose up "as one man" (*ke-ish echad*—כְּאִישׁ אֶחָד). In no place is the pluralistic unity of *echad* more graphic and appropriate than Genesis 2:24 where we read, "For this reason a man shall leave his father and his mother, and be joined to his wife; and they shall become one flesh (*basar echad*—בָּשָׂר אֶחָד)."

There is something about the marital union between a man and a woman that reflects the unity in God. Since God is a Triune Being, He has always expressed love within Himself—even before there were any other beings with whom to share the love. If we include the children, the family is the image of God here on earth, and the family that is really one reflects God even better. For that reason the Devil attacks families so much and tries to split them up.

But what is it that actually does keep families together? We need to understand what the words male and female mean in the Hebrew. First of all, the word male is *zachar* (זָכָר) in the Hebrew. The primary meaning of its Hebrew root is the verb "to remember" זָכַר). Remembering in Hebrew is somewhat different than the concept of remembering in English. The primary difference is that Hebrew words are action oriented. In Exodus 2:24 God responds to the suffering of the Israelites: "So God heard their groaning; and God remembered His covenant with Abraham, Isaac, and Jacob."

Did the Israelites suffer in Egypt 400 years because God had a poor memory? Of course not! God Himself had already told Abraham in Genesis 15:13-16 that his descendants would serve a foreign power 400 years, then would be delivered by Him. Why does it say that He *remembered* His covenant with the patriarchs? In the next chapter He reveals Himself to Moses and in verse 8 says, "So I have come down to deliver them from the power of the Egyptians." Here the word remember has a greater meaning that a merely cognitive one. God knew about the 400 years of slavery ahead of time, and He waited until 320 years of that had passed. Then He had Moses born, raised him forty years in Pharaoh's court, then made him serve a 40 year sentence of exile for manslaughter. Only after that He revealed Himself to Moses, ready to act.

Remembering in Hebrew is action. Taking into account the covenant with the patriarchs, God was ready to do something. The Israelites remember their Exodus from Egypt every year by obeying commandments to eat bitter herbs and unleavened bread, and to read the Biblical historical account. If they did not do what is required, they did not remember the Exodus. In the same way, we Christians are to remember the death, burial, resurrection and second coming of Jesus in the Communion service by eating the bread and drinking the cup of wine. If we don't eat and drink, we did not remember the death of Jesus.

Remembering in Hebrew is a two-way word. To be a real man, according to the Hebrew Scriptures, a man must remember the things of God, and taking them into account, put his family in order, beginning with himself. This is a rather complicated explanation of the Biblical word, but it covers the two-way sense it has: upward and downward. Upward towards God, man is to learn and understand, and downward towards others he is to put himself in order and then put the family in order, taking into account what he knows of God. Both directions are covered in the verb *zachar*.

In his book, *Men and Women: Enjoying the Difference*, Dr. Larry Crabb has given an interesting definition of masculinity: "Masculinity, I suggest, might therefore be thought of as *the satis-*

fying awareness of the substance God has placed within a man's being that can make an enduring contribution to God's purposes in this world, and will be deeply valued by others, especially his wife, as a reliable source of wise, sensitive, compassionate, and decisive involvement" (Emphasis the author's). [17]

This definition defines the main sphere of the man as in the world, where he uses his creative abilities to provide materially for his family. Here he is contributing to God's purposes in this world. When God passed sentence on Adam for the first sin, He did not invent work—Adam already was working. God added futility by cursing the ground, making man's work much more difficult. Thus, the sphere of man's activity was to be focused on his work to support the family economically, and this work was primarily outside of the home.

The second aspect of this definition is the guidance (through wisdom), sensitivity, compassion, and decision-making for the family by which the man is to demonstrate his leadership over himself and his family. The Lord has designed the male for active leadership. It is interesting to note that in the Old Testament, the "supermachos" were the prophets, priests, and kings, as they were to take into account the things of God and put the whole nation of Israel in order, according to them. This is a far cry from its meaning in popular culture.

The word female in Hebrew, *nekevah* (נְקֵבָה), also sheds light on the meaning of what it is to be a woman. The word comes from the Hebrew root meaning literally "to pierce," and, according to Gesenius means "pierced one."[18] This title refers to the sexual act, but goes beyond. As a man is to lead the family, his wife is to be filled up with the things of her husband. He initiates, hopefully sensitively, and she reacts, hopefully supportively.

Dr. Crabb also has given functional definition of femininity: "Femininity, at its core, might therefore be thought of as the secure awareness of the substance God has placed within a woman's being that enables her to confidently and warmly invite others into relationship with God and with herself, knowing that there is something in each relationship to be wonderfully enjoyed."[19]

These two identities are made for each other: narrowly focused, purpose-oriented leadership and wide focused, relationship-oriented invitation. Even the sexual act tends to reinforce these two roles. As Dr. Crabb concludes about the complementary nature of the human sexes: "The difference is noteworthy. The woman sees herself as *inviting others* to taste the Lord through her. The man sees himself as *moving toward others* with powerful impact. I do not think it stretches things too far to regard *physical* sexuality as a wonderful picture of *personal* sexuality: men feel complete as they strongly enter; women feel enjoyed as they warmly invite." (Emphasis author's)[20]

By creating human beings as male and female, God sets us up to find our greatest fulfillment by being drawn outside of ourselves in service in depth to someone else. In the union of one male and one female there is a great strength: what one is strong in the other is weak, and vice versa. It is the union that is fulfilling—not the individual. This is in keeping with the Lord's two great commandments: to love Him with all our heart, soul, and might, and to love our neighbor as ourselves.

God does not just have us fit together as two, though. There is a chain of command where everyone on the planet fits in—or should fit in. Picture for a moment a ladder with six rungs and a name on each rung. From top to bottom there is God the Father, God the Son, God the Holy Spirit, the father of the family, the mother of the family, and the children of the family. If we put together the Scripture references about these relationships, we come up with two basic ways to show love for everyone below one on the ladder and two basic ways to show to love for everyone above one on the ladder. To everyone below one, he is to supply provision and guidance. Everyone below one is to respond to the provision with gratitude (and praise, as it is included in the same word's meanings in Hebrew), and to the guidance with obedience.

Let us now check the different relationships on the ladder of authority to see if this explanation works. According to this model, God the Father provides and guides for all below Him, but has no one above Him. He provides for Jesus, and guides Jesus. Jesus resisted the temptation to turn stones into bread because He laid aside the self-operation of His Deity to depend willingly on the Father's provision through the Holy Spirit. Jesus also always obeyed the Father, as he said in John 5:30: "I can do nothing on My own initiative. As I hear, I judge: and My judgment is just; because I do not seek My own will, but the will of Him Who sent me" (see also John 5:19, 12:49-50, 14:31).

The Holy Spirit also fits in the chain of command below Jesus and above all people. In relation to Jesus and the Father, the Holy Spirit submits and glorifies them without drawing attention to Himself (John 16:13b): "for He will not speak on His own initiative, but whatever He hears, He shall speak; and He will disclose to you what is to come." We see here that the Holy Spirit's role upward on the chain of command is to submit to all orders and words from above, and to pass all glory to Jesus and the Father in that "He will not speak on His own initiative."

Towards believers, however, the Holy Spirit has the opposite roles: guidance and provision, and there is no distinction between men, women, and children with respect to their being under His authority. In Acts 2:17-18 Peter, quoting Joel about the coming of the Holy Spirit, says, "'And it shall be in the last days,' God says, 'That I will pour forth of My Spirit on all mankind; and your sons and your daughters shall prophesy, and your young men shall see visions, and your old men shall dream dreams; Even on My bondslaves, both men and women, I will in those days pour forth of My Spirit; and they shall prophesy.'"

Here we see that the Spirit is promised to be in every believer in Jesus. Since He has come, He gives prophecy, therefore guiding us, and He gives spiritual provision for our spiritual needs. The Holy Spirit is our life according to Romans 8:10: "If Christ is in you, though the body is dead because of sin, yet the Spirit is alive because of righteousness." The Spirit adopts us into God's family (Romans 8:15), provides corrected intercession to the Father for us (Romans 8:27), provides power for miracles (Romans 15:19), empowers us with respect to our spiritual gifts (I Corinthians 12:7-8), provides spiritual pleasure and satisfaction as a down payment of heaven (II Corinthians 5:5, Ephesians 1:13-14), equips us for our witness to others (II Corinthians 3:3), and provides the church to meet our social needs properly (Ephesians 2:2), among many other things. The Holy Spirit fulfills the two roles of provider and guider for all people who are believers.

Next we shall consider the father of the family. We have seen that the word male means basically "to put oneself and the family in order, taking into account the things of God." It is a two-way term, situating the father of the family properly with respect to God above and his family below. In this respect, the "remembering" of his maleness refers to his responsibility to get guidance from God, in order to have something to remember. In Deuteronomy 6:4-7 we have special instructions for fathers to memorize Scripture and teach it to their children in all life situations as specifically commanded in order to fulfill the great commandment: "Hear, o Israel, the Lord our God, the Lord is one! You shall love the Lord your God with all your heart and with all your soul and with all your might. These words, which I am commanding you today, shall be on your heart (memorized by heart). You shall teach them diligently unto your sons, and shall talk of them when you sit in your house and when you walk by the way and when you lie down, and you rise up."

The guidance is to come from God to the father of the family, and from him to the wife and children. We see that the husband is also responsible for teaching the wife, as indicated in I Corinthians 14:34-35: "The women are to keep silent in the churches; for they are not permitted to speak, but are to subject themselves, just as the Law also says. If they desire to learn anything, let them ask their own husbands at home; for it is improper for a woman to speak in church."

Though many modernists will chafe at the harsh language here, it is obvious that a man is to be responsible for the doctrinal teaching of his own wife, and she is to submit to his doctrinal teaching and discernment, as mentioned in I Timothy 2:11-15: "A woman must quietly receive instruction with entire submissiveness. But I do not allow a woman to teach or exercise authority over a man, but to remain quiet. For it was Adam who was first created, and then Eve. And it was not Adam who was deceived, but the woman, being deceived, fell into transgression. But women will be preserved through the bearing of children if they continue in faith and love and sanctity with self-restraint."

What will the wife be preserved from? According to this passage she will be preserved from being deceived by trusting her husband's discernment and dedicating herself to the bearing and training of the children. It is specifically the husband's responsibility to learn about God and teach his family—both by verbal instruction and by personal example.

The man as head of the home is also responsible to provide for the material needs of his wife and children. Paul says to Timothy (I Timothy 5:8): "But if anyone does not provide for his own, and especially for those of his household, he has denied the faith, and is worse than an unbeliever." It is in this work especially that man is like God, the Creator, because he has to labor with his hands creatively to provide good things for his family, similar to the way God labored to create the universe in the first place.

It is in this creativeness that the male at the head of the household is remembering God the Creator and putting that remembering to practice for the whole family. The man, however, receives the materials to work with from God. God provides the plants and makes them grow. The man has to plant, water, remove weeds, and harvest. God also provides in other ways for other occupations. Thus, the man takes God's primary provision and makes it effective for his wife and children. The man "remembers" (i.e. takes into account) God's provisions and labors to transform them to be usable for the whole family.

The female as wife also has the same responsibilities upward and downward on God's chain of command. Towards her husband and towards the Triune God, she is to receive guidance, as indicated above in I Timothy 2:11-15. She is to trust in her husband's doctrinal discernment, as well as to obey him, as mentioned in Ephesians 5:22-24 (see also I Peter 3:1-6): "Wives, be subject to your own husbands, as unto the Lord. For the husband is the head of the wife, as Christ also is the head of the church, He Himself being the Savior of the body. But as the church is subject to Christ, so also the wives ought to be to their husbands in everything."

As the wife is submitted to her own husband, she is also ready to lead the children. The mother, as well as the father, is to teach the children. That is why Solomon exhorts us in Proverbs 1:8: "Hear, my son, your father's instruction, or reproof (*musar*, מוּסָר), and do not forsake your mother's teaching (*torah* תּוֹרָה). Here we see that the child is to submit fully to all reproof and law the he receives from both parents equally. Of course, if the father is properly submitted to the Lord and the mother is properly submitted to the father, they will both say the same thing.

The provision for the children also comes through the mother, as well as the father. Initially, of course, the mother has a more direct role in the sustenance of the children through the womb and the breast milk. Thereafter, she is cooking, sewing, and doing other things to supplement the earnings of the father in the care of the children. A look at the virtuous woman in Proverbs 31:10-31 shows many efforts of taking the provision of the husband and further transforming it through work for the whole family. The father provides money for flour and the wife bakes bread and cake. The father provides money for cloth and the wife sews together clothes, as well as doing laundry. So we see that the wife receives the provision from her husband and further processes it for the benefit of the whole family.

Since they are on the bottom of the chain of command, the children are not over anyone. They are just to learn to receive instruction and provision, in order to prepare them to give them later as adults. The children are to learn from their parents, as was shown in Proverbs 1:8—equally from the father and mother. In Modern Hebrew the word for parents is *horim* (הוֹרִים). This means that they give torah, or instruction. This word is the same as the word torah as the name for the five books of Moses, or sometimes Scripture in general.

Children are to respond to this guidance with obedience, as mentioned in the Exodus 20:12: "Honor your father and your mother, that your days may be prolonged in the land which the LORD your God gives you." In Ephesians 6:1-3 the Apostle Paul expands on this command by saying (v.1): "Children, obey your parents in the Lord, for this is right."

So we see that the chain of command of God includes male and female, and they have exactly the same responsibilities to those above them on the chain of command, as well as the same responsibilities to those below them. The only difference between male and female in the marriage bond is their position in reference to each other. The husband is above the wife. The husband, however, is to see this position as a ministry. He is ministering to his wife the guidance he has received from God and he is ministering to his wife the product of his material provisions he has received from God and transformed through labor. This is an act of submission in loving and providing for her.

The wife also is to submit to her husband by receiving his instruction and following his leadership. Also, she is to receive his provision for her and the family and transform it through further labor for them. Both are to show gratitude to God for what they have received, and it would go a long way if the wife would show some gratitude to her husband for his part in the provision, as well.

In the twentieth century the world has suffered from the scourge of women's liberation. It is an attempt to reject the chain of command and make everyone an individual god for himself. We are even seeing the beginning of the children's liberation movement with certain decrees from the United Nations. Where did all of this rebellion come from? In the seventeenth century a philosopher named Descartes locked himself in his room to discover the beginning place for all of philosophy. He came out with the starting place: "Cogito ergo sum," or "I think, therefore I am." In Exodus 3 God reveals Himself to Moses as "I am that I am." Only God can be the "I am," a name that is then given in third person for us to call him: Jehovah (or "He Who is"). By attributing to man the essence of God, Descartes began what is called "the Enlightenment," but starting from that blasphemy, nothing good could result.

Today society, following this so-called enlightenment thinks of every man as an independent god for himself, and therefore the chain of command is a scandal for modern men. Using the illustration of the ladder, it has been removed from its vertical position, and it has been placed horizontally. They begin with Descartes by assuming that man is god for himself, and they end in Kant concluding it. However, modern man is also lost, lacking in guidance and morals, and he is fearful of his material sustenance, hiding behind socialist programs. We need a resurgence of teaching on the chain of command of God, which is also the chain of provision. So we see that the women's lib movement and the children's lib movement are a logical extension of the original "men's lib" movement of the enlightenment and a punishment for it. If our society is to get back to God, the men need to learn about God and put themselves and their families in order accordingly, the women need to submit to their husbands (who have already submitted themselves to God), and the children need to submit to both parents. This is God's solution to the problem, and it can be enacted one family at a time.

We need to remember that "God created man in His own image, in the image of God He created him; male and female He created them (Genesis 1:27). We need more of God's teaching about what that means, and we need to obey what God tells us to do in order to be a better male or female.

IV. Man as Son of Adam.

Another description of a human being in the Scriptures is Adam, or son of Adam. This description is based on our natural descent from the historic first created man, named Adam. This expression is used in several ways: the historic first-created man Adam, man (generic usage), and mankind in general. There is also the expression *beney-Adam* בְּנֵי־אָדָם), or children of Adam, which is used to refer to mankind in general, also.

Of course the most basic reference of the word Adam in the Scriptures is to the historical first person of the human race. He is the first human being, and from his rib Eve was made. Eve was Adam's wife, and from this married couple came the whole human race.

What can we learn about Adam from the Hebrew root of his name? We read in Genesis 2:7: "Then the Lord God formed man (*ha-Adam,* הָאָדָם) of dust from the ground (*adamah*—אֲדָמָה)..." The name Adam is the masculine form of the word, and the feminine, or abstract form means ground. It is interesting to note that all the elements in a person's body are also in common soil. In Genesis

3:19, God's judgment on Adam also relates to his origin from the soil: "By the sweat of your face You will eat bread, Till you return to the ground (*adamah*), Because from it you were taken; For you are dust, And to dust you shall return." As man began as soil, so man decomposes back into soil—at least, the material part of man. Genesis 2:7 also mentions the *neshamah* (נְשָׁמָה or spirit (breath of God) and the soul ("man became a living soul") together as the other elements of man. The name Adam, however, refers to our material origins in the dirt.

There are also other words derived from this root: Edom, red, reddish, and Carnelian (a precious stone, *odem,* אֹדֶם in Hebrew).[21] It is interesting to note that Esau was born with a ruddy complexion, and so was also called Edom. His descendants are called the Edomites. At first they are friends of Israel, as Jacob and Esau are reconciled after Jacob's return from Haran. However, after the Israelites return from Egypt, they are bitter enemies of Israel. What does this mean for us? I believe that Esau represents the nature of Adam that is in people at birth. There is nothing blameworthy about a child having inherited the nature of Adam. This is to be expected. Therefore, in the patriarchal period there is friendship there.

However, after one is saved, the old Adam is dead, but his works rise up through our flesh and fight against the believer. Esau is from the verb "to do," and emphasizes works. In Galatians 5:19-21 there is a list of the works of the flesh, and these are produced as we do things in the flesh. The Edomites live on Mt. Seir, which means Demon Mountain, as false spirits energize the works of the flesh.[22] Our only remedy is to crucify the flesh and walk in the spirit.

The color reddish is the color of a sore that indicates leprosy in Leviticus 13:24,43, & 49, and 14:37. Leprosy is a symbol of sin in the Bible and the color *adamdam,* (אֲדַמְדָּם) from this root is the color of a stain or sore that indicates the presence of leprosy. It is fitting that, as we received the sin nature from Adam, we also received it as a disease that destroys us, symbolized by leprosy. The word leprosy in Hebrew is *tzaraat* (צָרַעַת), and this root refers to prostrating of humbling one, according to Gesenius.[23] Our sin nature prostrates or humbles us and leaves us devastated. We need to crucify it and walk in the Holy Spirit or we will be brought down by it.

The gem that is called *odem,* אֹדֶם is translated in the Bible as *sardion* (*σάρδιον*) in the Septuagint. The King James renders it *sardius*, transliterating the Septuagint, while the NASB renders it ruby. This is a stone on the High Priest's Breastplate of Righteousness in Exodus 28:17, along with 11 other precious stones, but was one of nine taken from Satan, who had nine precious stones originally before the fall, including this one in Ezekiel 28:13, rendered *sardion* (LXX) and *sardius* (KJV) and ruby (NASB) again. It is noteworthy that in both lists it is the first mentioned. It appears to refer in some way to the brightness and attractiveness of the first Adam. As it is in the High Priest's Breastplate of Righteousness it may refer to the brightness of the Second Adam, or Jesus. Gesenius believes that this refers to the stone carnelian, which is reddish, but it could be a ruby, as ruby is not used to translate any other word in Scripture, and it is red also.

Secondly, the word Adam can refer to a man in general. In Leviticus 1:2 we read, "Speak to the sons of Israel, and say unto them, 'When any man of you brings an offering..." The expression "when any man of you brings" stands as *adam ki yakriv* (אָדָם כִּי־יַקְרִיב) or "a man that shall bring." This refers to any person at all that may need or desire to bring any sacrificial animal. It is not unlike the expression anybody in English. Obviously, what makes a person "Adam" here is a physical descent from the historical person Adam, but no more meaning is intended than any man in general. It does not specify anything about the person except that he is physically descended from Adam.

Another reference of the word Adam is for mankind in general. In Genesis 6:1-7 every verse has the expression *ha-adam*, meaning mankind. This is the articular form, literally "the Adam," and that form is used in many languages to describe the item generically. Here again there is no special thing implied about the person by means of this description except that he fits in the category by his descent from the historical Adam.

Sometimes one almost gets the impression in Hebrew that the historical Adam was still alive and doing whatever is described. For example, in Genesis 6:5 we read, "Then the LORD saw that the wickedness of man (the Adam) was great on the earth, and that every intent of the thoughts of his (singular) heart was only evil continually." It is obvious from the Biblical account that the historical Adam died in the year 930 after his creation. By calculating in chapter 5 the dates of the births of the early patriarchs, we note that Noah was born in the year 1056 after the creation, so this could not have referred to the historical Adam, even though it sounds like it could be referring to him.

This brings us to the most significant expression for people as descended from Adam: *beney-Adam* (בְּנֵי־אָדָם) or children of Adam. In this expression we have the most extreme statement of original sin. Original sin has been treated like a substance to be washed off, and a number of other things. It has been treated as culpable and not culpable, as well. We now need to look at original sin from the Semitic perspective.

Let us begin with the word *beney* (בְּנֵי), or "children of". The word son *ben* (בֵּן) and daughter *bath* (בַּת) both come from the root *bnh* in Hebrew. From this root comes the verb "to build" in the Hebrew. One's sons and daughters (children) are his "builders." They are building the same thing as the parents are building, according to the Semitic thought.

There is an understanding among Jewish people that they are part of *kol-Yisrael* (כָּל־יִשְׂרָאֵל) or "all Israel." This means that every Jewish person is actually a part of Israel, or Jacob, and has the same standing before God as he does. This is a good Semitic concept, but the Jewish people don't usually carry the principle back far enough. In fact, every human being is part of *kol-Adam* (כָּל־אָדָם), or "all Adam." This would mean that we all have the same standing before God that Adam had.

Adam was expelled from the Garden of Eden and the presence of God. That was Adam's position. Adam was a rebel against God, and that was Adam's character. Incidentally we must note, with respect to Israel, that Israel was born Jacob ("conniver" or "twisted one"), and only with his conversion did he receive the name Israel. The Jewish people are born "in Adam" with the character of Jacob, and need the same conversion as a Gentile to function as "sons of Israel."

What led to Adam and Eve's first sin? It was the three things that comprise the world (Genesis 3:6, cf. I John 2:15-17): the lust of the flesh ("the woman saw that the tree was good for food,"), the lust of the eyes ("and that it was a delight to the eyes,"), and the boastful pride of life ("and that the tree was desirable to make one wise").

We are all born "in Adam," and have the same desires for things of the world, rather than things of God. These desires are transmitted through the soul of Adam, which comes from our physical father, along with his DNA contribution to our body as was already mentioned. We are all born with a soul that is corrupted with self-exaltation and seeks fulfillment in the three things mentioned above: the lust of the flesh, the lust of the eyes, and the pride of life. This is what makes us children of Adam, or "builders of Adam."

In Psalm 14:2-3, repeated in Psalm 53:2-3, God gives us His evaluation on the goodness of man: "The Lord has looked down from heaven upon the sons of Adam (Heb. *al beney-Adam,* עַל־בְּנֵי אָדָם) to see if there are any that understand, who seek after God. They have all turned aside, together they have become corrupt; there is none who does good, not even one."

Now God saw every generation of people in every part of the earth during every period of their lives during all of history, and He did not find even one that was upright and acceptable on his own merits. We all inherited the sin nature in our souls from Adam via our fathers, not mothers, though they are sinners also through their fathers. The sin nature is in our soul, and that comes only from the father. Why the fathers only? The Lord preserved a way to be born without sin through a virgin. Mary did not pass sin to Jesus because she was perfect herself, or, worse, immaculately conceived. She did not pass on sin to her son Jesus because the sin nature is passed through the father. The sin nature is in our soul, and that comes only from the father. She did not pass on the sin nature because she is a woman, and the mother did not pass on the nature. That is why Adam's sin brought sin on the human race—not Eve's sin. Only Adam's soul with the sin nature could be passed to the next succeeding generations.

For most of us it makes no difference whether we are children of Adam because of our fathers or mothers, because both are descendants of Adam. However, it did so for Jesus because, as the angel of the Lord told Joseph (Matthew 1:20): "the Child who has been conceived in her is of the Holy Spirit." The Holy Spirit created a perfect male seed and placed it in her womb to combine with her egg. Thus Jesus did not have any sin nature. The word "seed" itself in Hebrew (*zera*—זֶרַע), refers to what the father places for procreation—not the mother, and it is a word that refers to one's descendants, as well.

So we see that we are all "builders of Adam" at birth, having inherited in our souls the nature of self-exaltation that Adam fell into through his sin. We are inevitably set to sin and rebel at the law when given, and that rebellion will lead to a sort of "individual fall" of our own. The result is separation from God, loss of personal identity, and alienation from others. This is the condition of lost people in the world today.

V. Man as Weakling (Enosh—אֱנֹשׁ)

Since being a son of Adam means being a sinner, why did Jesus take that name for Himself? Does this mean Jesus was a sinner? No! The last of the 5 descriptions of man that we will consider is *enosh* (אֱנֹשׁ) or man as weakling. Gesenius does not place the word *ish* (אִישׁ—man) under the same root as *enosh*,(אֱנוֹשׁ), but he does place *ishah* (אִשָּׁה—woman) under that root. In favor of including *ish* is its plural *anashim* (אֲנָשִׁים), which has all the radicals of that root. It would appear best to treat all three words, *ish*, *ishah*, and *enosh* as under the same root.[24]

Where did Jesus get the name "Son of Man" for Himself? I believe it was Daniel 7:13-14, the passage which He quoted to the High Priest when adjured to answer if he was "the Messiah, the Son of the Blessed One (Matthew 26:63)." He answered, "Hereafter shall ye see the Son of Man sitting on the right hand of power, and coming in the clouds of heaven." In Daniel 7:13-14 we read: "I saw in the night visions, and, behold, one like the Son of man (*ke-bar enash*—כְּבַר־אֱנָשׁ) came with the clouds of heaven, and came to the Ancient of Days, and they brought Him near before Him."

Here the expression "one like the Son of man" refers to man in his weakness, not as having sin. Here *enash* is the Aramaic equivalent of the Hebrew *enosh*. Jesus took on the weakness of our humanity, but not the sin nature. In contrast, God repeatedly calls Ezekiel *ben-Adam*, referring to him as a representative sinner of the human race. Jesus is *bar-enash* in Aramaic, or *ben-enosh* in Hebrew, and they both mean "son of weakness."

This weakness must stand in contrast to beings with strength. They are God, the angels (both good and bad), and political leaders among men. The name for a strong being in the Scriptures is *el* (אֵל) or *elohim* (אֱלֹהִים). In the absolute sense Jehovah is the only *Elohim*, for He alone is omnipotent. The Bible begins "In the beginning *Elohim* created the heavens and the earth." God in the character of this name has all power.

However, there are other beings called *elohim*. The clearest reference to angels as *elohim* is in Psalm 97:9: "For Thou, LORD, art high above all the earth: Thou art exalted far above all gods (*elohim*, אֱלֹהִים). Here the *elohim* are rebellious angels, or demons, or they could also be the good angels. The Psalmist exhorts us to fear Jehovah alone because, no matter how much power evil spirits have, they are no match for the omnipotence of the True God. He is far above them.

In addition to angels, people with high political power are referred to as *elohim*, by virtue of their power. In Psalm 82 there is a curious double usage of the word *elohim*. In verse 1 we read, "*Elohim* stands in the congregation of *el*. He judges among the *elohim*." The first *Elohim* refers to Jehovah, and the second refers to political rulers of this world. In verses 6-7 God says, "You are *elohim*, and all of you are children of the Most High. Surely as Adam you shall die, and as one of the princes you shall fall." Here *elohim* are rebellious human political leaders. Finally the Psalmist cries out to the True Powerful One in verse 8: "Arise, o *Elohim*. Judge the earth; for You shall inherit all nations" (author's translations).

God and angels are definitely *elohim*, and so are the highest political leaders among men. Though I tried to use capitalization by English convention above, capitalizing Elohim only when it referred to God, It must be stated that in Hebrew there are no capital and small letters, and so the distinction is artificial. But there is another group that is weak, but wields great power: born again New

Testament believers. In John 1:12 says: "But as many as received Him, to them He gave the right to become children of God, even to those who believe in His name." Even though Christians do not feel powerful, we have power. We have power given to us, but not in ourselves. We are channels of God's power. In and of ourselves, we are *anashim*, or weaklings. However, God moves within us with His power to accomplish His will. Therefore what we really have is not power, but authority.

When Jesus sent out his twelve disciples in Matthew 10:1, "He gave them *exousía* (ἐξουσία—authority) against unclean spirits, to cast them out, and to heal all manner of sickness and all manner of disease." The word *exousía* is better rendered here authority, rather than the KJV power. The disciples did not have the power in themselves. They were weaklings. They had authority, so that they spoke the word and the power of God came through them through the Holy Spirit and did the healing. If we remember our understanding of man as the image of God, God has the power, and God is in the believer. The believer is a weakling, but he brings the presence of God to the problem. He has God, the Being with Power within himself, but he doesn't have the power intrinsic to his nature.

Paul learned this fact well, as he tells us in II Corinthians 12:9: "And He (the Lord) has said to me, 'My grace is sufficient for you, for power is perfected in weakness.' Most gladly, therefore, I will rather boast about my weaknesses, so that the power of Christ may dwell in me." Paul gloried in the character of this name *enosh*, weakling, trusting in his authority, as well as God's grace, in order to meet the enemy with however much power he came.

Let us imagine we are looking at a short, weak-looking policewoman directing traffic in a downtown area. Large cars and trucks arrive at her intersection and she puts up her hands to stop traffic in two directions. All these huge vehicles come to a stop. Why? They have power, but she has authority. The whole police force, the government, the National Guard, and the armed forces of the nation stand behind her, ready to back her up. Though the cars and trucks could leave her flattened and dead on the pavement, they stop because they do not want to lose to her higher-ups. That is how we, as believers, have authority.

When God created Adam He gave him authority over the whole earth, but Adam lost that authority through sin. In Jesus it is restored, as the Holy Spirit takes up residence in His image, and takes control over His likeness. He has the only absolute power in the universe. All other power is just relative.

The policewoman needs two things in order to exercise her authority: cleanliness and faith. If she were to grovel in the mud with the pigs all night and then come to work covered with mud, the people would not stop for her because they would not see her uniform. Also, if she did not believe that she had authority, she would hide behind some bushes and stick up a finger and say, "Please stop," and nothing would happen, either. They would not see her. In this way we need cleanliness and faith in order to exercise our God-given authority. This is the way that we, as *anashim*, can operate in a world of beings much more powerful than we are. Authority wins out over power.

Conclusion: What it Means to Be a Human Being Today.

We have seen that man is the image of God—a dwelling place for the Spirit of God. Outside of salvation, the Spirit is not there and a great, God-sized vacuum exists, which only God can fill. After salvation God's Spirit is living in us, and we no longer feel empty. This is the result of justification.

We have seen that man is in the likeness of God. We have the elements of God's life. However, before salvation these elements are out of order. We hate what we should love and love what we should hate. Our lives are in disarray. However, after salvation, the Holy Spirit that comes in begins a process to bring order out of the chaos that is inside of us. This is the process of sanctification; and, though we will never arrive completely to act like Jesus in everything, we must surrender to the working of the Holy Spirit to transform us now.

We have seen that we are male or female, and that God has different roles for us. This fact shows us that true reality is bigger than any person, and that we need to live together with God and others. God has given men and women different gifts and roles for the good of both, and the union of a man and a woman in marriage is a glorious thing—better than the sum of the two individuals. We have seen the importance of God's chain of command and provision. Everyone has two ministries of love to all those below them on the chain: provision and guidance, and everyone has two ministries to respond to these ministries from those above: we respond to the guidance with obedience, and to the provision with gratefulness.

We have seen that we are sons of Adam and unable to get beyond the rebellion of Adam and Eve on our own. We need the God's ministries to us or we will be lost in our sins.

Finally, we have seen that we are just weaklings, in and of ourselves. We are matched up against spiritual powers that could crush us in a moment, were it not for the Lord's care. We need to remember to fight with authority by faith in God, exercised in cleanliness, rather in any intrinsic strength of our own. Let us, like the Apostle Paul rather glory in our weakness. That way all of the glory will go to God, and none will be for us.

Thousands of years ago, God took some dust, formed of it a body, and breathed into it His breath of life and man became a living soul. As we meditate on all of the things that God has done for us, may we be lost in wonder, love, and humble worship of Him that created us.

Chapter 4

The Problem of Sin: Seen in the Light of Israel's Bondage in Egypt

It is a long journey for the Israelites as they journey from the pristine simplicity of the relationship of the patriarchs with God to the bondage in Egypt, but God oversees the whole process, and they go into Egypt at His guidance. God sends Joseph ahead in chains of slavery to prepare the way for his family. God sends the dreams to Pharaoh to notify of the coming famine and to raise Joseph to second in command to prepare for the famine. God also sends the famine to bring Joseph's family to Egypt to save them during the famine. God places in Pharaoh's heart the desire to let Joseph's family stay in the land of Goshen in Egypt, where they prosper and are multiplied to the size of a nation. Finally, God tells Jacob to go there (Genesis 46:3-4): "He said, 'I am God, the God of your father; do not be afraid to go down to Egypt, for I will make you a great nation there. I will go down with you to Egypt, and I will also surely bring you up again; and Joseph will close your eyes."

God also raised up in Egypt a king who did not know Joseph, and the privileged status of Israel was exchanged for a terrible slavery. Worse than just slavery, Pharaoh made two attempts to have all of the male babies of Israel put to death: at birth, and then later by being thrown into the Nile River. As the Book of Exodus opens, the

Israelites are in a terrible slavery in Egypt, and we must conclude that that is exactly where the Lord wanted them to be. God even tells Abraham about this in advance (Gen. 15:13-14): "Know for certain that your descendants will be strangers in a land that is not theirs, where they will be enslaved and oppressed four hundred years. But I will also judge the nation whom they will serve, and afterward they will come out with many possessions."

God knew about the slavery in Egypt before it happened. He brought Israel down into Egypt and arranged things so that they would end up in slavery. He also promised to deliver Israel and give them riches to compensate their years of service. Israel's stay in Egypt was an integral part of God's plan for them.

To what does this correspond in the life of the New Testament believer? The Apostle Paul states in his famous chapter on his battle with sin (Rom. 7:9): "I was once alive apart from the Law; but when the commandment came, sin became alive, and I died." When was Paul alive, and when and how did he die? We have seen in the previous chapter on man that, according to Romans 7, Paul was conceived by a direct inbreathing of God's *neshamah* (roughly translated "spirit") at conception, and he was in spiritual contact with God from his conception onward. As his religious Jewish upbringing gave understanding of the Law, the sin nature inherited from Adam through his father in his soul led him into rebellion against it (vv. 9-11). The result was a bondage in which Paul does what he does not want to do and does not do what he wants to do (vv. 14-20). "For we know that the Law is spiritual, but I am of flesh, sold into bondage to sin. For what I am doing, I do not understand; for I am not practicing what I would like to do, but I am doing the very thing I hate. But if I do the very thing that I do not want to do, I agree with the Law, confessing that the Law is good. So now, no longer am I the one doing it, but the sin which dwells in me. For I know that nothing good dwells in me, that is, in my flesh; for the willing is present in me, but the doing of the good is not. For the good that I want I do not do, but I practice the very evil that I do not want. But if I am doing the very thing I do not want. I am no longer the one doing it, but sin which dwells in me."

It will be the purpose of this chapter to trace the course of events from Israel's patriarchal period leading to the bondage in Egypt. In the light of this, we will seek to understand how every person begins with some spiritual contact with God, and how he comes to be in bondage to sin. We will seek to explain the parallels between Israel's history and the Christian life by examining the roots of the words in Hebrew, historical circumstances, and New Testament passages for the applications to the life of the modern believer.

I. The Patriarchs of Israel in Canaan: Childhood Innocence.

The Land of Canaan (כְּנַעַן) in the Bible is a picture of humility, even as the root of the word Canaan (כנע) means "to be humbled or subdued" under someone.[1] In this case, we note that the child is humbled, or subdued under his parents, who, hopefully, are under God. Children know that they cannot run things, and that they are dependent on others for their sustenance, guidance, and all provisions. They live by being dependent on others, and they learn to trust their parents implicitly in everything.

It is for this reason that Jesus tells His disciples (Mat. 18:3), "Unless you are converted and become like children, you will not enter the kingdom of heaven." It seems that that implicit trust that children have needs to be redeveloped in us through a series of stages so that, at the end, *we are again fit for the Kingdom of Heaven.*

So it is also with Israel. They are living as patriarchs in a personal relation with God without laws or penalties. God gives direct commands, and they obey. They trust with simple faith and are prospered. However, through a series of events, they become enslaved in Egypt, are liberated, pass through the desert, and then cross the Jordan River, just to return to the Land of Canaan from which they began. Someone has said, "Happiness is the fulfillment of a childhood desire." In the life of Israel, it is the return to Canaan, from which they were separated. In the life of the Christian, it is the return to our childhood humility, faith, and dependence on God from which we were separated by our rebellion against God.

In the lives of Abraham, Isaac, and Jacob we see a picture of little children in relation with their Father. God took care of them, overlooked many sins that they committed, not holding their sins against them, and prospered them through all the difficulties of life. As for Abraham, so it was for the others (Gen. 15:6): "Then he (Abraham) believed in the Lord; and He reckoned it to him as righteousness." Abraham more than once passed his wife off as his sister to avoid conflicts with men who might be interested in her. God overruled and rebuked both Pharaoh and the King of the Philistines so they didn't take Sarah for a wife, and they repented. In the same way our Heavenly Father overlooks the temper tantrums and other wrong actions of a two year old, not holding it against him, and keeps the way open to Him.

When Abraham was called, he was living in Ur of the Chaldees. In the Hebrew Ur means flame, primarily in the sense of the light that it gives. The Hebrew word for light is *owr* (אוֹר), from the same root.[2] The word *Chaldees* (כַּשְׂדִּים) refers to a place in lower Mesopotamia, as well as a certain class of magicians and conjurers that come from this area.[3] Ur was well known as a city of moon-worship, and also Terah, Abraham's father is most likely named after the moon (*yareah*, יָרֵחַ), according to his name. It is not surprising that when Abraham is called, he is involved in moon-worship, his father is named after the moon, and his city is walking in the light of different types of witchcraft and other spiritual conjuring.

According to Genesis 11:31-32, Abraham's father Terah went with Abraham as far as Haran (חָרָן), where he died. <u>H</u>aran means "crossroads," according to Gesenius.[4] It was a junction of trade routes and an ancient seat of worship of a moon-god. Here God's call put Abraham at a crossroad. Abraham chose to follow the Creator God, rather than the moon-god of his father Terah, whose name means "Moonie," meaning Terah probably worshipped the moon-god.

In the same way, each one of us is in contact with rebellion against God from an early age. We get the light of this world and begin to follow it, as we follow our parents. The Apostle John warns us all (I John 5:19), "the whole world lies in the evil one" (my translation). It is not our fault that we start off in a dangerous place with false light and, in most cases, relatives that are going in the wrong direction. God called out to Abraham, and Abraham responded by obeying God's requirements to renounce his country, his relatives, and his father's house, including the false gods, false light and false conjuring.

At some point God wants to see from us a response to the truth. If we respond to the truth, He gives us more truth. Do we want the truth above our country, our relatives, and our father's house? The answer is up to us. As we move forward to accept the light we have, we are in the beginning of our gestation. Just as Jesus says that we must be born again to enter the Kingdom of God (John 3:3), so also God prepares us for that new birth through a period of gestation. Also, as Abraham crosses over the Euphrates River, so we need to cross over from the things of this world that hold our esteem in order to search for God.

Abraham "crossed over" for God, thus becoming the first Hebrew. The word Hebrew comes from the verb "to cross over,"[5] and refers to this commitment. Just as he crossed over from his country and family to follow God, his descendants crossed over the Red Sea (really the Reed Sea) to be separated from the other nations and to follow the One True God. To follow God through Jesus, we must also "cross over" from everything of this world that can move us in the wrong direction.

Another great event in the life of Abraham was his willingness to sacrifice Isaac in Genesis 22. This is a lesson from God as the Great Teacher Who, on Mount *Moriah* (מוֹרִיָּה, meaning "Jehovah is my teacher") was teaching Abraham to trust in Him. Later in his life, Abraham had more children by a lady named *Keturah* (קְטוּרָה, "smoke", Gen. 25:1). These were *Zimran* (זִמְרָן, "pruning"), *Yokshan* (יָקְשָׁן, "trapper"), *Medan* and *Midian* (מְדָן and מִדְיָן, perhaps duplicate names from the root "to judge" (דִּין), referring to the natural conscience), *Yishbak* (יִשְׁבָּק, "let go" or "leave," from the Heb. root שׁבק), and *Shuach* (שׁוּחַ, "sink down" in depression). While all of these names can be integrated into the identity of a child, there is none so interesting as that of the *Midian*.

The *Midianites* come from Abraham, and, through the root of their name, remind us of the natural conscience. In a child it is good. In fact, the *Midianites* are friends of Israel from the patriarchal period until Mt. Sinai. After that, they are mortal enemies. Why? The natural conscience condemns us, leading us to seek forgiveness of sins and be converted in the first place. After that, it continues accusing us saying, "Don't think that forgiveness was that easy. You are guilty." At some point later we have to defeat the weak human conscience and trust the Word of God for our forgiveness in order to enter into the Land to become the spiritual man. Nevertheless, in a child it is good, though its criteria have not been developed yet.

Isaac and Rebekah sinned in favoring one son above the other, but God overruled and Jacob was selected to continue the blessings of the Lord because Esau despised his birthright. Jacob (יַעֲקֹב) means "schemer" or "conniver," but that is closer to the plan of God than was Esau.[6] Esau (עֵשָׂו) is from the verb "to do," and refers to trusting in works to please God and despising the inheritance.[7]

After wrestling with others all his life, Jacob finally wrestled with the Lord and would not let him go until he received a blessing. The Lord renamed him Israel (יִשְׂרָאֵל), combining the words prince-שָׂר-and God-אֵל), meaning "Prince of God", reminding him to trust God, rather than his own schemes to get ahead. After that time, Jacob no longer tried to trick others. He even forced Esau to receive a gift from him, rather than tricking him to get things, as before (see Genesis 34:4-11). We see that, when a child fully trusts his father's provision, he is capable of much generosity.

II. The Descent into Egypt: Coming Under the Yolk of Sin.

During God's dealings with Jacob, 12 sons are born to him; and in this period, the family goes down to Egypt. We need to consider the events leading to the descent into Egypt to see that it was in the plan of God, as well as to see the steps of a child's descent into rebellion against God. A consideration of the steps into the fall needs to begin with the origin of all sin: the fall of Satan himself. After that, we will see how Adam and Eve fell, and then we will see how every person undergoes that same fall in his or her life at a certain stage of development.

A. The Fall of Satan.

The fall of Satan is the event that brings sin into the universe and begins an unraveling process in the history of God's creation—indeed, it begins history itself. Before sin, there were eternal beings worshipping their Creator in peace and harmony. There was no history, as there was no change. Sin, however, brought changes measuring the distance between God and some of His creatures, the progress of the conflict between them, and, eventually, the progress of God in reconciling some rebellious creatures to Himself. Before sin, there was no becoming—just being. Incidentally, for those of us who end up in heaven, after sin there will be no becoming anymore—just being.

In Ezekiel 28:12-19 we read about the fall of Satan, called here the King of Tyre, contrasted with the human ruler, called the prince of Tyre in verses 1-10. Satan, meaning the adversary, or enemy,[8] was not so called at first. Neither was he called the King of Tyre, or the King of oppression, according to the root of Tyre in Hebrew.[9] He was probably called, as in Isaiah 14:12, Lucifer, or <u>*Heyleyl*</u> <u>*Ben-Shachar*</u> (הֵילֵל בֶּן־שַׁחַר). This name means "Shining one, son of the dawn." He was one of 3 specially named angels, along with Gabriel (גַּבְרִיאֵל, "God is my mighty warrior") and Michael (מִיכָאֵל, "Who is like God?"). We may venture a guess that each one had rule over about a third of the angels because it is thought that about a third of the angels rebelled with Satan. This is evident from Revelation 12:4 where we read that, as Satan falls from heaven, "His tail swept away a third of the stars of heaven and threw them to the earth." Thus he will bring them with him when he is cast out of heaven.

As we continue in Ezekiel 28:12-19, we find out that *Heyleyl Ben-Shachar* (הֵילֵל בֶּן־שַׁחַר) "had the seal of perfection, full of wisdom, and perfect in beauty (v.12)." When he was created, *Heyleyl Ben-Shachar* was the wisest and most beautiful of created beings. He had nine precious stones in the day of his creation, and they were set in gold (v. 13). In verse 14 we read that he was "the anointed cherub that covers" (כְּרוּב מִמְשַׁח הַסּוֹכֵךְ). This means that he was over many in authority. Cherub means, literally, "approached one," or one who approaches God. These were the angels closest to God. *Heyleyl Ben-Shachar* also was in the holy mountain of God and walked around in the midst of the stones of fire. Not very much is known of the holy mountain of God or the stones of fire, but his presence among them was definitely indicative of a great position of power and authority among angels.

What happened to this powerful, beautiful, and wise cherub to turn him into the monster that we know him as today? Verse 15 even states, "You were blameless in your ways from the day you were created until unrighteousness was found in you." How could iniquity arise in a creature created perfect? What is sin, anyway, that it can arise in a perfect being? Thiessen asks what motive could be behind the revolt of Satan and settles on three: "Great prosperity and beauty seem to be thrown out as possible hints in this respect.[10] The Tyrian King seems to symbolize Satan in Ezekiel 28:11-19; and he is said to have fallen because of these things (cf. I Tim. 3:6). Undue ambition and the desire to surpass God seem to be another hint. The King of Babylon is charged with this ambition, and he, too, seems to symbolize Satan (Is. 14:13-14). It will be seen that in any case it was selfishness, discontentment with what he had, and the craving to get all that anyone else had" (emphasis mine).

I would like to rename these three motives of Satan so that they can be more readily understood with respect to the origin of sin in him. The first was self-focus. At the beginning, *Heyleyl Ben-Shachar* (הֵילֵל בֶּן־שַׁחַר), "the Shining One, Son of the Dawn," took his focus off of God, and began to look at himself. It may have been that he noticed his own beauty and appreciated it as coming from God, Who had created him. At this stage it is not a sin. Perhaps, next, he began looking around and comparing himself with others of God's created angels—even concluding that his beauty surpassed theirs. This in itself was still not sin, for God gives different glory and beauty to each one of His creatures, and surely one is entitled to his opinions as to the relative beauty of different ones.

The second step to sin was a comparison to those who were seen as better off than him, leading to discontentment. Discontentment is a dangerous feeling a good half of the way to sin. It is a beginning to judge God's creative decisions as being less than perfect. If *Heyleyl Ben-Shachar* at this point would have repented and concluded that things must be right because it was God Who arranged them this way, he still could have avoided sin.

The third step is a craving to move himself up above others. This would include wanting to get all that anyone else had, but also included a rejection of his God-created position and portion, and an attempt to obtain a greater position and portion through his own efforts apart from and against the wishes of God Himself. As this craving increased, he probably even recruited the third of the angels that were under him (as we have seen above), and challenged God Himself trying to take away God's throne.

After these three steps, the results come forth in actions. In verse 16 we read that by the multitude of his schemings, he was filled with violence and he sinned. I believe that "schemings" is a better translation of the Hebrew *rechullatchá* (רְכֻלָּתְךָ) because the base meaning of the root in Hebrew is "going about" (either to trade or gossip), which would indicate the scheming of the person, rather than the actual act of trading or the merchandise accumulated.[11]

At this point God dealt with the situation. First He declared *Heyleyl Ben-Shachar* as profane, meaning not fit to be in His presence or for His service, and cast him out of the Mountain of God. I believe that Satan and his angels were cast down to earth at this point, and earth became a quarantine place for rebellious creatures. This was, of course, before the creation of Adam and Eve. God continued by announcing that He would destroy Satan from the midst of the stones of fire (v.16).

Next in verse 17 God explains to Satan what he did that was sin: "Your heart was lifted up because of your beauty; and you corrupted your wisdom by reason of your splendor." *Heyleyl Ben-Shachar* focused on his own brightness and dedicated his once perfect wisdom to build up himself even further. This can only have one result: judgment from God.

God judges this first rebel by announcing that He will cast him to the ground and make an example of him for others. Also, God says that He will bring out a fire from the midst of him that would devour him to ashes. Not only does God judge him from above, but also God here condemns all sin to be self-defeating. The fire that he once walked in with the stones of fire now would consume him. God's fire can purify or consume, depending on what our relation to God is. The fire of Satan's own ambition, or craving to move himself above others actually consumes him and makes him suffer, along with all humans who are perpetually discontented with God's portion and craving to work their way up over others, as we shall see later. However, the fire of our ambition to glorify God drives men to saintly lives of beauty and dedication to God.

Thus, we see that God did not make Satan evil, as though evil was something in itself to be blamed on God. God made Satan perfect, and Satan began to value himself independently from God, focusing on himself. Comparing himself to others worse off than himself, he felt superior to them. Next, he compared himself unfavorably to God Himself, as well as others, whom he considered better off than himself in one or more categories, leading to discontent. Finally, he developed a craving to improve his position above others, and this craving began to consume him. The result was actions against God and others, resulting in judgment. It is this craving for self-exaltation that is the essence of the sin nature, and the actions that result are acts of sin.

B. The Fall of Adam and Eve.

After his fall from his position of authority with God, Satan witnessed the creation of Adam and Eve. He saw Adam exercised authority over the whole earth, helped God by naming the animals, and enjoyed the Garden of Eden. Satan then came to try to get man to join him in his rebellion, as he had already induced his angel subordinates to join him.

How was it that Satan succeeded in getting Eve to sin? Let us attempt to cast his temptations into the form of the processes that were going through his own heart when he rebelled against God in the first place. The first was to cast doubt on God's Word. In Genesis 3:1 he cast doubt on God's good counsel: "Indeed, has God said, 'You shall not eat from any tree of the garden'?" He was really implying that God could not be that good if He was holding something back from her. He also exaggerated God's commandment to include all of the trees.

Eve picks up on this attitude of doubting God's goodness by adding to God's word: "or touch it (3:3)." This addition makes God look worse than He would have appeared, had she quoted Him correctly. She was already playing into Satan's hands by beginning to act independently of God.

When Satan sees her willingness to alter God's revealed Word, he continues his attack with more directness (3:4): "You will not surely die (my translation)." Here the meaning is that it is not sure that Eve will die if she eats the fruit, not that it is sure that she will not die, as the NASV reads. He was leaving open space for the possibility that God would not carry out His threat. After she had thought about that for a few moments, he continued with a promise that tantalized her discontent which he had stirred up (3:5): "For God knows that in the day you eat from it your eyes will be opened, and you will be like God, knowing good and evil." At this point she began to focus on herself and compare herself unfavorably with God, Who knows good and evil, concluding that she was inferior to God and angels and should be dissatisfied with her abilities. After this there is a direct incitement to exert herself to act independently of God and do something to better her situation.

Therein follows the saddest verse in all of Scriptures. Genesis 3:6 describes the fall of mankind into sin. Eve then contemplates what both she and the Serpent have said, and there are three elements about the fruit that attract her. These are the essential elements today around which the battle of sin is centered: "When the woman saw that the tree was good for food (lust of the flesh), and that it was a delight to the eyes (lust of the eyes), and that the tree was desirable to make one wise, (pride of life), she took from its fruit and ate; and she gave also to her husband with her, and he ate."

When one seeks to improve his position, or exalt himself, as a human being, there are three basic areas of temptations through which Satan tempts us to exalt ourselves against God, and we are warned about them in I John 2:15-17: "Do not love the world nor the things in the world. If anyone loves the world, the love of the Father is not in him. For all that is in the world, the lust of the flesh and the lust of the eyes and the boastful pride of life, is not from the Father, but is from the world. The world is passing away, and also its lusts; but the one who does the will of God lives forever."

Eve first thought of herself independently of God and focused on herself. Then she accepted Satan's distortion of God's Word, including his insinuation that God was not really seeking her best interests by withholding the fruit of the tree of the knowledge of good and evil from her. As this thought was stirred up inside her, she thought upon the possible improvement in her situation through the fulfillment of the desire of her flesh, the desire of her eyes, and the satisfaction of her pride. Thus, the same mental processes were reproduced in her that had been working in Satan that brought about his sin and judgment.

Of course, like Satan, Adam and Eve were judged for their sin. As Satan was cast out from the Mountain of God, so Adam and Eve were cast out of the presence of God in the Garden of Eden. The expulsion from the presence of God, of course, left them out of God's revelation and precluded their doing anything else but sin. Sin is the attitude of seeking to glorify oneself independently of God. Now, without the presence of God, mankind can do nothing but sin, as everything is now done for self-glorification, and apart from God. However, God still took into consideration that some were seeking after Him.

In theology there is a dispute as to whether man is totally depraved or has some independent good in him that can seek God. Some men, such as Immanuel Kant begin well by declaring the absolute depravity of man, and then undercut the whole meaning of depravity. Berkhouwer explains about Kant: "Kant thus, in passing, mentions the Biblical idea of rebirth, but goes on then to ask how it would be possible for man to "bring this revolution to pass through his own powers and become a good man through himself." In answering this question, Kant suddenly sets a limit on the radicality of evil. For Kant is of the opinion that such a revolution is necessary and <u>therefore</u> must be possible for man to accomplish. It <u>is</u> possible through a 'unique unalterable decision' in which the tendency of the heart is transformed. There is a way from the "<u>Sollen</u> (what man <u>should</u> do)," the moral law, to the ability to conform to it. 'When the moral law commands, we are obliged to be better men, and it follows that we must, and thus that we can.'"[12]

It is important to see the reasoning of Kant here because so much of Western Civilization has been moved to liberal modernism through his influence. Kant, in effect, is saying that man needs to be born again; but if he doesn't want to be born again, he can make a moral regeneration and become acceptable to God on his own. How should we react to this idea? The reaction of the traditional reformed theologians was to point out that Luther supported total depravity, and only referred to any of man's moral understanding to result in his just condemnation for sin, but could not result in his acceptance by God through his self-efforts.

I believe that Kant, being a philosopher more than a theologian, was moved more by the influence of Descartes' "I think, therefore I am," than the Bible. As this error in the guise of a qualification of his Biblical teaching slipped in, it crowded out the truth of Scripture. By starting from man himself as an independent and autonomous moral being and reasoning out to all truth, Descartes—far from establishing the truth of Christianity and the Bible—set up a mindset of self-awareness, dissatisfaction, and striving in words and deeds for human improvement that is the crystallization of sin in its purest form. Far from leading to noble truths and selfless service, it brought the world wars, the holocaust, communism, abortion, and a whole host of other modern evils.

We men are not independent and autonomous moral agents—only Adam and Eve were. We are worse off than Adam and Eve, in that we inherited their rebellious, self-exalting nature in our souls. In us Satan is not tempting an innocent being, as were Adam and Eve. He is simply seeking to activate his ally in us—the nature of sin we inherited from our parents. Though the outcome of Satan's temptation of Eve was in doubt, each human being since was born in his camp and falls easily into his clutches. As surely as we learn the law of God, we surely rebel against it, and we all go through the equivalent experience of being expelled from the Garden in Eden, even as Paul described it above. At that point man is without God, and cannot find or will his way back. That is what total depravity refers to.

Without God there is no fixed moral standard, and everyone can invent his own criteria to justify himself to a god of his imagining. With man as the starting point of philosophy, man has become the ending point, not God. Once a Transcendent God is denied in the universe, total chaos will result. This is the spirit of lawlessness (Greek, anomía, ἀνομία) that we are encountering today in the world. Just as man turned out to be incapable of arriving at true ideas by beginning with himself and reasoning outward, so man was equally incapable of defining good actions beginning with himself, let alone acting in accordance with them.

Kant also transformed or limited sin to the commission of certain external acts, rather than the inward state of separation from God leading to independent efforts of self-exaltation. This is only a superficial treatment of sin, allowing a superficial answer, as we shall see.

What would the acceptance by God through man's self-efforts represent, anyway? It would be the same thing that man did in the original sin. It would represent perception of being independent from God, dissatisfaction in his position, the desire to improve his situation through self-effort, and a strong self-effort to achieve a goal. This would result in a major achievement that he could boast about and feed his pride. Thus, the natural religions, as well as modern liberalism, all make human religion a stepladder to achieve union with God by achieving the moral law that God demands. The very act of going up that ladder involves every major thought process of sin itself. Therefore, far from being the means of liberation from a difficult situation, human religion, philosophy, and moral effort of any kind is the essence of sin itself. It is the person standing up to God in striving and saying, "With my own effort, I will be like the Most High." Thus, Kant makes the law a means of reconciliation with God, rather than the means of revealing of sin and motivation for man to seek salvation by grace through faith.

It is for this reason that we need to hold to the doctrine of the total depravity of man, but not as though man were a piece of garbage. Apart from a personal relation with God, man is incapable of having the desire to glory in his standing as God created him, praising God, and submitting to God's authority and God's Holy Spirit. Depravity may be a harsh term for modern ears, but it is the guaranteed inability of man to work for his own salvation. In his discussion of the "remnants" of God's knowledge that are in unregenerate man, Berkouwer concludes: "We must always measure every discussion of "remnants" against one standard—in what context and with what aim is the discussion carried on; that is, whether it is an attempt to escape from "totus homo peccator" (man as completely sinful) to some untouched human reserve, or whether the aim is to stress the seriousness of fallen man's humanity in the sight of God, his humanness *while* he is a sinner, so that his innocence is not vindicated, but rather is the force of the Divine indictment."[13]

We may leave no place in man isolated from the fall which could provide his way back to God unaided. We need a radical rebirth. Yes, there is a statement that we must be born again because "God has shut up all in disobedience that He may show mercy to all (Romans 11:32)." The fact of the separation is not a logical imperative to believe that bridging it is within our ability. We cannot say with Kant, "When the moral law commands, we are obliged to be better men, and it follows that we must, and thus that we can." We must, but we can't. Thus, it follows that God needs to intervene or we will all perish.

C. The Fall of Each Person.

Having provided the proper background for the entrance of sin into the universe in Satan, and its entrance in the human race in Adam and Eve, we are now in a position to understand how sin becomes a problem for each individual person. At this point of the discussion, we will consider the parallels between the story of Israel's descent into Egypt and bondage there and the way each one of us comes under bondage to sin as we grow up as children.

Let us now rejoin the narrative of Israel's descent into Egypt. We want to see the elements of the story, and then we need to analyze the process as internalized in an individual person, leading him from infant innocence to adult bondage to sin.

The story of Israel's descent into Egypt began with Joseph and his brothers. In Genesis 37 Joseph told his father what some of his brothers had done and brought an evil report about them. They thus became angry with him for this. Then Joseph had a dream and told his brothers that they would eventually end up bowing down to him. They became enraged with him and began to plot against him.

One day when Joseph's brothers were busy tending sheep at Shechem (שְׁכֶם), his father sent him from the valley of Hebron (חֶבְרוֹן) to check up on them. Hebron means "league," and Joseph was still in league with his family at this point. When he arrived in Shechem, he did not find them, and a man told him that they had gone to Dothan. Shechem means "shoulder", and comes from the root, referring to "rising early," or diligence.[14] Joseph here was diligent in fulfilling his father's business, but his brothers were not.

As he was arriving at Dothan, his brothers consulted together to get rid of him. Dothan (דֹּתָן) is from the root referring to law (*dath*, דָּת), or decree, and this is the Modern Hebrew word for religion, as well. Here, however, we see that some sort of "religion," whether of Israel or of another nation is just what a child is brought up with. The religion and cultural content vary from one nation to another, but a child is usually brought up to believe that there is a right and wrong, and this process eventually ends the childhood innocence.

Joseph's brothers were divided as to what to do with him. Reuben (רְאוּבֵן, translated means, "Behold, a son") wanted to rescue him and send him back to their father. Simeon (שִׁמְעוֹן), translation, "hearing") and Levi (לֵוִי, translation, "joined") wanted to kill him. Judah's (יְהוּדָה, translation, "praise") counsel prevailed, and they sold him into slavery to some Midianites (מִדְיָנִים) and Ishmaelites (יִשְׁמְעֵאלִים) merchants that were passing by. Joseph was sold in Egypt to "Potiphar (פּוֹטִיפַר), an officer of Pharaoh's, and captain of the guard (Gen. 37:36)." It is interesting to note that Potiphar in Egyptian means "belonging to the sun." At this stage the child is making his transition from seeing spiritually on the inside to seeing on the outside where the sun illuminates. In Ecclesiastes the expression for this sphere of existence is "under the sun" (Ecclesiastes 1:3, 1:9, 2:11, 2:17, etc.) As his focus changes, his ambitions begin to stir, and he begins to follow others in the things of this world.

What happens when a young child passes through the process of being taught a religion? At first he is confident that he can do everything that is asked of him, and he starts out optimistic. Then, as he fails to do everything asked of him, he begins to make a discovery: the laws that are given him are much different than his natural desires. The Apostle Paul in Romans 7 wrote of the conflicts that he faced as a growing child (7:8-9): "But sin, taking opportunity through the commandment, produced in me coveting of every kind; for apart from the law sin is dead. I was once alive apart from the Law; but when the commandment came, sin became alive and I died."

This, I believe, speaks of the growing up process of a child. As was mentioned in the previous chapters on man and revelation, the child begins with an inherited sin nature through his soul, which comes biologically along with his body. This self-worshipping soul will lead each person to do nothing but sin when it takes over. However, each person is also born with a spirit (neshamah) that is directly "breathed in" by God, as He breathed it in the first man Adam, as mentioned in Genesis 2:7: "Then the Lord God formed man of dust from the ground, and breathed into his nostrils the breath of life; and man became a living being." In Job 33:4 Elihu mentions that this is true of every person born subsequently: "the breath (*neshamah*) of the Almighty gives me life."

Paul explains this process from the beginning in Romans 7:9: "I was once alive apart from the Law; but when the commandment came, sin became alive and I died." Paul began in spiritual contact with God because of the breath of God that was breathed into him at his conception. However, when, through his Jewish upbringing, he learned the Jewish Law, the sin attitude of selfishness, discontentment, and craving to get what others have, which was inherited in his soul, came to life and led him to rebel against that law. The result was that he died, i.e., he lost the spiritual connection with God that he had from his conception. His human spirit was now dead, in that it could no longer contact God. It is not clear at what age God considers the person responsible for his own decisions, and therefore accountable for his sins. The Jewish people consider a boy to be responsible at his 13th birthday. However, the only place that God held people responsible by age, it was twenty years old. Every man that was twenty years of age and older could not enter the land of Canaan and had to die in the wilderness because they did not believe the Lord.

Though we do not know the exact age at which a child is considered accountable—and it probably varies from person to person—we do know the end result. The contact between the person's human spirit and God's Holy Spirit is broken, and the person can no longer perceive God spiritually. I believe there is a memory of that original contact with God. That is why everyone starts out knowing God, and so many have a clear idea of which God they are rejecting. In fact, Paul mentions that each person in the worst sins imaginable begins with knowledge of God, which he rejects. In Romans 1:21, Paul starts describing all of the worst types of rebels against God with this phrase, "For even though they knew God, they did not honor Him as God or give thanks."

The child is alive to start out. This does not imply that the child has no inherited sin nature, but that there is nothing blamable for the child, up to the point at which he sins and cuts himself from God's presence and care. As Paul says in Romans 5:13, "Sin is not imputed when there is no law." It is as though the child is in the Garden of Eden with God's presence until his sin nature expresses itself in rebellion against the law that is taught him in the growing-up process. Then he passes his equivalent of being expelled from the Garden of Eden. This is the same difference between the relationship of the patriarchs and God, on the one hand, and the relationship of the later Israelites and God after the Law was given at Mt. Sinai. The patriarchs have almost no knowledge of the Law, and they talk with God directly. The later Israelites have many laws from God, and God only reveals Himself to a few through His Holy Spirit.

Though God waits for our rebellion before He cuts us off, this hardly means that we are left with a viable option to sin or not to sin as Adam and Eve had. The nature that we inherited from them will automatically choose to rebel against God when given the opportunity. There is no suspense anymore, as to whether or not the fruit of the Tree of the Knowledge of Good and Evil will be eaten. The sin in us grabs for it as soon as God's voice says no.

As Thiessen states, "Paul distinguishes between *sin* and *sins*, the one the nature, and the other the expression of that nature. Sin is present in every one as a nature before it expresses itself in deeds."[15] It is not the nature itself that is culpable, or the Apostle Paul, or the rest of us as well, never would have been "alive without the law once." It is only when the individual acts according to this nature in rebelling against the law after it is presented and understood that renders blame and results in his death. This death is spiritual death, meaning being cut off from God's presence, as Adam and Eve were when expelled from the Garden of Eden (Gen. 3:23-24).

What is this process of development to which we all were subjected as children? First of all, there is our natural conscience, which indicates to us what is right and wrong. The conscience begins to show evidence of being active around the age of one and a half to two years of age. The child's knowledge of good and evil is on the level of a "gut reaction," but he cannot understand the principles of right and wrong yet at this stage.

The natural conscience corresponds to the Midianites (Heb. מְדָיְנִים), who brought Joseph down into Egypt. The word *Midianites* comes from the Hebrew root (דין) which means, "to judge."[16] These people were descended from Abraham directly (through Keturah, Gen. 25:1-2), and present a curious paradox throughout the various stages of Israel's history. Here they are seen carrying Joseph down into Egypt. Later Moses marries a Midianite lady, and the Midianites are on the side of Israel up to Mount Sinai. From the point of Mt. Sinai onward, they are bitter enemies of Israel. Why is this?

The natural conscience of a man will lead him to try to follow the law, leading to his failure and resulting bondage to sin. This corresponds to the Midianites that brought Joseph down to Egypt. Next, the natural conscience will be distraught at the sin that the person is committing, leading him to seek to receive Jesus as his Savior. This corresponds to the Exodus. The natural conscience then leads one to affirm that the "law of the Spirit of Life in Christ Jesus (Rom. 8:2)" is just and good. Then the natural conscience condemns him every time he steps out of line—even doubting or denying the facts of our salvation and forgiveness.

If we are cowering under the accusations of the natural conscience, we will not have confidence to enter into the Land of Canaan, or spiritual maturity. Even after Israel is in the Land of Canaan, the Midianites at times attack from outside, trying to bring Israel again into bondage, even as our natural conscience might try to bring us again into bondage to the law as a means of being perfected through works. We eventually need to say, as the Apostle John did (I John 3:19-20): "(We)...will assure our heart before Him in whatever our heart condemns us; for God is greater than our heart and knows all things." Even if we are not keeping everything perfectly, we need to throw ourselves on God's mercy, repent of any known sin, and claim the victory through God's grace. So much for the future of the Midianites. At this point, however, they bring Joseph down into Egypt, as the conscience moves the child closer to bondage to the law.

Accompanying the Midianites were Ishmaelites. These were the people descended from Ishmael, also a son of Abraham. The word Ishmael (Heb. Yishma-el, יִשְׁמָעֵאל) means "God Hears," and there were Ishmaelites that were also with the Midianites bringing Joseph into Egypt. This illustrates the fact that, even as the child is being brought under bondage to sin and entering spiritual death, God hears his cries for help and understands his predicament.

Why would God give us the law, since it has the result of bringing us into bondage? Thiessen tells us what the law is not for: "We need to be clear as to the purpose of the law. It was not given as a means whereby a man might be saved. 'If there had been a law given which could make alive, verily righteousness would have been of the law' (Gal. 3:21). It could not make alive because "it was weak through the flesh" (Rom. 8:3). ... Since, however, man is hopelessly enslaved to self, he cannot keep God's law, and consequently neither life nor righteousness are possible by the law."[17]

What then is the purpose of the law, given to those who cannot keep it? Thiessen continues with three reasons for the giving of the Law of God: "It was given, however, to intensify man's knowledge of sin, to reveal the holiness of God, and to lead the sinner to Christ."[17]

How did sin intensify the sinner's knowledge of sin? We began with a little child and his conscience. If the little child sins, his conscience gives him an uncomfortable feeling, but no definite understanding of his disobedience to a definite commandment of God. After the law is given, the act for which the conscience made him feel uncomfortable is now revealed to be sin. In Romans 7:7 Paul states: "I would not have come to know sin except through the law." Paul had known sin as a bad feeling in the conscience before the law; but as his training in the Hebrew religion of the Old Testament progressed, so did his understanding of the seriousness of his rebellion against God's revealed Law on the tablets. The giving of the law intensified the receiver's knowledge of sin.

The entrance of the law into Paul's life also revealed the holiness of God. All of the ceremonial law showed that there was only one way to approach God—His way. The law also showed God's holiness by the very nature of the commandments (Romans 7:12): "So then, the Law is holy, and the commandment is holy and righteous and good." Paul's conscience confirmed the written Word, which had more content than the gut feelings of the conscience; but Paul was worse off because his understanding of his sin was heightened. What was he to do?

Thank God for the third purpose of the law. Paul writes of his experience (Gal. 3:24): "therefore the Law has become our tutor to lead us to Christ so that we may be justified by faith." As the child grows up, the law shows him that he is a great sinner, that God is Holy, and that he cannot live up to God's standard. This leaves the child conscious of his separation from God and his unworthiness to approach God on the basis of works, or merit, though he still tries. He should also then be open to the plan of salvation when he hears it. This is the opposite of Kant's idea mentioned above that the obligation to do what is right implies the ability to do what is right. The law rather shows man the helplessness of the lost condition into which he has fallen through his rebellion.

There is another ingredient in the descent into Egypt: the famine. There was a worldwide famine, and Joseph's brothers had to go to Egypt to buy food. There Joseph recognized them and made them confess their sin. Afterwards, Pharaoh extended an invitation for Jacob and his whole family to come to live permanently in Egypt. Since there were many years left for the famine, Jacob accepted, and they moved into the province of Goshen, where they prospered at first, and were satisfied with their new life in Egypt. Goshen means "drawing near" and refers to the child's drawing near to discover this world and the things that are there.[18]

Here we see the child's initial satisfaction in things of the world. If he hears about heaven or some place of God's blessing, he does not want to leave his concentration on the things of the world, which he is experiencing as his education proceeds. His focus is on his schoolwork and his social upbringing by his parents, and his focus is necessarily on the things of this world. As the young child enters more and more into his education and progresses in the things of this world, his competition with other children, and his craving to get ahead of the others, he looks back with disdain on the innocence he had as a baby, and perhaps on a younger sibling, and proudly plunges on into the darkness of self-effort, self-improvement, emptiness and loneliness, as his perception of God fades, becoming a distant memory.

III. Living in Egypt: Under the Yolk of Slavery.

The Book of Exodus opens with a change of Pharaohs in Egypt. The new Pharaoh did not know Joseph (Ex. 1:8), and the Israelites lost their favored status. Pharaoh then decided to enslave the Israelites (1:10-11). However, when he found out that the Israelites were prospering in spite of the slavery, he tried to get the midwives to kill all male infants, but they refused. Finally, he ordered all male babies thrown into the Nile River. The slavery continued generation after generation. When would the daily drudgery end? When would they find true fulfillment as human beings, Hebrews, and Israelites?

The same scenario can be set up with respect to the young person who is on track to make his way in the world. He is in his own Egypt and ruled by his own Pharaoh. The word Egypt in Hebrew is *Mitzráyim* (מִצְרַיִם). The Hebrew root (צרר) carries words with the following various meanings: bind, tie up, be restricted, narrow, tight, straits, distress, suffer distress, a bundle (as something bound up), show hostility to, vex, adversary, and foe, among others.[19] This could well be translated "the two oppressors." Why two? In Hebrew there are endings for singular nouns, dual nouns, and plural nouns. The singular nouns have one of them, the dual nouns have two of them (most often body parts in pairs, but not always), and the plural nouns indicate three or more of them. The *áyim* ending of Egypt indicates that there are two of them, and the Hebrew letter "m" at the front indicates a participle.

Why would the word for Egypt be a dual noun? First of all, there were two kingdoms of Egypt: the Upper Kingdom stretched from what was Memphis, near present Cairo, southward about 330 miles to what is today the Aswan Dam, which is at the first cataract of the Nile. From Memphis northward was the Lower Kingdom, which was mainly the Nile Delta. This is where the Israelites were. The New Bible Dictionary describes the duality of Egypt this way: 'When the pre-historic kingdoms of Upper and Lower Egypt were united under one king at the start of their history, the ultra-conservative Egyptians retained the dual nature of the kingdom in the title assumed by each Pharaoh: 'King of Upper and Lower Egypt' and 'Lord of the Two Lands.' In periods of political weakness, Egypt regularly tended to fall back into her two natural divisions."[20] These two natural divisions would then require two separate Pharaohs.

Having established Egypt's duality linguistically and politically, we now need to see what the duality means for us on the spiritual plane. I believe that the duality of Egypt refers to the bondage of the human being to the flesh and the world, which are ruled over by Satan, in the character of his name Pharaoh.

We will deal with these three traditional enemies of the Christian: the world, the flesh, and the Devil; but first we need to understand how the name Pharaoh is appropriate for the Devil as the slave master of all people in the world, between their childhood innocence and their conversion to Christ. The word Pharaoh (פַּרְעֹה) is from the Hebrew root (פרע) that means "leader" (questionable), "long hair" (let loose from being tied up), "to remove restraint" (from the people so that they do their own thing).[21] When Aaron cooperated with the Israelites to make the golden calf, Moses said (Ex. 32:25, my literal translation): "And when Moses saw that the people were let loose (from following the Lord, Heb. let loose, פָּרֻעַ); (for Aaron had set them loose (פְּרָעֹה) from following the Lord unto their shame among their enemies)." The use of the word naked by the AV is not indicated by the Hebrew word in either occurrence in this verse. The idea is the removal of restraint, such as law or the authority of another. The result is that the person feels free to do his own thing without feeling obligated to submit to any criteria external to him.

How does the Devil do this? He casts doubt on the authority of God's Word, as he did with Eve. In Genesis 3:1, he said to Eve, "Did God really say, 'You must not eat from any tree in the garden?'" Here he expresses disbelief that God would keep back anything from Adam and Eve. Later he denied God's Word directly (v.4): "You will not surely die." This is an outright lie.

The second step of Satan into sin is also in verse 4. Satan led Eve to doubt the certainty of God's judgment. He said, "You will not surely die." If she had believed God, she would have drawn back and refused to consider the temptation further. However, she also began to doubt the certainty of God's judgment, and went ahead with the temptation. When they ate, they died spiritually by being expelled from God's presence in the garden; and only through the grace of God the physical death they deserved was transferred to some animals, whose skins were then used to make clothing for our first parents. God's Word was true, and Satan was a liar. Here is the essence of the second step of Satan's acting in the character of his name Pharaoh: casting doubt on the certainty of judgment for sin.

Satan then goes further in verse 5 by claiming that eating the fruit will open their eyes to understand good and evil and make them wise. The third step is to make the alternative action to God's revealed will to seem attractive so that it will be chosen above God's will. Thus he did what he could to remove the restraint of God's Word from Eve, and to make the alternative attractive so that she would sin.

Satan also moves people to act independently of God to seek to glorify themselves in the three areas of the lust of the flesh, the lust of the eyes, and the pride of life. These three items together constitute the world (Greek, *kósmos*, *κòσμος*). As the Apostle John says (I John. 2: 15-17): "Do not love the world nor the things in the world. If anyone loves the world, the love of the father is not in him. <u>For all that is in the world, the lust of the flesh, and the lust of the eyes, and the boastful pride of life,</u> is not from the Father, but is from the world. And the world is passing away, and also its lusts; but the one who does the will of God lives forever."

The world is a collection of sinners that are enticing each other to seek self-gratification or self-glorification independent of God and His Word through fulfillment of these three things: the lust of the flesh, the lust of the eyes, and the pride of life. All acts of sin are attempts of individuals to seek satisfaction of these things independent of God and His Word. Human beings will commit acts of sin continually, as long as they are sold on these 3 ideas: 1. God's Word is not true, or at least not for them, 2. the judgment of God won't come, or is, at best, doubtful, and 3. the alternative action to God's plan is more attractive than God's will, in the criteria of fulfilling the lusts of the flesh, the lusts of the eyes, and the pride of life. In fact, the more that they focus on these three items and value them, the less they will worry about God's revealed will or the probability of punishment. Most people lack good criteria of their own, and so Satan sees to it that there are many bad worldly examples of other people to follow. The result is a self-perpetuating sin system: the world.

Of course, the flesh is that part of us that is directly involved in these items of the lust of the flesh, the lust of the eyes, and the pride of life. It is what is left of us when we have died spiritually and we are no longer alive to God anymore. Its focus is on things of the world at this stage because there is no alternative, therefore no option.

A further factor tightens Satan's grip as Pharaoh even more on the people in the world: self-esteem. Separated from the true basis of self-esteem in the Bible, which fits within the plan of God, the natural man seeks to earn esteem from others to fill the emptiness he feels within. Many writers have tried to find the best basis for self-esteem, but almost all have come up with bases that are temporal and can change with the wind. Aaron Wildavsky says, "Self-esteem cannot be sought as an end in itself but must come as a byproduct of meeting standards of excellence—taking pride in work, supporting a family, bringing up decent children, learning about life and imparting that wisdom."[22]

The problem with these criteria is that one can lose his job, or his children can turn out bad, and then he would have no self-esteem. Not only that, but some form of self-esteem is already established long before one has a job, marriage, or children. This type of criteria could well be the type of lie that Satan as Pharaoh tells you. The result is that you will be vulnerable to an opportunity to lie to make your job more secure, or you might be too possessive of your spouse and alienate him or her. You might be either too strict or too lenient with your children, and they might rebel partially because of your treatment. Your very act of making something a base of your self-esteem could actually ruin it.

The three elements of the world are very commonly the items upon which we base our self-image as unbelievers. The lusts of the flesh can include food, liquor, sex, drugs, and other things that pamper the cravings of our flesh. If these are fulfilled on demand, we may have a good self-esteem of providing for our needs and wants. The lusts of the eyes can also be a source of self-esteem. This would be true for the materialistic person. The self-esteem would be due to his value in earning the money for these things. A great delusion of the Devil is to convince one to calculate his "net worth" in dollars, and then compare it to that of others. This can lead to pride towards those below him or greed and envy towards those above him on his false scale. The option of pride of life can take on many forms: ethnic pride, racial pride, national pride, sports achievements, music achievements, etc.

As long as one thinks that he has to earn his self-esteem, he will work hard at whatever he has to do to get it. At this point, it becomes very strong for the person to resist temptation. As his memory of God weakens, sin becomes stronger and stronger. It eventually takes over in his focus and the act of sin results. In this case, he will also say to himself that he does not have worth while he has not yet achieved that which would give him value. As a result, it is easy for man to justify himself to an adverse conscience. By justifying himself, he really represses his guilt. The guilt, however, does not just go away. It resurfaces as a generalized anxiety. The anxiety is worse, in that it cannot be dealt with, as it is just a generalized feeling.

As we consider the focus of the mind of the unbeliever who is a slave to sin, we do well to remember that Egypt is well-called "the Gift of the Nile." Satan, as Pharaoh, the promoter of lawlessness, has a river from which everyone under him drinks: the Nile. In Hebrew the word Nile is *Ye-ór* (יְאֹר), or "enlightener." Here Satan appears in the character of his name *Heyleyl Ben-Shachar* (הֵילֵל בֶּן־שָׁחַר, Isaiah 14:12), or "Shining one, Son of the Dawn." Satan is an angel of light. The Apostle Paul warns us about false teachers in the church saying (II Cor. 11:14): "No wonder, for even Satan disguises himself as an angel of light." We must realize, as the Apostle John says (I John. 5:19), "the whole world lies in the evil one." Here "evil one," following Bauer,[23] is to be preferred over the AV "wickedness" because the Greek is "*en to poneró* (ἐν τῷ πονηρῷ)," not "*en te ponería* (ἐν τῇ πονερία)," and there are no significant textual variants. Also, the world is contrasted to the believer who is "from God" (ἐκ τοὺ Θεοῦ), rather than from goodness. Here the contrast favors the personal, rather than the generic usage. The world is therefore said to be in the power of Satan himself.

As Pharaoh giving people water from the Nile, Satan is a lawless one giving people a false light in the world: a false light of self-glorification, and this false light maintains them in slavery to him. The believer is to realize what the Psalmist learned (Ps. 36:9): "For with You is the fountain of life; in Your light we see light." There is a True Light and there is a false light. *Heyleyl Ben-Shachar* gives the false light from his Nile ("Enlightener") River, and his slaves drink in this false light continually. One only has to think of the modern person imbibing a continual stream of input from television, radio, newspapers, magazines, school, etc. to see how people are continually receiving messages to seek to glorify themselves by seeking lusts of the flesh, lusts of the eyes, and pride of life. The input from the world sheds a light on all these things and brings them to our attention continually.

In direct contrast to Satan, Jesus is "the True Light which enlightens every man who comes into the world (my translation, John 1:9)." In our infancy, when we "were alive without the Law once," it was Jesus who was shining His light in our hearts. Later, after His presence is driven away by our rebellion, we have access to the True Light through the Word of God, since "faith comes from hearing, and hearing by the Word of Christ (Romans 10:17)." However at this stage, the lost person does not recognize the truth to which he is exposed through the Word of God until the Spirit of God works on his heart.

In addition to drinking in the Nile River, the Israelites are slaves by building for Pharaoh two store cities named *Pithom* (פִּתֹם) and *Raamses* (רַעַמְסֵס, Ex. 1:11). These two cities represent for us two different aspects of reality into which our perception is shattered by our spiritual death: the material and the spiritual. The word *Raamses* is made up of two Hebrew roots. The first is *Rá-am* (רָעַם), which means "to move violently," or "to thunder."[24] The word "vibration" also comes from this root. The other root is *sws* (סוּס), meaning swift.[25] The Hebrew words for horse and swallow come from this root. Therefore we can combine these two roots to mean something like "swift thunder" or "swift vibrations."

The pace at which people live today is frantic. They seem to be building *Raamses* for Satan with more effort than ever. This name would be the opposite of the Hebrew word *Shabbat* (שַׁבָּת), or Sabbath. The Sabbath was designed as a day of rest for mankind, in which he may rest and "cease" from his daily activities. The Jewish people rightfully say, "The Sabbath has kept the Jews more than the Jews have kept the Sabbath." When one rests one day per week, he does so because he is obeying the Lord and trusting that God will provide for him. However, when one trusts himself instead of God, there is no rest, as one doesn't want to lose any opportunity to "get ahead." Here again we see that *Raamses* includes the three elements of sin, as it developed in Satan as the first sinner: selfishness (an exaggerated focus on self as the most important for one), discontentment with what one has, compared to others, and an incessant craving to get beyond the perceived material level of life that others have.

On the other hand, there is the city of *Pithom* (פִּתֹם). According to Gesenius, this means the "house of (the god) Atum."[26] The person who is lost in sin also serves evil spirits, represented by their idols, including here by Atum, the Egyptian god of suffocating heat. We human beings are incurably religious, and it is most natural to worship something or someone. If we are not worshipping the True God, then we will end up worshipping one of the many false gods: Satan or one of his angels. While we are worshipping false gods our conscience is burning up against us, even as Atum is the god of suffocating heat. It is clear that these are rebellious angels, as the angels that stayed with the True God neither seek nor receive worship (see Revelation 22:8-9).

While Raamses represents the frenzied activity of materialism, Pithom represents the emotional high of idolatry. To understand the seriousness of this type of idolatry better, we need to understand man as the image of God. In Genesis 1:26-27 we read: "Then God said, "Let Us make man in our image, according to Our likeness: and let them have rule…" So God created man in His own image, in the image of God created He him; male and female He created him; male and female He created them."

What does it mean to be in the image of God? First of all, the Hebrew root meaning is something "cut out."[27] The expression is often in parallel with the word *pesel* (פֶּסֶל), which means something "cut into shape," usually, though not always, in the negative sense of an idol. For more discussion on this subject, it is recommended to review chapter 3 in the section under man as the image of God. We will consider only a brief summary of that section here.

The pagans cut their idols into the shape of the spirits that they represented. In fact there are 3 major ways that the image is related to the spirit that it represents. The first way is that the image resembles the spirit that it represents. The original thing must be there first before the "cut out" is made of it. In this regard it becomes apparent that God had hands, arms, legs, etc. before man was created. When Jesus was going forth ages before he was born on earth (Micah 5:2, 5:1 in the MT), he went forth in a theophany (preincarnate appearance of Christ), such as that in which he appeared to Isaiah in chapter 6 of his book, as well as Joshua 5:13-15.

In the light of this order of appearance, and the fact that the idol is a "cut out" copy of a spirit who was there first, then it appears improper to talk of "anthropomorphisms" in reference to descriptive language about God. We should rather speak of theomorphisms in reference to man. For example, the Bible does not say that the arm of the Lord did something because it is trying to describe a spiritual being in human language to facilitate communication. Rather, we should think that when the reference is to a certain man doing something by the strength of his own hand, he has a hand because the God in whose image he was created has a hand. Human language thus becomes a series of theomorphisms. God was there first and then we appeared as the "cut out" copy. It is amazing that God's existence should be disputed when He has over 6 billion "portraits" in the world today, and even more amazing that the "portraits" themselves should dispute His existence!

The second significance of an image is that it is a dwelling place for the spirit it represents. The Apostle Paul in I Corinthians 10:20 states: "No, but I say that the things which the Gentiles sacrifice, they sacrifice to demons, and not to God." What were they doing? They were sacrificing the animals for meat before an idol representing a particular spirit because the spirit was living in that idol. Man had degenerated to seeking false spirits—even making "cut outs" (i.e. idols) of them—for a very important reason: with the advent of sin in human existence, man was spiritually dead. This death meant that the Spirit of Whom he was created to be the dwelling place was now not dwelling in him. He was now an empty dwelling place, and therefore had to seek spiritual contact outside of himself.

The third significance of an image is that the way it is treated is seen as the way that the spirit it represents is being treated. If one were to smash an idol that belonged to a pagan, he would react with fury and try to take vengeance. Similarly, since we are in the image of God, we are to show love to others as a means of showing our love to God, which is the first priority. As we treat others, we are seen as treating God Himself. That is why in I John 4:20 the Lord says: "for the one who does not love his brother whom he has seen, cannot love God whom he has not seen." Also, when Jesus comes to judge all nations at the end of time in Matthew 25, he says (v. 40), "to the extent that you did it to one of these brothers of Mine, even the least of them, you did it to Me."

There is only one way in which God approves of idolatry. According to God, we are the images, or idols. These words are equivalent in the Hebrew. Therefore we should not be worshipping idols because we **<u>are</u>** the idols. Obviously, God is not the worshipper, either, because He is the Spirit that is supposed to be dwelling in us. Who are to be the approved idolaters? For this answer, we must turn to God's instructions in Genesis 1:26 when He made us as His images: "let them rule over the fish of the sea and over the birds of the sky, and over the cattle and over all the earth, and over every creeping thing that creeps on the earth."

The animals are the ones that God intended to be the idolaters. In Genesis 9:2, God says to Noah, as representative of all human beings: "The fear of you and the terror of you will be on every beast of the earth and on every bird of the sky; with everything that creeps on the ground, and on all the fish of the sea; into your hand they are given."

Here we see that the animals are to fear human beings. The first word for fear is from the same root as the expression the "fear of the Lord." This is the good kind of fear. The other type is next: the dread. This is the kind of fear we are not to have. The animals are said to have the good kind of fear of the Lord, and in Daniel 4 Nebuchadnezzar was changed into a beast of the field for seven years to learn at least the fear of the Lord that an animal had, since he was too proud to have any as a human being.

Thus we see that God intended animals to be the idolaters, and the people to be the idols. However, devoid of the Spirit of God, Who is supposed to dwell in him, man takes the role of an animal and makes an image to worship in order to seek spiritual contact. Thus man's enslavement to sin degrades him to the level of the animals when he is sunken in idolatry. Such is the bondage of labor to build *Pithom.* No matter how much spiritual contact one has, no matter what emotional thrills are stirred up by such contact, and no matter how many different spirits are contacted, they cannot fill up the empty place left by the initial spiritual contact with God and so the person is left empty, unfulfilled, and miserable, trapped in a vicious cycle of ever deepening spiritual quests leaving an ever deepening spiritual void.

A discussion of the depths to which man has fallen in his sin would not be complete without tying it in to the modern scene. In twentieth century America there are two movements that illustrate man's bondage to Satan in building the two cities of Pithom and Raamses. They are explained well by Dick Keyes in his book *Beyond Identity: Finding Your Self in the Image and Character of God.* Corresponding to the building of *Raamses* is what Keyes calls New Victorianism, and corresponding to the building of *Pithom* is what he calls New Romanticism.

Describing New Victorianism, Keyes says, "It resembles the old Victorianism in its deeply rooted materialism. Personal security is to be found in one's possessions, a house at least half paid for, life insurance, investments, and prospect of job advancement. These material goods promise to provide the adequacy and sense of self that is lacking."[28]

New Victorianism then is a modern movement to fill up the spiritual void that is in people, due to the absence of the Holy Spirit. It is an attempt to deny or reduce the importance of the spiritual dimension of existence and to seek fulfillment entirely in the material dimension. These are the people that say things implying that the person with the most and best toys is the one that wins in the game of life. They also tend to calculate every man's "net worth" in money, possessions, stocks, etc., while playing down the importance of "religion," or tolerating it benignly as something which one invents to help him get along. The spiritual dimension is not recognized, or at least, not valued. It is curious to note that both the Western materialist, who is obsessed with the accumulation of material wealth, and the Communist, who is opposed to him with a religiously motivated hatred, are both building *Raamses*. The Communist even denies all spiritual values, claiming that the material reality is all that exists.

At the other extreme are the people that "tune in, turn on, and drop out." These are the people that labor just as hard and with as great discipline to build Pithom. Keyes describes these people as being involved in the New Romanticism: "The New Romanticism is the polar opposite of the New Victorianism... its newer form lashes out against the technological demands and obligations of the New Victorianism. While the New Victorianism says that your identity is to be found in what you do, the New Romantic says that your identity is in what you feel yourself to be. Feelings rule. The Romantic's personal emotions are the highest authority. Spontaneity is the Holy Grail. He is convinced that the inner goodness of man can emerge if he is freed from prescribed moral systems, organized religion, and the octopus of technology."[29]

While the New Victorian is convinced that fulfillment is through doing and achieving, thus combining mind and will, the New Romanticist denies both intellectual endeavor and effort of the will and focuses on his emotions. Neither can he integrate all three elements of the soul: mind, will, and emotions, in a single focus without the Holy Spirit, and so is content to see his world fractured into two irreconcilable compartments: the spiritual, where his emotions rule, and the material, where the mind and will operate. The

New Romanticist focuses on the former, while the New Victorian focuses on the latter

There are many, however, who switch off between the two, as though recognizing the importance of both, and are content to live with the contradictions. Thus, today we see a university professor that engages in i-ching, an ancient Chinese form of divination, and others of the intellectual elite forming part of a witch's coven. Also, we see modern gurus driving around in Rolls Royces and swimming in luxury, while deploring materialism. There are also many of the modern common people who live during the week as New Victorians working overtime on jobs and being obsessed constantly about their material wealth, but who, on weekends experiment with liquor, wild parties, drugs, séances, or anything else that might fill the spiritual void. They build Raamses during the week and Pithom during the weekend, accepting the contradiction between the two as a something to live with.

Keyes concludes with a dangerous observation: whether of the New Victorians or the New Romanticists, one becomes a slave of the values of the group with which one identifies—a compulsive copycat. The rule of the day is conformity: "Conformity... involves an enslavement to the whims of the group, a commitment to which many mass movements owe their strength. Only in acceptance by the group does one find the self-confidence needed to face life. ...Of course, the person who has sold his soul to a group has not solved his problem. There still remains nagging anxiety and inauthenticity."[30]

This is because conformity to an earthly group will not fill the void inside one. Neither will conformity to the entire "shtick," or way of operating, of any spirit other than the Holy Spirit. Modern man is caught in the dilemma of choosing which of many equally worthless groups he will imitate, and the resulting emptiness and disillusionment continue even if he jumps from group to group. His human freedom to choose his master is not satisfying because all of the masters he sees are equally empty of that which would satisfy him. As Allen Wheelis describes modern man: "Without meaningful goals modern man has, understandably, no sense of direction; for he does not look where he is going. Like an anxious soldier on a drill field he covertly watches those around him to make sure he stays in step. He sticks to the group, and where the group will go next nobody knows."[31]

One might better say without knowing God man cannot have ultimately meaningful goals, but Wheelis makes an excellent observation without the benefit of a personal relation with God, as far as this writer can determine.

In his book, Kingdoms in Conflict, Charles Colson shows how this separation from God leads to self-worship, which is the essence of sin: "Separated from God, men seek satisfaction in their senses. This is more than mindless hedonism; it is a worldview in which, according to Professor Allen Bloom, 'The self has become the modern substitute for the soul.' A 1985 study titled Habits of the Heart calls this attitude 'utilitarian individualism,' arguing that the two primary ways Americans attempt to order their lives are through 'the dream of personal success' and 'vivid personal feelings.'"[32]

Again here we have the fulfillment of the two types of bondage—of Pithom and of Raamses. Raamses, the materialistic grind of endless planning, work, and material aspirations cast as "the dream of personal success," and Pithom, the idolatry of spiritual "turn-on" described as "vivid personal feelings."

Once the spiritual contact between man and God is broken, his world is shattered. Even his worship of "god" becomes worship of self. Here man is fully enslaved wherever he turns. The unity of his world is shattered hopelessly, for what his own efforts can restore. He has no rest from his material pursuits and no fulfillment in his spiritual pursuits. He is as truly a slave as were the Israelites in Egypt building Pithom and Raamses and crying out to God in each generation for relief. Underneath the smug, follow-the-leader veneer of modern man there is a tired, confused, despairing child seeking to put his world view back together and return to the Garden of Eden and a love relation with a Loving Heavenly Father. The daily grind of emotional trips and/or materialistic accumulation weight him down, and occasionally a disaster hits near him to remind him that death awaits him. Whether or not he believes in the Devil, as Pharaoh, the Devil is telling him to do his own thing, and then accumulating a long list of sins of which to accuse him and weigh down on his conscience as guilt or, when repressed, surfaces as a free-floating anxiety. What could be done to rescue him from this situation?

We leave Israel at this point enslaved in Egypt. They were building two cities, Pithom and Raamses, for Pharaoh. They made bricks and built with them seven days per week. They were slaves with no rights. In the beginning of the Book of Exodus, Pharaoh turned even more against them and ordered that the male children were to be killed at birth. What had been difficult had become intolerable, and something had to be done. What could be done to rescue them from this situation?

I will repeat a few lines from the preface to this book, as they express appropriately the dilemma of modern man trapped in his rebellion against the True God, unable to reconcile in his *Weldbild* (world view) the material with the spiritual, trapped in a meaningless existence, and trying to substitute the self for the soul. The West was building Raamses and the East was building Pithom, but there are changes today. As I said before:

Today one can stand back and see the limitations of these two perspectives on existence-the Eastern and the Western. People throughout the world have noticed these limitations and have sought to learn from the others. The West has long been deluged with gurus, and much of the psychotherapy in the West has consciously adopted Eastern thought into its methodology. The highly prized individualists of the West cannot handle the pressures and tensions of facing a world in which they are in constant struggle with others to survive, and the accumulation of riches is a hopeless, never ending, self-inflicted burden which can never bring peace because one never has enough.

In addition to the dissatisfaction with materialism and other practical exercises of the will, Western philosophy has fallen in shambles at the end of the 20th century. The optimism of Descartes who began all philosophy with man's independent human reasoning through the statement, "I think, therefore I am," has given way to modern nihilism and cynicism. Time and time again the optimistic philosophers have thought that they had a good line of reasoning starting from themselves and working outward, only to be shot down. Starting with himself, man has not been able to reason his way up to God, Ultimate Knowledge, Cosmic Consciousness or any other thing transcendent. Thus the West is bankrupt in itself and dabbling in Eastern mysticism through various leaps of faith, seeking fulfillment in the spiritual dimension.

Meanwhile, those of the East have been discovering that man's individuality is not so bad, after all. The colonial era, followed by independence, has left these nations seeking fulfillment in the material sphere. The postwar development of the Asian countries is the greatest illustration of this revolution. It is not enough for these people to revere their ancestors and seek unity with the Cosmos, they want to live better here now.

Yes, those on both sides of the Tigris and Euphrates rivers are dissatisfied with their limited viewpoints, and now have imported and adapted many elements from the other side of the rivers. Are they now satisfied? No. Modern man still holds two separate compartments in his mind, and cannot reconcile them: the material and the spiritual. They both lead different directions and tend to pull him apart. The science of his workaday world cannot coordinate with his weekend binges of alcohol, drugs, Eastern Religion, or whatever spiritual fulfillment he seeks. His individual consciousness-so important for his 8 to 5 job Monday through Friday-is left behind as he "blows his mind" on the weekend.

What is the answer that can unify all of existence for man? Where is the Spirit that can sustain the law of gravity and fill us with peace and joy at the same time? How can my individuality be valued without overcoming me with neuroses and psychoses? What is the answer that can put together all of the pieces?

In the next chapter, we will see God's answer to forgive man, restore him to the position from which he had fallen—and an even better one, heal him, and enter into a love relationship with him. All of this will be in parallel with His plan to save Israel in the Book of Exodus.

Chapter 5

Doctrine of Salvation— Egypt and the Exodus: Our New Birth into Spiritual Life

At the end of the previous chapter, we found Israel in total slavery to Egypt building two store cities, Pithom and Raamses. They could not serve God as they needed to do it, and they had no choice as to what to do. If God did not send Moses and the plagues to force Egypt to its knees, the Israelites would have had no way out. The Jewish people recognize this fact in their Passover celebration every year by admitting that if the Lord had not liberated them from slavery in Egypt, they would still be slaves there. There was no other way out for Israel.

In the same way, by the time that a person is lost in his sins, it is obvious that he cannot find his way back to God. He cannot find a way to God or make a way to God. He is not sick in his sinful rebellion, he is dead spiritually, as far as contacting God is concerned. We have also seen that he is trying to find satisfaction through a combination of material possessions, as well as emotional experiences. Far from liberating him, they represent the very nature of his slavery. In fact, all of his self-will is the problem, not the solution, as we saw in the previous chapter.

The history of Israel falls broadly into four stages: the patriarchal, the stay in Egypt, the stay in the desert, and the stay in the

Promised Land. These stages correspond to the believer's infancy, time as a natural man, time as a carnal believer, and time as a spiritual believer, respectively. The transition periods are also important. As the patriarchs left Canaan and moved down to Egypt, we have seen how every man loses the pristine innocence and spiritual contact with God from the time of the creation of his spirit at conception. Corresponding to Israel's descent into Egypt, each person experiences his or her own personal fall; and just as Adam and Eve were expelled from the Garden of Eden, we were expelled from all contact with God through our rebellion as we learned God's Law. And so each one of us found himself as slave in the world, as the Israelites found themselves in Egypt.

But Israel did not stay in Egypt. The second transition period is that of the Exodus. This transition takes Israel from slavery to freedom, from Egypt to the desert, from daily work to a day of Sabbath each week, from the security of the slave's routine to the insecurity of the faith life, and from the visible master with the whip to the invisible God of the Universe with His Law, power, and provision.

No human being needs to stay in slavery to the world, either. We can also go from slavery to freedom, from the world to the desert, from the bondage of fear and perpetual work to a peaceful rest in the promise of God, from the security of personal routine in this life to the insecurity of the faith life with its security in the goodness of God, and from the invisible enemy of our souls, Satan, to the Invisible God of the Universe with His Holy Spirit as our guide, power, water, oil, and all other provisions.

The New Testament believer's salvation experience is so glorious that the Lord put many Old Testament background items there in order for man to understand it better, and one item that directly anticipates the overall salvation experience of the believer in the New Testament times is the Israelite Exodus from Egypt.

The purpose of this chapter will be to examine the elements of the New Testament believer's conversion experience in the light of the salvation of Israel from Egypt. It is not an accident that Jesus institutes the celebration of the New Testament out of a celebration of the Old Testament Passover. The word for covenant in the

Hebrew is *brit* (בְּרִית), which has in its root a reference to eating and drinking. It is by eating and drinking in the Passover celebration that the Israelites celebrate their covenant with God, and it is by our eating and drinking at the Lord's Table that we believers celebrate our New Covenant with that same God, through Jesus Christ.[1]

In order to see this connection better, we will consider the story of the first Passover and show the relation to our salvation experience at each point. Our procedure will be threefold. 1. First of all, we will seek to understand the events surrounding the Exodus, giving special attention to Hebrew words with special applications. 2. Second, we will consider the special meanings of the Hebrew words and tie them in with references from the New Testament about the Christian's salvation. We shall observe how they have the same basic meanings, though on different parallel planes. 3. Finally, we shall attempt to shed light on our salvation experience in a practical way so that we will be filled with more gratitude to God for our salvation, a fuller assurance of our salvation, and a greater desire to serve God now in our life.

As we reflect on this narrative from the Christian viewpoint, several applications suggest themselves to us from the beginning. First of all, we know that it was God's will for the Israelites to go down to Egypt. He stated to Abram in Genesis 15:13: "Know for certain that your descendants will be strangers in a land that is not theirs, where they will be enslaved and oppressed four hundred years." Also, the Lord appeared to Jacob in a dream in Genesis 46:3 and said: "Do not be afraid to go down to Egypt; for I will make you a great nation there." Because of this revelation from God, Jacob loaded up the carts that Joseph sent and took his whole family to Egypt.

We have already considered how Israel made the transition from Canaan to Egypt, but we will summarize it here. Because of jealousy, nine of Joseph's brothers sold him into slavery when He visited them to check up on them at Dothan, after missing them at Shechem. Reuben was opposed to harming Joseph, Joseph was the victim, and Benjamin was too young to be involved. Joseph was bought by the Midianites and Ishmaelites, who sold him to an Egyptian named "Potiphar, an officer of Pharaoh." The Hebrew here is *Potiphar, serís Pharaoh*, literally, Potiphar, a eunuch of Pharaoh. This might explain why his wife was attracted sexually to Joseph, more than to her husband. Because Joseph refused her advances, Potiphar's wife lied, claiming that he had tried to force her sexually, and Joseph was sent to the royal prison.

Joseph spent a number of years in the prison when Pharaoh's butler (Hebrew *mashqeh*, or "supervisor of drinks") and baker were sent to prison and had strange dreams, which Joseph interpreted for them. Things worked out as Joseph had predicted in the interpretation: the baker was hanged in three days, and the drink supervisor was restored to his former position in three days, but he forgot to tell Pharaoh about Joseph and try to get him out of prison, where Joseph languished two more years.

One night Pharaoh had two dreams and nobody could interpret them. The drink supervisor remembered Joseph, and he was brought out of prison. Joseph interpreted the dreams, which foretold seven years of prosperity, followed by seven years of famine. When Joseph recommended that Pharaoh store up for the years of famine, Pharaoh put Joseph over this project.

During the years of famine, Joseph's brothers came to buy grain, and he recognized them. After dealing with them harshly and getting them to confess their sin and show real repentance, he revealed himself to them, forgave them, and invited them to come to live in Egypt in the land of Goshen. The Book of Genesis ends with the Israelites living in Goshen in relative prosperity with the good will of Pharaoh, and things looked good for them.

Let us now see what going down to Egypt corresponds to for the New Testament believer. "Joseph" means "may he add," and refers to the fact that Rachel wanted God to add to her another son. To us it means "May God add" blessings to the person, save him, and restore him to Canaan. Just as God has allowed things to work out that each person who reached the age of accountability will rebel against Him and be expelled from His presence, so God is "not wishing for any to perish (i.e. remain in spiritual death) but for all to come to repentance (II Peter 3:9)." Even though we head from spiritual contact with God to the darkness of this world, God is for us, and wants us to come to repentance and find His way back to Him.

Joseph went to visit his brothers at Shechem, and did not find them there, but rather at Dothan. Shechem means "shoulder" in Hebrew, Gesenius explains this word as a symbol for responsible toil, as in Genesis 49:15, where Issachar was as a strong donkey, bearing a double burden and bowing his shoulder to the task.[2] Just as Joseph was not betrayed at Shechem, so responsible toil is not a stumbling block for a child. Joseph was betrayed at Dothan. I believe that Dothan refers to the Law, or *dat* in Hebrew. A child can learn to work and help his parents, but when it becomes a law, he begins to rebel at it. The word *dat* even develops into the word for religion in Modern Hebrew, as Jews tend to see religion as a body of commandments that are to be observed, rather than a personal relationship with God. So Joseph is betrayed by his brothers at Dothan, as a child's nature, inherited from Adam, rebels at law.

As Joseph was taken by the Midianites (Genesis 37:36) and Ishmaelites (Gen. 39:1) to Egypt, so the young child is guided by his conscience and confidence that God hears him to trust that he can please God with his own efforts in things of this world. The word "Midianites" comes from the root word meaning "to discern" or "to judge," and the word "Ishmaelites" means "God hears."

Once in Egypt, Potiphar, an official of Pharaoh, bought Joseph as a slave. Gesenius believes that it is an abbreviation of Potiphera, the name of the priest of On, who became the father-in-law to Joseph later.[3] The name is hard to break down in Hebrew, but Gesenius gives its meaning in Egyptian as "He whom Ra gave." Ra was a god of the Egyptians, but the word means "evil" in Biblical Hebrew. Thus, it is not hard to see that the child is coming into the domain of the enemy at this stage. The enemy cannot make the child rebel, but he can give many temptations for it to happen.

Joseph was brought out of prison and set up to be second in command to Pharaoh in Egypt. In the same way, children can become very good at focusing on things of this world as they learn to look on the outside and copy what others are doing. This is a part of our enculturation process, whereby we learn our language and ethnic behavior and customs. As god of this world, the Devil has no objection to our being cultured. In fact, it is by this process that we learn to think on the things of this world, for culture is just a pattern for gratifying the lust of the flesh, the lust of the eyes, and the pride of life.

Every culture has a preference for foods and food preparation, sexual gratification, clothing, etc. Also, every culture has a value system by which we judge things more or less attractive to our eyes. Finally, every culture has a hierarchy of importance that it assigns to people and through which relative value or status of people is judged. This gives us a false sense of pride or worthlessness, depending on our position in that society's scale. Because he is looking on the outside and learning about the world from those around him, a child is far from obeying the injunction of John the Apostle who says (I John 2:15-16): "Do not love the world nor the things in the world. If anyone loves the world, the love of the Father is not in him. For all that is in the world, the lust of the flesh and the lust of the eyes and the boastful pride of life, is not from the father, but is from the world."

At this stage, the child is learning about the world and learning to love the world because God made it. He is not ready to reject it yet in favor of something better. In fact, he needs to learn about the world to be prepared for what comes next. Just as God wanted Jacob and his family to go down into Egypt, so God wants children to learn about the world and the things of the world as part of their initial upbringing.

Joseph received a new name when Pharaoh promoted him to second in command. In Genesis 41:45 we find that Pharaoh called him *tzaphenat pa-néach* (צָפְנַת פַּעְנֵחַ) if we combine the different Hebrew roots of these words we can get a name meaning, "treasure of the groaning rest." This is appropriate in that the child that is entering the domain of training is still God's treasure, there is a lot of groaning and bondage ahead, and he is resting still before the big battle.

Joseph married Asenath, the daughter of Potiphera, priest of On, who bore him Manasseh and Ephraim, and he lived well and was treated well by Pharaoh and all Egypt. Also, the Egyptians accepted his family because they had royal connections. It seemed that Israel had found its place in the world, and the people had few aspirations to return to the lowly Canaan that the mysterious God of their fathers promised to them. Would they want to go back?

There are applications for the Christian here in this stage of his life. He has settled in to the world and the routine of learning about the world. Manasseh means "payback," in that in that God had paid back Joseph for his suffering in his exaltation to the number two position in Egypt. He also had a son he named Ephraim, which means "two fruitfulnesses." The Hebrew ending "*aim*" is a dual ending, referring to two of something. Here the child is fruitful in both things of the flesh and things of the spirit and he sees no contradiction in them, as yet. Everything seems his friend, and his parents do not tell him about so many dangers that are there in the world.

At this stage the developing child is shielded from danger, and seeks to learn about the things around him. He retains a spiritual connection to God so far, but he is also learning about and participating in the lusts of the flesh as he learns to eat different foods. His eyes are continually open to what they can discover, and he demands things that appeal to his eyes. Also, he begins to discover that certain things seem better to him than others and begins to assert his will to demand that he get what he wants because of his self-exalting pride. He is getting further into seeking fulfillment of the three things that God warns us about in this world, and God is silent. It is necessary for the child at this stage to learn about the world so that he can live in it.

In an earlier chapter, we discussed the difference between the traducianists and the creationists in theology. The resolution to this controversy can set us up to understand the steps whereby a child passes from childhood innocence to become the natural man, dead in his trespasses and sins.[4] We inherit our sin nature from our father, along with our body from both father and mother. God breathes in the human spirit at conception.

Having established the elements of man and their source, we may now continue with what happens within man after birth. We have seen that the human spirit is created as a special act of God. It is obvious that the spirit was created without sin. The sin nature, which we inherit, comes from our father through the soul, not the spirit. Since the spirit is created as a special act of God, and it is without sin at the beginning, it must be concluded that man begins in spiritual contact with God. This is what the Apostle Paul affirms of his case, and by extrapolation, to all men in Romans 7:9: "I was once alive apart from the Law: but when the commandment came, sin became alive, and I died."

Let us go through the sequence of events for Paul. He is born with a body and soul, which came from his parents and inherited a sin nature in the soul. He also possessed at birth a perfect spirit without sin, which was a special and direct creative act of God. Now the human spirit is the part of us that has God—consciousness. Since it begins without sin, we are alive in a relation with God spiritually at birth. Therefore, Paul stated that at that time he was alive without the law.

This spiritual relation with God lasts from conception until the child comes into an understanding of the law and inevitably rebels against it. It was the sin he inherited in his soul that rose up against the commandment of God, and he chose to rebel against the commandment. At that point during his childhood, Paul then died spiritually.

Paul was not born separated from God, and likewise, neither is any other person. He had a perfect spirit and was alive in some relation with God. Paul also states in Romans 5:13: "For until the Law, sin was in the world: but sin is not imputed when there is no law." In the same way, sin is not imputed to a child before the Law comes to his attention and knowledge. Then, when he rebels, he dies, i.e. his spiritual relation with, or at least, perception of God ends. He then becomes dead in his sins without God's presence to guide him.

It appears that each one of us goes through the same willful rebellion against God that Adam himself experienced, except that we begin with a sinful soul, which leads us into rebellion when the understanding of the Law is present later in life. In this way, we are fully responsible for our rebellion against God, even though we have inherited a sinful nature from Adam. Each one of us goes through his own personal fall and expulsion from the presence of God.

As it was in God's plan for Israel to go down into Egypt, and become hopelessly enslaved there, so also God's plan anticipates that each person will go through the process of rebelling against Him and become a slave to sin. However, it is important to notice that everybody began in a spiritual relationship with God from conception until their rebellion. In is interesting to note that in Titus 3:5 Paul says: "He saved us, not on the basis of deeds which we have done in righteousness, but according to His mercy, by the washing of regeneration and the renewing (*anakainósis, ἀνακαινώσεως*) of the Holy Spirit." The word translated "renewing" suggests that we may have here the reestablishment of something that had already existed. Paul uses the same word in the form of a verb (*anakainóo, ἀνακαινόω*) in 2 Cor. 4:16: "Though our outer man is decaying, yet our inward man is being renewed day by day." Bauer translates this, "the renewal of your spirit."[5]

What is renewed at our salvation? On the spiritual level, our spiritual connection to God, which was breathed into us at conception and lost at our personal fall, was lost. Though our human spirit, which was "inblown" by God at conception did not die at our rebellion, the spiritual contact with God that it had was cut off. This lack of spiritual contact is called death. Therefore we were dead in our trespasses and sins. This connection is renewed, or restored at our salvation through the work of the Holy Spirit. At this point it is sufficient to say that we have hereby traced the process whereby each person passes through his own personal fall and expulsion from God's presence. It is this expulsion from God's presence and cutting of the spiritual contact, which is restored at salvation.

The book of Exodus begins with the Israelites as slaves in Egypt. As we saw in the last chapter, Egypt means literally "the two oppressors," translated from the Hebrew. There were two kingdoms of Egypt: Lower Egypt and Upper Egypt, representing the Nile delta area in the north and the southern area of Egypt, respectively. These two kingdoms were sometimes ruled over by two different Pharaohs and sometimes by one Pharaoh who wore two crowns.

Israel's trouble began with the death of Joseph and his whole generation. In verse 8 of chapter 1 we read, "Now there arose up a new king over Egypt, which knew not Joseph." This king did not know about all of Joseph's help for the country and for a previous Pharaoh personally. He was afraid and mistrustful of the Israelites and had them placed into slavery. The slavery of the Israelites consisted of building the cities of Pithom and Raamses, cities of supply or storage (v.11). The Hebrew word *are-miskenoth* (עָרֵי־מִסְכְּנֹאת) is better rendered "cities of supply or storage" than the AV "treasure cities," being from the verb meaning "to be of use, service, or benefit."[6] The Israelites were truly of service to Pharaoh, the King of Egypt, in their labors. They were slaves with no human hope of ever getting out of Egypt, except through their death, which they dreaded even more than their slavery. As Pharaoh rules over both Upper and Lower Egypt, so Satan rules over this world, organized to provide outlets for our lusts and pride, and our flesh, so ready to lead us astray into any of these wrongful paths.

The Israelites were multiplying rapidly and Pharaoh feared that they would take sides with any invading enemy and lead to their defeat. Thus, they were forced into bondage, and two different efforts were made to wipe out the nation through the killing of the newborn males. First of all Pharaoh ordered the Hebrew midwives, Shifrah and Puah, to kill the male children, but to save the females. This would have left the girls to marry foreigners, and the children would have been of the other nation, as the father, not the mother counted in mixed marriages back then.

The midwives told Pharaoh that the Hebrew women delivered too quickly for them to be able to kill the male babies. Shifrah means "beautiful one," and Puah means "one who is made to groan"[7] In the same way, the believing child, after rebelling against the knowledge of the Lord that he has, still shows beauty, but is being made to groan under the many desires that invading his mind through his senses. At this stage, there are many lusts and thoughts of self-exalting pride that are welling up within him from his soul, which was inherited from Adam, and he leaves behind the "babyish" spiritual peace and joy for the never-ending pursuit of self-gratification. He becomes sensually oriented, rather than spiritually oriented, and at this point he is lost in his trespasses and sins. From this point on, the child is in an odyssey to find his fulfillment. This fulfillment is only to be found in the reestablishment of the spiritual bond with God, enhanced by personal memory of God and His self-revelation in nature and the Bible; but the older child is fleshly and sensual (being dead spiritually), and always seeks that fulfillment in the things that cannot really satisfy his deepest need.

The Israelites built the two cities Pithom and Raamses, and these cities correspond to the bondage of the unbelieving natural man. According to Gesenius, Pithom means "the House of Atum."[8] If we spell the word Atum with an ayin (there is no root with aleph), we find that Atum is the god of suffocating heat. As the natural man labors to fulfill his lusts, they burn within him. Also, the natural man's conscience is burning against him with an ever-growing list of accusations, which he cannot remove by his own efforts.

So we see that the natural man is burning up with lust and/or a contrary conscience that cries out against him. This is the origin of all of the foolish rationalizations that people give when confronted with the Gospel. They think that they will eventually be able to work off the individual bad things that they have done and be accepted by God. As an undergrad in college, the present author was studying Freud's defense mechanisms, which are devices that the human ego uses to defend itself from truth that it does not want to acknowledge. The natural man who is resisting the Gospel message has used each one of the mechanisms. The bondage of Pithom is very great for the unbeliever.

But he is also in bondage to Raamses. If we combine two roots to form this longer word, we have the meaning "swift vibrations." This name has two basic meanings. The first refers to the fast pace of life with no rest. The swiftness of life gives us many problems related to our bodies. In his book <u>Adrenaline and Stress</u>, Dr. Archibald Hart calls stress the "hurry sickness:" "A large part of the damage we experience in our lives is caused by "hurry sickness." It comes from our urge to live and do everything in haste. As a consequence, we live at a pace too fast for our bodies. This hurried lifestyle creates a persistent *internal state of emergency* that keeps our stress hormones elevated."[9]

Dr. Hart goes on to list all of the many human diseases that are the result of excessive stress, due chiefly to the fast pace of life. From headaches to stiffness in the neck to digestive disorders and many more, most of the illnesses of modern Americans are chiefly due to the fast pace of their life. The converse of this is also true. God commanded Israel to rest one day per week, and more than one Jewish friend has told me, "More than the Jews' keeping the Sabbath, the Sabbath has kept the Jews."

In Hebrew, the word *shalom* means more than peace. It also means good health, having all of one's economic debts paid, and universal friendship, as well as the absence of war. As the natural man goes about building Raamses, the swiftness of his lifestyle is killing him with many health problems, but there is another problem in Raamses—the vibrations. Lacking spiritual receptivity, the natural man building Raamses needs sensory stimulation. Many take drugs for "medicinal" purposes—some by prescription. Others seek to reestablish the lost spiritual connection by dabbling in drugs or alcohol. Still others engage in activities that stimulate their adrenalin to give them a "high," such as compulsive stealing, various sexual addictions (both heterosexual and homosexual), and gambling, among others.

The vast majority in modern times turn on some type of rock music and turn the beat way up, in order to feel the vibrations directly. This produces an adrenalin rush, not unlike the other addictions and can be addictive, as well. In this case, the person becomes addicted to his own adrenaline. All of these activities or substances, as well as many others are engaged in as an attempt to fill in the empty feeling inside because of spiritual death. The natural man senses the void left by the lost spiritual contact with God and tries to fill it by something from the world outside. However, these attempts are doomed to fail from the beginning because they can only meet physical needs. The only remedy for spiritual needs is the Holy Spirit of God, and for this contact to be restored, the natural man needs to be saved from his sins. Pithom and Raamses—far from providing the satisfaction that people are seeking for—are really the slavery and bondage that they need to be delivered from.

Being devoid of any chance of spiritual input from God, the natural man is forced to drink in a continual stream of things of the world for his sustenance and enlightenment. In the same way the Israelites had no option in Egypt except to drink from the Nile River (*ye-or,* יְאֹר). This word means "enlightener" in Hebrew and represents the continual river of sensory input from the world, which takes the place of the spiritual perception of God that was the primary input.

With that false light, the natural man will do nothing but sin. In Psalm 36:9 (36:10 in Masoretic text) we read: "For with you is the fountain of life: in Your light we see light." According to Scriptures there is a true light and a false light. One of the names of the Devil is *Heyleyl Ben-Shachar* in Isaiah 14:12. This is rendered in the AV as Lucifer, following the Vulgate. The Hebrew means "Shining One, Son of the Dawn," and the Latin means "Light Bringer." Satan blinds people by "enlightening" them with a continual river of three things—the same three things that he tempted Eve with: the lusts of the flesh, the lusts of the eyes, and the pride of life. These are the water of the Nile as "enlightener," and through them, Satan controls people, filling them with desires to sin in order to get more and more "fulfillment" in these areas of life.

There is another name that the Devil operates under, and that is Pharaoh. In Egyptian the word means "Great House," as he is leader of the nation. However, in Hebrew the name means "lawless maker," as he sets people free from the law of God to do their own thing. When Moses rebukes Aaron for making the golden calf, we read (Exodus 32:25, my translation): "And when Moses saw that the people were *loosed (from the law—*Heb. *parua)*, (for Aaron had *loosed* them (from the law) to their shame among their enemies)..." The idea of being loosed from the law to do one's own thing is the idea here, rather than the AV translation of "naked" and "had made them naked," respectively. Gesenius prefers the reading "to let go, of let loose the people," meaning "to remove restraint from them."[10] The very word *parua* in Modern Hebrew refers to one who lives licentiously without any regard for God or His Law. As the Devil pours out a continuous river of worldly enticements and pride into people, he also tells them to do their own thing, removing restraints of their conscience. This is how the god of This World (Satan) "has blinded the minds of the unbelieving, so that they might not see the light of the gospel of the glory of Christ, who is the image of God. (II Cor. 4:4)." As they sin more and more, the conscience becomes duller and duller, and the light dimmer and dimmer, and thus, the slavery becomes worse and worse.

Even though Jesus is the "True light that lighteth every man that cometh into the world (John 1:9, AV)," once the person rebels and becomes the natural man, his spiritual connection with God is severed and he is spiritually dead. After that, the only light left from God will be the person's conscience and the fading memory of a contact with a good spirit from an ever more distant past. Living in a world of other people in the same condition makes sure that the natural man will have little inclination to search for the way back to God.

Just as Israel is unable to conquer the Egyptians in order to leave Egypt in their own strength, so the natural man cannot save himself. The theological term for this inability of man to save himself is called the total depravity of man. This does not mean that man himself has nothing good in him, but rather the mixture of good and evil is unacceptable to God, and he cannot get beyond this condition, once he has rebelled against the law as he understands it. God has created man to be filled with His Spirit and operate on earth in parallel with what He is doing in heavenly places. Once man sins and the spiritual connection between him and God is severed, he is in a state of sin, and can no longer function as a channel of the Holy Spirit. Thus, nothing that he does can please God.

When talking about the total depravity of man, Thiessen mentions that man's inability to keep the Law does not excuse him: "Ability to keep the Law is not essential to make the non-fulfillment sin. Man's inability to fulfill the law is due to his own part in the sin of Adam, and is not an original condition. Since the law of God expresses the holiness of God as the only standard for the creature, ability to obey cannot be the measure of obligation or the test of sin."[11]

Thiessen is mentioning specific acts of sin here, but the conclusion is even more obvious when seen in the light of the sin nature. The breaking of the spiritual bond between God and the creature came about at the rebellion against God at the age in which the child understood the will of God and directly rebelled against it. The result was spiritual death—the removal of the spiritual contact between the creature and Creator. This initial culpable sin by the creature, which resulted in spiritual death, was really the fault of each one of us. Therefore, all sin that was committed after our coming under the power of the devil is our fault as a result of our original committed sin, which put us there in the first place.

The Israelites were slaves in Egypt, such that they could never deliver themselves through their own efforts—not even one of them could. In the same way, each man voluntarily rebels against God and dies spiritually. The spiritual connection from conception onward is broken. Each one of us becomes a slave under Satan, as Pharaoh, who sets us loose from God to do our own thing. As the natural man each of us was drinking in a continual "river of light" full of diverse enticements to the lusts of the flesh, lusts of the eyes, and pride of life. What we thought was enlightenment was just darkness.

The broken spiritual contact with God left a God-sized vacuum that only God could fill, but we had lost our way, and the bridge was burned behind us. Once we sinned willfully and rebelled against God, we could no longer return to our childlike innocence. Salvation, the return to God, would have to be a work of God's, reaching out to us. It would be a forward trek through deserts and a continual war waged against the enemy within us (the flesh), the enemies around us (the world), and the spiritual hosts of rebellion (the Devil and his fallen angels), who would have us exalt ourselves and reject God at every turn. From the beginning to the end, God has to take the initiative to bring to us so great salvation, as He did to the Israelite slaves in Egypt, but we need to do our part, as well.

For the Israelite people, their story of salvation from Egypt begins with Moses. Moses means the "drawn out one," so named by Pharaoh's daughter, who drew him out of the Nile River and cared for him.[12] This is a picture of our conversion experience, for we also were "drawn out" of This World to enjoy the World to Come. If God does not draw us, we will not respond or come. The initiative must be God's.

This brings us to the unpopular but controversial doctrine of predestination, election, and calling. There are believers on the Calvinistic extreme who believe that God is totally sovereign in predestination, election, and calling to the degree that man is a mere puppet and everything is on God's part. There are others on the Arminian extreme that believe that God votes for you, Satan votes against you, and you cast the deciding vote.

From the human viewpoint it seems impossible to reconcile these apparently contradictory viewpoints, but both appear in the Bible.

The same Jesus who said (John 3:16) "whoever believes in Him shall not perish, but have eternal life," also said (John 6:44) "No one can come to Me unless the Father who sent me draws him."

Let us consider the situation with Israel. When did God decide to save them from Egypt? In Genesis 15:13-14 God had already told Abraham about what was to come: "Know for certain that your descendants will be strangers in a land that is not theirs, where they will be enslaved and oppressed four hundred years. But I will also judge the nation whom they will serve, and afterward they will come out with many possessions."

This passage tells us that God foreknew that Israel would be in Egypt 400 years, most of the time in bondage, and that He would judge that nation and bring them out with much material wealth. God was going to oversee the process of migration for that nation, their fall into bondage, their material payback, and their exodus, as well as their return to that same land where He and Abraham were talking in the first place. From beginning to end, the work was to be of God. He would be responsible that the people would be willing to go down into Egypt; and by bringing on the bondage, He would make sure that they wanted to leave. He already had in mind the different plagues that He would send on the Egyptians so that they would be willing to let the Israelites go, and He knew that they would come, as well as those of other countries that would also leave Egypt with the Israelites.

When we read Romans 8:29-30 we have this impression about the way that God goes about saving a lost person: "For those whom He foreknew, He also predestined to become conformed to the image of His Son, so that He would be the firstborn among many brethren; and these whom He predestined, He also called; and these whom He called, He also justified; and these whom He justified, He also glorified."

Just like God knew all of the Israelites 400 years into the future and how He would deliver them, Paul says that God "chose us in Him (Jesus) before the foundation of the world (Ephesians 1:4)." However, at the time of the Exodus itself, the invitation was open for anyone to leave Egypt, and many non-Jews took advantage of this opportunity, as well as the whole people of Israel. As Moses tells in Exodus 12:38: "And a mixed multitude also went up with them, along with flocks and herds, a very large number of livestock." This mixed multitude included people of many nationalities who converted to follow the God of Israel and who were accepted into the nation of Israel.

It is clear also that many people chose to stay in Egypt. They saw the 10 plagues, which demonstrated that the God of the Hebrews was superior to all of the gods of Egypt, but they chose to continue to worship the gods of Egypt. They chose the status quo and continued drinking from the Nile, the false "enlightener," and continued to be comfortable with their false gods. That is why the first two groups of people mentioned in Revelation 21:8 as going to the lake of fire are the fearful and the unbelieving. They just don't want to rock the boat.

In his Systematic Theology, Berkhof posits both a general grace that is offered to all men and a special efficacious grace that is granted only to the elect. He attributes to God both the election of some to salvation and the choice by God to pass by the salvation of others. He calls the latter reprobation and defines it this way: "Reprobation may be defined as *that eternal decree of God whereby He has determined to pass some men by with the operations of His special grace, and to punish them for their sins, to the manifestation of His justice*."[13]

In terms of our narrative of Israel in Egypt, this would be equivalent to God's arbitrarily killing some Israelites and Egyptians on Passover while saving others without taking into account their sprinkling of the blood. While it is probable that many Egyptian families did not know about the orders to sprinkle blood on the doorposts to save the firstborn, it is also probable that many did know and obeyed the command.

As on the Day of Atonement, God gave the requirements and provided the way for people to be reconciled with Him in a general way. It was up to the people to do two things to show their faith to appropriate it for themselves. They had to afflict their souls, recognizing that what happened to the two goats—dying and going to hell, symbolized by the hot, dry desert—was what they deserved. The second thing was to refrain from working, as God did not want anyone to think that he was earning he acceptance with God through his own merits. In Leviticus 23:29-30, God threatens to cut off from his people anyone who fails to do either of these two acts of faith on the Day of Atonement. God provides everything in salvation, but the people have to take a step of faith to apply it to themselves. Otherwise it does not count for them.

Does each one of us need a special grace of God to respond and appropriate the provisions of salvation through faith? I like to think of this question in terms of II Thessalonians 2:10-12: "And with all the deception of wickedness for those who perish, because they did not receive the love of the truth so as to be saved. For this reason God will send upon them a deluding influence so that they will believe what is false, in order that they all may be judged who did not believe the truth, but took pleasure in wickedness."

Here we notice that God is said to be sending people strong delusion. How can one send darkness? By removing the light. How does God send strong delusion? By removing the truth and the witness of His church in the world. It is not a positive act of sending delusion, but rather the removal of God's Light and Truth. I believe that this involves the removal of the church, in what is known as the Premilenial and Pretribulational Rapture of the Church.

If we can reverse the process, we may see how God does reach out to people in the church age before His universal grace is exhausted at the Rapture. Let us say that a person comes into contact with the Scripture. As Paul says in Romans 10:17, "So faith comes from hearing, and hearing by the Word of Christ." Since the Word of Christ is perfect Truth, the conscience of the person will bear witness to them that this is truth. At this point the person will have to decide whether to accept or reject the truth. Even after admitting to me, many to whom I have witnessed have said they prefer to stay where they were because it was better for them. Jewish people have told me that they might lose their business, family, and nation for believing that Jesus is the Messiah; and that they preferred to stay with Israel, even though they intellectually agreed with me that Jesus is probably the Messiah of Israel. They did not want the truth, and therefore would not "receive the love of the truth so as to be saved."

At this point, I usually remind them that God's Word (Deuteronomy 6:5) commands us to "love **God** with all our heart, soul, and might," not our Rabbi, parents, or the Nation of Israel. For many, however, the truth is low priority and they are fearful and unbelieving. These people will not receive a love of the Truth in order to be saved. Therefore, God leaves them with their darkness and comfortable delusions. In these cases, however, it should be considered inappropriate to attribute to God an *a priori* decree of reprobation for these people. God's decree is on the basis of His foreknowledge, not simply a sovereign acting of His will.

One time I met a young Jewish lady from Israel who was a believer in Jesus. She commented that she could see clearly the truth that Jesus was the Messiah of Israel, and wondered why so few of her people could see the truth. I asked her, "what did you most want in life: a good ethnic shtick, a close family, good ties with neighbors, and a good career with many friends, or the truth?"

She answered, "I wanted the truth more than anything else in the world."

I pointed out, "Then that is what God gave you. And what do think the majority of the Jews, who reject Jesus, want?"

"I guess they want a good ethnic shtick, a close family, good ties with neighbors, and a good career with many friends," she replied.

"Well," I concluded, "it appears as God gave each of you what you were looking for. If they want the truth above all else, then God will show them, too."

I have seen the same reaction from other people, whether Muslim, Hindu, atheist, agnostic, materialist, or of any ethnic group there is. The issue is whether they want the One True God above all else, or they want their own ethnic, materialistic, or social arrangement—whatever that may be. We need to remember that Jesus "was the True Light that lights every man that comes into the world" (John 1:9). Jesus was the Light that they perceived spiritually from their conception onward. Upon hearing the Scripture, the person has testimony of his or her conscience, and possibly memory, that this is the truth, but they also think of the cost of believing it, and they may want convenience, friendships with unsaved people, or some pet sin above truth. God proceeds according to their openness to the light that they do have.

Let us analyze the paradox of Divine Sovereignty and human free will in the light of the different parts of the person, as mentioned above. Man, as created, is made up of soul and body, which come through biological procreation, and a spirit, which is directly "breathed in" at conception. We have already seen how the human spirit is continuously in contact with God until the person comes to enough age to understand the will of God and rebel against it. At that time spiritual death occurs.

In the time between the occurrence of this spiritual death and the new birth, the person has nothing to operate with except the body, which includes his five senses, and the soul. This person operates without spiritual input, though he does have a conscience and, perhaps, some memory of his spiritual contact with God. He also should have a thirst for God. This may survive as just an idea of how God is, but is a byproduct of the initial revelation of God in him, nonetheless. This person is called by Paul the natural man, as in I Corinthians 2:14: "But a natural man does not accept the things of the Spirit of God, for they are foolishness to him; and he cannot understand them, because they are spiritually appraised."

The natural man (*psychikos, ψύχικος*) operates only through the unaided soul (*psyche, ψυχή*). He is "psychological," or "soulish," in his orientation because he has no input from the Holy Spirit. He reasons on the basis of the input from his five senses and the influence of his conscience. Bauer says that the person who is *psychikos* is totally involved in "the life of the natural world and whatever belongs to it, in contrast to the supernatural world, which is characterized by *pnéuma* (*πνεῦμα*)."[14] The product of this reasoning is condemned by James (3:15): "This wisdom is not that which comes down from above, but is earthly, natural (*psychiké, ψυχική*), demonic." Thus, the natural man is unable to reason his way back to God. He must depend on God to take the initiative to reach out to him. And he must want the truth, as was mentioned earlier.

It is important to remember that the body represents our awareness of the world, through its 5 senses. The soul represents our awareness of ourselves, through mind, will, and emotions. However the spirit represents our awareness of God, and even other spirits. When we passed through the transition of being cut off from God because of our rebellion, we became dead in our trespasses and sins. However, this death meant—not that the spirit died—but rather that the relation to God was cut off. The spirit continued functioning and was even able to contact other spirits that were not related to the True God. These other spirits or no spirit at all will never satisfy us, however. As Image and likeness of the One True God, we will never be satisfied until we are filled and controlled by the right Spirit—the Spirit of the One True God. Salvation refers to the restoration of the presence of the One True God in us, and sanctification refers to the gradual and progressive restoration of the control of the Spirit of the One True God in our lives. In this chapter we are concentrating salvation: the restoration of the indwelling presence of the One True God in us.

We will now consider the ten plagues that God used to show up the impotence of the gods of Egypt and their counterpart in the redemption of New Testament believers. It is interesting that the first plague was to turn the Nile River into blood. As mentioned earlier, the Nile means "the Enlightener." The world was drinking in a continuous river of filth of the world's "enlightening," thus reinforcing their lost condition. Now suddenly that false "enlightener" turns into blood. It is interesting to contemplate the different ways that God brings the wisdom and enlightenment of the world to nothing to frustrate people of this world so they seek meaning elsewhere. That it should be blood that it is turned into is further meaningful because Jesus shed His blood as the central act in purchasing our salvation. People need to see the limitations of earthly "wisdom" to that they begin to pursue the true wisdom and see the need for the blood of atonement.

The second plague is frogs (*tzefardéa*, צְפַרְדֵּעַ). This is a composite root, made up of two other roots. The first root is *tz-f-r* (צפר) yielding the idea of chirping or twittering,[15] and the second yields the word knowledge. The combined roots mean "chirping knowledge." The Egyptians worshipped frogs, and so many people in the world worship worldly knowledge. As this backfired for the Egyptians when God sent them too many frogs, so God can make this backfire as our worldly knowledge is shown to be vain and unsatisfying, no matter how much of it we get. Nowadays there is more knowledge, technology, and technological gadgets than ever and people are spiritually emptier and hungrier than ever. The false god of knowledge cannot satisfy.

The third plague was gnats, or lice, as some translations read. God created them directly out of the dust of the ground, as we read in Exodus 8:17: "Aaron stretched out his hand with his staff, and struck the dust of the earth, and there were gnats on man and beast. All the dust of the earth became gnats through all the land of Egypt." This is the first miracle that the magicians of Egypt could not imitate. They could fake the turning of the Nile to blood, and they could bring frogs out of the Nile. However, they could not create life. Only the True God can do that.

The natural man also needs to see that its greatest knowledge—whether esoteric or scientific—is nothing in reference to the matter of the creation of life itself. As gnats or lice make men itch, so God also plants dissatisfaction with the things of the world in us. Solomon said in Ecclesiastes 3:11: "He has made everything beautiful in its time. He has also set eternity (Heb. *olam*) in their heart, yet so man will not find out the work which God has done from the beginning even to the end."

The Hebrew word *olam* is rather complicated. Its meaning includes both *time* and *world*. As *world* it refers either to this world (*ha-olam hazzeh*) or the world to come (*ha-olam habba'*). Also, in referring to the notion of a long time, it would appear that the best translation is "as long as this world lasts and you are in it."[16] There is an element of reference to a "long time," almost beyond human calculation in the expression. However, when absolute eternity is indicated, the word is either in the plural (Psalm 45:17, cf. Paul's reference to "the ages to come") or otherwise amplified by adding other words, such as *le-olam va-ad*, which means "for the age and beyond." It would seem that Solomon is mentioning here that God has put some quest for eternity, or, at least, that goes beyond death, in the heart of every man; and man cannot be satisfied by just meeting his physiological needs as an animal. Man aspires to more than he is at, but the natural man, being an unsaved man, does not quite know what that aspiration is. He itches, however, with spiritual lice, and cannot be satisfied with just food, clothing, a house and a family.

After the lice, God sends the fourth plague: a swarm of flies. The Hebrew word is (*aróv*), which means simply swarm, from the root meaning "to mingle or mix." The reference is to the swarming motion that the flies make as they fly in a group, each in an almost random trajectory. Gesenius believes that they are some kind of stinging flies coming in a swarm.[17] It was a terrible plague for the Egyptians and their cattle, but the plague did not come to Goshen, where the Hebrews were.

From the same Hebrew root is the word for a mixed company, "a heterogeneous body attached to a people." In Exodus 12:38 this word refers to the mixed multitude of people from many nations that left Egypt with the Israelites, as mentioned earlier. It is easy to see this as God's election of the people to be saved. He sees the human race as a whole group of people who are "in Adam," for we are all rebellious by the rebellious soul we inherited from Adam. However, God sees this group as a mixed multitude because He sees those who are going to be saved as "in Christ," even at this time before they personally receive Him as their Savior. This is because of God's foreknowledge of who will receive Jesus. As was said before, God's judgments on Pharaoh were enough to allow anyone to leave Egypt, but only those who had faith and acted on this truth and applied it to themselves benefited by salvation from Egypt.

It is very probable that the flies were of a stinging variety, and may have brought the fifth plague, called simply a plague. It was some kind of disease that affected the Egyptians' animals, killing most of them, including all of the cattle. The Israelites, living up in Goshen, were spared, as were all of their animals.

As far as the New Testament believer is concerned, the word "plague" in the Hebrew comes from the same root as the word *word*. In Romans 10:17 we read, "So faith comes from hearing, and hearing by the Word of Christ." At this point it is necessary for the lost person to hear the words of Scripture from the Lord. This is through somebody witnessing to him or from reading the Bible while alone. The Word of God is living and active, and can bring salvation to the one believing in it, but it is a plague to the spirits of the enemy who have the person held captive. Thus God sends His Word as a mighty plague against the enemy to drive him away so that the person can believe.

In Hebrews 4:12 we read that "the word of God is living and active and sharper than any two-edged sword, and piercing as far as the division of soul and spirit, of both joints and marrow, and able to judge the thoughts and intents of the heart." Here the word translated "two-edged" really says "two-mouthed." The edge of the sword is the "mouth of the sword", both here in the Greek, as well as in the Hebrew (see Exodus 17:13). As the Word of God is spoken, it cuts against both the spirits of the enemy and our flesh that wants to respond to the temptation. It is two-mouthed. The spoken word is also important because the spirits of the enemy cannot read our thoughts. They can only hear our words. Therefore we must speak out the Word of God, and the mouth of the Word will defeat the enemy.

The sixth plague was boils, which erupted on both the Egyptians and their animals. This type of boil may or may not be leprous, as noted in Leviticus 13:18-20. The Hebrew root from which this word *shechín* (שְׁחִין) comes refers to heat, as the boils are inflamed.[18] It seems logical that after the Lord puts a plague on the enemy, He should also turn up the heat to drive him away. This type of eruption may or may not be leprous (Lev. 13:18-20). It may also be fatal, as in the case of King Hezekiah, who was about to die from it. When God healed him, Hezekiah was told to put a compress of figs on the *shechin*, and he recovered (Isaiah 38:21). Because of the hot nature of this eruption, it could also be cancerous, as cancerous growths are also hotter than the regular body temperature.

The seventh plague was hail, which destroyed much of the crops, as well as killing any man or beast outdoors. The root of this word has the basic idea of cold. After the heat of the boils come large, round balls of ice from the sky. These are large enough to kill any man or animal not under a roof. Pharaoh and the other Egyptians were warned about the hail and told to bring in their servants and cattle into the houses and other buildings. Those who feared the Lord and made provision were saved, and those who, like Pharaoh, "paid no regard to the Word of the Lord left his servants and his livestock in the field" (Exodus 9:21), where they died.

The seventh plague was a direct attack against false gods of Egypt. This plague was directed against two nature gods of the Egyptians, Isis and Osiris, who were thought to control the rains. That the God of the Hebrews could overrule these two Egyptian gods and bring destructive hail was evidence that the whole religious system of Egypt was false. With this plague, God was demanding people to choose between Him and the false gods of their nation. Those who feared God and brought their animals and workers into houses were saved. Those who trusted Isis and Osiris to protect them were killed.

The same lesson is true for the natural man to be saved. In Hebrews 11:6 we find: "And without faith it is impossible to please Him, for he who comes to God must believe that He is and that He is a rewarder of those who seek Him." Some of Pharaoh's servants believed that the God of the Hebrews existed, and they took precautions, rather than trusting in Isis and Osiris. It is probable that a number of them later left with the Israelites because of their belief in His word, as a part of the large multitude of foreigners who joined Israel in leaving Egypt.

In the same way, all people are servants of the Devil, as Pharaoh, "the lawless one." However, some have faith in the Word of the God of the Hebrews and some trust in other gods. Those who trust false gods die in the world without salvation, and one day will be thrown into the Lake of Fire along with Isis, Osiris, and any other false god they are worshipping. Those who have faith, however, may become a part of the church, the mixed multitude from all nations that follows the God of Israel. They received the salvation, which was originally promised to Israel and then opened to everyone on earth.

The eighth plague was the greatest swarm of locusts that had ever invaded Egypt. They ate up everything that the hail did not destroy, leaving nothing edible except themselves. Egypt was totally devastated.

For us the locusts speak of God's multiplied efforts to fight against Satan, who has usurped man as ruler of this world. The Hebrew root from which this word comes means "to multiply" or "to become great." God's salvation is abundant and capable of saving every person that ever lived. Man himself is the one that places limits on God's great accomplishments in salvation.

The ninth plague was a total darkness that made all activity to cease for three days, though there was light in the dwellings of the Israelites. This was a direct attack on the highest of all of the Egyptian gods, Ra, the sun god. The Pharaohs were highly devoted to the worship of the sun, along with the rest of Egypt, and sun worship was very prominent in Egypt. In Joseph's day, Potiphera (which means "He whom Ra gave," according to Gesenius) was the priest of On (later called Heliópolis, or "sun city") and Joseph's father-in-law.[19] On was located in the Nile delta, near to Goshen, where the Israelites lived. That the God of the Hebrews could shut down the sun for three days was the final evidence that He was supreme in the universe—at least supreme in the Egyptian territory.

It is not surprising that there is a connection between the highest god of Egypt and the sun. In Isaiah 14:12 we read about Satan in his rebellion: "How you have fallen from heaven, o star of the morning, son of the dawn!" The name given at the end in Hebrew is *heyleyl ben-shachar*, literally, shining one, son of the dawn. Hence, it should not surprise us to find countries in which Satan is worshipped as the sun god. The three days of darkness remind us of Jesus' three days in the tomb. In Jesus' death, Satan was really the one who was defeated. Because Jesus died in our place, Satan, whose name means the accuser, can no longer accuse us when we have believed in Jesus because the penalty has already been paid.

The last of the ten plagues is the killing of the firstborn, which is explained in Exodus 12. The Israelites were to kill a lamb and sprinkle its blood on the two side doorposts and the upper door-post of their house. Then they were to roast the lamb in fire and eat it. After that they were to stay indoors all night until the morning. The people that obeyed these orders were spared any harm; but in the houses where these orders were not observed, every firstborn was killed, whether the firstborn of people or animals that were in the house. In every house where the people did not observe these rules there was at least one dead person. In reaction to this killing,

Pharaoh ordered the Israelites to leave Egypt, and was glad to get rid of them—especially since he was burying his own firstborn son.

For Christians, the killing of the firstborn reminds us of Jesus as the Firstborn, as in Colossians 1:15, where Jesus is referred to as "the image of the invisible God, the firstborn of all creation." The most popular verse for summarizing the Gospel message in one verse is John 3:16: "For God so loved the world, that He gave His only begotten Son: that whoever believes in Him, shall not perish, but have eternal life." It is noteworthy that, as the Israelites had to sprinkle the blood on the two side doorposts and the top doorpost of their houses, the wounds in Jesus' hands, head, and feet also made three bloodstains on the cross. The stains were in the same shape, as well.

The life of the lamb was necessarily taken in the place of the firstborn of each household. Where the lamb was not killed and its blood sprinkled on the doorposts, the firstborn of that house died. Through this commandment the God of Israel was teaching the Israelites about substitutionary atonement, as well as the necessity of the shedding of blood for redemption.

At this point the Israelites were, in effect, free from Pharaoh's power, but they were not yet out of his territory. They still had to walk out of Egypt by faith. They proceeded from the city of Rameses and stopped the first night at Succoth, which means booths (Numbers 33:5 ff.). This was a special step for the Israelites, as they left the security of the Nile River and its continuous water supply and set out towards the desert, where everything was uncertain and they had to trust the God of their fathers for every provision. The word Succoth, or "booths," was also significant because it was the first night that they had to live in temporary shelters. It must have been a real lesson on how vulnerable and temporary our existence was on the earth. This lesson was so important that God later made Israel live in temporary shelters for seven days every year as a part of the celebration of the Feast of Booths (Lev. 23:42-43): "You shall live in booths for seven days; all the native-born in Israel shall live in booths, so that your generations may know that I had the sons of Israel live in booths when I brought them out of the land of Egypt. I am the Lord your God."

The same lesson is important for the beginning believer in Jesus. As he becomes detached from the "enlightener," the continuous river of false worldly desires, he realizes that he is now alone and headed towards the desert. He is separated unto the True God and he is dependent upon the provision of that God. His body is a booth for him to dwell in and move around in on the earth, but he is vulnerable and temporary on the earth. At the same time, he can see the greatness of the God Who is now sustaining him, and he begins to focus on the eternal values of his inheritance, even as the Israelites at this stage looked forward to Canaan as they turned their backs on Egypt.

At this point the believer is a wanderer—no longer at home on the earth, even as the Israelite was no longer at home in Egypt. He has taken the first step in becoming like his Savior Jesus, for in Jesus, "the Word became flesh and "tabernacled" or "boothed" among us (John 1:14)." Here John uses the Greek verb (*eskénosen*, *ἐσκήνωσεν*) from which the Greek translation of the Hebrew word "booths" (*skenai*, *σκηναί*) comes. Jesus walked on this earth in his temporary and vulnerable existence, completely dependent on God the Father, and living a life foreign to this place, ever the example of what the believer should be. This Feast of Booths will also be obligatory for all nations in the Millennial Kingdom (Zechariah 14:16-17).

The second day out the Israelites stopped "in Etham, which is in the edge of the wilderness (Num. 33:6)." If we follow Gesenius' suggestion of the Egyptian spelling *chethem*[20] and seek the Hebrew root accordingly, we find two basic meanings: be stained with blood, and gold.[21] This describes the new believer. He is stained with the blood of Jesus, and he is gold. This is the positional truth of what the believer is in Jesus, though he has not as yet learned to function according to what he is.

The third day out the Israelites were put in a very vulnerable position. They camped at *Pi-hahiroth*. To the north was *Baal-tzephón*, to the south was *Migdol*, behind them the Egyptian army was approaching in chariots, and in front of them lay the Reed Sea. They were trapped. With no place to go, they called out to the Lord. Where could they go?

For the new believer in Jesus there is a similar problem. *Pi-hahiroth* means "mouth of paleness." The latter root can mean white, pale, or hollow. The believer is weak at this stage, and he is between two temptations of the enemy on each side. To the north *Baal-tzephón* means "Lord of the Treasure," by which Satan seeks to tempt him with the loss of worldly riches. To the South is *Migdol*, where he is tempted with the loss of "greatness." He can see that by dying to self, he can never achieve greatness with his own efforts. Behind him is the army of Egypt, the "two oppressors," the world and the flesh demanding conformity to worldly norms and self-gratification, respectively. Where can he go?

God's answered the Israelites by placing columns of fire between the Israelites and the pursuing Egyptians while He was parting the Reed Sea and drying out the seabed with a dry east wind all night. In the morning, He ordered the Israelites forward through the Reed Sea. As they are finishing their passage through the seabed, God removed the columns of fire and the Egyptians drove forward to attack the Israelites. As soon as the Israelites were out on the shore, God released the water to its original place and drowned all of the pursuing Egyptians. Thus the Israelites were safe on the eastern shore of the Reed Sea with no fear that the Egyptians would ever pursue them. In I Corinthians 10:2 Paul says that the Israelites "were baptized into Moses in the cloud and in the sea."

For the believers in Jesus, the answer is similar—baptism. According to Romans 6 the believer in Jesus is baptized into Jesus' death, burial, and resurrection in his baptism, spiritually speaking. Therefore, a physical baptism in water is administered as a public testimony of the spiritual reality. At this point it is important to note that the sea that the Israelites crossed was called the Reed Sea (*yam suf*) in Hebrew, not the Red Sea (*yam adom*). This is important to the meaning of Christian baptism, as the word "reed" is from the same root as the word "end" in Hebrew.[22] This is the "sea which makes an end," for the believer, symbolizing death, burial, and resurrection.

In the Book of Jonah (2:6), Jonah declares, "a reed was wrapped around my head." It would appear from the Hebrew root connection that Jonah actually died (met his "end") and was resurrected in the belly of the fish. In Jesus' case, this reminds one of the "face-cloth (Greek *soudárion*), which had been on his head, not lying with the linen wrappings, but rolled up in a place by itself (John 20:7)." These things are outward symbols of the inward reality of the "end," or death of the person.

We read in Romans 6 about the Christian's baptism (vv. 3-7), "Or do you not know that all of us that have been baptized into Christ Jesus have been baptized into His death? Therefore we have been buried with Him through baptism into death, so that as Christ was raised from the dead through the glory of the Father, so we too might walk in newness of life. For if we have become united with Him in the likeness of His death, certainly we shall also be in the likeness of His resurrection, knowing this, that our old man was crucified with Him, in order that our body of sin might be done away with, so that we would no longer be slaves to sin; for he who has died is freed from sin."

As the Israelites passed through the Reed Sea, it made an "end" of their Egyptian slavery. They were, in effect, dead to Egypt and being Egyptians and alive to the "God of the Hebrews" and being Israelites in the desert. Here death and life are functional terms, as are most Hebrew terms. For example, when one man was ready to follow Jesus, but wanted to bury his father first, Jesus said (Matthew 8:22), "Follow Me; and allow the dead bury their own dead." Did Jesus expect some literal corpses to come out of their graves and bury the dead father and then return? No! The dead people for Jesus are the ones not in a right relationship with God. They are dead in their trespasses and sins because they are not acting under the leading and empowering of the Holy Spirit.

In the same way, the Israelites died to Egypt and Pharaoh's dominion over them as they passed through the Reed Sea, "the sea that makes an end." On the other side there was freedom from Egypt and a new Lord—the God of the Hebrews. They were freed from the "two oppressors" (the meaning of "Egypt" in Hebrew), the world and the flesh, so that they can now serve the God of their Fathers. When a Gentile converts to become a Jew, the last step in the conversion process is a ritual immersion in water, so that, like the Israelites, they also went through a "sea which makes an end" and across to the Jewish people on the other side.

This crossing is also the main meaning of the word Hebrew—"one who crossed over." This name is used of the Israelites because Abraham "crossed over" the Euphrates, renouncing his family and nation in order to receive the True God (Gen. 12:1-3). After his descendants have been multiplied in the oven of affliction in Egypt, they were born as a nation as they "crossed over" to God through the Reed Sea. From then on, it has been forbidden to number them among the nations. There could be seventy nations plus Israel, but not seventy-one, to use the traditional number of nations.

Israel's Exodus and the Christian's Salvation Experience: a Retrospect and Conclusion.

What the crossing of the Reed Sea was to Israel, Christian baptism is to the believer in Jesus Christ. It represents our death to the world and life to the True God. As Pharaoh could no longer give orders to the Israelites, so the new believer in Jesus is no longer obligated to yield to the temptations of the Devil. He is not free from the possibility of sinning, as the old behavioral patterns, called "the flesh," still clamor for control of him; but for the first time, he is now free not to sin. He may yield to the Holy Spirit or he may yield to the indwelling sin within him. However, whenever he tries to do his best in his own strength, he is in the state of sin—the state of operating as though in bondage to Pharaoh ("the one who sets free from the law to do our own thing"). As the Israelites recently liberated from Egypt were more Egyptian than Israelite in their thinking, so the new believer in Jesus, though a new creature in Christ (II Cor. 5:17), still has the habits and behavioral patterns of the old man.

The Israelites were about to embark on a journey through hot, burning deserts while trusting in the daily provision of food and water from their God. Many times in this journey they sinned by craving the things of Egypt and complaining about the Lord's provision for them. Nevertheless, they were no longer Egyptians demanding their ethnic foods, but rather Israelites craving something outside their proper upbringing. That is, they were bad Israelites at that point, rather than good Egyptians. In many ways they were out of sorts as Israelites until they had their own land, and there they could begin to function as a national and ethnic entity.

In the same way, the Christian, after his salvation experience and baptism in water as outward testimony, is embarking on a journey through a spiritually dry time. He ceases to drink from the false river of filth (lusts of the flesh, lusts of the eyes, and pride of life) that formerly "enlightened" him. He sees that he is no longer under Satan, and a slave to "doing his own thing." He sees that he is directly under God, and can personally know God, through the Holy Spirit.

The "journey across the desert" that is before him is really a journey into the Word, as the Hebrew word for desert is *midbar*, which is from the same root as the word "word".[23] As the new believer in Christ sets out across the desert toward Canaan, or "humility," as the root indicates, he must begin to memorize Scripture. The Apostle Peter exhorts believers at this stage (I Peter 2:2), "like newborn babes, long for the pure milk of the word, so that by it you may grow in respect to salvation."

The new believer in Jesus should learn to seek to satisfy his thirst from Jesus, the Rock that follows him in his wilderness, rather than the continuous river of filth from the world. He is no longer under self as a slave to Satan in the character of his name Pharaoh, but rather he is under the "law of the Spirit of Life in Christ Jesus, (which) has set (him) free from the law of sin and of death (Rom. 8:2)."

Finally, one day the God of the Hebrews will make His final judgment on the gods of This World, as He judged the gods of Egypt. Instead of 10 plagues to show for all time their impotence before Him, He will personally throw all of the false gods of This World into the Lake of Fire, in addition to every person who has followed them, instead of being saved by exiting from the world through faith in Jesus and the new birth. The most real and pressing need of salvation for all men should be seen in that fate that awaits those who do not believe in Jesus. Instead of taking the long way around and returning to the Canaan of humility, from which they were expelled when they rebelled against the Lord in the first place, they just stay in Egypt and perish with their accursed false gods, while in bondage to the god of This World, who, as Pharaoh, has set them loose from the law to do their own thing. He who does nothing perishes with this world, but he who believes in the Lamb of God and sprinkles

His blood on his heart is saved with a great salvation for all of eternity, crosses the Reed Sea, and sets out on the adventure through the desert as Israel did.

Chapter 6

From the Reed Sea to Mt. Sinai And Covenant Enactment: Entering into a Covenant with the Creator God

After their glorious crossing of the *Yam Suf*, (Reed Sea, not Red Sea, according to the Hebrew), the Israelites have a long way to travel to Mt. Sinai, at the south end of the Sinai Peninsula, the isthmus joining Africa and Asia. That is where they will enter into a covenant with the God of Israel.

The Christian lives his life in a parallel dimension, and sees the fulfillment of his life in a similar way as the Israelites. After he has received Jesus as his Savior, the believer in Jesus is baptized in water as public testimony of his deliverance from the dominion of Satan and transference into the kingdom of God's Dear Son (Col. 1:13). According to its root in Hebrew, the Sea of Reeds is the "sea that makes an end."[1] He is freed from Satan, even as the Israelites were freed from the tyranny of Pharaoh. However, this is only the beginning of a long journey in a relationship with God. Though it is a glorious birth, it is only a beginning.

As the Israelites next must travel to Mt. Sinai to enter into a covenant with the God of Israel, the next step for the believer is to enter into the New Covenant with the Lord. While this is automatic for the believer, and simultaneous with his conversion, we need to see this great event in terms of a number of events in the national life of Israel in order to understand the various elements of it: first, in this chapter, we will discuss nine steps to the preparation of the Israelites for the receiving of the covenant at Sinai, and then see the fulfillment in the life of the New Testament believer as nine lessons leading to a frame of mind to receive and understand the New Covenant. After that, we will consider the ceremony of enactment of the Mosaic covenant and relate it to the New Covenant. Finally we will compare the New Covenant to the Old Covenant along the main difference: the difference between law and grace. We will use samples from the thought of John Calvin and Lewis Sperry Chafer.

I. Nine Lessons of Preparation for the Covenant.

As the Israelites proceed from the Reed Sea, they enter the Desert of Shur (Ex. 15:22), "And they went three days in the wilderness and found no water." The wilderness, or desert is from the same Hebrew root as the word word.[2] At this point the new believer needs to be filled up with the Word of God in preparation for being the spiritual man later. We need a certain base of knowledge and nourishment by the Word of God in order to be ready for the Spirit of God to empower us and use us in humble service and ministry to others. Even the Apostle Paul, after his Jewish upbringing still spent 3 years in the desert after his conversion.

1. Follow the example of older believers. After crossing the Reed Sea and entering the desert, the first place that the Israelites entered was the Desert of Shur. This is the first lesson for the believer. Gesenius notes that the root for Shur has two basic meanings, "to travel, or journey", and "to behold, or regard."[3] The new believer in Jesus just after his conversion and baptism begins to travel by beholding, or looking at other believers. Thus, he learns to imitate other believers and look the same on the outside, but he soon learns that the outward arranging of his actions does not produce the same results as the mature believer has. Thus, there is no water, symbol of the blessing of the Holy Spirit.

The regular blessings of the Holy Spirit in the believer's life correspond with the regular rains in the Land of Canaan, or spiritual stage. The young believer cannot understand and hold great quantities of God's blessings yet. There is no "instant Christianity" in the Bible. Our journey is a marathon—not a sprint. We need patience and a teachable heart. God spends about 2000 years of Israel's history to develop a perceptual model that will be lived out in its fulfillment in a mature Christian in about seventy years or less.

This lesson is that we are not to be satisfied with just going through the motions of copying what other believers are doing. We need to pursue our own relation with God, and we need patience. We will feel thirsty and unfulfilled at this stage because we have ceased drinking from the Nile ("that which gives light," according to the Hebrew)—the false light of this world—but we are not yet equipped to drink in the blessings of the Holy Spirit. We need to press on, anyway, however.

2. Keep returning to the cross. The second lesson is at *Marah* (Exodus 15:23-26). *Marah* means bitter because the waters were bitter there. After imitating mature believers without the same results, there is a tendency for new believers to be bitter about the lack of results. What they don't realize is that they may be very advanced in physical age, but they have just been "born again," and they are spiritual infants.

Not only was the water bitter, but also the waters of the souls of the Israelites were also bitter. The bitter water on the outside was a picture of the bitterness on the inside of the Israelites. The result was murmuring against Moses. At this stage of events, the Lord puts up with the murmuring, though later He deals with it as a sin. As we make progress in our spiritual lives, the Lord expects more of us, and doesn't accept our more immature responses.

What is the remedy for the bitter waters? The same remedy as for all bitterness in the human soul: the cross. As the Israelites complained to Moses, Moses cried out to the Lord, Who showed him a tree. Moses threw this tree into the waters and the bitter waters became sweet, or drinkable. In the same way, the cross of Jesus is also called a tree. By applying the cross of Jesus to our lives, the bitterness is sweetened as we remember that our life is not about our self-glorification, but rather about the Lord's glory.

The lesson at this stage is clear: we need to be patient, rather than bitter. Also, the cross is the continual means of progress in the Christian life. It does not just constitute the beginning point for salvation only. As we progress in the Christian life, we need to keep returning to the cross. As the flesh gets in the way, and we are tempted to murmur or quit, the cross crucifies the flesh so that we can appropriate the life of Christ in exchange. In this way, we are "fleshing out" Christ, rather than ourselves.

We need to realize that we already died with Christ in our baptism and conversion seen as a single event, just as the Israelites died to Pharaoh and his control as they passed through the Reed Sea. Often, however, we lose sight of this fact and begin to seek our own goals and worldly fulfillments. When these fail to satisfy, or we fail to achieve them, then we can become bitter. Returning to the cross means renouncing these things that we shouldn't have aimed for in the first place. As we surrender again, we can then drink of God's provision of the sweet waters of His Spirit. This lesson appears in various different forms again later.

3. Good Health through Faith. There is another good lesson here. God promises physical health to the Israelites if they obey Him in everything. He says (15:26), "I will put none of the diseases on you which I have put on the Egyptians; for I, the Lord, am your healer." What does physical health have to do with obedience to the Lord? If we trust God and relax, we can save our physical resources for just what God leads us to do. However, if we spend large amounts of time and energy setting our own agenda and worrying about it, we will probably subject our bodies to a stress overload. Over a long period of time, the stress overload will lead to some physiological breakdown and medical symptoms.

Our bodies are like chains, and different people have different weakest links. That is why doctors ask people about diseases of our family members. Where we are weakest is where we are most likely to break down, due to long-term excessive stress. In his book, *Adrenaline and Stress*, Dr. Archibald D. Hart mentions a number of negative effects of what he calls "stress disease:" "Stress disease is not confined to the heart. It attacks many parts of the body. While the other symptoms of stress are not as life threatening as heart disease, they certainly have a negative effect on the quality of our lives. Vast numbers of people suffer from debilitating stress symptoms, such as headaches, ulcers, digestive problems, or muscle spasms, and live very painful and intolerable lives."[4]

It is the Lord's desire that we submit to Him and let Him lead us one step at a time. That is why He says to Israel, that He is going to put a foundation stone in Zion. This stone turns out to be Jesus. Then God says (Isaiah 28:16, AV): "He that believeth shall not make haste." Believing in Jesus will allow one to relax and trust God one step at a time. Dr. Hart dedicates a whole chapter to what he calls stress as "hurry sickness."

Dr. Hart describes two different types of people. People with type A personalities tend to live with a much higher stress level than those with type B personalities. They are more competitive, more easily irritated, more hard-driving and ambitious, more aggressive, easily angered, and more likely to feel guilty when they are relaxing and not doing anything. Dr. Hart then warns about these people: "But there is a physical penalty to be paid for being a predominantly Type-A person. Type-A people recruit very much more adrenaline than Type-B. And research has shown that Type-A men have three times the incidence of heart disease as Type-B men."[4]

This lesson is clear. We need to relax and trust in God and His provision as preparation for operating under the covenant. Here God associates our obedience with physical health. In addition to the positive psychosomatic effects of our faith and obedience, it is very probable that our immune system itself will function better against the invasion of live germs and the diseases that they bring if we are relaxed, faithful, and obedient to our Lord. When the Lord rebukes Israel for their unfaithfulness in the days of Isaiah, He tells them (Isaiah 30:15): "In repentance and rest you will be saved; in quietness and trust is your strength." We prepare for a life lived under the watch care of the Almighty and Omniscient God, we need to prepare to follow Him and trust in Him, rather than running ahead of Him, and becoming defeated, dejected, bitter, and even sick.

4. A taste of the Promised Land. The third lesson that prepared the Israelites for the covenant is the lesson learned at *Elim* in Exodus 15:27: "And they came to *Elim*, where there were 12 wells of water and 70 palm trees: and they encamped there by the waters." While it is true that at this stage the Israelites are not yet in the Land of Canaan, with its seasonal rains and flowing rivers, they need a taste of the blessing and prosperity, so abundant in the Land of Canaan, in order to have something to look forward to. Here the Israelites have a taste of the abundance of water and see some great trees.

It is noteworthy that there is a symbolism in the number of the blessings. First of all, there are 12 wells—one for each tribe. God is faithful and will remember everyone under the covenant—not just a few. Secondly, there are 70 great palm trees. Just as the number of 70 symbolically represents the 70 nations, so Israel is promised greatness over the 70 nations.

It is often the case that at times new believers will go through a special period of their lives and appear well beyond believers of many years. At this stage the Lord might be just giving them a taste of what true spirituality will be later on down the line as an encouragement to continue in the way of the Lord. This is not the time to give them a leadership position, as they will need to mature more in order to face the tests that leadership requires. The Apostle Paul warns us in this light (I Timothy 5:22): "Do not lay hands upon anyone too hastily." This means that new believers should not be placed in positions of authority very soon. They may just be in their "*Elim*," and may soon plunge into the Desert of carnality again. This is not to say anything against a new believer—he is just not ready at this point, and is not as far along with the Lord as he may appear.

5. Becoming flexible. The fifth lesson to be learned in preparation for the covenant was learned in the Desert of Sin. The word sin is not as it appears in English, obviously. Gesenius sees this name as coming from a common Semitic base as the Egyptian and Aramaic words for "clay."[6] This suits our study, as we will see that the Israelites at this stage need to become flexible like clay, so that God, the Divine Potter, can begin the work them into another form. For centuries the Israelites had been drinking from the Nile River and feeding on the food of Egypt around them. As we have seen, the word Nile (יְאוֹר) means, "Light giver," as there is a false light to the carnal view of the world we learn as we grow up. The unbelievers spend their whole lives "drinking in" the things of the world and being sustained by them. But what about the Israelites wandering around in the desert drinking from a rock? How could this be better, or lead to something better?

The food of Egypt also has many attractions for the believer to draw him back, as they complain in Exodus 16:3: "when we sat by the pots of meat, when we ate bread to the full." What were the Israelites craving? —the things of Egypt. What do they represent for the Christian? The flesh is always considered a major enemy for the believer in Jesus, but what specifically does the flesh represent? The word flesh in Hebrew is from the same root as the word Gospel. What is the flesh, then? It would appear to represent best the false gospel (good news) of our self-promotion. It is the promotion of our interests in the world above the interests of others, and often at the expense of others.[7]

The Israelites also craved bread to the full. When people strive to promote themselves above others the result is a war. The word bread comes from the same Hebrew root as the word battle.[8] Often the new believer still has ambition to be "a Christian above the others" and strives to "get ahead" of others in spirituality. He may do this sincerely, though focused still on the external items. The result will usually be strife with others, or feelings of superiority over others. We may well face the question again and again in different forms at different stages of our spiritual walk, "What is our diet?" Do we seek our own "flesh and bread," or do we wait on the Lord for His provision?

In Numbers 11:4 the Israelites again crave the foods of Egypt, and the list includes six other items, as well: fish, cucumbers, melons, leeks, onions, and garlic. The word fish in Hebrew comes from the root that means "to multiply" or "to increase."[9] I believe that fish represent the idea of the worldly people that one must always be striving at increasing his portion in life. In the extreme they do this because they are perpetually fearful of lacking what they need. The opposite of this fearful activity to increase one's portion is the

Sabbath, in which one "ceases" from his activity by resting. One can rest one day per week because he trusts in God for his portion in life, instead of fearfully and feverishly working to increase it constantly without rest. In I Timothy 6:6-10 Paul explains this truth to Timothy: "But godliness actually is a means of great gain when accompanied by contentment. For we have brought nothing into the world, so we cannot take anything out of it either. If we have food and covering, with these we shall be content. But those who want to get rich fall into temptation and a snare and many foolish and harmful desires which plunge men into ruin and destruction. For the love of money is a root of all sorts of evil, and some by longing for it have wandered away from the faith and pierced themselves with many griefs."

The second of the additional foods of Egypt was cucumbers. The original root indicates nothing more than cucumbers; but there are two cognate roots that refer to more. One refers to being hard or severe, and the other old or dried up.[10] There are many people in this world that pride themselves on being hard people to deal with, and they always trust themselves, and do not rely on any spirit to help them. This is really a front that people put up to look self-made to others, but it is really hiding a miserable person. As a new believer, we may actually crave the front that we put on before we knew the Lord because it was comfortable. It is easy to forget the misery and fear that go with "self-sufficiency."

The third food was melons. The Hebrew root behind this food is the word trust.[11] Many people in this world have a trust in a false object that gives them a sense of security. The current idea that everyone is right for himself further adds to this mentality. There is therefore no reason to check if the object of the trust is valid, or trustworthy. The current idea is that the trust of the person makes the experience valid. It is easy to live with the careless idea that your belief makes anything valid; but after learning the truth and being converted, one can no longer look to the inadequate objects of faith that the world has in preference to the Omnipotent Creator God. However, in the dry desert of early Christian experience, some of us may be tempted to look nostalgically at our earlier naïve trust in a worthless object when life was much simpler.

The fourth food was leeks. The Hebrew root behind this food refers to the idea of an enclosure and protection, as well as grass, leeks, and other herbage that grows abundantly.[12] Protection and prosperity are not so important to one in the world who eventually sees through them and their fleeting nature. This root also refers to grass as a type of what is quickly perishing in Psalm 90:6: "In the morning it flourishes and sprouts anew; toward evening it fades and withers away." During trying times in our early development as Christians, we are tempted to crave the unsure earthly riches that we sought before without thinking on the fact that they will not last.

The fifth food that the Israelites craved from Egypt while in the desert was onions. The basic meaning of the root is "to strip off," as onions have many layers to peel off.[13] This refers to the various layers of false front that we may put on so that others do not see us as we really are. It is scary to reveal what we are really like to others so that they can see us with all of our flaws and weaknesses. Very few people want to be that vulnerable. It may seem frustrating to follow a God that knows everything because we cannot hide anything from Him; but if we learn to be open with Him and let Him change us, then we can be transparent with others. At this stage, though, the believer may wish that he could cover up himself so others-and even God-cannot see him. We should resist the urge to cover up our sins, faults, and other problems before God especially. Watch out for the craving for onions!

The sixth food that the Israelites craved from Egypt was garlic. Garlic in Hebrew comes from the root for the word *name*, which is from the root that Gesenius says refers to being high or lofty.[14] The word *heaven* comes from this root. Garlic refers to our making a name for ourselves. This can refer to being popular with friends or being famous in general. There is a real desire to be "someone" among people of this world, and it is sad that people think that popularity will solve all their ills. One has only to look at the currently popular television show *American Idol* to see how desperately some people crave acceptance by others. We Christians at this stage must learn to give up on popularity and seek to please Jesus—the opposite of pleasing others. This is repulsive to the unsaved people, as the Apostle Paul comments in II Corinthians 2:14-17: "But thanks be to God, who always leads us in triumph in Christ, and manifests through us the sweet aroma of the knowledge of him in every place. For we are a fragrance of Christ to God among those who are being saved and among those who are perishing; to the one an aroma from death to death, to the other an aroma from life to life. And who is adequate for these things? For we are not like many, peddling the word of God, but as from sincerity, but as from God, we speak in Christ in the sight of God." For the unsaved person, our dedication to God is like pouring ourselves out for nothing, and so it has a spiritual fragrance like death to him. To the believers, our sacrifices for Christ are a fragrance of life, because they perceive that they have eternal rewards. Now from God's point of view, all of the effort of people to build up a name for themselves stinks, even as garlic gives our breath a bad odor. From the time of the Tower of Babel (Genesis 11:4), mankind has said, "let us make for ourselves a name," and all of our efforts to do that are a stench to God—like breathing in someone's breath filled with garlic smell. Our entire craving for "fame" in this world is an offence to God. Let's give up the spiritual garlic!

The meat, bread, fish, cucumbers, melons, leeks, onions, and garlic of Egypt could not satisfy the Israelites even if they did get them in abundance. In the same way, our "false gospel" of self glorification, our false battle to promote our own interests, our seeking material abundance in this world, our hardness to get ahead, our false confidence, our temporary prosperity, our many layers of facades that protect us from being known, and our craving for popularity or fame cannot satisfy us New Testament believers in our lives now. God has something better for us!

The Israelites are more flexible spiritually after a month outside of Egypt. They had been brought up under the evil spirits that the Egyptians worshipped, and there is ample evidence that they had been, and still were idolaters, like their masters. However, for one month the Israelites have been traveling outside of Egypt now. After being outside of the influence of these evil spirits, having escaped the territory where they have their power, they are now becoming flexible for God to begin changing them spiritually.

God, however, could not take away the provision of the Nile, the pots of meat, the bread of Egypt, and the other various cravings without substituting something else, that was according to His plan for the Israelites. The same is true for the believer in Jesus. After the Lord removes his worldly things, he begins to fill him up with His good provisions. The major provisions for food immediately were quail for meat and the bread of heaven.

The Lord promised meat at evening, and so at evening the Israelites had meat: God sent quails. "So it came about at evening that the quails came up and covered the camp," as we read in Exodus 16:13. All the Israelites had to do was to club them, clean them, and cook them. Here in the middle of the desert a nation of about 2 million people had all the meat they could eat without slaughtering their precious herd animals. What a blessing and miracle! According to Koehler and Baumgartner, the word *quail* refers to fatness, according to the only cognate root available from Arabic. This is probably correct, as they mention that the residents of Egypt often club these quail today in the same way, as they are fat, clumsy, and awkward.[15]

The question here is not whether the Israelites will eat meat, but rather which meat they will eat—the pots of meat from Egypt or the quail. In the same way, the believer will evangelize a message (i.e. "flesh out" a message). We have to choose whether it is the message of our own exaltation or the message of the exaltation of Jesus. The Lord can give us the miracle of showing the Gospel through us to encourage us along the way! We just have to seek Him and stop seeking the fulfillment of the gospel of our own self-fulfillment. This is the lesson for us, since the root for flesh is also that of gospel and the verb *to evangelize.*[7] The Israelites sought the flesh and bread of Egypt, and God gave them flesh and bread—but not of Egypt.

God also gave them the bread of heaven. In Exodus 16:14-15 we read, "When the layer of dew evaporated, behold, on the surface of the wilderness there was a fine flake-like thing, fine as the frost on the ground. When the sons of Israel saw it, they said to one another, *"What is it?" For they did not know what it was.* And Moses said to them, 'It is the bread which the Lord has given you to eat.'" (italics mine)

Manna means "Whatchamacallit," and is not exactly a flattering expression for God's gracious provision of bread in the desert. Jesus prefers to call it the "bread out of Heaven" in John 6:32. Moses describes this "bread out of Heaven" in four ways in Exodus 16:31: "it was like coriander seed, white, and its taste was like wafers with honey." In Numbers 11:7-8 there is additional information about the manna. We are told here in addition that its appearance was like bdellium, and that "its taste was as the taste of cakes baked with oil." Here Gesenius prefers "a dainty item" over "cakes" of the NASV.[16] Also, it is different than *ugoth*, translated "cakes" earlier in this verse, and the word "baked" is not in the Hebrew. This description of "manna" serves to show us the difference between the diet of Egypt and the diet of the Lord.

As we consider that God's bread is also from the Hebrew root for battle, we see by the ingredients that the battle is different. The Egyptian bread was leavened. Leaven makes the dough ferment and rise up. People who are in sin are continually fermenting, or boiling up in their spirit and prone to bitterness and rebellion. Also, they do not submit to self-abasement, but rather are trying to exalt themselves and rise up against God, just as the dough "rises up".

The bread of Heaven, on the other hand is made differently. The word coriander (gad, in Hebrew) comes from the root that means, "to penetrate or cut."[17] God first penetrates and cuts us as His best provision for us. To be penetrated by God is our best way of being strengthened, as He is beginning to replace the old Adam, who died and was raised with God in baptism, symbolized by the crossing of the Reed Sea. As we feed upon God's presence every day, more and more of Him penetrates us and we become more and more like Him. How is this done? John says at the beginning of his Gospel (1:14): "The word became flesh and dwelt among us." This was in the person of Jesus of Nazareth. As we read, memorize, and meditate on the word of God, the Lord is becoming more and more a part of us. The Hebrew word for meditation comes from the root meaning, "to chew the cud."[18] We need to think over what we read and memorize of the Scriptures in order for them to penetrate, or they do not become "like coriander seed" for us.

The second description of manna is that it was white. We need to realize that the Word of God is white, i.e. totally truthful and without error. We must have the highest view of the truth and inerrancy of

Scripture or we will begin to judge the Scriptures by some other criteria that we put above it. We will then fall into all types of error. Let's remember that "Every word of God is tested: He is a shield to those who take refuge in Him. Do not add to His words, or He will reprove you, and you will be proved a liar (Proverbs 30:5-6)." We must judge everything else by the Scriptures, but never judge the Scriptures by anything else. If we feed on the truth, we will be able to distinguish error because it is different; but if we study a mixture of truth and error, as is in the world, we will never be able to separate the truth from the error.

The third description of the manna is that of wafers. The word in Hebrew comes from a root that means, "to make wide or broad."[19] The name Jesus comes from a different root meaning to make wide or broad, as well. In the sense of Jesus' name, it means, "to make wide or broad" for someone bound up by sickness, evil spirits, or one's own sins. Here, the sense can refer to spreading us out in preparation to work on us as a Divine Potter. From this root comes the word for a flat, or broad jug—one that was literally "spread out" by the potter into its shape. What could be more appropriate in the Desert of Sin (clay), than being spread out by the Divine Potter? We need to expose ourselves to the Word of God for it to affect us.

The fourth ingredient of Manna was "honey." Though the Scripture says it was "like wafers made with honey (16:31)," we need to know about honey to know why manna is like honey in some way. According to Gesenius, honey comes from the root referring to its color of reddish brown.[20] It is interesting to think that pottery jars are this color. This is symbolic of the fact that at this stage, God, as the Divine Potter, is preparing Israel for His labor of love to transform them in the future. While the whiteness describes the purity, the honey describes the clay-colored material. The human being is made of the same elements as clay and is formed from the clay, but God breathed into him the breath of life. In that we differ from clay. This fact reminds us that all of the glory must go to God. As Paul writes in II Corinthians 4:7: "But we have this treasure in earthen vessels, so that the surpassing greatness of the power will be of God, and not from ourselves."

The "dainty item of the oil" also reminds us of several truths. First of all, God always gives the best. A dainty item would be something special on the menu, and anything from God should have top priority and approval. The oil reminds us that we are special, and God's anointing is on us and on His provision for us. We are holy, meaning, "set aside" for God.

What does this stage mean for the new believer? It means that shortly after his baptism, he needs to begin to have his private time with God every morning. At this stage, he does not know the proper steps in the procedure. These will be provided in the instructions for the Tabernacle at Mt. Sinai later. However, he needs this time alone with the Lord every day. As the Israelites gathered the manna on the ground early in the morning, so the new believer should have his time with the Lord early before the day proceeds and it melts. There are many simple devotionals that contain a brief meditation and a Bible passage that can help us get started. The daily nourishment in the Word and prayer will provide four things for the believer in preparation for an understanding of the covenant: penetration and cutting of the flesh (coriander seed), whiteness (purity), spreading out in preparation for God's work in us (wafers), and our remembering our claylike nature, weak and vulnerable, but moldable (honey). As we acquire a taste for it, it will become a "dainty item of the oil"—something exquisitely wonderful.

6. Becoming consciously dependent on God. Chapter 16 ends with the preservation of a memorial portion of manna to remind Israel how they were sustained in the wilderness with the bread of heaven. The new believer needs to see his dependence on God as preparation to understand his relation to God under the covenant better. Here, God put Israel into a position in which they could not provide for themselves, and then provided for them so that they could learn that He was faithful, able, and willing to provide for their every need. By the time they entered into the covenant at Mt. Sinai, they already had proof that God was able to carry out His part of the covenant and God was trustworthy. That is why 40 years later in Deuteronomy 8:3 Moses reminds them: "He humbled you, and let you be hungry, and fed you with manna which you did not know, nor did your fathers know, *that He might make you understand that man does not live by bread alone, but man lives by everything that proceeds out of the mouth of the Lord.*" (Emphasis mine.)

God deliberately put Israel in a position of need, and then fulfilled that need so that every person in Israel might know His faithfulness, ability, and trustworthiness. They were to live by the bread He sent; but more than that, they were to live by every word that He gave them—whether to obey the command, or to believe and act on the promise. That was to be their part under the covenant that was later to be given: to live by God's words.

The manna that the Israelites were to gather every morning kept them through that day only. We need to remember to begin have our daily quiet time with prayer and Bible study every day in the morning. We cannot read the Bible and pray for a long time one day, and then skip the next. Just like a newborn baby needs regular feedings—not just a big dose on Wednesday and a super mega dose on Sunday with nothing the rest of the week—so the new believer in Jesus especially needs to meet with Him every morning. Just like a little baby, he will not be able to hold much at a time, but he should put forth the effort—even for a brief devotional every day—in order to grow in the Lord.

It is amazing how the Israelites were so hard-hearted about the commands through Moses. First, many tried to gather more than an omer per person (Exodus 16:16-18). The Lord saw to it that whatever they gathered was equal to an omer, whether they gathered a lot or a little. The Lord didn't want them to be worried with accumulation of manna, but to trust Him that the amount would be enough for the day. According to Gesenius, the root for omer is related to a root meaning abundant.[21] New believers do not have to devour vast Scripture passages or huge theological tomes each day in order to have sufficient nourishment. They just need their daily manna, which for them is sufficient.

Secondly, many tried to store up manna for the next day in fear that there would be nothing on the ground the next morning (16:19-21). Whatever was left over for the next morning "bred worms and became foul." Here the Israelites needed to learn that the Lord's mercies were fresh every morning. They didn't have to stockpile His blessings in case He failed to provide later, or worry primarily over material things.

In Matthew 6:24-34 Jesus uses the birds of the air and the lilies of the field as examples of the Father's provision. They depended on God daily for their provision without accumulating anything. This is the example for the believer. Take one step at a time and trust God for the provision one day at a time. Throughout many days, though, you will grow into a spiritual adult of full stature if you are faithful one day at a time.

The third lesson that the Israelites learned about the manna was that God could make exceptions. Because God wanted them to rest on the Sabbath, He made two exceptions to the normal rule of gathering and preparation: He gave a double portion on Friday which did not breed worms and become foul when they had leftovers for the next day, and He gave no manna on the Sabbath. The people were, of course, surprised that the double portion of food cooked on Friday lasted for Sabbath without spoiling, but some went out on Sabbath to look for manna and did not find any. Here, again God was irritated with them because they did not simply believe what He had said. We also need to learn that God can make exceptions to His own rules and specific provisions. We are to simply follow without asking questions or doubting.

We can easily be tempted to think how hard-hearted the Israelites were until we reflect on our own hard-heartedness. How many times has the Lord promised us something and then fulfilled it, only to see us doubt the next time He promises something, or balk at His next promise or ignore His next warning. The Israelites are surely a visible picture of what is going on inside of us as we grumble our way through the desert of life, treating God's beautiful promises as though they were a mockery!

7. Be thankful and patient instead of complaining. From the Desert of Sin, the Israelites moved on to Rephidim in Exodus 17:1-7. Here they found no water, and the people grumbled against the Lord again. God told Moses to strike the rock in Horeb, and water would come out. Moses did this in the sight of the leaders of Israel so that they could see God's provision. God was displeased with Israel for accusing Him of bringing them there to kill them with thirst; but they were still immature, so He did not punish them directly for this lack of faith. God puts up with a lot of complaining from new believers that He does not tolerate from older believers. His expectations of us are according to the level where we are. Moses renames the place Massah (testing) and Meribah (striving) because the people had tested God and were striving with God there.

It is amazing that the name of the place Rephidim means "helps" or "protected places," according to its Hebrew root.[22] It was right while they were in the Lord's protection and help that they were complaining that God had just brought them there to slay them with thirst. They didn't recognize God's helps until they saw the water gushing from the rock. The rock was in Horeb, which means "the dry place" in Hebrew.[23] God knew that He was taking Israel through a dry place—In fact, no other nation could have made it through this place without God—but God was ready with every provision for their needs.

The same lesson is there for new believers. As we move away from our source of spiritual nourishment of things of this world (equivalent to drinking out of the Nile River), we sense a spiritual dryness in our souls because we as yet do not experience the abundance of the Holy Spirit in our lives. However, the Lord is there like the Rock in the Dry Place (Horeb), and will provide all that is needed to continue.

The Israelites needed to pray for the provision—not grumble for it. They had the Creator God of the Universe accompanying them through a humanly impossible journey, and they would need Him constantly. This is another lesson in preparation for life under the covenant: pray for needs, don't grumble because of needs. This lesson of water from the rock was the seventh of the lessons and prepared the way for the eighth: military warfare.

8. Military Warfare. The last half of Exodus, chapter 17 tells of an attack by the Amalekites. This time, the Israelites had just seen God's provision of water for their thirst and were ready to respond to the threat against their physical safety. We need to note at this point that the Amalekites were a strong, desert people, who were experienced warriors and well-equipped with weapons for warfare, while the Israelites were recently-liberated slaves with hardly any weapons. The outcome of this battle looked as hopeless against Israel as did the lack of water, which God supplied out of the rock, but God also provided here.

Just as Rephidim might mean "helps," as indicated above, it may also mean "protected places." Here we see the second meaning of the name Rephidim. As Major W. Ian Thomas says, "Amalek here is a picture of the flesh, seeking at all costs to bar the onward journey of God's redeemed people, through the wilderness, into the Land of Promise."[24]

The name Amalek is from a four-letter root in Hebrew, and I believe it should be better split into two smaller roots. This gives as a base meaning "the people that lap up (the strength)." When we walk in the flesh, it sucks up all of our strength and leaves us weak. Conversely, when we crucify the flesh and walk in the spirit, we are strong. At this stage, the Israelites are not strong to fight against the Amalekites, as the new believer is not strong to fight against the flesh.

In verse 9 of chapter 17, Moses tells Joshua to choose out men and go to fight Amalek. At the same time, Moses, Aaron, and Hur went up to the top of the hill with the rod of God in Moses' hand. As the battle progressed, Moses discovered that when he held up his hand with the rod Israel was winning, and when he lowered his hand, Amalek was winning. Thus Moses sat on a rock and Aaron and Hur each held a hand up until Amalek was defeated.

There are also many lessons for the believer at this stage. Speaking about victory over the flesh, Thomas concludes, "The principle is plain. Victory over Amalek is God-given; it cannot be won, it can only be received, and that by the appropriation of faith."[25]

This is the lesson in preparation for warfare in the covenant relation with God. Protection from the enemy is through faith. Also, the believer needs to believe that the victory over the flesh is through faith in God's provision through the cross. The victory has already been won, but we need to appropriate it through faith.

There is another lesson in spiritual warfare: perseverance. Moses saw that when his hands drooped, the tide of battle changed.

His response was first to sit down on a stone. We need to rest on Jesus in prevailing prayer, but he is "the stone which the builders rejected" who "has become the chief corner stone (Psalm 118:22)." Also, Moses asks Aaron and Hur to join him. New believers need to learn the lesson of trusting in Jesus alone for the victory, and of getting together with other believers to pray for the victory. The new believer needs to see that the Lord can protect him from all attacks of the enemy, and trust in God for the victory. The lesson was clear: victory came less through the methods of fighting than through God's response to the intercession of Moses.

There is another means beside prayer employed in the victory. We read in verse 13: "So Joshua overwhelmed Amalek and his people with the edge of the sword." First we see that Joshua is the leader of the army. Moses never leads the army or engages in actual battle. Moses means "the drawn out one."[26] As long as Israel is under Moses it is just "drawn out" from the world, and not good for winning any battle. On the other hand, Joshua means "Jehovah is salvation,"[27] reminding us that only God wins the battle. That is the lesson here "that the Lord will have war with Amalek from generation to generation." The battle is the Lord's and the victory is the Lord's, as well.

For the believer, the difference between Joshua and Jesus in the Hebrew is that Joshua means "Jehovah is Savior" and Jesus means "Savior." This is because Joshua refers to another one doing the saving (Jehovah), and Jesus refers to the same person doing the saving, because he is Jehovah. When Jesus wins the battle, only God wins the battle, and, as believers, we know more about God because we see Jesus.

Besides Joshua, the "edge of the sword" is used to defeat (literally, "make weak") Amalek (by killing off many of his offspring). In the Hebrew the expression is literally, "with the mouth of the sword."[28] This idiom in Hebrew either carries over into Greek or is imitated in the Greek of Hebrews 4:12: "For the Word of God is living and active, and sharper than any two-edged (literally, "two mouthed") sword."[29] It is the Word of God that defeats the enemy, under the direction of Jesus, and while used in an attitude of constant prayer and delivered through our mouth out loud. The Word should be spoken out loud because the evil spirits cannot read the believer's mind. We must speak the Word of God out loud.

The lessons from the war against Amalek are so important to God that He orders Moses to write down a memorial that He will utterly blot out the remembrance of Amalek from under heaven. Then Moses also builds an altar, and calls it Jehovah Nissi, which means, "Jehovah is my standard," or "Jehovah is my miracle."[30] Israel was to trust in the Lord that Amalek would eventually be blotted out from under heaven. This was eventually accomplished, as far as we can tell, in the Book of Esther, when Haman, the direct descendant of Agag, an Amalekite king, and his family were destroyed through the miracles God arranged in that book.

For the believer, the lesson is essentially the same. The battle with the flesh is the Lord's, and He will wage warfare against the flesh throughout our life here. When we have our new resurrection bodies, there will be no more battle with the flesh; just as in the Millennial Kingdom Amalek no longer exists. While Israel had a memorial written in a book, the believer in Jesus has the written record of the New Testament, where in Romans 6:1-6 we read about the victory Jesus won over our old man: "our old self was crucified with Him, in order that our body of sin might be done away with, so that we would no longer be slaves to sin." As Israel was to rehearse the writing about God's victory over the Amalekites, we believers are to rehearse the truths about Jesus' victory over sin and our participation in that victory by dying and rising with Him.

It is absolutely imperative that the new believer memorize key Scripture portions in order to fight against the temptations of the flesh. When Jesus was in the desert, he fought off the tempter Satan by quoting appropriate Scripture verses. Jesus did not have time to go running to Jerusalem for a scroll of the Law of God to read against Satan. He quoted the verses by memory.

Why does the Scripture have two edges, or two mouths? I believe that the first is to cut against the flesh and defeat it, while the other is to be directed against the evil spirits that work through the flesh. Jesus quoted the Scriptures to tell himself what to do, not to tell Satan what to do. As our flesh rises up within us to sin, we may quote the Scripture about what we should be doing at that moment instead of the sin to fight against it. Where Israel often failed in the wilderness, and where we believers also often fail in our "wilderness," Jesus never failed. He maintained Himself perfect throughout his life, and his perfection now counts for us believers. That way Jesus is the victor in the wilderness for us believers as Joshua was the victor in the wilderness for Israel.

Also, the edge of the sword is called the mouth of the sword because the Scriptures should be spoken out loud in the battle. Only God can read our thoughts. Evil spirits cannot read our minds. They only respond to what we speak out loud. As we speak the Scriptures out loud, we are wielding the sword of the Spirit, and the mouth of that sword is mighty in battle against the flesh and against the evil spirits that try to stir up the flesh.

9. Dealing with the natural conscience. The final lesson in the wilderness that prepared the Israelites for the covenant was the dealings with Midian, just before reaching Mt. Sinai. While believers are not under the Law, we still need discernment as to what is right and what is wrong. The word Midian comes from the Hebrew root meaning "to judge."[31] The Midianites are, in my consideration, the most peculiar of all of the enemies of Israel. From their origin through Abraham and Keturah up until the Israelites arrive at Mt. Sinai, they are friends and allies of the Israelites. Moses even marries Zipporah, the daughter of Jethro, the high priest of Midian and ruler of the people. However, from the time Israel starts northward from Mt. Sinai, they become mortal enemies of Israel and need to be destroyed. How can this be?

The root for Midianites has as its meaning "to judge," and I believe that they represent for the Christian the natural conscience. Our natural conscience cries out against us, leading us to feel uncomfortable. This helps us to want to receive Jesus as our personal Savior, be baptized, join a church, and seek to know what God's Law is. The content of the Law of God guides our conscience. However, after receiving the Law, the conscience continues to condemn us, denying the effectiveness of the shed blood of Christ, preventing us from going on for God in faith.

This double bent of the natural conscience is because we tend to use the law to justify ourselves against an adverse conscience, rather than to continue to plead the shed blood of Christ. In I Timothy 1:8-10 the Apostle Paul declares that "the Law is good, if one uses it lawfully," or in the correct way. He then states that the law wasn't given for righteous, but for rebels to see their sin and repent. The real righteousness is in verse 15: "that Christ Jesus came into the world to save sinners; among whom I am foremost of all." When believers see themselves as the chiefest of sinners and plead only the death, burial, and resurrection of Jesus for their standing, they use the law the right way, and their consciences cannot keep them from being mired down in legalism, once they know the law. Instead, they can go on in the Lord.

Here Jethro, Moses' father-in-law is on his side and rejoices that the Lord delivered Israel from Egypt. If we remember that Egypt represents "the two oppressors," the world and the flesh, ruled over by Satan in the character of his name Pharaoh, which means "one who releases from the law to do one's own thing," it is easy to see why the natural conscience would oppose Egypt. The Midianites are glad that Israel has been delivered from Egypt and are coming to their place, the mountain where the law will be given. The natural conscience thrives on the Law of God. It finds its nourishment from the Law.

In Exodus 18 Jethro gives Moses advice to delegate the matter of judging to others, while hearing only the hardest cases. Here is the judgment of the human conscience honing itself for the best it can do, but it has a false optimism. To judge the truth is not necessarily to do the truth. However, at this stage of Israel's history, in preparation for the receiving of the covenant, it is natural and good for the conscience to be on the alert and sharp in preparation for God's revelation to man.

At this point we have traced nine scenarios in the learning experience of Israel in preparation to enter into a covenant relation with their God. We have also seen nine corresponding lessons that the young Christian needs to learn to prepare for the covenant relation with his God under the New Covenant. Now we shall consider the enactment of the Old Covenant and its comparison to the enactment of the New Covenant.

II. The Ceremony of Enactment of the Covenant.

The difference between "The Desert of Sin" and "The Desert of Sinai" is small but significant. While "Sin" means clay, "Sinai" means "My Clays," undoubtedly spoken from the viewpoint of God.[32] The difference is commitment. When the people of Israel left Egypt, they were a rag-tag bunch of former slaves, rejoicing in their newfound freedom, and grumbling whenever anything went wrong. They were a "free people" placed at liberty in the desert.

God, though he conquered Egypt and led the Israelites out, did not want to declare them simply to be His slaves. He could have done this, though, taking possession of them as the spoils of war. He preferred rather to exhort them to enter into a covenant relation with Him, giving them the option to receive or reject it.

There are five elements to the ceremony of ratification of the covenant on Mt. Sinai, and each one corresponds to a lesson that we need about the New Covenant.

The first element: God's perspective on the covenant. This comes in the famous "Eagles' wings" speech which God gives Moses to tell to the people. In Exodus 19:4-6 God says: "You yourselves have seen what I did to the Egyptians, and how I bore you on eagles' wings, and brought you to Myself. Now then if you will indeed obey My voice and keep My covenant, then you shall be My own possession among all peoples, for all the earth is Mine: and you shall be to Me a kingdom of priests and a holy nation. These are the words that you shall speak to the sons of Israel."

The Lord begins with an historical reminder of what He had already done for them. He had smitten the mightiest nation on earth at the time, Egypt, with 10 plagues that had beaten them to a pulp and made desolation and a mockery of their false gods. Then He had taken Israel by the hand and led them out of bondage to Egypt. After that He had led them back southeast toward the Reed Sea. After parting the Reed Sea for them, He subsequently drowned the Egyptian army in it.

He then bore Israel on eagles' wings by providing water from the Rock, quail for meat, and the bread of heaven, which they called Manna, or "Whatchamacallit." He had protected them from an attack of the Amalekites and had brought them safely to the foot of Mt. Sinai, where they were at that moment. He had certainly brought them unto Himself there, and they were in a position to receive the covenant that He was offering. This speech is a reminder of where Israel came from and their needs, as well as the greatness and love of God, Who delivered them and brought them safely up to the point where they were at that moment.

This speech is to ready the Israelites to submit willingly to the Lord by reminding them of the past, in which He delivered them from slavery to Egypt. Also, it is to promise them good for the future under the covenant, that they would be a peculiar treasure and Chosen People of the God Who created and owns the whole world. Also, they were to be above all the other peoples of the earth because they would be the priests, or mediators, of that God to present Him to the other nations. By receiving this covenant and submitting to this God, the Israelites would be above all peoples on the earth and in a special love relation with the Creator God of the Universe. How exciting!

It is similar for the Christian. In I Peter 2, Peter alludes to this passage as he writes to new believers. In verse 2 he exhorts the new believers, "like newborn babies, long for the pure milk of the word, so that by it you may grow in respect to salvation." While the Old Covenant has a definite sequence of events from the blood of the lambs, to the crossing of the Reed Sea, and enactment of the covenant at Mt. Sinai, the New Covenant equivalent truths are simultaneous with conversion. However, we may study these truths in the order of the Old Testament in order to gain a step-by-step understanding of the multifaceted blessings we have under the New Covenant. This is useful, considering our human limitations.

When we are recently converted, we need to understand little by little the blessings of the covenant, though we are already under it. We need "the pure milk of the Word" in order to grow into what we already are. Peter then mentions how Jesus is the Living Stone, rejected by the leaders of Israel in verse 4. This refers to the fact that the Old Covenant is conditional and dependent upon the people's obeying God's voice and keeping His Covenant (Exodus 19:5), while the New Covenant is conditional only upon our receiving Jesus as our Personal Savior in the first place. The blessings then follow unconditionally through grace.

Israel, in fact, did not keep God's conditional covenant, as mentioned, and in verses 4-7 of I Peter 2, Peter draws a sharp contrast between unbelieving Israel and the believers to whom he is writing, who are coming to Jesus (v.4), being built up into a spiritual house, being a holy priesthood, offering spiritual sacrifices, acceptable to God by Jesus Christ (v.5), to whom Jesus is precious (v.7). Concerning unbelieving Israel he alludes to the fact that God's promise to make them His peculiar treasure, a kingdom of priests, and a holy nation is **conditional**, and that they did not fulfill the condition.

What is the result? Believers in Jesus are to see themselves as "a chosen race" (*génos eklektón, γένος ἐκλεκτόν*). Here we should read *génos* as "race," not "generation" as the AV. Though Bauer prefers the reading "chosen nation" here, his other suggested meanings for *génos* seem to fit the context better. His meaning "descendants of a common ancestor" fits well with our common new birth in Christ, and his meaning "family or relatives" is more suitable to our relations within the church body, based on that common birth. Instead of a common physical descent from Jacob, or Israel, we have a common new spiritual birth in Jesus through our conversion.[33]

Our new birth in common is not that physical birth of the Israelites, and therefore we are a different group of people in Jesus. We include the remnant of the Jewish people who did not rebel against God and the remnant of the Gentiles who did believe. Peter's description is of one who has already received the blessing and the new birth—not of one preparing to enter into a covenant, and a conditional one at that. As we seek to see the applications for Christians under the New Covenant at this stage, we need to keep in mind the differences arising from the fact that the New Covenant is of grace, while the Old Covenant is of law.

Peter continues in verse 9 that we are also "a royal priesthood" (*Basíleion hieráteuma, βασίλειον ἱεράτευμα*). This is an allusion from Exodus 19:6, where Israel was to be a "kingdom of priests" (*mamlechet cohanim,* מַמְלֶכֶת כֹּהֲנִים) The Greek of I Peter is identical to the Septuagint of Exodus 19:6, and so these two expressions should be seen as equivalent. In olden times God had told Israel that the Gentiles would have to come to Him through them, and that they would be the priests to make a bridge between the Gentiles and God. Now this responsibility was given to all people that were under Christ and the New Covenant to reconcile unbelieving Jews and Gentiles to God.

Peter's third description of New Covenant believers is "holy nation" (*éthnos hágion, ἔθνος ἅγιον*). This copies verbatim with the Septuaginta rendering of Exodus 19:6, and refers to our being "set apart" from all other nations. Israel had been set apart ("made holy") by passing them through the Reed Sea, a figurative death to the other nations (especially Egypt) and life to God under Moses as mediator on the other side. The believer is now made dead to This World and living in the resurrection life of the World to Come under Jesus direct through the new birth. We are "made holy," or set apart from the other nations and Israel in that the other nations and the Israelites did not pass through death into The World to Come while we did. This is a past action by the time a believer has believed, passed baptism, and is learning about the new covenant, and therefore it is a certain blessing that is not dependent on his subsequent obedience.

Peter's final description is *láos eis peripoíesin* (*λαὸς εἰς περιποίησιν*). The King James rendering, "a peculiar people," should be rendered "a people for (God's own) possession," following the sense of the Hebrew *segulláh* in Exodus 19:5, though the Septuagint *perioúsios*, (*περιούσιος*) indicates "property owned as a rich and distinctive possession", according to Friberg.[34] The New Covenant believer is God's special possession now, and there is no demand placed upon him to earn or maintain this status. The covenant has already been enacted by the time he has reached this phase. The New Covenant believer is now learning about what he already has in Christ, while the Old Covenant believer is being prepared to receive something not yet his, and the continued possession of which will be conditional upon his obedience. Here again, we see a significant difference between the two covenants.

Peter then gives the purpose of these new changes: "that you may proclaim the excellencies of Him who has called you out of darkness into His marvelous light." This is a major purpose of God's call to the Israelites, and not significantly different from that of the church. Whether one is a member of Israel or the church, God expects him to glorify Him and tell the world about His greatness. This is the meaning of the "Eagles' Wings" speech which God gives to prepare the Israelites for the covenant relation with Him.

After giving the Israelites this major "pep talk," God then orders them to prepare for the covenant enactment ceremony. In Exodus 19:7-9 there is a preliminary explanation of the covenant and the people said, "All that the Lord has spoken we will do." This part is not unlike the initial part of a wedding ceremony, called the statement of intentions, in which the bride is asked if she takes the groom for her lawfully wedded husband and vise versa. This is like a prelude to the formal ceremony, which states the intent of the two people to continue on with the ceremony and the covenant.

In verse 10 there is a formal preparation ordered by the Lord: the people are to sanctify themselves and wash their clothes. This procedure is to impress upon them the greatness of the God that will be appearing to make a covenant with them, and fix on their minds the importance of the covenant. They are told that God will come down on the third day to the mountaintop in the sight of all Israel (v.11). Added to this measure in verse 15 was the order to abstain from sexual intercourse—not because it is bad—but in order to dedicate oneself to his relation with the Lord. This is the same reason—and the only reason—given in the New Testament for abstinence from normal sexual intercourse in I Corinthians 7:5: to dedicate themselves to the Lord in fasting and prayer for a time. We need to remember that God does miracles and reveals Himself to **all** believers in Jesus, not just some of them.

The next provision was to set apart Mount Sinai by putting barriers of some kind and announcing that any man or beast that crossed the line would be put to death (v. 12). This is to show the seriousness of dealing with God, and the absolute respect that He is due. In verse 9 God gives His reason for making a personal appearance in a cloud "so that the people may hear when I speak with you, and may also believe in you forever." The new Christian needs to have a sense of the awesomeness and holiness of God as a perceptual background for appreciating how accessible God is under the New Covenant. In Hebrews 10:19-39 the author gives a strong exhortation to follow God and take Him seriously. After mentioning how those who despised Moses' law died without mercy by two or three witnesses, he then reminds us that the Lord will judge His people even under the New Covenant, and continues (v.31), "It is terrifying thing to fall into the hands of the living God." When we fear God and understand His justice, only then can we appreciate all that He has accomplished in providing our salvation, and only then can we love Him as we should.

The final preparation is for the people to stand before the mount when they hear the trumpet. The Hebrew word translated trumpet in verse 13, *hayyovél* (הַיֹּבֵל) means a ram's horn, according to Gesenius.[35] Its name comes from the root meaning "to bear along," especially as in a procession. The image that we might have here is that of the father of the bride bearing along his daughter to the altar for the wedding ceremony. Here the ram's horn will be played to bear along the people to the base of the mount for the ceremony of institution of the covenant.

The third part of the ceremony of enactment of the covenant was scary signs, sent by God to impress upon the Israelites of all generations the seriousness of the covenant and the reality of His presence. The signs include thunder (literally, "voices") and lightning, a thick (literally, "heavy") cloud upon the mount and the voice of the *shofar* (שֹׁפָר) very loud.[36] The *shofar* was in addition to the *yovél*, or cornet used to assemble the people. There were also smoke and fire because the Lord descended upon the mount in fire. In verse 18 we read that the whole mount quaked, and so there was some sort of earthquake, as well.

We read here also that the smoke ascended "as the smoke of a *kivshán*" (הַכִּבְשָׁן) in verse 18. The word means specifically a "potter's oven." This is especially appropriate because the Israelites are on Mt. Sinai, the "mountain of my clays," where God is working on them as a Divine Potter. The Hebrew root gives us more insight about this matter. Gesenius shows us that the main verb from this root means, "to subdue or bring into bondage."[37] This reminds us of the Apostle Paul's favorite self-description (see Romans 1:1, etc): "Paul, the bond-servant (*doulos*, *δοῦλος*) of Jesus Christ." The New Covenant believer must see that he is being prepared to be a bond-servant of Jesus Christ, fully possessed by the Holy Spirit in every way, in order to be free from the bondage to self-exalting sin, which is such an abomination to the Lord.

The new believer needs to have a mindset to want to bring his whole self into total servitude to the Lord so that he can please Him in everything. Otherwise he is in bondage to the self-exalting flesh, which cannot please God. Either way, he will be a slave at the level of doing. His freedom lies in choosing his master—whether the flesh or the Lord Jesus, through the Holy Spirit. Romans 6 explains this paradox. Paul begins the chapter by explaining that the believer's old man has been crucified with Christ, "that the body of sin might be rendered inoperable (v.6, my translation)." "Rendered inoperable" is to be preferred as a translation of *katargethé* (*καταργηθῄ*). According to Bauer, the primary meaning of the verb is "make ineffective, powerless, or idle," and the base verb argéo (*ἀργέω*) means "be idle."[38] Our death, burial, and resurrection with Christ have rendered our body of sin inoperable, but there is still a battle.

What is the battle that remains for the believer? He must decide consciously to yield his members to God for the Holy Spirit to have full control in his life. Otherwise, he has yielded them to sin, and they will obey the dictates of the flesh when the opportunity arises through temptation. The new believer needs to know, though, that the real goal of the Christian life is total control by the Holy Spirit, not self-actualization, as in the world. In fact, self-actualization is really the problem, not the solution. There was no greater lesson for Israel in preparing to receive the Old Covenant, and there is no greater lesson for a believer in Jesus Christ in order to understand the New Covenant he is already under.

5. The Summary of the Law. The fourth part of the ceremony of enactment of the Old Covenant was the giving of a summary of the Law. Since Israel was obligated by the covenant to obey everything that God told them to do, God could, and would surely be adding many things in the long history of relating to His covenant people. However, what was needed now was a summary of what was expected of the people under the covenant. This was both a protection for the people and a protection for God.

The Ten Commandments were a protection for the people because they knew basically what the Lord required of them. Every person could apply it to his own situation and have a relatively stable lifestyle and understanding of what God required of him under the covenant. They would not incur God's displeasure suddenly without knowing why. The commandments were a protection to God in that the people ratified them; and any punishment He meted out—whether to the individual or to the nation as a whole—would be understood and justified before them all. God could not be charged with wrongdoing because He enforced the covenant. Also, even the Gentiles would not have a bad opinion of God because He judged His own people. They would rather fear Him.

In Exodus 20, the Ten Commandments are given orally, though they are also later written on two stone tablets (Exodus 24:12), which were later kept in the Ark of the Covenant as testimony. The first four deal with the people's relation to God. They were not to have any other gods before the LORD. This does not mean that there could be a group of gods that the people dealt with, as long as Jehovah was at the head of the line. Rather, it means, literally (my translation), "There shall not be for you other gods in addition to my face." This means that they were not to recognize or treat any other god as god for them, except for Jehovah alone. They knew that there were other gods. The word *elohim* as gods exists in Scripture in many places, and refers to angels in contrast to Jehovah in Psalm 97:7: "Worship Him (Jehovah) all you *elohim* (angels)." However, they were not to deal directly with any of these *elohim* or attribute to them any power, compared to the power of Jehovah. Neither were they to bow down to nor serve the images of these rebellious angels, as the second commandment says.

The third commandment is not to take the name of the Lord in vain. This preserves the reverential respect for Jehovah alone that they are to have under the Old Covenant. Finally, the fourth is to keep the Sabbath, which would be like their special actions to receive the Lord for the covenant ceremony, only every week. Obedience to this commandment would teach them to show their respect and worship of God by setting apart one day per week to obey Him by resting. Each time they rested on the seventh day of the week, they were reminded that God is ruling in His universe, and that they were resting because they were under His authority. Also, they were following His example, since He rested on the seventh day of creation. Thus the first four commandments have to do with the first and great commandment, which was to be given in Deuteronomy 6:5, about forty years later at the end of the wilderness wanderings: "You shall love the LORD your God with all your heart and with all your soul and with all your might."

The last six commandments deal with what will be the second great commandment soon to be given as Leviticus 19:18: "you shall love your neighbor as yourself; I am the LORD." These are designed to instruct people to treat others, as well as themselves, with love. They are: 5. Honor your father and mother, 6. You shall not murder (a better translation of the Hebrew than the King James' "Thou shalt not kill."), 7. You shall not commit adultery, 8. You shall not steal, 9. You shall not bear false witness, and 10. You shall not covet.

The True God seeks what is best for each person from God's point of view, which results in the best thing overall for everyone individually and society as a whole. As a result, God promises His blessings for obedience and curses for disobedience. There is a natural dynamic built into the blessings and curses, in addition to God's Divine intervention in weather, sickness, war, etc. If we accept to limit ourselves in these areas, we give to others the blessings we would like to enjoy from them. As we honor our parents, we teach our children to honor us when we are older. As we refrain from taking the life of other people for our benefit in any matter, we give them the freedom to live—and that without fear—the same we receive from them, and all society benefits.

There are other benefits for society, as well. As we restrict all sexual expression to a strictly monogamous heterosexual relationship, avoiding sexual relations before marriage (fornication), and outside of marriage (adultery), we protect each other from sexually transmitted diseases, and we form strong marriages with clearly defined sexual roles. Both restrictions have a special benefit for us, for our children, and for society in general. If everyone in society were to avoid fornication and adultery for one or two generations, all sexually transmitted diseases would disappear. In our generation, however, they have multiplied from two when I was in high school (syphilis and gonorrhea) to 23, including AIDS today.

Also, we are bringing up a generation of kids spaced out and psychologically crippled because of inadequate family ministry—yes, ministry. In the absence of a proper father figure and mother figure and also the sexual role redefining in society, there is a sharp increase in all crime, suicide, gender disorders (such as homosexuality and lesbianism), and a generally unteachable attitude among students in our schools.

In my school days, a threat to report bad behavior was sufficient to effect immediate order in the classroom. Almost no mothers worked outside the home, and they would be at the school very quickly to take an unruly child home, only to face his father's strict attention and discipline in the evening. Learning was serious business, and everyone knew that the real truth was "out there," and we had to seek it and change into conformity with it. Now sexual roles are seen as self-constructed for self-fulfillment, with "educators" there to provide a myriad of "equally valid lifestyles" as alternatives. Each person is seen as god for himself, but what a poor and pathetic god he is—lonely, rejected, confused, and abandoned! How beautiful in contrast are God's words for children to honor parents and for parents to portray the right role models for their children and succeeding generations.

God also told the Israelites not to steal. Stealing only benefits the thief on a short-term basis, and hurts the victim. After the thief is caught, he is publicly disgraced, in addition to the requirement to make restitution double or fourfold, according to what was stolen. What benefits would there be to society if nobody stole anything! There would be no need to buy expensive alarms, locks, of safes, and no need for security agents in stores, housing developments, or businesses. With the extra money not spent on these things businesses could lower prices and people would have more money to spend on things to generate more productive jobs. "You shall not steal" is the freedom to have property rights that we give each other by loving each other as ourselves.

Also, God forbad His people all lying. "You shall not bear false witness" prohibits all lying. People often lie for immediate personal advantage in a situation; but in the long run, losing their credibility hurts more than any short-term gain. It is obvious that the person lied to would benefit more by hearing the truth. Access to the truth is a blessing we give others by always telling the truth ourselves.

Finally, God says, "You shall not covet." This is the only commandment that is fulfilled or broken totally within the heart of the person, and visible only to that person and God. However, coveting, if allowed to continue, usually gives rise to the other visible social evils, such as murder, adultery, stealing, and lying. Our satisfaction with our portion in life, and willingness to ask God for things needed and to wait upon Him in everything is national peace and prosperity, and our gift to others' well-being and security.

As God gives the Ten Commandments, He gives the Israelites a social plan for the nation, cast in ten calls for personal morality, which will transform the people. They are the greatest blessings because they are blessings that we give others, as we love them as ourselves. The benefits are for everyone for a greater good than anyone can achieve on his own by trampling on others. Praise the Lord for His blessings! As the Israelites understand these Ten Commandments, they know the content of the program, or *shtick*, of the particular God they are receiving in the covenant relation, and they know what they are committing themselves to. These commandments then become binding on all in the nation, and the tablets are eventually stored in the Ark of the Covenant as a permanent testimony between God and His Chosen People.

The fifth and final element of the ceremony is the people's reaction and ratification. The immediate reaction of the people is found in Exodus 20:18-21. They stood afar off trembling at the thunder, lightning, noise of the trumpet, and the smoking mountain. They promised to obey what God said, but did not want to approach the mountain for fear of death. Then Moses gives the reason for the scary signs in verse 20: "Do not be afraid; for God has come in order to test you, and in order that the fear of Him may remain with you, so that you may not sin." In other words, God was showing some of His power in order that the Israelites might see His glory and fear Him and be afraid to sin later, when things were calm and they did not see Him.

Ten steps in the ratification ceremony of Exodus 24. Next come three chapters of Divinely decreed legal precedents in chapters 21-23. The word in Hebrew in the singular is מִשְׁפָּט, and comes from the root שׁפט, from which comes the word שׁוֹפֵט, or judge.[39] After these chapters of diverse "judgments," they are ready for the ratification ceremony in Exodus, chapter 24.

The first step: Moses tells all God's words. In verse three, we read "Moses came and recounted to the people also the words of the LORD, and all the ordinances." It was important that Israel know formally what requirements were being made of them under the covenant so that their decision to receive the covenant was not through ignorance. There would be no bad surprises later that would make them change their minds about the covenant.

It is important also that people know what they are getting into by receiving Jesus as their Savior. Jesus tells us to "count the cost" before deciding to follow Him in Luke 14:25-33. He says that He demands that a man love Him above his own life, his family, and friends, and take up his cross and follow him. This means to be dead to what your own desires are and to present yourself so God's Spirit can take over control completely of your life. God is not looking for independent self-worshipping gods to vote for Him to be President of the Universe, so they can get a kickback in favors from Him later as they do their own thing, He is King of the Universe with right to full worship from every created being, and the only one worthy to be sovereign and determine what we should do. Our receiving of the New Covenant is the only reasonable thing we can do in the light of this truth.

The second step: The people formally commit themselves. The second step to the covenant enactment ceremony is in the last part of Exodus 24:3: "All the people answered with one voice and said, 'All the words which the Lord has spoken we will do!'" The children of Israel individually and collectively accepted the covenant just as God offered it with no modifications. We are in no position to dicker with God concerning the provisions of the particular covenant that He offers us. We simply accept it or reject it. Here all Israel as a whole and every Israelite in particular received this covenant. It was now to be binding on every one of them, and on all their subsequent generations.

The third step: a written copy of God's words. The third step to the enactment of the covenant was the making of a written copy of all the words of the Lord (v.4A). It is important to understand that communication is made through words, not general ideas, and the inspiration of the Bible goes down to the very words through which the revelation came. Jesus even goes beyond this in Matthew 5:18: "Till heaven and earth pass, one jot (the smallest Hebrew letter yod) or one tittle (the smallest part of a letter that makes distinctions between Hebrew letters, such as dalet and resh, beth and caph, and vav and zayin) shall in no wise pass from the Law, till all be fulfilled" (AV). The Israelites are responsible to know and obey all the words of the covenant, and so they are given a written copy at this stage. Later, of course, many copies would be made so that the leaders could know for themselves and teach the people. Any subsequent revelation given by God would not contradict what was already given, and any comments by men would have no weight in themselves, but would only have value as they explained the revelation of God.

Fourth step: construction of an altar. Next, Moses built an altar at the bottom of Mount Sinai (v.4B) with twelve pillars, representing the twelve tribes of Israel. The altar was needed for sacrifices. All covenants required sacrifices in order to be enacted, and this was not an exception.

Fifth step: animal sacrifices. Next, the Israelites sacrificed on the altar burnt offerings and peace offerings of oxen to the Lord (v.5). This represented the devotedness of the Israelites to the Lord.

Also, in Hebrew there is no expression "to make a covenant," as is often translated. The word used is "to cut a covenant." The "cutting" is done in the sacrifice that is made to enact the covenant. For Christians, Jesus is both the covenant mediator (in the same place as Moses) and the sacrifice, in that the thorns, lance, and nails of the Romans cut Him.

Sixth Step: the application of the blood. The sixth step was for the blood to be applied to the two parties of the covenant. Moses poured half of the blood on the altar, representing the Lord, and put the other half of the blood in basins for later use on the people (v.6). Again, the same truth was fulfilled in Jesus for the New Covenant believer. Jesus sprinkled His blood on us (Hebrews 12:24), and on the altar in heaven (Hebrews 9:12). God first obligated Himself as covenant provider, and then, as we received Jesus, we came under the sprinkling and covenant. The blood has already been applied in heaven since the day of Jesus' resurrection from the dead. It is applied to us at the point of time when we receive Jesus as our personal Savior. By the time we are at the equivalent of Mt. Sinai as New Covenant believers, we are learning about what we have already received in Christ at conversion in preparation for living the New Covenant life under God.

Seventh step: the reading and acceptance of the book of the covenant. The seventh step in verse 7 was for Moses to read the entire book of the words of the Lord up to that time, to which they responded, "All that the Lord has spoken we will do, and we will be obedient!" By this statement they officially accepted the covenant, and became legally bound. God had already committed Himself by offering the covenant, and the blood had been thrown on the altar, representing Him, as testimony of His acceptance.

The eighth step: sprinkling the blood on the people. The eighth step was for Moses to sprinkle the remaining half of the blood, which had been collected in basins, on the people. While he did this in verse 8 he said, "Behold the blood of the covenant, which the

Lord has made (literally, *cut*) with you in accordance with all these words." This made the enactment officially binding on the people.

The ninth step: a commemorative meal. The ninth step is a commemorative meal in verses 9-11. It is interesting that the word for covenant (בְּרִית) comes from a Hebrew root with several meanings, according to Gesenius. One meaning he cites is "to bind, or fetter," in that both sides are bound to fulfill it. However, this is only from the Assyrian cognate language. The parallel Aramaic word also means covenant, as translated by the Greek *diathéke* (διαθήκη) and Latin *constitutio*, from which our word constitution comes. However, as Gesenius' work shows, the only use of this root in Hebrew is a verb meaning "to eat," and two different words that mean food.[40] Thus, celebrating the covenant is related to eating and drinking, as Jewish people do today in the Passover celebration, and Christians do at the Communion service.

In verse eleven it is said of Moses, Aaron, and the seventy elders of Israel, "they saw God, and they ate and drank." Here, I believe, in the light of the problem of nobody being able to see God and live, they either saw Jesus or the eating and drinking was seen as beholding God. If the former is the case, it is a pre-incarnate appearance of Jesus. However, if the latter is the case, we have an interesting parallel with the account of the disciples whom Jesus met on the road to Emmaus the day of his resurrection in Luke 24: 13-35. Verses 30, 31, and 35 put together an interesting connection. In verses 30 and 31 we read: "When He had reclined at the table with them, He took the bread and blessed it, and braking it, He began giving it to them. Then their eyes were opened and they recognized Him; and He vanished from their sight."

Here it was the breaking of the bread with Jesus that opened their eyes to recognize Him and really "see" him. They realized this and ran all the way back to Jerusalem and announced the news to the 11 remaining apostles, along with other believers (v. 35), "They began to relate their experiences on the road and *how He was recognized by them in the breaking of the bread.*" It is significant that eating is from the same root as the word covenant, and that the elders of Israel in Exodus 24:11 "saw God, and they ate and drank." It is also significant that the disciples who met Jesus on the road to Emmaus recognized Jesus specifically in the breaking of bread with Him, and then told the others "how He was recognized by them in the breaking of the bread."

When we celebrate the Lord's Table, we also break bread with the Lord, and we can see Him more clearly then, as well. It is eating that is a celebration of the covenant, even as the word covenant and one word for eating are from the same root in Hebrew. Today, the Jewish Passover celebration is a celebration of the covenant that God "cut" with Israel, and the Lord's Table is the celebration of the New Covenant, which Christians participate in.

The "cutting" produces blood and food. The blood was sprinkled on the two parties of the covenant, and the food of the bodies of the animals was eaten. For the Christian, Jesus' teaches that His flesh is meat, and His blood is drink, for He is the sacrifice, as well. In John 6:53 Jesus says, "Unless you eat the flesh of the Son of Man and drink His blood, you have no life in yourselves." These terms are in reference to their function, the last statement refers to being dead in trespasses and sins, and outside of the New Covenant. It is eating and drinking that refers to our being in this covenant relation with God through Christ Jesus, and, our eating and drinking with Jesus opens our eyes to understand God better. This may be behind Luther's teaching that Christ is present "by, with, and under the elements of the Eucharist."

The tenth step: the meeting on the top of Mt. Sinai. The tenth step to the covenant enactment ceremony on Mt. Sinai is God's bringing Moses up to the top of Mt. Sinai to receive the materials of the covenant that God wrote with His own hand. The materials are described in the following way (Exodus 24:12): "I will give you the stone tablets with the law and the commandment which I have written for their instruction." The Hebrew of the last phrase could equally read "in order to teach them," meaning "in order for Me (God) to teach them."

The first of the three things God wrote with His own hand were the tables of stone. Almost all scholars believe that these contained the Ten Commandments, and most people think that this is all of the written material that God gave Moses. However, God says He also wrote "the Torah (Hebrew *hattoráh*)," here translated "the law" in the NASV. The reading "the Torah" or "the law," is to be preferred, following the Hebrew, the Samaritan Pentateuch, and the Septuagint, over "a law" in the AV. There is a definite article in front of the word in all early sources, hence the favorite Jewish title for all five books of Moses: "the Torah" (*Hattoráh*, or הַתּוֹרָה).

The last of the three things that God left written with His own hand, according to Exodus 24:12 was rendered "commandment" in the NASV. Here the Hebrew word is *ve-hammitzváh*, literally, "and the commandment." It is singular, not plural, in the Hebrew, though the Septuagint has the variant plural reading "and the commandments" (*kai tas entolás*, καὶ τὰς ἐντολάς), reading as the AV. It appears that God wrote down a considerable body of material with His own hand, and did not just rely on Moses to take down dictation at this point. According to Exodus 24:4, Moses had written much down by himself earlier. We will never know exactly how much of the Scripture here the Lord actually wrote with His own hand, but it appears to have been considerably more than just the Ten Commandments.

III. The Main Difference Between the Covenants: Law and Grace.

While it is relatively easy to point up provisions for law and grace in both the Old Covenant and the New Covenant, there is a major difference in the way that this difference is to be treated. Representing Covenant Theology, John Calvin emphasized the continuity. For him, there was a difference in the treatments of law and grace between the Old Covenant and the New Covenant, but, he says, "all men adopted by God into the company of His people since the beginning of the world were covenanted to Him by the same law and by the bond of the same doctrine as obtains among us."[41] This means that the differences between the application of law and grace are relatively insignificant.

He states further that the Old Covenant believer was bound to the covenant by the mercy of God alone without merit: "The covenant by which they were bound to the Lord was supported, not by their own merits, but solely by the mercy of the God who called them."[42] Thus, Calvin thought that the Old Covenant believer had hope of eternal life solely on the basis of God's mercy.

It is not disputed that God's mercy was necessary for atonement and a right relation with God under the Old Covenant, but it was hardly the only thing, as in the New Covenant. There were certain rules in the Old Covenant, the breaking of which led to being cut off from Israel. All of the faith of the individual and all of the mercy of God given previously, and the covenant eternal life that the believer was confident of earlier could be lost by committing certain sins. In Ezekiel 18:21-24, the condition in which one ends his life appears to be the determining factor where he goes after death: "But if the wicked man turns from all his sins which he has committed and observes all My statutes, and practices justice and righteousness, he shall surely live; he shall not die. All his transgressions which he has committed will not be remembered against him; *because of his righteousness which he has practiced, he will live.*"

The opposite is true of the believer that turns away from God (v.24): "But when a righteous man turns away from his righteousness, commits iniquity and does according to all the abominations that a wicked man does, will he live? All his righteous deeds which he has done shall not be remembered for his treachery which he has committed and his sin which he has committed; *for them he will die.*"

This last expression, "for them (his sins) he will die," is the equivalent of Jesus' statement (John 8:24), "Unless you believe that I am He, you will die in your sins." This is the equivalent of saying that they were going to hell. But in what does the Old Testament believer live? In grace? In Christ? No. As we see above, the repentant sinner that is reconciled to God lives somewhere else: *in his righteousness that he hath done he shall live.* This implies a certain focus on the Law in the life of the believer of the Old Covenant that is absent in the life of the believer of the New Covenant. There is a different relation to the law.

The best explanation that I have found about the differences between the Old Covenant and the New Covenant does not see just one covenant from the Garden of Eden with occasional minor modifications in subsequent generations, as John Calvin alluded to above, but rather allows for greater differences in content and separate covenants at different periods of human history. These changes in the covenants are not due to some changing nature of God Who never changes, but rather to the changing circumstances of the people with whom God "cut" the covenants.

There is a special difference between the Old Covenant and the New Covenant over the difference in the treatment of law and grace. In his book, *Grace: The Glorious Theme*, Dr. Louis Sperry Chafer explains three spheres of dominion under which a person may be: under Law (unbelieving Israel), under Grace (the church), and under Sin (the unbelieving Gentiles). He establishes that the Israelite is under the Law. Few scholars will dispute this. He next recognizes that only unbelieving Gentiles are under sin, and then addresses the issue of whether the believing Christian is under Law. He continues: "The issue is, therefore, between law and grace as governing principles in the life of the Christian. Must Christians turn to the Decalogue for a basis of divine government in their daily lives? Scripture answers this question with a positive assertion: "Ye are not under the law, but under grace."[43]

We must understand, therefore, the differences between being under law and under grace in order to understand the covenants better, as well as to make a more precise application of the Old Covenant truths to the Christian life, as is the purpose of this chapter, but Chafer takes his case even farther: the two principles of law and grace cannot be mixed. "By such co-mingling of opposing principles, all that is vital in each system is sacrificed. On the one hand, the sharp edge of the law, which constitutes its sole effectiveness, is dulled by an admixture of supposed divine leniency; on the other hand, the truth concerning the absolute graciousness of God is corrupted by being commercialized, conditioned on the merit of man, and made subject to the persuasion of man. ... God is never reluctant in the exercise of grace: instead, He seeks, draws, and entreats man. The principles of law and grace are mutually destructive, and doctrinal confusion follows the intrusion of any legal principal unto the reign of grace."[44]

So we see that the principle of law governs Israel in the sphere of this world, where their national life and history are lived, and the principle of grace governs in the church, in the sphere of the world to come. For we pass through Jesus' death, burial, and resurrection into the world to come, even though we are still present in this world externally. We are born again. Though there are similarities between the two spheres of operation—law for this world and grace for the world to come—the differences force us to modify the perceptual model of Israel's history in its application to the life of the New Covenant believer, even as I have made some observations already.

Conclusion: Some Modifications of the Old Covenant Truths are needed For Application to the New Covenant Believer's Life.

The differences between living under the grace principle and living under the law principle necessitate adjustments in applying the truths of the Old Covenant life of Israel and the New Covenant applications for doctrinal understanding. First of all, under grace, the believer begins lost and must accept Jesus as his savior before he can have any standing before God. The Old Covenant believer was born under the law and had the privileges of the covenant by virtue of birth to Israelite parents.

The New Covenant believer, upon receiving Jesus as his Savior, receives with Jesus every blessing of the New covenant without further decision and apart from the issue of merit. The Old Testament believer lived with the real possibility of "being cut off from his people," and "dying in his sins." This gave the law a real edge in its power over him, for he could be cut off from the covenant. This word "to cut off" is the same verb in Hebrew that describes God as cutting the covenant in the first place.

Thus, there is one conditional element and one unconditional element in each covenant, but they are reversed. Under the Old Covenant, one was born unconditionally under the covenant by virtue of his birth to Israelite parents. However, he could be cut off from the covenant by turning his back on the law and disobeying God. His position within the blessings of the covenant was conditional and could be lost. On the other hand, no one can be born under the

New Covenant. Everyone is born a Jew or a Gentile, but nobody is born a Christian, according to physical birth. It is 100% conditional upon one's acceptance of Jesus personally to enter into the New Covenant, but then something wonderful happens: one receives all of the blessings of the New Covenant right away, conditioned only on his choice to receive Jesus in the first place, and he can never be cut off. His permanence under the covenant is unconditionally guaranteed forever.

For the purposes of this chapter then, all of the items under discussion in Israel's history, from the Passover to and including Mt. Sinai, are all available to the Christian from the moment he accepts Jesus as his Savior, along with other blessings mentioned for him later in this book.. However, though every blessing in the New Covenant is there and available to the believer from the moment that he receives Jesus, his ability to enjoy them is not. To enjoy them he must learn about them, and then appropriate them through faith.

Thus, at conversion, the New Covenant believer already has everything. The sequence of the Old Testament events and the lessons learned then form an excellent chronology for learning about the manifold grace of God available in Christ at conversion, so that he can apply it to his life progressively through faith. It represents the learning steps to understand what he has from the beginning in Christ.

Our conversion corresponds to Passover and Baptism to the crossing of the Reed Sea. Israel's seven lessons in the desert in preparation to enter into covenant with the Lord represent seven lessons Christians need to learn to prepare us to understand the New Covenant we are already under, which was received along with the "blood of the lamb" at our conversion (the equivalent of way back in Egypt).

The lessons at Mt. Sinai also need to be modified in the light of the differences in the covenants. New believers need the historical perspective of the "Eagles' wings" speech (exodus 19) to understand of God's love for them in reaching out to them and cutting the New Covenant, which they already have. All of the covenant ceremony preparations of Israel instruct the New Covenant believer to love and serve the Lord and sanctify himself for service because he already has received the covenant, not in order to receive it. The scary signs shown to Israel should instruct the New Covenant believer that, if God was that harsh with Israel under the law, how much stricter is He in His demands under the New Covenant (see Hebrews 10:26-31)!

If the 10 commandments instruct the Old Covenant believer about God's standards, how much more does our direct knowledge of God's Holy Spirit instruct us about God's Person, which should be expressed through our whole being! If the 10 commandments are to be observed in the energy of the flesh, how much more should the New Covenant believer depend on the power of the Holy Spirit to live through him the only possible fulfillment of God's much greater expectations under grace!

If the blood of the lamb in Egypt did not end sacrifices for Israel, but only led to a continuous daily sacrifice, how much more should the New Covenant believer seek the daily applications of the once-and-for-all sacrifice of Jesus! If the cutting of the sacrifice resulted in the sprinkling of blood on the altar and on the Israelites, as well as their eating and drinking together with God under their covenant, how much more should we rejoice that the cutting of the body of Jesus resulted in our being sprinkled once-and-for-all with the blood of Jesus, as well as daily for cleansing, and also our eating and drinking together as a church with God at the Lord's table, remembering His body and blood. As the eating and drinking of the elders of Israel led to their "seeing God," How much more should our eating Jesus' flesh and drinking His blood at the Lord's Table result in our "seeing God!"

Israel arrived at Mt. Sinai, which means "Mount of My Clays," where God, as Divine Potter began to work on them to transform them to be like Him through the giving of the Law, and the whole mountain smoked like a potter's oven. The New Covenant believer is born again and made dead to the world and alive in Jesus as a new creation in order to be transformed by the direct intervention of the same Holy Spirit that hovered over and supervised the creation of this world in Genesis 1:2. He also works all things out for good so that we will be made in the image of Christ (Romans 8:28-29). How much better is the image of Christ than some moral laws that people are trying to observe in the energy of the flesh in order to begin to be what God wants on the outside!

The Israelites said, "All that the Lord says, that we will do." Then they failed to do it, generation after generation. The New Covenant believer says, "I believe in Jesus, and identify with Him in His death, burial, and resurrection." Then he takes his seat in heavenly places, and Jesus lives out His life in the believer's body down here. Hallelujah! There is always a point that corresponds, but it means something a bit different to us who are under grace in the World to Come. Praise God!

In this study we see the special blessings of the Lord to Israel in their application to believers under the New Covenant from the crossing of the Reed Sea until the establishment of the covenant at Mt. Sinai. We have also applied them to the life of the New Covenant believer, making needed modifications to take into account the different natures of the two covenants, as well as the differences between life in This World and life in the World To Come.

At Sinai there are three more topics that need to be addressed. The second topic will be the topic of the sacrifices at Mt. Sinai and the Christian's riches through Christ's sacrifice seen in the light of the sacrifices in Leviticus. The third topic will be access to God under the tabernacle as a pattern for the Christian's access to God each day in our daily devotional time. Finally, we will consider the manifold guidance of God through the diverse laws given at Mt. Sinai and their relation to our being led personally by the Spirit of God.

Chapter 7

Mt. Sinai I: The Believer's Riches in Jesus' Sacrifice: God's Provision for Continuous Cleansing And Fellowship with Him

After the Israelites cross the Reed Sea (not Red Sea, according to the Hebrew), they wend their way in stages southward, ending up in the Desert of Sinai before Mt. Sinai. Here they pass almost a year learning valuable lessons about their relation to God and each other. After the Christian accepts Jesus and is baptized, he also needs to learn lessons about cultivating his relation with God and other believers. So it is that Mt. Sinai provides many lessons for the New Testament believer, as well as the Israelites that stood before Moses. As in the previous chapter, we see that the Israelites are preparing to implement different provisions of the covenant, while the Christian at this stage is learning about what he already has received in Christ. Again, the different provisions of the Old Covenant here correspond to blessings of the New Covenant. However, though the Old Covenant believer is seeking to enter in to the covenantal provisions here, the New Covenant believer is preparing to discover what he already has received through receiving Jesus as his personal Savior.

The Bible passages during this sojourn before Mt. Sinai (Exodus 19:1—Numbers 10:11) can be grouped into three major categories: the Sacrifices, the Tabernacle, and Diverse laws. We will consider them in chapters 7, 8, and 9, respectively. For the Christian these three categories of God's revelation are important in the following ways: the sacrifices show the external form of the many facets of the sacrifice of Jesus and its application to our lives, blessing us in our relation to God and to others. The tabernacle shows us the external form of the 7 steps that the believer can follow to approach God in his personal devotional time each day: the door, the bronze altar, the bronze laver, the bread of the presence, the lampstand, the altar of incense, and the Ark of the Covenant with the Mercy Seat. Of course, the diverse laws about how to get along with others in a society have been the foundation of our legal system in the United States, as well as yielding the good principles of the Judaeo-Christian ethic to get along with one another even today. We will also see why the Christian is not under the Old Testament Laws once he believes in Jesus.

Before we get to the main topic of this chapter, which is the relation of the sacrifices in Leviticus to Jesus' sacrifice for us, it is necessary to understand the place and the purpose of he Law of Moses for Old Testament Israel, as well as Jesus' commandments for the New Testament believer.

If the Israelites could have been saved by keeping the Law, then the Lord would have given them the Law when they were in Egypt. Everyone, then, who kept the Law, could leave Egypt, and everyone who did not keep the Law would not have been allowed to leave Egypt. The Law did not save the Israelites—they were saved by the blood of the lamb, sprinkled on the doorposts of their homes. Then they were baptized into Moses in the crossing of the Reed Sea (I Corinthians 10:2). They were set at liberty in the desert, and came before Mount Sinai, where they said unanimously, "All that the LORD has spoken we will do (Exodus 19:8)." Then the Lord gave them the Law through Moses, His mediator.

If we understand the passage in Hebrew, we have a beautiful picture of what was happening there. As we saw in the previous chapter,[1] the word <u>sin</u> is an Egyptian word for clay, and the ending <u>ay</u> is the plural form with a first person singular pronoun, here showing possession. Thus, a good translation for Sinai is "My Clays." To continue the scenario of the Divine Potter and Israel, His clays, in verse 18 of Exodus 19 we read "its smoke ascended like the smoke of a furnace." The word translated furnace here is kivshan, which means specifically a kiln, used for pottery. This kiln is from the verb *kavash*, which means to subdue or bring into bondage.[2] Israel needed to be worked by the Divine Potter and passed through the potter's oven to be subdued under Him. They were more Egyptians than Hebrews at this point, even as the word for clay, *sin*, is really an Egyptian word.

The Christian follows the same sequence. He is saved from the world by the blood of the Lamb, Jesus. Then he is baptized in water as testimony of his salvation experience. Then he is set at liberty in the desert, where he begins his Christian walk as an immature, or carnal, believer. Next he arrives to the place where the Lord Jesus says to him, "If you love me, you will keep my commandments (John 14:15)." If he then says as Israel (Exodus 19:8), "All that the Lord has spoken we will do," then he is ready for the Lord as the Heavenly Potter to begin working on him with His Divine Commandments.

These commandments of Christ are for discipleship—not for salvation. He doesn't say, "If you want to be saved, you will keep my commandments," He says, "If you love me, you will keep my commandments." In the same way, he says, "Whoever does not carry his own cross and come after Me cannot be My disciple (Luke 14:27)." He doesn't say, "Whoever does not bear his cross cannot be saved." If salvation corresponds to the Passover and Reed Sea crossing, seen as one event, then discipleship is presented here at Mt. Sinai, the Mountain of My Clays, as a statement of commitment to the Lord as Potter to mold and make and change the believer in preparation for a victorious life in the Spirit.

As the Divine Potter, God begins teaching Israel with the 10 commandments, along with various other laws. Secondly, there is a long teaching about the Tabernacle, and the Book of Exodus ends with the Tabernacle erected. The Book of Leviticus begins with 7 chapters on the various sacrifices, followed by the installation of Aaron as High Priest, and his sons with him. After various laws that priests are to administer, such as purification from leprosy and other uncleanness, there is a discussion of the various holidays, which are annual reminders of various things that God did for Israel.

The purpose of this chapter is to focus on the third section of the teachings at Mt. Sinai: the Christian's riches through Christ's sacrifice seen in the light of the sacrifices in Leviticus, chapters 1-7. It is important to see the Old Testament sacrifices as each presenting different aspects of Jesus' atonement, as it is applied to the believer for both salvation and sanctification. For the purposes of this paper, we will apply the sacrifices in the order that they really are applied to the New Testament believer, and not in the order of Leviticus. We will consider first the trespass offering, the sin offering, the whole burnt offering, the grain offering, and, finally, the peace offering in that order.

When the worshipper puts his hand on the head of the offering, a change of identities takes place: the offering is treated as the worshipper deserves to be treated, and the worshipper is treated as the offering deserves to be treated. The first two offerings we will deal with here show that the believer's sin and sin nature have been transferred to Jesus by faith, corresponding to the trespass and the sin offering. The next two offerings, the whole burnt offering and the grain offering, show how Jesus' perfect nature and actions, including perfect fulfillment of all obligations toward God and fellow men, are transferred to the believer by God's reckoning. The peace offering is the celebration of the perfection of Jesus' sacrifice as it unites God and all believers together in the church. We will start with the sacrifices that show that our acts of sin (trespass offering) and sin nature (sin offering) have been removed in Christ.

I. The Trespass Offering (*asham*—Leviticus 5:1-6:7, & 7:1-7).

The first thing that an unbeliever notes in coming to faith in Jesus is his individual sins—the acts of sin that he has committed. Probably, as an unbeliever, he tried to cancel these out with good deeds. I believe that the most powerful lie of the Devil—one that sends more people to hell than all other lies combined—is that if one's good deeds outweigh his bad deeds, he will be acceptable to God. Unbelievers know nothing about the sin nature, and, therefore, only deal with the acts of sin, not the nature of sin from which they came. On this level the Lord Jesus actually does cover the penalty for our trespasses—the acts of sin that we have committed.

However, "the wages of sin is death (Romans 6:23)," not an equal and opposite good deed that supposedly cancels out the effects of the sin. Therefore, the New Covenant believer needs to understand first of all that the sacrifice of Jesus covered all of the sins that he has committed or ever will commit in one single act, without respect of time. As we consider the elements of the trespass offering, we will see how Jesus' sacrifice for sin, in fulfillment of the trespass offering, canceled out all of our sinful deeds ever committed in our whole lifetime.

The trespass offering (*asham*) is revealed in Leviticus 5:1 through 6:7 and chapter 7, verses 1-7. The trespass offering covers sins committed directly against God or sins committed directly against other human beings and therefore indirectly against God.

The passage begins with several possible circumstances in which a person may be found to have committed a sin against God or his fellow man. For example, his refusal to bear witness to someone's oath, when needed for a legal matter, results in guilt for the person refusing to testify. Also, the touching of any unclean person or animal, or other similar prohibitions in the Law is seen as a guilty act. Guilt is something that the person has to deal with. We all have done something that we knew was wrong and felt a heavy weight on our chest. We also have felt the weight removed when we "got it off of our chest" by confession and restitution. This sacrifice takes care of this level of human sin.

The first thing we note about the sacrifice itself is that the guilty person "shall confess that in which he has sinned (Leviticus 5:5)." We cannot get rid of sin unless we confess it as sin. Any self-justification, rationalization, projection onto others, and other defense mechanisms are strictly forbidden.

On the other hand, modern psychology sees each man as god for himself, and therefore, guilt as a negative emotion or energy representing the acceptance of the dictates of others. From this perspective, if one could only free himself from the demands of society, one would then be free of guilt. One such movement in psychology was Freudian psychoanalysis. Tal Brooke sums up psychoanalysis this way: "What psychoanalysis did offer to sophisticated society... was freedom from the dictates of the conscience and moral restriction. It offered sexual liberation to a world still under the dictates of moral propriety and Biblical moral law. Moral customs still created pangs of conscience; they still inhibited free expression. And liberated intellectuals were trying desperately to break down the doors of sexual "repression" and find a haven of free expression. Freud helped provide the door; but behind that door...was the deeper despair of determinism of man's lack of significance in a godless universe."[3]

If there is no God and each man is god for himself, then everything is all right for that man. For Freud sin does not exist. It is a deviation from the norms established by society and held in ignorance by fanatical devotion to religious myths, such as those found in the Bible. In Freud, man sees himself as autonomous from all illusions, such as religion, but he is also without meaning, and he has to construct it for himself. Man is free to make his own choices, but those choices are seen as determined by a mechanistic universe.

Psychology left the True God permanently out of the picture. This is the ultimate justification of any type of behavior, but it was achieved at a high cost. The resulting alienation from others (i.e. other gods) is painful, and the real guilt, which was imagined away, with the help of the psychoanalyst, surfaces again as free-floating anxiety, to be dealt with by a variety of tranquilizers, electric shocks, and drugs. Among the more insightful, there was the despair of being a meaningless god in a meaningless universe, choosing or inventing a religion or philosophy, which one knows us untrue, to help one get along, waiting for the certain death, which will obliterate one's existence. *Is there any reason to doubt why the Bible says that these people are lost?*

The other waves of psychology did not solve these problems, they only applied techniques to cure the wound of the people slightly, crying "peace, peace," when there was no peace. The behaviorists treated man as material only, and erased all morality. Behavior was to be modified by social engineers, not a free response to Divine decrees. Therefore there was no guilt, either, but great suffering under Communists in the East and Fabian socialists in the West, who have been trying their social experiments on society.

Rogerian psychology also tried to kill the conscience. This non-directive therapist said that every man (being a god to himself) had all the answers within and just needed someone to interact with so they would surface. As Brooke continues: "Respectability and conformity were limitations to radical human freedom that were carryovers from the old order. I was assured that human nature was basically good, so why be afraid to change?"[4]

While this teaching helped each person deal with the problem of their own guilt by repressing it, and declaring everything all right, it has a downside: the abolition of all morality. I have noticed that the vast majority of modern Jewish people are absolutely sold on these teachings. One time I was discussing the Bible with a Jewish man and he said the following to me, "If there exists a God so rotten that He would send anyone to burn forever in hell, I don't want to hear about such an evil God, and I don't want to know him. If He exists and I end up in hell, it will just prove how rotten He is. If, however, there exists a God Who is loving, He will send everyone to heaven, no matter what they do. Either way I don't need your message, so why don't you just bug off."

This was quite a shock to me, and I sent up a hurried prayer to God for a wise answer. I answered what He gave me, "Let's assume for a moment that you are right, and there exists a God that is all loving, and He sends everyone to heaven. You arrive there all happy to be in heaven and go to greet your neighbors. On the right is Adolph Hitler, on the left is Himmler, behind you are Goering, Goebels, and Eichmann. Across the street are Yasser Arafat, Haman (from the Book of Esther), and Saddam Hussein. Would you call that heaven?"

He became nervous and tried to elude the logical results of his beliefs. "**You** let everyone into heaven," I continued. "Now you have to live with them." He continued squirming in his seat while I concluded: "I think that if God sent all the people in the world to the same place, that would be hell, not heaven. All of us have the same wicked, self-serving nature that Adam and Eve had, and anyone of us could make heaven into hell for others. That is why the God of

Israel gave us His law and offers to change us. Only if He changes us can we live in heaven without making it into hell for someone else—or even for ourselves."

Still the modern psychologists seek to escape into spiritual experiences of heightened consciousness apart from conscience. The effort was still to transcend both guilt and conscience by oriental mysticism. When Dr. William Kirk Kirkpatrick attended the Fifth International Conference of Transpersonal Psychology in 1979, he was interviewing a typical psychologist there: "I asked if he thought there was anything of value in the Western tradition or in Christianity. 'Christianity,' he explained with an amused smile, 'makes people feel guilty; guilt is a crippling emotion. The others at the table nodded assent, and the psychologist settled comfortably back in his chair. It was an open and shut case."[5]

This is why God requires everyone to confess completely all of the sin that he has. Unlike modern psychologists, God has a remedy for it. God's remedy for guilt brings peace instead of anxiety, health instead of medicines, and order in society instead of chaos. Confession of our sin accepts all of the reality. It recognizes God's presence, His Law, our guilt, and the consequences that come as a result of that guilt. God has judged the penalty for even one sin to be that of death, and the death sentence must be executed.

His remedy is elaborated as God continues in Leviticus 5. The requirement is for a female lamb or goat from the flock. The animal is switched with the person. The sin of the person is transferred to the animal through faith, and the animal is killed in the place of the guilty person. This is a safe and realistic form of displacement of the guilt. God actually commands the Israelites to place their guilty deeds on an animal substitute, which is then executed in their place.

How does this solution work out for the person? First of all, he has to confess his sins, thus bringing him to the reality of what he has done. Next he brings a substitute animal and transfers the individual acts of sin to the animal. This is a public recognition that God loves him while hating his sin. Thirdly, he recognizes that what he did is worthy of death as he sees the priest kill the animal which has his acts of sin on it. Finally, the actual guilt is removed without avoiding justice, and so the believer can leave with a clear conscience, as well as a deeper love for the God Who provided this forgiveness. What a marvelous way for dealing with sin! "If we confess our sins, He is faithful **and righteous** to forgive us our sins and to cleanse us from all unrighteousness (I John 1:9)."

The New Covenant brings up full guilt to the maximum degree by raising the standard to that of Jesus himself. The psychologists are right in mentioning this fact. The Christian feels more and more of his guilt as he draws closer and closer to the Lord. However, there is grace, forgiveness, and healing to deal with that guilt and get rid of it. Though the psychologists try to reduce and avoid guilt, all they have is a false peace through rationalization, denial, anxiety, and, perhaps, drugs. As these false strategies for dealing with guilt fail, the guilt filters back through their psyche as generalized feelings of anxiety that cannot be treated.

The certainty of forgiveness for the believer gives us the boldness to face up to our failures and resulting guilt while not denying the seriousness of the offense or our own worth. ***At the same time, in Jesus, God hates our sins enough to declare the death penalty for even one sin, and God loves us enough to become a man and take our sins upon Himself and take that penalty of death for us. Thus we are simultaneously drawn to our own guilt and our own worth.*** Thus, guilt does not become a "crippling emotion" for the believer, but a reminder of God's love in taking our guilt and deserved death upon Himself, and another reminder of His love for us in doing it.

II. The Sin Offering (*hattat*—Leviticus 4:1-35, & 6:24-30)

While the trespass offering deals with our acts of sin, the sin offering deals with the sin nature, which gave rise to the acts of sin. When Jesus died on the cross, he not only died for the acts of sin that we committed, but he also died for the sin nature that we inherited from Adam. This sacrifice completes the two things that are transferred to Jesus in His High Priestly work for us: our sins and our sin nature.

I would like to use an analogy to explain the difference between the acts of sin and the sin nature, as well as why God is offended at the presence of the sin nature. It is as if we are born pigs at physical birth. Everything we do and think is self-centered and self-worshipping. All of the acts that we do—even our good deeds—are for self-glorification in some way, at least for the sake of earning our way into heaven, at best. All human religion is just a system for the natural pig to accumulate merits to earn his way into heaven. This self-glorification is the way to please God, according to the natural man, and it itself is a fault.

However, the natural man also has other worse faults. He squeals at the least provocation from others, and fights are common. His greatest delight is to wallow in the mud of unclean desires: the lusts of the flesh, the lusts of the eyes, and the pride of life (I John 2:15-17). The attendance at church is something to be endured if he even goes, for the worship of God may earn him some acceptance. God is totally displeased with this whole orientation of the unregenerate man, and no efforts of his to please God can be accepted because the pig himself is an abomination. We are reminded how the Old Testament declares pigs as unclean animals, and people became unclean by even touching one. This is apart from the question of whether the pig behaves well or not. The fact of its being a pig was enough to make it unacceptable before God.

When we accepted Jesus as our personal savior, God killed the old pig and resurrected him a new creation: a humble lamb—DNA and all. As II Corinthians 5:17 says: "Therefore if anyone is in Christ, he is a new creature: the old things passed away; behold new things have come." At that point of time, the believer has all the nature and capacity of the lamb, but all the habits of the old pig.

When Jesus died on the cross, the nature of the pig died with him, and the lamb nature is what is transferred to the believer by faith, symbolized by the burnt offering, which we will consider later. After conversion, the carnal believer continues to think that he is still a pig, and therefore yields to the old habits of the pig. *However, now he is a lamb who is acting like a pig*. God is pleased with the "lambness" (the lamb nature) of the new lamb, but not the "pig acts" it is still doing. The process of sanctification is then the process of getting a lamb to act like a lamb because he is now a lamb, instead of a pig.

The sacrifice is carried out in a similar fashion to that of the trespass offering: the offering for a common person is a female of the flock, representing them in the subservient role as a failure before God. Also, something is removed from the offerer, instead of added to the offerer: the sinful deeds (in the case of the trespass offering), and the sinful nature (in the case of the sin offering).

There are also differences between the two offerings: first of all, the offering is killed by the offerer, instead of the priest, as in the trespass offering. Also, some of the blood is sprinkled before the veil of the sanctuary and put on the horns of the altar of incense before the rest is poured out at the bottom of the bronze altar. Thirdly, there is no restitution to be paid to God or to our fellow man in this offering, as it is the acts of sin, not the nature producing them, which require restitution. In addition, the whole animal is burned and none is eaten. This represents the fact that our old nature is good for nothing and for nobody, while God and others can receive something from our restitution for our evil deeds.

III. The Whole Burnt Offering (*olah*—Leviticus 1:1-17, 6:8-13).

The sacrifice that is the complement of the sin offering is the whole burnt offering. While the sin offering transfers our sin nature to Jesus, so that Jesus died for our sin nature, the whole burnt offering transfers Jesus' perfect nature in fulfillment of everything that God the Father requires of a person on earth to the believer.

As the whole burnt offering is wholly given up to the fire, so Jesus' life was wholly given up to do the Father's will to be burning with the Holy Spirit. Jesus said (John 5:19): "The Son can do nothing of Himself, unless it is something He sees the Father doing; for whatever the Father does, these things the Son also does in like manner." This would be a blasphemous statement if it were not true. However, the Father's appraisal of Jesus is exactly the same. At Jesus' baptism, as well as the Transfiguration, the Father's voice calls out from heaven and says (Matthew 3:17, 17:5): "This is My beloved Son, in whom I am well-pleased."

The sacrifice of the burnt offering brings that statement of the Father to be His evaluation of every believer in Jesus because the life that the Father judged acceptable in these words is reckoned to be the believer's life. Also, in the practical day-to-day living, this righteous living is available to be lived out through the believer by faith. Thus, in fulfillment of this sacrifice, Jesus can live out His righteous life through the believer.

We will first discuss the requirements of this sacrifice, and then its effect on the believer. In Leviticus 1 the instructions for this sacrifice are given. First of all, the sacrifice must be a male without blemish. We know that Jesus was among men the only one without sin. Concerning all sons of Adam, the Lord judges the following (Psalm 14:2-3, 53:2-3), "The LORD has looked down from heaven upon the sons of men (literally, "the sons of Adam") to see if there are any who understand, who seek after God. They have all turned aside, together they have become corrupt; there is no one who does good, not even one." Does this then mean that Jesus also had sin? No! Jesus is not a son of Adam because the father, not the mother, counts in mixed marriages.

Concerning Jesus, we read in Isaiah 53:9: "He had done no violence, nor was there any deceit in His mouth." Jesus had a totally different quality of life than that which we inherited from Adam. When Jesus came to earth born of Mary, God said (Matthew 1:20): "the Child who has been conceived in her is of the Holy Spirit." The burnt offering shows us how that different quality of life is transferred to the believer by faith—both in reckoning for salvation and for empowering for daily living.

Another requirement is that the believer offer the burnt offering "of his own voluntary will (Leviticus 1:3, AV)." Nobody can choose for us. We can be saved without understanding the lordship of Jesus Christ in our lives (through the trespass and the sin offerings), but we cannot be the Lord's disciples until we approach him by our own will and voluntarily surrender to his lordship. Jesus' offering, in fulfillment of the burnt offering, was his body. Jesus says in Hebrews 10:5-7: "Sacrifice and offering You have not desired, but a body you have prepared for me; In *whole burnt offerings* and sacrifices for sin You have taken no pleasure. Then I said, "Behold, I have come (in the scroll of the book it is written of Me) to do Your will, O God."

What does Jesus say here? He says that the true burnt offering would be his body totally given over to the fire of the Holy Spirit like the burnt offering was wholly given over to the fire. This obedience counts for the believer through his identification with Christ in his sacrifice. Here we need to deal with the subject of shame. As the trespass offering takes care of guilt and restitution, the sin offering and the burnt offering take away shame and replace it with acceptance. The sin offering removes our sin nature, transferring it to Jesus, and the burnt offering transfers Jesus' perfect obedience to us, thus dealing with our shame.

Guilt is something real and objective, received because of wrong deeds, and is dealt with by restitution. Shame is much more diffuse and difficult to deal with. It is the failure to live up to a role model. Shame can be felt even when nothing wrong has been done. Shame is the pig surrounded by lambs, excluded from the Temple because he is "unkosher," while the others enter. He is rejected and poked away with poles, lest someone touch him and become unclean. It doesn't matter if he washes himself and is as clean and appears as well behaved on the surface, he will be rejected automatically because he is a pig. A pig cannot fill the role model of a lamb.

Let us continue the analogy. At conversion the pig is killed and resurrected as a lamb. Now he is just as acceptable as the other lambs, but he still feels like a pig. He no longer has any cause for shame and can approach with the other lambs, but he still remembers his time as a pig and expects others to treat him as a pig again. He forgets his conversion and acts more like the pig that he was than the lamb he is now. In his second epistle, Peter mentions seven characteristics of the Christ life (lamb life) and says (II Peter 1:9): "For he that lacks these qualities is blind or short-sighted, having forgotten his purification from his former sins." We need to remember that there is no more need to have any shame in Christ. In Christ the believer walks into the Temple as a lamb because he **is** a lamb.

Shame is the violation of a role model, and Christ is our role model. In the Old Testament, the God of Israel says, "Be holy, for I am holy (Leviticus 11:44)." The Lord Jesus also says the same (Matthew 5:48): "Therefore you are to be perfect, as your heavenly Father is perfect." At first glance from a human viewpoint, this is obviously impossible. Doesn't this commandment guarantee permanent shame, then? It guarantees shame only to the carnal believer that is trying to live the Christian life in his own strength. For the spiritual believer the result need not be shame, but rather the opposite: heroism.

In his book, Beyond Identity: Finding Yourself in the Image and Character of God, Dick Keyes mentions the type of person who gets accustomed to a certain sin or sins and seems unaffected by committing them. However, he then commits a great sin and reaches a crisis. He thinks that he is not the type of person that would do such a thing, but he just did it. What bothers him is not guilt (everyone does wrong things), but shame. He concludes, "First of all, God does not distinguish between respectable and unrespectable sins. For Him, sin is sin. Any perimeter dividing them is only in our minds. This sort of experience shows that we are not so much bothered by breaking God's laws as we are of breaking our little china models of ourselves. We are not terribly bothered by being guilty (nobody is perfect, after all); but when faced with having acted unheroically, the end of the world seems upon us. This suffering of shame therefore is more of a fall from ourselves, a blow to our pride in our own heroism than it is a fall from obedience to God."[6]

What is the resolution for the problem? —Our identification with Christ. When we change places with Jesus, we turn over to Him the old nature and the acts proceeding from the old nature. In exchange, we receive His perfection on our account, as well as His Life within us. As Jesus is living through us, we are perfect in His perfection. We are heroic in His heroism.

How can the spiritual believer find heroism in the very thing that should bring shame for him? It is in the fact that the person who is the role model for him (Jesus) is actually living in him. That the role model is the one living through one actually guarantees perfect fulfillment of the role ***to the degree by which that one is allowed to live his life through us.***

Therefore, we find the case that, to the extent that we allow Jesus to live through us, we will act heroically and follow Jesus' role model perfectly. However, to the extent that we do not follow the role model of Jesus, it is no longer we, but sin that dwells in us

(Romans 7:20). Either way, we, as rebellious sinners, are dead, and dead people do not act unheroically or wickedly. They do not act at all. As obedient sons of God with Jesus' obedience, we are heroic and perfect "in Christ." As we relax and believe by faith in our death with Jesus, we can trust God to bring out, more and more every day, the perfection of Jesus. All the while, we can claim to ourselves His approval: "This is my beloved son, in whom I am well-pleased."

Having this sacrifice with Jesus' righteousness attributed to us frees us from making "china models" of ourselves that can be broken, generating a crisis every time we fall into a gross sin. True, we need to confess our sin before moving on, but we can truly disassociate ourselves with the sin because we are dead and it was indwelling sin that worked out the evil action. Our mistake was in leaving something in us outside of the control of the Holy Spirit.

Mr. Keyes continues describing what is the accessible and inaccessible heroism that believers might have in the Christian walk. What is the actual heroic thing that they can do in imitating Christ and Christian leaders? "We are not to imitate the specific ways they lead their lives, their calling, their gifts, their opportunities, their mannerisms, or vocabulary. Such imitation inevitably fails. When Paul told the Corinthians, "Be imitators of me," he did not want them all to become missionaries (no one would have been left in the churches that he started), tentmakers, Roman citizens, or to wear the kind of clothes he did. He wanted them to imitate his "ways in Christ" (I Cor. 4:16-17) which he taught wherever he went."[7]

This imitation focuses on things of the spiritual sphere of existence and our relation to God, not on the details of living it out down here on the earth. This heroism is possible for the believer. Also, when we fall, we need to confess our sin, and it is gone from the record of our life that will be reviewed in glory.

To understand this difference better, one need only read the history of the kings of Israel and Judah in the books of Samuel and Kings to see all of the sin, imperfections, and flaws of each king faithfully recorded alongside their accomplishments. When, however, we read alongside it the account of Chronicles, we see how God looks back on it. The sin, for the most part, is erased, and the history is glorious. We, as believers, need to have that "Chronicles" perspective on our life to see the heroism of Christ living through us, and our failures blotted out by the blood of Christ.

It is this perspective through which we can develop a positive appreciation of Jesus' work through us, and we can see our value as a vehicle of God's presence—not as an independent god achieving things through self-effort. Either way, Jesus receives the glory both for blotting out our sins and for doing His works through us. Jesus blots out our evil deeds with the trespass offering, and he removes our evil nature with the sin offering. It is his fulfillment of the whole burnt offering whereby He imputes, implants, and then lives out His righteousness toward God through us.

It is noteworthy that in Leviticus 1: 5-6 the believer has the responsibility of killing the sacrifice, skinning it, and cutting it into pieces. There are several lessons for the believer in this procedure. First of all, just because Jesus has done everything necessary to make our sanctification possible, we may not lie back passively and develop Godliness. We need to be active in applying what is necessary to develop Godliness. In Ephesians 6:11 we are told: "Put on the full armor of God, so that you will be able to stand firm against the schemes of the devil." God makes the armor available, but we have to put it on.

Also, the skin of the burnt offering goes to the priest. In Galatians 3:27 believers are told: "For all of you who were baptized into Christ have clothed yourselves with Christ." Just as the priest receives the skin of the sacrifice to wear, so we are to be instrumental in applying the sacrifice of the burnt offering and to "cloth ourselves with" the Lord Jesus Christ. This is in the aorist in the Greek and indicates in one point of time in the past "clothing ourselves with" Christ, and afterward, we are accepted before the Father as Christ Himself.

Verse 9 of Leviticus mentions that the priest "shall burn all on the altar." This reminds one of the hymn that says, "Is your all on the altar of sacrifice laid?" Jesus' all was on the altar for us and for our acceptance before the Father. As we identify with Jesus' work in this aspect, then his acceptance by the Father in service to God is attributed to us. Thus in Ephesians 1:6 (AV) we read, "He hath made us accepted in the beloved." The "Beloved" is the Beloved One, or Jesus.

In Leviticus 6: 8-13 there are more instructions for the priests. In verse 9 the fire of the burnt offering is to be burnt all night until the morning, when another of these sacrifices was offered. This shows us that we are to claim Jesus righteousness and bask in Jesus' acceptance by the Father continually. Every morning in our devotional time, we are to claim Jesus' fullness for us that day.

In verse 13 we read that the fire on the altar is to burn continually. "It shall never go out." Jesus' perfection is always counted for the believer, and therefore we can always approach the Father with confidence. In verse 12 we find that the fat of the peace offering is burned upon the burnt offering. This shows that total surrender is the basis of peace with God.

IV. The Grain Offering (Leviticus 2: 1-16, 6:14-18).

While the burnt offering shows us how Jesus' total submission and obedience to the Father has been made available to us in Him, the grain offering shows us how Jesus' perfect service to His fellow man is available to us in Him. The grain offering is a sweet savor offering-a soothing aroma. The issue of sin is not dealt with in this offering. Rather, it is an oblation for acceptance and worship.

In Genesis 1:29 God gave the plant kingdom to man for food. Since this refers to relations between men, it is of plant production. While the burnt offering represents giving God His due, the grain offering represents man giving to man a gift of service in order to honor God. These two offerings represent our fulfillment in Christ of the two great commandments: to love God with all our heart, soul, and might, and to love our neighbor as ourselves. These two sacrifices go together and are offered together, as noted in Numbers 28:12-13. We cannot separate obedience to God from meeting man's need. Both are necessary and required.

It must be noted here that there is a logical order of these two sacrifices: first the burnt offering and then the grain offering. This is because we have to give ourselves to God first before our service to others is acceptable. In fact, giving ourselves to God first provides the motivation for giving ourselves unto others. This was discussed in an earlier chapter about man as the image of God. As one treated the image, he is seen as treating the spirit that dwells in the image.

Thus, as one loves God more and more, he wants to show that love for God the True Spirit by showing love and service to His images, which represent His presence in the world.

In Leviticus 2:1, the ingredients of this sacrifice are given. First of all it contains fine flour. The fine flour has been crushed completely, even as Jesus was crushed in his suffering for us. Jesus was hurt more than any of us because of human rejection and hatred. Jesus treated people perfectly, but received evil for good. His suffering was deepened further in that He loves every human being more than we love each other.

The fine flour was anointed with oil, even as Jesus was anointed with the Holy Spirit. Jesus emptied Himself of all function of Deity and relied on the Holy Spirit for everything in order to be an example to the world of what God could do through one person perfectly submitted to the Holy Spirit. Also for us, this is a reminder that the Holy Spirit's ability to use us is limited to the degree that we submit to Him. Our potential in the control of the Holy Spirit is theoretically the same as that of Jesus, except for the many subtractions we make through our lack of yielding to the Holy Spirit.

In his excellent book Christ Esteem: Where the Search for Self-Esteem Ends, Don Matzat puts this problem in a proper perspective. "A popular advocate of the positive self-image teaching wrote, '*What* you think of yourself influences every part of your life.' It is far more Biblically correct to say, '*That* you think of yourself influences every part of your life'! We could even say, '*When* you are thinking of yourself, every part of your life is being negatively influenced.' The real question is: '*Why* are you thinking about yourself?'"[8]

As we maintain our focus on glorifying Jesus, He fills us and we can endure the crushing that comes in human disappointments. This is also pleasing to the Father if we allow ourselves to be agents of His grace in the situation to produce healing, rather than serving the interests of self.

The sacrifice also has frankincense on it (2:1), but not honey (2:11). Frankincense is sweet, and only releases its fragrance under fire, but it does not ferment like honey, which is also sweet. Honey represents our own graces, which will ferment under fire and over time. However, frankincense does not. It is interesting to note here that frankincense (levonah) in Hebrew comes from the same root as the word white. In a sense, it is this purity of heart that the Holy Spirit produces in the believer that even under fire gives off a pleasing aroma.[9]

This offering is to be partaken of by the Lord, who receives a handful burned on the altar. Also, the priest and his sons are allowed to eat of this offering. This is a good picture that both the Lord and others are to benefit from our service to others. There is no portion to be eaten by the one who brings the offering. Why? Because our motive in serving others should not be personal benefit, but rather service in love. This reminds us of Jesus' warnings in the Sermon on the Mount that if one does his service to be seen of others he has his reward in the praise of men, and will receive nothing from God. It is one way or the other.

If we abandon ourselves in service to the Lord through serving other people without thought of recompense, then our service is well pleasing to the Lord. However, if we are looking for personal gain through our service—whether recognition, financial recompense, or some other gain—God sees it that we were doing it for that gain, and it is not an act of service to God.

There is one ingredient left that assures that our motives are right: salt. In verse 13 we find the requirement that all offerings must be seasoned with salt. This reminds us of a statement that Jesus made (Mark 9:49, AV): "Every sacrifice shall be salted with salt." Why is this so? In the Hebrew the word salt comes from the same root as the verb that means "to tear away" or "to dissipate."[10] It seems that God at times allows our sacrificial efforts to come to nothing to test our motives.

Many times we end up saying, like the Pre-incarnate Christ (Isaiah 49:4), "I have toiled in vain, I have spent My strength for nothing, and in vanity; yet surely the justice due to Me is with the Lord, and My reward with My God." He then tells the answer. He is promised that God will be his strength. Also, he is promised that his program will succeed to all peoples "to the end of the earth." He has to live his life of sacrifice "salted with salt." All of his efforts are apparently in vain. Even after his three years of discipling efforts, one disciple betrayed him directly and the rest ran like cowards at his arrest. It looked like Jesus' whole life was wasted. He did everything for the glory of the Lord while receiving little glory or recognition during his lifetime. His motive was his love for the Father and desire to serve Him, as well as human beings. This service was accepted because the motive was pure. Like Jesus, we should keep serving God out of love when things are going bad. We have to accept the salt on our sacrifice, as well.

God wants our service for Him, but He wants our surrender of ourselves first. Without our surrender of ourselves, the service is not acceptable. The liberals of last century and earlier this century have overemphasized that we are to love our fellow men. In fact, they have so overemphasized service to others that they have ignored the atonement for salvation. This is a deplorable act that will cost many people eternal perdition.

However, while good deeds done to others will not gain us salvation, the life of Jesus with which we are born again should issue forth in service to others. This, of course, is to be a result of salvation—not the means of obtaining it. We conservative believers often shrink back from serving others because of the stigma of the "social gospel" mentality, but Jesus expects it of us. The difference is between "dead works," that an unsaved person is doing to gain acceptance with God, and "living works," which God produces in and through the believer as a result of salvation. This distinction is best explained by Ephesians 2:8-10, especially verse 10: "For by grace you have been saved through faith; and that not of yourselves, it is the gift of God; not as a result of works, so that no one may boast. For we are His workmanship, created in Christ Jesus for good works, which God prepared beforehand so that we would walk in them."

The good works of the believer are living works because they arise from his living relationship with the Lord Jesus. Jesus lives in and through them (Galatians 2:20), God the Father arranges the circumstances, and then (Philippians 2:13), "it is God who is at work in you, both to will and to work for His good pleasure." These are living works because they come from a living relation with Jesus Christ. They are not dead works, which are invented by us on the spur of the moment and done in the energy of the flesh, according to our human insight and ability. As a result, Jesus gets the credit and glory for the works.

Jesus' selfless service to others is imputed to us as the grain offering in His sacrifice. As we lose our identity with Jesus, He takes over and continues to do His works through us as the continuation of the grain offering and our life becomes a blessing to others and "a soothing aroma to the Lord."

V. The Peace Offering (Leviticus 3:1-17, & 7:11-34).

The culmination of all sacrifices is the peace offering, and that is to be expected. The word peace (shalom in Hebrew) is from a root that means many things: absence of war, the payment of all economic debts, health, universal friendship, and completeness.[11] It is this completeness that places this sacrifice at the pinnacle of all sacrifices. It is the goal of a complete relation with the Lord towards which other sacrifices were just steps. This sacrifice makes us perfect (complete) in Christ, as we are exhorted to "Therefore you are to be perfect, as your heavenly Father is perfect" (Matthew 5:48).

This time the animal may be either male of female (v. 1) because there is no longer any difference in the fullness of our relation with the Lord. The believer is to bring the offering to the door of the "tent of meeting" with the Lord. Here the approach is for the deepest fellowship. Again, the worshipper lays his hand on the head of the offering, identifying with it (exchanging identities with it), and kills it. Then the priests (more than one) sprinkle the blood around the altar as testimony that the sacrifice had died, the blood being shed. When we realize our identity with Christ and enter into the fullness of fellowship, we have the real peace of God in us. This is possible, though, only after we realize the death of the old nature in us and we praise God for the new nature that we have.

In Leviticus 7:11-34 there is also mentioned the thanksgiving variation of the peace offering. This is accompanied by both leavened and unleavened bread (vv. 12-13). When we are at peace with God, God accepts Jesus' offering through us (unleavened loaves), and also our efforts (leavened loaves) on the basis of Jesus' work. There is full confidence and full acceptance.

The peace offering is unique in that it is the only one in which the worshipper is allowed to eat anything. The other offerings have a portion for God alone, or for God and the priests, but nothing for the worshipper. The peace offering is like a party of fellowship with God as the host, inviting the priests and their families, the worshipper and his family, and even friends of the worshipper. Thus, this is the only sacrifice from which the worshipper is nourished. If he only brings the other sacrifices, he may still be weak and malnourished. Only the peace offering leads to spiritual health.

The peace offering feast is a picture of the Lord's Table celebration in the New Testament. Everyone is there together, God, the leaders, and other people. There is peace and harmony at the table together. In Corinth there had been abuses, which were corrected by the removal of some brothers in premature death (11: 30). God takes this celebration of love very seriously, and so should we. Many people can benefit from the peace offering of a particular person, but each person should develop to the point that he is bringing peace offerings for himself and others, instead of depending on the offerings of others for his sustenance.

Such fellowship between God and many people is really a celebration of the covenant. As has already been explained, the word covenant, *berit* in Hebrew, is from the same root as a word for food (*biryah*) and a verb to eat (*barah*).[12] It is this fellowship of peace to which the covenant leads. In the Middle East, to be in this type of covenant with another person means that, if necessary, one would die for the other person. Jesus has already died for us, and we have died in our union with Him. If necessary, we should be ready to die for the honor of the name of Jesus as martyrs, also. This is the depth of the fellowship of the covenant of peace as explained in the peace offering.

In the peace offering, Jesus offers Himself as the offering, and we are "accepted in the Beloved one (AV)." In Revelation 3:18 Jesus counsels the Laodiceans to buy from Him "white garments, so that you may cloth yourself, and that the shame of your nakedness will not be revealed." This was done when we "clothed ourselves with Christ" (Gal. 3:27, Eph. 4:24, and Col. 3:10). There is perfect heroism and no shame, as we are covered with His righteous nature and acts, therefore seen as perfectly fulfilling the role model of absolute perfection that the Father demands. There is also perfect pardon for our sinful acts and Jesus' full righteousness, thus removing our guilt and providing God's righteous acts in its place.

The Parts of the Animal used in the Sacrifice and the Application for us.

At this point, it is very important to consider the different parts of the animal sacrificed and for whom they are. In Leviticus 3:9-11 and 7:22-27 there is a list of parts of the sacrifice that are strictly for the Lord only. As we analyze these, we will see how they are applied to us today, and the reasons the Lord reserves them for Himself.

Leviticus 7:25 mentions that whoever eats the fat of any sacrifice offered to the Lord "even the person who eats shall be cut off from his people." Why the fat? In Hebrew the root for fat (*helev*) also includes milk, but nothing else. We must see how the word fat is used in Bible passages. In Genesis 25:18, Pharaoh told Joseph to invite his relatives to come and settle in the best area of Egypt and "eat of the fat of the land." The fat was seen as the best part of the animal, and is used as a symbol of the best there is. The fat of every animal, whether for sacrifice or not, was considered given to God. God must have the best there is. Therefore, the Israelites never ate the fat of any animal by Divine order (Leviticus 7:23). Even if God was not seen as consuming the fat as part of a sacrifice that went up in smoke, still, the fat was forbidden for the Israelite, even if the animal was not sacrificed.

The lesson for the New Testament believer is obvious: God is worthy of the best. We should give Him our best effort (Col. 3:23) at all times in everything we do. We should give Him our best offering in everything, so that in all things Jesus might have the preeminence in our lives. Many young people think that they want to keep their best years for themselves and then receive Jesus when they are old and need some "fire insurance" against hell. We should offer to the Lord the strength of our youth, our best time (even if we have to jumble our schedule and miss the Superbowl or something else important to us—or even go to a foreign country to preach the word), the first fruits of our income (the tithe should come off the top of our money—it is not a pittance from our leftovers), and the first priority in every consideration. Every believer needs to make sure that he is "giving God the fat." Thus, fat is the first item on the checklist of our sacrifice for God.

The next item must always be for God, also. In Leviticus 7:26 God says, "You are not to eat any blood, either of bird or animal, in any of your dwellings." The blood was always to be for God. It was sprinkled on the bronze altar, the altar of incense, the veil before the Holy of Holies, or the Mercy seat. The rest was poured out at the base of the bronze altar (Deuteronomy 12:27). If the animal was not being sacrificed to God, it was still to be poured out on the ground (Deuteronomy 12:15-16).

There are three reasons why Old Testament believers were not to eat blood: First, the soul of the flesh is in the blood, and the blood was therefore accepted in substitute for the soul of the worshipper in the sacrifice. In Leviticus 17:11-12 the word *nephesh* is translated life in most translations: "For the life (*nephesh*) of the flesh is in the blood, and I have given it to you on the altar to make atonement for your souls (*nephesh*); for it is the blood, by reason of the soul (*nephesh*) that makes atonement. Therefore I said to the sons of Israel; No person (*nephesh*) among you may eat blood, nor may any alien who sojourns among you eat blood."

The Hebrew word *nephesh* is translated life, soul, soul, and person in these two verses. It is best to translate it soul all four times to make the application. Therefore we see that the believer was not to eat blood because the soul in that blood was from God and was to go exclusively to God. The soul is sacred. It comes from God and is to return to God only.

The second reason that the believers were not to eat blood is the other side of the coin: that it would mix the soul of the animal whose blood was shed with that of the Israelite. This mixing is seen as an abomination. God sets up clear categories in the Old Testament, and does not want things mixed wrongly. The very disgust and abomination of Babylon was that it stood for mixing—in religion, politics, and everything else. This was the essence of Babylon. Even the name comes from the verb "to mix." In that sense, Babylon was the essence of what God most hates. The world system that dominates until the Second Coming of Christ receives the name Babylon for that reason. There is little that God hates today more than the illegitimate mixing that comes from Western humanism. Its goal is to mix the holy things and holy people of God with horrible crass sins like homosexuality and rebels of all types and call them and their activities all equally valid lifestyles. God does not want us to mix the soul of another being with our own soul by drinking or eating the blood.

The third reason why we dedicate the blood for God is that the word *blood* in Hebrew is from the same root as the word *likeness*, and the verb *to be* like.[13] We are in the likeness of God through the life (soul) that is in our flesh in our blood. Thus the term "likeness of God," refers to the quality of life that we received from God: the ability to love, hate, choose, get angry, etc. The unregenerate man has these qualities, but they are in disorder. When a man is born again through the shed blood of Christ and receives the Holy Spirit, he has the potential to be under the control of the Holy Spirit. When he is submitted to the Holy Spirit, he is in parallel with God, expressing those qualities of life on the earth in parallel with what God feels in heaven. As Jesus says to the church, "whatever you bind on earth shall have been bound in heaven and whatever you loose on earth shall have been loosed in heaven (Matthew 16:19)." The quality of life in animals is inferior to that of humans, but it also came from God and must return to God. *Thus, we see that the blood and fat at all times, not just from the sacrifice, are only for God.*

In addition to the blood and fat, which are always reserved for God, the peace offering has some special other body parts of the sacrificial animal which are exclusively reserved for God, as mentioned in Leviticus 3:3-4: the fat in various places, the kidneys, and the liver. We will consider the kidneys, the fatty appendage above the liver, and the liver, as well as the importance of giving them to the Lord.

The kidneys (*kelayoth*, in Hebrew) are from the root meaning, "to be complete, at an end, accomplished, spent".[14] There is a cognate root in the Hebrew that covers the same meaning and also includes the meanings *complete, perfect, all, entire, and bride (as one who completes one*). The kidneys are seen as the seat of the emotions and affections in the person. In what sense? The adrenal glands are considered part of the kidneys, and what "turns you on" will get the adrenalin going.

In Psalm 16 David shows us how he learned to "give his kidneys to the Lord." In verses 1-3 David cries to the Lord for help. He recognizes that his plea for help is based on his trust in the Lord and his identity on the Lord's side in the war between good and bad. In verse 4 David reiterates his faith that the evil people will not prosper, and he will not follow them.

In verses 5-7 David rehearses all of the Lord's promises to him and reminds himself that the Lord is the one sustaining him, and giving him counsel, but he is still so nervous that he cannot sleep at night. He says (AV), "my reins (kidneys) also instruct me in the night seasons." Here the AV is better than the NASV "my mind instructs me," because the Hebrew word is *kilyothay*, which is literally, "my kidneys". How did his kidneys instruct him? As he was thinking about all of his enemies and troubles here on the earth, his fear reaction turned on the kidneys (adrenal glands), which pumped adrenalin into his system so he could not sleep at night. That is how his kidneys were reproving him that he was taking the wrong course of action by focusing on his problems. The latter verb is *yasar*, which means "to admonish," or "to chasten".[15]

Verse 8 is the turning point in the Psalm. As a result of his problem, David decides to change his focus and think about the Lord. He says "I have set the Lord continually before me; because He is at my right hand, I will not be shaken." Here David changes his focus. He takes his problems away from being in front of him and replaces them with God. As he thinks about God's presence and power, there are three changes in him physiologically in verse 9: first of all, his heart is glad. We know that a merry heart will change the state of mind. Happiness will relax us so that we can sleep better. The second change, I believe, is that his liver rejoices. There is a textual variant that reads *liver*, instead of *glory*. Both are from the same root, and I believe that the liver is involved here for reasons already noted.

The third effect is that his flesh shall rest in hope. This rest is of a dual reference. First of all, David can now sleep at night in hope of God's protection and deliverance, and secondly, his flesh shall rest in hope in that he will have hope in the Lord to resurrect him when he dies. David finishes with a triumphant affirmation of his own future resurrection from the dead, as well as his descendant the Messiah's resurrection without decaying, and sees far into the future for all of eternity. He ends with this dual affirmation of faith: that the Lord will guide him now, and give him joy in His presence for all eternity (v. 11). "You will make known to me the path of life; in Your presence is fullness of joy; in Your right hand there are pleasures forever." David sees beyond his difficult circumstances. He sees a Loving God that is taking care of him right now, and will continue to take care of him for all of eternity. Death has no power over him during his life because he has accepted that he will die, anyway. The time of his transfer to be with God is of no consequence when compared to his sure eternity at God's right hand with pleasures forever.

We Christians need to refocus our thoughts on Jesus and our eternity with Him, as well as His protection for us now. We have an even closer relation with God than David did, and the Apostle Paul instructs us how to take this even farther in Colossians 3:1-4: "Therefore if you have been raised up with Christ, keep seeking the things above, where Christ is, seated at the right hand of God. Set your mind on the things above, not on the things that are on earth. For you have died and your life is hidden with Christ in God. When Christ, who is our life, is revealed, then you also will be revealed with Him in glory."

Paul has the same counsel here. He tells us to think about the things above, where Jesus is. Where he says to "Set your mind on the things above, not on the things that are on earth," he is telling us to change our focus to think on heavenly things, which are sure and much better than the things on the earth. As we view the meaning of our identity with Christ, we understand our death, burial, and resurrection with Him. This moves us to change our focus, treating everything about us on the earth as already dead and raised up. The conclusion follows in the rest of the chapter that we should treat as dead desires we feel in us that focus on this earth and treat as alive desires that are from above, especially love.

The result of this change of focus for the Apostle Paul is a rest for the kidneys, as he continues in Colossians 3, because they are turned over to God. Because of the immorality, impurity, passion, evil desire, and greed (v.5), anger, wrath, malice, slander, and abusive speech (v.8), the kidneys were pumping adrenaline into our systems continually as unbelievers. This led to a life of dissipation and physiological suffering, as well as a loss of sleep. Now that we know the Lord Jesus, we can refocus on Jesus and "things above," which include compassion, kindness, humility, gentleness, and patience (v.12), forgiveness (v.13), love (v.14), peace, thanksgiving (v.15), singing, and thankfulness (v.16).

In this case, just as Jerusalem, the City of Peace, rules over all the cities of Israel, so the peace of God is to rule in our hearts (v.15). Because of these different emotions, the kidneys are relaxed and the person tranquil. When the believer needs energy, the Lord directs his kidneys to release adrenaline over things that matter concerning the kingdom, which are much fewer, and the person is able to function in a generally peaceful manner the rest of the time. In this way, the person is complete in God. The root meaning "to be complete" is from a cognate root to the root fulfill and kidney in the Hebrew. It would appear that this would suggest a connection between our fulfillment and our being complete. These two roots may be variants of the same background, though it is not certain.[16]

In his book, Adrenaline and Stress, Dr. Archibald Hart deals with the problem of stress damage in people. He warns about excessive stress and the damage it causes in the body. If you do not limit the excessive use of the stress response system in the body, the result will be stress disease. Hart mentions various diseases that can result in excessive triggering of the stress defense system over a long period of time: migraine headaches, panic attacks, rapid heartbeat, irregular heartbeat, high blood pressure, dizziness, heart palpitations, nausea, acid stomach, heartburn, diarrhea, indigestion, constipation, neck ache, shoulder pain, teeth grinding, high and low back pain, skin rash, cold hands, some asthma, and many others.[17]

All stress response results in adrenaline being secreted into our bloodstream, giving us an increased capacity to face a threatening situation. It is important and necessary for us to recuperate from the adrenaline response and rest for our bodies to recover from the heightened state of activity. In this, even an imagined stimulus receives a full response. As Hart mentions, "The stress response cannot tell the difference between real and imagined threats; it responds the same way to both sets of stimuli."[18]

This explains why we may wake up in a cold sweat from a bad dream, but it also explains the importance of not letting our mind wander into fantasies. These fantasies can be as taxing on the body as facing the real events or activities that are fantasized about. The addictions of television, video games, pornography, sports events, and other similar events or fantasies can wear out our kidneys (adrenal glands) and lead us to burnout. Hart mentions that people can become addicted to their own adrenaline high, and through it become addicted to the activities that give them this high. "But the trouble with any kind with any kind of dependent or addictive behavior is that people can come to use it for other purposes, such as an escape from problems and to relieve anxiety. This causes them to rely on the dependent activity too heavily and to "run away" from the problems and the reality of their lives. It is this aspect of addiction that is unhealthy—as well as the physical damage that it might do."[19]

In terms of our study here, it is absolutely necessary to give God our kidneys. Only when this complex stress defense system is under the control of the Holy Spirit can we avoid the bondage of excessive use, which leads to the many symptoms mentioned above. In the New Testament over and over we find the Apostles desiring grace and peace for the believers. These are great blessings that are available to us, but we need to give God our kidneys—let God make the reactions to things in our lives, and let God be our "turn on."

What responses does God make that are different from our responses in the flesh? Dr. Hart gives three solutions for excessive stress, and I consider that these three responses will effectively maintain our kidneys under the control of the Lord and fulfill this benefit of the Lord's sacrifice for us in this matter: faith, love, and forgiveness.

Hart mentions Jesus' life as a perfect example of a life of faith. "What sort of life did Jesus model for us? First, I would say that his life was a model of unhurriedness. One could argue that unhurriedness was characteristic of Jewish life in the New Testament times, but I think there is more to it than this. A life of perfect faith—faith that understands that God is in control even when nature is turbulent—cannot be anything but a life of peace."[20]

Jesus was with His disciples crossing the Sea of Galilee in a storm in Mark 4:35-41. While His disciples were yelling and screaming and rowing and bailing, Jesus was asleep in the boat. When they woke him, he rebuked the storm, and all was peaceful. Jesus did not use a big adrenal rush to row harder. He spoke the word through faith and there was a great calm. Then he rebuked them for having fear instead of faith. We need to surrender completely to God's leading and will, and maybe then we will be calm enough to hear His order to rebuke the storm, using this attack of the enemy to glorify Him. The same is true of other obstacles if we see things through the eyes of faith from God's perspective.

Besides faith, Hart recommends that we seek to love others. He states simply after years of study, "The role of love in reducing stress can be quite remarkable."[21] This shouldn't surprise us that the two greatest commandments—to love God and to love others—should reduce stress and help to bring healing from stress-related diseases. Also, as Jesus loves others through us more and more, our kidneys will be given to God so that God can respond in love where before we burned with anger, hatred, and bitterness toward others. We need to love others more.

The last of the three prescriptions from this doctor for making sure that our kidneys are given to God is forgiveness. He says, "Freedom from the destructive force of anger in only possible through two mechanisms: revenge or forgiveness. Since revenge is not always possible or desirable, forgiveness is the only way out of the prison of resentment."[22]

Forgiveness frees us from our past so we can live in the present. I heard from an unknown source that forgiveness is setting a prisoner free, and discovering that that prisoner was you. Forgiving others is one other way to give our kidneys to God. Jesus must have had something like the physiological suffering of bitterness in mind when he warned about the unforgiving servant who was thrown in the prison because he would not forgive another servant, even after he was forgiven of a greater debt. Let's give our kidneys to God by seeking faith, love, and forgiveness.

Another part of the sacrifice of the peace offering that belongs exclusively to God is "the caul above the liver (AV)." The Hebrew word translated *caul* is *yoteret*. This word means the "fatty appendage" and is from the Hebrew root meaning *remainder, excess, or abundance*. The lesson here is clear. We are not to dedicate ourselves to heaping up riches here on earth. There are strong warnings to Timothy in I Timothy 6:6-10. We are to be content with our portion in life and not have a lot of love of money, which is a root of all evil. If we trust God for our sustenance, we will not be fretting about accumulating material wealth so that we won't have to trust God in the future. In Hebrews 13:5 we read: "Make sure that your character is free from the love of money, being content with what you have; for He Himself has said, 'I will never desert you, nor will I ever forsake you.'" If we give God the excess, we won't be so preoccupied with ourselves that we can't serve God or others. God must have the excess.

The last item mentioned is the liver. While it is not specifically stated that the liver went to God, most scholars think that it did. This would be for a good reason: the liver in Hebrew is *caved*, or heavy organ, and is from the same Hebrew root as *cavod*, which means glory. It is obvious that God must have all the glory in our lives in order for there to be peace. When God has the glory, the believer will not be unloving, unforgiving, or unfaithful to God. Also, when the believer is focused on seeking God's glory in all things, his liver will be able to relax, and heal itself because it won't be pouring out bile into the digestive tract in reaction to the stress which comes as a result of the self-centered life.

In fact, in giving to God his liver, i.e. all the glory, the believer will cease to be conscious of himself as an active ego, responding to the stimuli in the environment as they threaten or benefit him and his goal of self-promotion. Matzat mentions the result of a radical surrender of self to God: "Because the death of Jesus was our death, living with ourselves and unto ourselves means living with a 'dead thing.' Jesus calls us to separate from the 'dead thing,' to lose our lives, to deny ourselves and cling in faith to him. Paul wrote: 'We are convinced that one died for all, and therefore all died. And he died for all, that those who live should no longer live for themselves but for him who died for them and was raised again' (2 Corinthians 5:14-15). A person who dies is free—free from any good works and free from any evil works. The person is free from worry and fear, free from sin and death. Centering and focusing attention upon self is merely digging up the corpse, so to speak. If you know that you have died with Christ, how can you feel good about yourself? A funeral director may make up and neatly dress a corpse, and the family may gather around the open casket and say, 'Doesn't he look good?' but the cold facts are, the corpse is dead no matter how good it may look."[23]

This radical surrender to God will live out only as Christ is resurrected in him and the life the world sees will be Christ in us, the hope of glory. God will have the blood, the fat, the kidneys, the appendage above the liver, and the liver. This true worship of God will be quite an offense and stench in the nostrils of the world, as Paul mentions in 2 Corinthians 2:15-16, "For we are a fragrance of Christ to God among those w ho are being saved and among those who are perishing; to the one an aroma from death to death, to the other an aroma from life to life." Our manner is as death because the world only sees our self-denial, which it finds repulsive because the world is totally energized by the lust of the flesh, the lust of the eyes, and the boastful pride of life (1 John 2:15-17). To God and other believers this life is an aroma from life to life because they can see the life of Jesus manifest through our death, His strength through our weakness, His wisdom through our ignorance, His forgiveness and love through our surrender, and His faith through our surrender. And Jesus is our life!

The peace offering caps off all offerings as the pinnacle of the Christian experience. In the same way, we should remember that the word for peace in Hebrew means absence of war, the payment of all economic debts, health, universal friendship, and completeness. Christ's sacrifice brings us all of these benefits in our lives. The absence of war is the absence of war with God, and often with our neighbors because "when a man's ways are pleasing to the Lord, He makes even his enemies to be at peace with him (Proverbs 16:7)." The peace includes the payment of all economic debts because we are living within our means and having faith in God, instead of the bank.

The riches of Christ include also physical health because, we has been seen, when God has control over our responses of the kidneys, liver, appendage, fat, and blood, we are not hyper about our circumstances and energized in the flesh constantly until we develop burnout. Thus we are healthier. While universal friendship is not always possible with unbelievers, we will live, as far as it lies with us, in peace and friendship with all men. In the church especially we will find universal friendship as Christ in each member overcomes all human barriers and reaches out to others. Finally, in Christ we will find completeness because we are the bride of Christ. Remember that the word *bride* comes from the verb *to complete*, as she is the complement of the groom. As Paul says in Colossians 2:9-10: "For in Him all the fullness of Deity dwells in bodily form, and in Him you have been made complete, and He is the head over all rule and authority."

Conclusion:

The Christian's riches through Christ's sacrifice seen in the light of the sacrifices in Leviticus 1-7 are many. They are appropriated through faith in the finished work of Jesus. As we look at the 5 separate sacrifices of Leviticus 1-7, we see that each one shows different riches that we receive through Christ's death and resurrection life.

The first two sacrifices, the trespass offering and the sin offering, transferred our sin and sin nature to Jesus: "He made Him who knew no sin to be sin on our behalf, so that we might become the righteousness of God in Him" (II Corinthians 5:21). The trespass offering transferred our evil works from us to Jesus, who paid the death penalty for them. The sin offering transferred our old nature to Jesus, who paid the penalty for it. These two sacrifices remove sins and sin nature from us. They also give us Jesus' perfection and perfect nature as gifts in exchange.

The next two sacrifices are the complement of the first two. They fill us up with Jesus after we are emptied of our sins and sin nature. The burnt offering shows how Jesus was totally given over to the Father's will and served Him as a perfectly obedient son. In our identification with Him we receive this obedience and good favor with the Father by faith. In this way we are "partakers of the Divine nature" (II Peter 1:4). In the grain offering we see how Jesus fulfilled perfectly everything that God expects of us in service to our fellow men because of a love for God. Jesus perfectly fulfilled these requirements and now attributes them to us by faith in His fulfillment of this sacrificial type from the Old Testament. Through this offering we are set to do Divine deeds, as the Holy Spirit works through us (Ephesians2:10).

Jesus' blessings to the believer in fulfillment of the peace offering are the final touch to our lives. Peace includes completeness; and the enjoyment of these blessings includes all of the others because all of the others are applied to get us to this point. Peace means completeness, tranquility, universal friendship, the absence of war, physical health, and the payment of all economic debts. It includes God's friendship and help now, and it promises an eternity of pleasures with the Lord forever. It is the down payment of heaven through the Holy Spirit's presence in our lives now, and it is the restoration of everything lost in the Fall, and more. It is the realization of our potential through God's strength, made perfect in our weakness, and it is a love, joy, and peace that transcend our existence here.

It is yet another blessing. The people of Eastern thought seek as a blessing the death of the evil, greedy, grasping ego in them that they might have peace by merging their identities into an impersonal universe. Those of Western thought try to find self-actualization and fulfillment in that same evil, greedy, grasping ego. Neither is satisfied, and mankind today is opting for one or the other pathway or trying to make a synthesis of the two. They are lost in their sins.

In Christ, we have the answer. It is not a synthesis of the two, but rather the truth that was shattered into a false dichotomy at our expulsion from the Garden of Eden. It is restored now to us. Beginning from Mesopotamia, the divider between East and West, with the call of Abraham, it began to be restored when the Creator God revealed His Truth to the Jewish people through Moses and the prophets. Now through Jesus we can be born again. We have the blessing that the Eastern mystics are seeking: the death of that evil, greedy, grasping ego that we inherited from Adam. However, we are not merged into a faceless, impersonal universe. The Perfect Creator lives in us and leads us into a perfect, personal, love relationship with Him.

We have a new nature that can do what it wants without getting into trouble—the fruit of the Spirit has no law against it. It is guaranteed to be self-actualized, fulfilled, heroic, eternal, and perfectly without sin, and it comes to us through Jesus' sacrifice for us. That is the mature believer's standing in God's glory for eternity. Let us praise the Lord for His sacrifice and the riches of His grace made available to us believers now, while we are in the process of being changed more and more to be like Jesus. Let us also praise the Lord for the oracles He gave to ancient Israel as a light to help us understand and claim these blessings, and let us praise Him for the Jewish people that have preserved them for all humanity.

Chapter 8

Mt. Sinai II: Approaching God Regularly: The Tabernacle and Our Daily Time Of Personal Fellowship with God

When the Israelites arrived at Mt. Sinai, fresh out of 400 years of slavery, they entered into a covenant with the God of Israel. Under this covenant, God was to provide guidance, blessing and protection, and Israel was to obey the guidance and show gratitude for the blessing and protection. Israel's training at Mt. Sinai can be classified into four parts: the covenant enactment and the sacrificial system, which we have considered in the last two chapters, the approach to God (involving the erection of the Tabernacle), and diverse laws. This chapter will deal with the third of these four parts: the approach to God, following the form of the Tabernacle.

The four steps of Israel at Sinai correspond with those of the new Christian. Early in his life as a believer, he needs to understand about the New Covenant with God, the deeper meaning of Christ's sacrifice for him and its various applications in his life, how to have his personal devotional time daily (as well as how to approach God at all times), and various instructions about how to follow God. These four training steps correspond with the four steps of Israel mentioned above. In the life of the New Testament believer, there is very little more important to him than his access to God. The unbeliever may think about God from afar and philosophize about Him, but the believer in Christ actually enters into the presence of the Creator God of the Universe and can have fellowship, converse, bring petitions, and receive answers. What a blessing!

In this chapter we will see in some detail what was the Tabernacle, as presented in the Book of Exodus, and how it taught about the presence of God, as well as teaching the way to approach God. At each point we will seek to see the fulfillment of the truth of the Tabernacle, as applied to the internal spiritual life of the New Testament believer, particularly with reference to the establishment of a daily "quiet time," or time set apart to approach God and have fellowship with Him.

The Tabernacle pointed the Israelite to God, but still placed many limits upon him. Only certain people were allowed to approach God on certain times and in a certain way. The others had to stand back and wait while the priests did their work, as prescribed by God. Under the New Testament we may all enter into the Heavenly Sanctuary whenever we want. Nobody is left standing outside. However, by looking in depth at the model of the Old Testament access to God, which is a shadow of the New Testament access to God, one may see in detail that there is yet a protocol, a right procedure for entering into the presence of the One True God in the Heavenly Sanctuary.

It will be the purpose of this chapter to compare and contrast the third of these steps at Sinai with our fulfillment in Jesus: the Tabernacle and the Christian's daily devotional time. We will seek to understand in some detail what was the Tabernacle, as presented in the Book of Exodus, and how it represented the presence of God, as well as teaching the way to approach God. At each point we will seek to see the fulfillment of the truth of the Tabernacle, as applied to the internal spiritual life of the New Testament believer in his approach to God. First we will review background truths about the names of the Tabernacle, the work leaders, measurements and layout, and materials. In Part II we will consider, step by step, the seven steps to intimacy with God, as explained by seven steps of approaching God in the Tabernacle, indicated by the furniture, in the order that one would approach God. At each step we will consider how that step would be important in a believer's daily devotional time with the Lord in the order discussed.

This chapter is a special blessing to me, the author, as I have followed these seven steps to fellowship with God daily for many years. I hope that the reader will be able to internalize and follow these seven steps with God daily, and I guarantee that you will not be disappointed.

I. Background Material on the Tabernacle.

A. Names for the Tabernacle. There are three main names for the tabernacle in the Old Testament. They are *mishkán* (מִשְׁכָּן), *óhel* (אֹהֶל), and *sukkáh* (סֻכָּה). The word *mishkán* refers to the Tabernacle as "the dwelling place," meaning the dwelling place of God. This term comes from the Hebrew root meaning "to dwell." It is also used about human dwelling places of Israel (Num. 24:5), or other nations (Jeremiah 51:30). When it was used with the article and no other explanation, then it referred to "the dwelling place (of God)," or tabernacle.

The second word used to describe the Tabernacle is *óhel.* This word means specifically "tent," but is followed by the word *moéd* to refer specifically to the Tabernacle as Tent of Meeting. The word *moéd* refers to a meeting at an appointed place. While describing the Ark of the Covenant, the Lord says to Moses in Exodus 25:22: "There I will meet with you; and from above the mercy seat, from between the two cherubim which are upon the ark of the testimony." God says that He will meet with Moses at the Tent of Meeting, or Tent of the Appointed Meeting. This imagery is helpful in understanding Hebrews 4:16 where we are exhorted: "Therefore let us draw near with confidence to the throne of grace, so that we may receive mercy and find grace to help in time of need."

The *óhel moéd* is distinguished in technical terms from the *mishkán* in Exodus 26:12. The tent refers to the outer covering and the *mishkán* to the structure underneath: "The overlapping part that is left over in the curtains of the tent (*óhel*), the half curtain that is left over, shall lap over the back of the tabernacle (*mishkán*)." The Tabernacle is sometimes called *óhel Adonay*, or "The Tent of the

Lord" in the period just before the Temple, as in I Kings 2:28. Here the emphasis is that it is a tent where one can meet the Lord.

The third word used to refer to the tabernacle is *sukkah*, or booth. This is the same name as occurs in the holiday the Feast of Booths (*hag hassukkoth*). In Psalm 76:2 (76:3 in MT), Asaph says, "His Tabernacle (*sukkó*) is in Salem (Jerusalem), and His dwelling place also is in Zion." This use is much rarer than the others, but makes a closer synonym of the Greek *skéne* (σκήνη), used in the New Testament to refer to it, as in Hebrews 8:5. This expression refers to the mobility of the tent. The *sukkáh* was a temporary shelter that was movable. The Israelites picked up their booth materials and took them with them and set them up at night again. This is the imagery of the Apostle John in his Gospel when he makes a verb out of this noun *skéne* and says concerning Jesus (John 1:14): "And the Word became flesh, and dwelt (*eskénosen*) among us." Jesus' body was the walking Tabernacle of God, moving around on the earth with God's presence inside.

So we can see that the three basic names for the Tabernacle refer to God's dwelling with His people (*mishkán*), God's tent where He meets with His people (*óhel moéd*), and God's portable, movable presence, going everywhere with His people (*sukkah*).

B. Work Leaders. It is obvious that Moses would have to be considered the primary leader in the whole project of the Tabernacle. He was the one that received instructions from the Lord and passed them on to the Israelites. The name Moses means "drawn out one," in Hebrew.[1] Under Moses, Israel is merely "drawn out" of Egypt, but still not ready to accomplish great things for God yet. Moses leads Israel through the wilderness up until they are ready to cross the Jordan River into Canaan.

Just as the word "wilderness" comes from the root for the word "word" in Hebrew,[2] the New Testament believer needs to study the Word of God greatly in the first stage of his pilgrimage from Egypt. "Canaan" refers to humility,[3] and Israel is under Joshua ("Jehovah saves") when they are conquering Canaan, as well as all of their battles in the desert. While the Israelites are under Moses, they are merely "drawn out" of Egypt. They are not good for accomplishing anything for the Lord; they are simply "drawn out." When they are under Joshua (Jehovah saves), they are finally good for winning the victory and accomplishing things for the Lord.

The new believer in Jesus is recently "drawn out" from the world. He is baptized into Christ's death, raised to newness of life, and separated unto God by his conversion. He needs to reaffirm his understanding of the covenant that he has entered into with the Lord as the first step. This involves assurance of salvation and reaffirmation of his commitment to the Lord. The second step is to understand the meaning of Jesus' sacrifice. The believer needs to know how to apply the different aspects of Christ's sacrifice, as they apply to his individual needs. These are illuminated in the various sacrifices that are ordered in the Levitical priesthood. The third step is the establishment of his regular devotional time. He needs to approach God continually and interact with Him. He also needs to study the Scriptures to find out what the Lord expects of him. Thus, we understand why Moses, the "drawn out" one is over the whole project at Mt. Sinai.

Next under Moses is his brother Aaron, the High Priest. It is hard to determine the root for the name Aaron in Hebrew, and Gesenius opts to list the name without a root,[4] though Koehler and Baumgartner list an Egyptian root meaning *the name is great*.[5] In this case, we would understand that the new believer is to glorify God's name as great. A common addition to a root to form a name is the aleph prefix. If this were true for Aaron's name, it would come from the root (*hrn*), which refers to conception.[6] One might conjecture that that name suggests that Aaron's priestly office was bringing life to the nation, in some form. It is far less common to ignore a "*he*" letter in the middle of a word in order to form a root, but this gives Aaron's name a better sense for Christians. This (*aron*) would make him a "box," as in the expression "the Ark (box) of the Covenant," or the "box" that Joseph was buried in in Egypt.[7]

What does Aaron have to do with a box? We need to remember that at conversion we actually pass through death and resurrection and are therefore dead to this world. We become vessels for Jesus' life to be present in us. Paul put it this way (2 Corinthians 4:7): "But we have this treasure in earthen vessels, so that the surpassing greatness of the power will be of God and not from ourselves." There is no better identity for a man that would be a mediator between God and men than to humble himself as a dead box that brings the treasure of the presence of God inside.

The other two overseers are appointed of God by name for the specific task of making the Tabernacle and everything related: Bezalel and Oholiab. In Exodus 31:2-3 we read about the first: "See, I have called by name Bezalel, the son of Uri, the son of Hur, of the tribe of Judah. I have filled him with the Spirit of God, in wisdom, in understanding, in knowledge, and in all kinds of craftsmanship." Since these men were going to make a copy of something invisible, the Heavenly Sanctuary, they needed revelation from the Holy Spirit in order to work properly.

The name of this person is especially appropriate for a chief worker on the Tabernacle, as it means "In the shadow of God." Also, he is son of Uri, short for Uriah, "My flame of Jehovah", and grandson of Hur, "white stuff (cotton or linen cloth)." His tribe is Judah, and this word comes from a root with 3 meanings: to praise God (Psalm 118:1), to confess one's sins to God (Proverbs 28: 13), and to confess God's names (i.e. attributes, II Chronicles 6:24).

If we are to combine the instructions in all of these names, we learn that the Tabernacle was made "in the shadow of God." The things of the Tabernacle are not the actual things in the heavens, but they are good copies. Since they are copies, the original items have the primary importance and existed first. As God instructs Moses (Exodus 26:30): "Then you shall erect the tabernacle according to its plan which you have been shown in the mountain." Even the individual items of furniture were to be copies of things already existing (Exodus 25:40): "See that you make them after the pattern for them, which was shown to you on the mountain." So we see that the items of the Tabernacle were not to be ends in themselves, but rather copies of heavenly items made for teaching purposes. The Tabernacle was to be "in the shadow of God."

Though the Tabernacle was a shadow, compared to the brightness of God Himself, it was a flame of light to the Israelite nation, and could be called by every Israelite "my flame of Jehovah." Hur reminds us of the need to approach God wearing "white stuff."

Whether cotton or linen, our clothing must be white to approach God. Thus, we come clothed in the righteousness of Jesus as we approach God, even as white garments are worn in heaven by angels (Revelation 15:6), the 24 elders (Revelation 4:4), and all of the saints (Revelation 7:9). Hur's name reminds us that we need to be clothed in Jesus' righteousness as we enter the presence of God.

The tribe of Judah reminds us of three things to do that will put God in His rightful place and us in our place: to praise God, to confess our sins to God, and to confess God's names, thereby affirming God's attributes. As we do this, we are affirmed in the proper relation to God, and we please Him. So we see why God chose Bezalel to head up the work on the Tabernacle.

God also chose "Oholiab, the son of Ahisamach, of the tribe of Dan." Oholiab means "My tent of the Father." This is appropriate because the Israelite can say it is "my tent," but it comes from the Father. The Tabernacle was not conceived by people on earth. It was revealed by the Heavenly Father to men of God through special revelation. The Jewish people cannot boast that it is a product of their religious genius, as they simply made what God revealed to them. The glory is for God, not Israel, but Israel did have the benefit of its presence among them, rather than among another people. Israel's advantage over the Gentiles was that they had received God's revelation and made a copy of it here, not that they were clev-erer than the Gentiles and could invent a better or more interesting religious "shtick." To the degree that they added any of the best inventions they could have thought of, it would have detracted from the structure, the additions being merely human, rather than Divine in origin.

"Ahisamach" means "my brother supports," and reminds us that the Tabernacle was a project of the whole nation. Everyone pitched in with offerings and labor until Moses and Aaron had to announce that the offering was too much and they should stop giving (Exodus 36:4-6). The greater believers sense the presence of the Lord, the better they cooperate and support each other.

The tribe of Dan (judgment) reminds us that the Tabernacle is involved with judgment, and that the believers have to judge their sin in order to approach God. Paul sums this up well in I Corinthians

11:31-32: "But if we judged ourselves rightly, we would not be judged. But when we are judged, we are disciplined by the Lord, so that we will not be condemned along with the world." When we come to the Tabernacle, we come for judgment now, so that we will not face judgment later.

So we see that the names of the work leaders are important in order to understand the Tabernacle better.

C. Measurements and Layout. The physical layout of the Tabernacle reinforces the idea, central to the Old Testament religion, that one must come to God His way, and not our way. There ***was*** access to the God of Israel, but it had to be on His terms. Around the outside of the Tabernacle was a courtyard measuring about 150 by 75 feet (considering a cubit to be 18 inches) with only one opening in the middle of the eastern side. The eastern and western sides were narrow (75 ft.) and the northern and southern sides were long (150 ft.). These curtains were 7.5 feet high. There was no other entrance, and there was not even an emergency exit anywhere.

This sole entrance, which had to be on the East wherever the Tabernacle was erected, lies in stark contrast to the currently popular wheel as the model of the ways to God. The Eastern mystics think of people as standing on the outside of the old-fashioned spoked wheel. The object is to get to the center, where there was peace and calm and god. The spokes represent different religions, and it does not matter which spoke one travels to get to the center of the wheel—any spoke will get you there. Once one gets to the center of the wheel he will realize that it does not matter which spoke he has taken, all spokes led to the same place. *This is the direct opposite of the God of the Bible, Who has only one way for people to approach Him. Anyone who approached God any other way would have been killed on the spot.*

After entering through the only door, the priest arrived first at an altar, then a washbowl. After these two outside items, one arrived at the actual Tabernacle structure. The structure itself measured 45 feet long, 15 feet wide, and 15 feet high. Inside there was a front section 30 by 15 feet called the Holy Place, and in the back there was a section called the Holy of Holies, which measured 15 by 15 feet.

Some authors think that the roof of the structure was flat because of the way the measurements are given, and others think that the sides sloped down from a point, like an A-frame house, only they were of cloth.

I believe that these two ideas can be made compatible if we look at the text of the Bible in Exodus 26:12-13: "The overlapping part that is left over in the curtains of the tent (*ha-óhel*), the half curtain that is left over, shall lap over the back of the tabernacle (*hammis-hkán*). The cubit on one side and the cubit on the other, of what is left over in the length of the curtains of the tent (*ha-óhel*), shall lap over the sides of the tabernacle (*hammishkán*) on one side and on the other, to cover it." So we see that the Tabernacle structure measured like an oblong box, with the east side having an entrance, and the tent covering peaked higher up and covered the Tabernacle.

There is a controversy as to where the cloths were hung. The inside cloth covering over the Tabernacle has cherubim in a design on it, presumably so that they could be seen from within. In the *International Standard Bible Encyclopaedia* Caldecott and Orr summarize the problem of the hanging of the cloths this way: "To avoid the difficulty of the ordinary view that the coverings, hanging down *outside* the framework, are unseen from within, except on the roof, it has sometimes been argued that the tapestry covering hung down, not outside, but inside the Tabernacle (Keil, Bahr, etc.). It is generally thought that this arrangement is inadmissible. A newer and more ingenious theory ... is that the "boards" constituting the framework of the Tabernacle were not solid planks, but really open "frames," through which the finely wrought covering could be seen from within."[8]

The most probable of the above arrangements was that the cherubim were visible from below, but we are not sure exactly how.

D. The Objects and Materials of the Tabernacle. The objects of the Tabernacle teach us many things about approaching God. From the outside, all that can be seen is the seven and a half foot tall linen curtain, the brass bases, the wooden pillars, and the silver pillar tops (AV, chapiters), with the outside of the Tabernacle structure at a distance. Speaking of the linen curtain, Olford says, "It speaks of righteousness, for Revelation 19:8 tells us that "fine linen is the righteousness of saints." This righteousness is imputed and imparted by God, through our Lord Jesus Christ."[9]

This linen represents our positional righteousness that is "in Christ." Every Christian has this righteousness by virtue of having received Jesus. The progressive righteousness, whereby we are becoming more and more like Jesus, is very different. Christians are on different levels of progressive righteousness, according to a combination of time and level of commitment to the Lord. Our positional righteousness is the righteousness of Christ on our account before the Father.

The pillars and their sockets were made of bronze, according to Exodus 27:10. Brass speaks of endurance through the fires of judgment, as brass is refined and strengthened copper. Thus, in Revelation 2:18 Jesus is described as "The Son of God, who has eyes like a flame of fire, and His feet are like burnished bronze." As fine bronze has passed through the refining fires, so Jesus has passed through the fire of testing and has come out perfect.

The last outside perimeter item is the chapiters, or silver caps on top of the pillars. Olford explains their significance this way: "All silver used in the building of the Tabernacle was melted down from redemption money. This was the half shekel that every man over twenty had to pay for the ransom of his soul (see Ex. 30:12-16). Thus silver speaks ever and always of redemption; and therefore of the Captain of our salvation."[10] As the chapiter is the top of the pillar, it is interesting to note that the Christian is to wear the helmet of salvation on his head.

The silver has a deeper meaning when we look at the Hebrew root from which the word comes. This Hebrew root also comprises the verb "to long for," and the word silver is commonly used to mean "money," as that was the common currency.[11] It is true that what we really long for is what we spend our money on. Jesus says, "for where your treasure is, there your heart will be also (Matthew 6:21)." It is true that when the members of the church all long for the same thing, they are unified. That is the reason that silver ("longings") is used for the connectors in the Tabernacle. Besides the chapiters, the hooks are silver, as they keep the curtains together and in place.

In addition to the hooks, there are connecting bars, made out of acacia (*shittim*) wood. This represents Jesus' perfect humanity, which we are being changed into. Our new nature also helps keep us together in Christ. The closer the believers are to Jesus, the closer they are to each other.

To complete the perimeter structure, there are cords and pegs. The pegs are of brass, and remind us that Jesus triumphed in judgment over death by his resurrection. He conquered the ground in that the grave could not hold him. The cords represent God's love for us, as God says in Hosea's day (Hosea 11:4): "I led them with cords of a man, with bonds of love."

The basic interior structure of the Tabernacle itself has some of the same items as the outer fence. The base consisted of about a hundred sockets of silver. As mentioned above, the silver represents our redemption, as it came from the half-shekel redemption money for every man over twenty. As this is the base upon which the Tabernacle stands, so our access to God stands solely on our salvation. Apart from salvation, there is no presence of God in our life and no access to God at all, except to repent and seek salvation.

The basic support for the Tabernacle was Acacia (*shittim*) wood, covered with gold. Olford says: "These boards speak of Christ in His perfect humanity and deity: imperishable wood, covered with pure gold. How wonderfully He stands out before us in the Gospels as the Son of Man and the Son of God. These boards also speak to us of the believer who has been cut down, as was Saul of Tarsus on the way to Damascus, shaped and fashioned, and made a partaker of the divine nature" (see 2 Peter 1:4). [12]

The pattern continues the same: we receive the fullness of Christ first at the time we believe, and then we grow in reality into what we already are in Christ.

There were also bars of the same wood, covered with gold, which held the boards together from above. I once asked a Rabbi friend what was the basic meaning behind the root that "gold" came from, and he said that it was "the shine of the presence of God." This explains why all of the gold is in the inside of the Tabernacle—that is where God's presence was. This author was unable to find a deeper meaning behind the root for gold in the Hebrew, and so we will stay with the rabbi's explanation.

There were four coverings to the Tabernacle. The first layer was made up of a series of small bands of curtain coupled together with gold clasps. They were to measure 28 cubits, which was enough to go over the breadth of the top and hang down to the height of one cubit (1.5 feet) above the ground on both sides. This was probably because it had cherubim on it and they were in a flying position.

The materials of this covering, mentioned in Exodus 26:1, are very beautiful. The first is *shésh moshzár*, rendered "fine twined linen." The word for linen is the same as the number six in Hebrew, the number of man. This refers to Jesus' perfect humanity. The expression *moshzár* means literally "twisted." Our humanity does not appeal to God as it is. It must be twisted out of its own self-will and led to say, "Not my will, but God's will be done."

This linen has blue thread (Heb. *tekhélet*) sewn into it. Gesenius says it is a violet thread, which was used to sew in the designs of the cherubim. The word appears to be from the Hebrew root meaning completion (*klh*). God is complete in Himself, and our satisfaction in Him should be total.[13]

The next color mentioned is purple (Heb. *argamán*). This needs to be broken into two words. The verb *arág* means, "to weave," and *man* is the name for mannah, which the Israelites ate in the wilderness. Combining the two would give us "woven mannah." The priests inside the Tabernacle could look upon this layer of coverings. We can also be fed by contemplating the Royal Jesus, as Jesus says in John 6:35: "I am the bread of life; he who comes to Me will not hunger, and he who believes in Me will never thirst." The purple color speaks of royalty, as Jesus is kingly in character. We need to understand and experience the glory of Jesus' presence in our experience with Him.

The last color is scarlet (Heb. *toláat shoní*). This means literally "worm of scarlet." This was a worm that produced a bright red dye upon being crushed, and is therefore a symbol of Christ's humility. In Psalm 22, a Psalm about Jesus' crucifixion, he says (v.6): "But I am a worm (*toláat*), and not a man; a reproach of men and despised by the people." The scarlet thus speaks of Jesus' humility, and even death.

What was made with the woven threads? "Cherubim, the work of a skillful workman (Heb. *cherubim ma-aséh hoshév*). This expression is literally, "cherubim, the work of a thinker." *Cherubim* comes from the verb "to approach" because these are the angels that are closest to the Lord—i.e. those who approach God. Satan himself was a cherub, according to Ezekiel 28:14, "You were the anointed cherub who covers." These *cherubim* are to be the work of a thinker. The word thinker is the participle of the verb "to think." In order to understand the things of God to approach God, the believer has to be a thinker. We are to meditate on the things of God day and night (Joshua 1:8, and Psalm 1:3). Unlike eastern mystic meditations, designed to empty the mind, our meditation is on the content of the Scriptures that God has revealed to man, to fill up the mind with God's truth.

The second covering was of "goats' hair," or just "goats" (Heb. *izzim*). The goat was used for a sacrifice in general (Leviticus 22:27), in a covenant enacting ceremony (Genesis 15:9), for Passover (Exodus 12:5), whole burnt offering (Leviticus 22:19), peace offering (Leviticus 3:12), sacrifice by fire (Numbers 18:17), and a sin offering (Leviticus 4:28). This covering speaks of Jesus as our sacrifice, indeed, every type of sacrifice for us. This covering did reach all the way down to the ground, like Jesus, as our sacrifice, came all the way down to man.

The third covering was of rams' skins. In Exodus 29 at the consecration of Aaron and his sons, the ram is a symbol of consecration. In verse 31 it is called "the ram of ordination" because of its part in the ceremony of ordaining of Aaron and his sons. Jesus was consecrated totally to the Father, even as He said in John 17:19: "For their sakes I sanctify Myself, that they themselves also may be sanctified in truth." The Hebrew root for "ram" means "to be in front of" or "to lead."[14] Jesus leads us in consecration by providing the example in his own personal conduct of submission to the Father. The ram skins are "dyed red" (Heb. *me-oddamím*). The Hebrew comes from the same root as "Adam" and "red," as the earth is reddish in the Middle East. Jesus in his consecration to the Father was "humanized" for his mission here, and "reddened" with his own blood from the whipping and crucifixion. Through it all, he remained dedicated to the Father to the utmost.

The final and outermost covering is that of badger's skins, though the Hebrew could have meant a dolphin or seal. The identity of the animal is not clear, but Olford says that the skin of this animal "was a hard, unattractive leather, calculated to resist beating rain, baking sun, or biting frost."[15] The outside of the Tabernacle was thus not attractive to the eye, even as Jesus was not attractive to the eye, according to Isaiah 53:2-3: "He has no stately form or majesty that we should look upon Him, nor appearance that we should be attracted to Him. He was despised and forsaken of men, a man of sorrows, and acquainted with grief; and like one from whom men hide their face He was despised, and we did not esteem Him."

II. Seven Steps to Intimacy with God Following the Seven Furniture Items in the Tabernacle.

In Hebrews 4:16 the believer in Jesus is exhorted to come before God continually: "Therefore let us draw near with confidence to the throne of grace, so that we may receive mercy and find grace to help in time of need." This is an invitation to come continually before God for mercy and grace. The verb "let us draw near" in the Greek (*προσερχώμεθα*) is a continuous action verb and suggests an open invitation for continual coming and going before the Lord.

We must remember that the throne of grace was on top of the Ark of the Covenant in the Holy of Holies in the Old Testament Tabernacle. The High Priest could only enter there once each year with sacrificial blood to atone for the sins of Israel. He even had a cord tied around his ankle so that if he was struck dead, the other priests could pull him out of there without entering there themselves and being struck dead. To this holiest of places in the Heavenly Tabernacle the New Testament believer has continuous access, according to this verse. Praise the Lord!

Though we have an open invitation to come before the Lord continually, there is still a protocol to follow in approaching Him. If an Israelite had wanted to see God in the Tabernacle and lifted up the western curtain and then went in under the other curtains directly into the Holy of Holies, he would not have made it alive. Even though a Christian has the Holy Spirit dwelling within him, he still needs to learn the steps to follow to approach that Throne of Grace.

A study of the seven steps to follow in approaching God in the Tabernacle is especially useful here because even the Throne of Grace in the Tabernacle takes its name from the Throne of Grace in the Heavenly Sanctuary. F. F. Bruce affirms that the Author of the Epistle to the Hebrews made this connection: "The lid of the ark was a golden slab called the mercy seat or place of propitiation, viewed by our author as the earthly counterpart of the "throne of grace" to which he has already exhorted his readers to draw near for help in the hour of need" (Chap. 4:16).[16]

Since the earthly Tabernacle was made as a copy of the Heavenly Sanctuary, it is especially useful for a Christian to learn the steps to approach God in the earthly Tabernacle and their equivalent items in the Heavenly Tabernacle. As we learn to include these steps in our approach to God every day, we will not forget any element of our relationship with God. In the order of approaching God, they are as follows: 1. the door, 2. the altar of bronze, 3. the laver of bronze, 4. the bread of the Presence, 5. the lampstand, 6. the altar of incense, and 7. the Ark of the Covenant. The first three involve a prayer in three parts, the fourth is our personal Bible study, and the last three are another prayer in three parts. This is an ideal form for the personal devotional time that this author has followed for many years.

1. The Door. As mentioned earlier, there is only one door in the Tabernacle, and it is on the east side. It consists of the middle 30 feet of the 75 feet of that side. There are four sections of curtain that form the door, and the door is made of four items (Exodus 27:16): fine twined linen with blue, purple, and scarlet threads sewn into it. Olford suggests that the door represents Jesus and that these four items mentioned suggest the four Gospels. The blue represents Jesus as the Divine Son, as in John's Gospel. The purple represents Jesus as the Divine Sovereign, as in Matthew's Gospel. The Scarlet represents Jesus as Divine Savior, as in Luke's Gospel. And finally, the white represents Jesus as the Divine Servant, as in Mark's Gospel.[17] The four materials on the earthly Tabernacle door point to the four Gospels, which are the way that we have access to Jesus, for "So faith comes from hearing, and hearing by the Word of Christ (Romans 10:17)."

It is clear that Jesus taught the He was the door of access to the Father. In John 10:9, using the metaphor of the sheepfold, Jesus says: "I am the door; if anyone enters through Me, he will be saved, and will go in and out, and find pasture." When we think of the Heavenly Tabernacle and our relation to the Father, we see that Jesus is the only way of access. Just as there is only one door in the earthly tabernacle, there is only one door in the Heavenly Tabernacle: Jesus. If one tried to enter the Old Testament Tabernacle some other way than prescribed by God, he would have been put to death—probably by God. In a similar way, one cannot get to God's presence another way, except through Jesus, the Door. Jesus says (John 10:1), "He who does not enter by the door into the fold of the sheep, but climbs up some other way, he is a thief and a robber." Anyone who tries to get in some other way will surely end up on hell. It cannot be any plainer than that!

It has been my experience to take my family to an amusement park. Near the entrance was a person who had a special material that could be stamped on one's hand and revealed only under a special light that they had. Anyone who had paid his ticked could have his hand stamped so that he could leave and re-enter without paying again for the rest of the day. In a similar way, the believer, upon believing in Jesus as his Savior is sealed with the Holy Spirit (Ephesians 1:13-14). This sealing with the Holy Spirit gives the believer unlimited access to the holiest site in the universe, the Throne of Grace in the Heavenly Tabernacle, from the point of his conversion through all eternity.

In our normal prayers, we usually say at the end, "in Jesus' name, Amen." However, the pattern of the Tabernacle suggests that this might be more appropriate as a beginning of a prayer, for in the name of Jesus we have access to God for salvation in the first place ("if anyone enters through Me, he will be saved."); and in Jesus' name we have continual access thereafter ("and will go in and out, and find pasture"). Thus, it is good to begin our prayer with a reminder that our only access to God is the name of Jesus, and also that that access is perfect forever after that.

2. The Bronze Altar. After the Old Testament Levite passed through the only door, he came to the bronze altar. This altar measured seven and a half feet squared and four and a half feet high. There were four horns on the top—one out of each corner. The AV reads (27:2), "Thou shalt make the horns of it." Keil explains this better the following way: "At its four corners shall its horns be from (out of) it," i.e. not removable, but as if growing out of it.[18] The NASV expresses this latter rendering well: "its horns shall be of one piece with it."

The altar was used to offer the blood sacrifices for the sins of the people. The Old Testament priesthood had to offer many sacrifices. There was a morning and an evening sacrifice, as well as others for the sins of the people and for certain feast days.

For the New Testament believer, things are different. Jesus has made a once and for all sacrifice, and it is not repeated. As the author of the Epistle to the Hebrews tells us (Heb. 10:11,12, & 14): "Every priest stands daily ministering and offering time after time the same sacrifices, which can never take away sins; but He (Jesus), having offered one sacrifice for sins for all time, sat down at the right hand of God. For by one offering he has perfected for all time those who are sanctified."

What need then could a Christian have of returning to the altar, if Jesus' priesthood was consummated by one sacrifice that was not repeated? We need a continual application of the blood for the sins that keep coming up in our lives, and we need to crucify the flesh daily.

In I John 1:7 we have instructions for the regular application of the blood for the continuous cleansing of sins: "But if we walk in the light, as He Himself is in the Light, we have fellowship with one another, and the blood of Jesus His Son cleanses us from all sin." Here the word "cleanses" (*katharíze*, *καθαρίζει*) is in continuous action, which means that the blood "keeps on cleansing us from all sin." The cleansing is regular. All we have to do to continue walking in the light is to confess our sins regularly and renounce them. At this step we want to deal with any sins that the Spirit brings to our attention. As we confess them and ask God to give us victory over them, we are cleansed from them with the blood of Jesus.

There is a once and for all application of the blood of Jesus for our eternal salvation, and there is the continuous, or daily application of the blood of Jesus as we confess our sins regularly. Once we are saved, our sin will not result in the cutting off of our relationship with Jesus, but it will cut the fellowship. When we confess that sin, the fellowship is also restored. As we remember the Altar of Bronze, we are reminded to deal with this step in our daily approach to God.

The blood has two functions in the human body: it removes toxic substances and brings nourishment. In the same way, the application of Jesus' blood removes sin and imparts Jesus' life. In Leviticus 17:11 we read, "the life of the flesh is in the blood." This should read, however, "the *soul* of the flesh is in the blood." The Hebrew word there is *nefesh*, which is usually translated as *soul*." As Jesus' blood is applied to our lives, then, He is our very life. This suggests what the Apostle Paul mentions about Jesus' living in us in Galatians 2:20: "I have been crucified with Christ: and it is no longer I who live, but *Christ lives in me*; and the life which I now live in the flesh I live by faith in the Son of God, who loved me and gave Himself up for me." So we see that the altar is the place where we seek the application of the blood with its twofold purpose.

In addition to the application of the blood of Jesus with its twofold purpose, there is another purpose for the altar of bronze. In Romans 12:1 we are exhorted to do the following: "Therefore I urge you brethren, by the mercies of God, to present your bodies a living and holy sacrifice, acceptable to God, which is your spiritual service of worship."

The verb translated here "to present" (*parastésai*, *παραστῆσαι*) is an aorist in the Greek, implying a single decision in a point of time. However, though the decision has to be made in a point of time, it must be lived out daily. While this is a once and for all decision in Romans 12, we are exhorted to make this decision regularly in Romans 6:16, where the daily battle is continuous: "Do you not know that when you present (*paristanete*, παριστάνετε, lit. "keep on presenting") yourselves to someone as slaves for obedience, you are slaves of the one you obey (*hupakouete*, ὑπακούετε, lit. "keep on obeying"), either of sin resulting in death, or of obedience resulting in righteousness?" This passage speaks of our daily habits, and it is at the altar that we turn over our flesh for crucifixion and our body for obedience to the Holy Spirit.

Though our old man is to be reckoned as dead after conversion, the flesh is the Christian's greatest enemy. As Paul explains in Galatians 5:16-17: "But I say, walk by the Spirit, and you will not carry out the desire of the flesh. For the flesh sets its desire against the Spirit and the Spirit against the flesh; for these are in opposition to one another, so that you may not do the things that you please."

For Paul then, the problem was that the flesh continues rising up against God, and there exists a very real conflict in the believer between choosing to walk in the Spirit and choosing to walk in the flesh. This brings us to the other application of the altar: the death of the flesh.

In Hebrew the terms are functional, and so death here means that the flesh is rendered inoperable. Though Paul mentions in Galatians 5:24, "Now those who belong to Christ Jesus have crucified the flesh with its passions and desires," there must also be a daily application of the cross, which is our altar. To this end Paul says (I Corinthians 15:31), "I die daily." We need to die daily to our flesh and its three motivating factors, as mentioned in I John 2:15-17: "the lust of the flesh and the lust of the eyes and the boastful pride of life."

We can dedicate our flesh to destruction by presenting our body to God and claiming the death of our flesh as a blessing from Jesus through His crucifixion each day. We then also claim his life living through us and abandon ourselves to His control for that day. That is how we die to the flesh. To this end it is helpful to me to offer my flesh as a sacrifice to God and claim Psalm 118:27b as a blessing from the Lord that day, "Bind the festival sacrifice (my flesh) with cords, to the horns of the altar." It is the job of Jesus as our High Priest to bring it about at this point, but we must be willing to hand it over.

3. The Bronze Laver. After leaving the bronze altar, the next item is the bronze laver. The bronze laver is mentioned in Exodus 30:17-21 near the end of the description of the items of the Tabernacle. Keil says, concerning the bronze laver: "The making of this vessel is not only mentioned in a supplementary manner, but no description is given of it because of the subordinate position which it occupied, and from the fact that it was not directly connected with the sanctuary, but was only used by the priests to cleanse themselves for the performance of their duties."[19]

There is good reason to suggest that Keil is wrong on this conjecture. First of all, in verse 21 God says, "So they shall wash their hands and their feet, so that they will not die." It would seem more logical to conclude that anything that prevented the priests from death when they went in to minister was both important and an integral part of their priestly duties.

Like the altar before it, the laver is of bronze, which speaks of Jesus' perfection that has passed through testing. The laver is made of a basin above and its foot, or its support below. According to Keil, the support probably was "something separate from the basin which was no doubt used for drawing off as much water as was required for washing the officiating priests."[20]

It is interesting to note from Exodus 38:8 that the bronze for this laver was made "from the mirrors of the serving women assembling who served at the doorway of the tent of meeting." First of all, the Hebrew does not refer to these women as "assembling" at the door of the congregation as the AV reads. The Hebrew word is *hatzovóth* (הַצֹּבְאֹת), which here means "who were serving." A better translation yet could be "who were waging war." The Hebrew word for army and for waging warfare comes from this root, rather than the word to assemble. The application for us is that every believer is in the Lord's army, even the lady that serves tables at our social events.

It is also significant that these ladies gave up their mirrors to make the altar of bronze, for when we give up focusing on our vanity, we are ready to be cleansed and prepared for God's service. In the same way, the ladies had to give up their focus on the exterior to focus on interior beautification. As Peter mentions in I Peter 3:3-4: "Your adornment must not be merely external—braiding the hair and wearing gold jewelry, or putting on dresses; but let it be the hidden person of the heart, with the imperishable quality of a gentle and quiet spirit, which is precious in the sight of God." The same is true of men, obviously. People should tell that we are different on the inside when we are around.

There is no mention of dimensions of the laver. I believe that this was to focus attention to the water itself, which has no dimensions of its own, but rather takes on the dimensions of the vessel it is in. In the same way, the Holy Spirit ministers to every believer with no limits, except as our lack of dedication may limit Him.

What is the purpose of the cleansing at the laver of bronze? At the Altar of Bronze all sin has been dealt with, but this is another cleansing. What is it for? The Aaronic priests cleansed themselves from sin at the bronze altar and from dirt at the bronze laver. What does dirt represent to the Christian? Dirt represents contamination from contact with the world. Just as the world is a dirty place, and the priests' hands and feet got dirty just from contact with the world around them, so the New Testament believer is in the world and he gets dirty from just touching the things around him.

But what is the world for the Christian? In I John 2:16 we have an exhaustive list of what a Christian picks up from contact with the world that defiles him: "For all that is in the world, the lust of the flesh and the lust of the eyes and the boastful pride of life, is not from the Father, but is from the world." A Christian picks up these desires just by contact with the world. For example when this author goes out on visitation to evangelize, something of the effects of the Holy Spirit in his life touch the people he is visiting, but he can return with anger, materialism, or other desires that touch him from the other people. There is a need to wash off this "dirt" before entering the presence of the Lord, as well as one's own sin.

In Ephesians 5:26 we find that Jesus gave Himself for the church "so that He might sanctify her, having cleansed her by the washing of water with the word." This is the equivalent of the washing at the laver. Just as the priests had to wash daily, so the believers in Jesus should be in the Word of God daily, letting the Holy Spirit bring to mind what is not right and cleanse them from it.

Finally, we need to look at what was to be washed in the laver. At the laver the priests only washed their hands and feet. They were to come already bathed from their own tents. In the same way the believer in Jesus is bathed once and for all at salvation, and only needs to wash his hands and feet regularly. At the last supper, Jesus wrapped himself with a towel and washed the feet of His disciples. When He came to Peter, Peter would not let him. Jesus said, "If I do not wash you, you have no part with Me (John 13:8)." Upon hearing this, Peter wanted a full bath, to which Jesus responds (v.10), "He who has bathed, needs only to wash his feet, but is completely clean." The full bath corresponds to salvation and the washings of feet and hands refer to our daily cleansing from contact with the world.

It is interesting to note that the Hebrew sheds additional light on the meaning of washing the hands and feet for the Christian. The Hebrew root from which the word for hands comes has 3 basic meanings for the verb, as well as the name Jew itself. The first is to praise the Lord (Psalm 118:1), "Give thanks (Heb. *hodu*, הוֹדוּ) to the LORD, for He is good; for His lovingkindness is everlasting." Here praise and the giving of thanks are seen as the same thing and are from the same Hebrew root.[21]

The second basic meaning from that root is to confess the names of God, including confessing the character of God revealed by that name. In II Chronicles 6:24 we read, "If Your people Israel are defeated before an enemy because they have sinned against You, and they return to You and *confess Your name* (Heb. *ve-hodu* et-shimecha, וְהוֹדוּ אֶת־שְׁמֶךָ), and pray and make supplication before You in this house…" This is part of repentance.

The third meaning behind the Hebrew root from which the word hand comes is to confess our sins to God. In Proverbs 28:13 we read: "He who conceals his transgressions will not prosper, *but he who confesses* (Heb. *umodeh*, וּמוֹדֶה) and forsakes them will find compassion." After praising God and confessing God's attributes, the natural response is to want to confess our sins before Him and seek forgiveness. These three practices put God in His rightful place and us in our rightful place. If we were to make an etymological translation of the word for hands from the Hebrew, they would be our "praisers." We need for the Holy Spirit to wash away the worldliness of self-glorification at the laver in order for our "praisers" to work right.

The other part of our body that needs regular cleansing is our feet. Our feet refer to our walk, and especially our witness. In Isaiah 52:7 we read, "How lovely on the mountains are the feet *of him that brings good news*". Here the Hebrew word for bringing good tidings is the participle *mebassér*. מְבַשֵּׂר). This is from the first verb *to evangelize*. The Hebrew idea behind evangelism is to "flesh out" the message. The word flesh is from the same root.[22] The Hebrew term for evangelism is holistic. It implies living out the message through our faith, in addition to announcing it with words. Our life should back up our words.

The Greek Septuagint translated this word with the verb *euangelízesthai*, (εὐαγγελίζεσθαι), combining two words *eu*, meaning "good" and *angelizesthai*, meaning "to announce." Combined they give us our modern word "to evangelize," and mean literally, "to announce good." Here the emphasis is on the proclamation of the message. Sometimes we emphasize the Greek background too much and emphasize the proclamation of the message without any emphasis on living the message. Both are necessary parts of real evangelism. When we come into contact with the world by "fleshing out the message" or "announcing good," we can get dirty with self-will from others and lag in our zeal to glorify God and evangelize. This also needs cleansing.

Both hands and feet explain different aspects of the same attitude. God puts His glory on us believers. We direct it upward as we "lift holy hands to the Lord" to praise God, confess God's name, and confess our sins to God. We direct it outward to others when we tell of the glory of the Lord and what He did for them in evangelism. Praise and evangelism both are the first parts of our walk that get cold, and they need to be cleansed every day at the laver of God. When we pray and ask the Holy Spirit to cleanse us from all contact with the world and with any bad effects of our own sin on our life, He washes us from these bad effects of the world through the water of the Holy Spirit and fills us with zeal for Him in preparation for the next steps with Him.

The issue is not only the bad effects of the world, though. Paul says in Galatians 6:14 that through the cross, "the world has been crucified to me, and I to the world." When the believer has contact with the world, he has touched a dead thing. All of the "lust of the flesh and the lust of the eyes and the boastful pride of life" are dead things for the believer. It is impossible to avoid coming into contact with them as it was for the resident of Canaan in Bible times to avoid getting dirty feet while walking on dusty roads with open sandals. However, as the Israelite priest had to wash his hands and feet before serving before the Lord in order not to die, so the modern Christian needs this cleansing from the contamination of the world before entering the Heavenly Tabernacle.

Numbers 19 gives us a clearer picture of this washing. Here we are told about a special sacrifice of a red heifer that purifies those who had touched a dead body. That is what the world is for the believer in Jesus—a dead thing. The heifer is sacrificed outside of the camp of Israel. Eleazer was to sprinkle some if its blood on the front of the tent of meeting seven times, and then the rest of the offering was to be burned as a whole burnt offering (v.5).

To this burning offering were added cedar wood, hyssop, and scarlet material. The cedar is a symbol of strength, as cedar beams were used as supports for the Temple later. This is symbolic of Jesus' strength to resist the influences of the world. The hyssop was a plant used to sprinkle fluids, and was thought to have healing qualities. It was used to sprinkle blood, as well as water. In this case the applied fluid was water, but even it was sanctified by a whole burnt offering. The scarlet material is the same as the scarlet above—a worm that gave off a red dye when crushed. As we have the attitude of Jesus in Psalm 22:6, we are ready to give up the effects of the world and take the attitude of Jesus by not exalting ourselves: "But I am a worm and not a man." Here the word worm is the same as the one that gave off the red dye: *tolaath* (תּוֹלַעַת).

It is interesting to note that the priest that slaughtered the animal and sprinkled its blood on the Tabernacle, the man who burned the animal, and the man that gathered the ashes and picked them up and carried them to a clean place outside the camp were then unclean until the evening. The sacrifice itself was in a sense unclean, but it made the people clean after touching a dead body (vv. 7-10). This reminds us believers that we can become unclean from the contamination in others and need to be cleansed from contact with them, even though we have no sin in the matter.

Concerning this purification, Moses says (Numbers 19: 11-13), "The one who touches the corpse of any person shall be unclean seven days. That one shall purify himself from uncleanness with the water on the third day and on the seventh day, and then he will be clean; but if he does not purify himself on the third day and on the seventh day, he will not be clean. Anyone who touches the corpse, the body of a man that has died, and does not purify himself, defiles the tabernacle of the Lord; and that person shall be cut off from Israel. Because the water for impurity was not sprinkled on him, he shall be unclean; his uncleanness is still on him."

So we see the importance of the water of purification, but how could this purification rite relate to the New Testament believer? In order to apply this rite to the New Testament believer, we need to see how the water is applied. In verses 17-18 we read, "Then for the unclean person they shall take some of the ashes of the burnt purification from sin and flowing water (Heb. living water) shall be added to them in a vessel. A clean person shall take hyssop and dip it in the water and sprinkle it." So we see that the rite of purification required that any person that had been defiled by touching a dead body, or grave, or a human bone had to be quarantined for seven days. On the third and on the seventh days he had to have special water sprinkled on him. After that, he had to wash his clothes and bathe himself, and then he was clean by the evening that began the eighth day.

The water of purification included the elements that we considered earlier, but they were to be applied with living water, as it says in Hebrew. Living water is mentioned in the New Testament in John 8:38-39, where Jesus says: "'He who believes in Me, as the Scripture said, 'From his innermost being will flow rivers of living water.' But this He spoke of the Spirit, whom those who believed in Him were to receive."

The Holy Spirit, who lives in the New Testament believer, removes the contamination of the lusts and pride of this world from the believer and produces in us the pure will of Jesus, which was totally given over to the Father, as the red heifer was wholly given over to the fire. This is what makes the New Testament believer ready to enter the presence of the Lord in the Heavenly Tabernacle. Without this application of the living water, the believer remains contaminated with the desires of this world, just through contact with this world, and is unfit to continue to the next step.

The First Prayer: The Door, the Bronze Altar, and the Bronze Laver.

These first three items, the door, the altar, and the laver, are fulfilled in a three-part prayer. In it we remember that we are coming only in the name of Jesus. We also must confess any known sin, as well as claim the death of the flesh that day so that Jesus can have full rule through the Holy Spirit through the daily application of the blood. Next, we ask God for the Holy Spirit's cleansing from all contact with the world so that we are prepared to go on with Him in everything. Thus we are prepared to partake of the bread (the Word of God) after the door, the application of the blood, and the application of the Living Water.

4. The Table and the Bread of God's Presence. As the Old Testament believer leaves the bronze laver, he arrives at the Tabernacle itself. When he passes through the door, he enters into the first chamber, called the Holy Place. In this chamber on his right there is a table with twelve pieces of bread in two rows of six. On his left there is a huge lampstand, or *menorah*, of seven branches. The seven oil lamps on top are burning with a continual light, day and night. At the back before the entrance to the second chamber there is the altar of incense, where incense is offered to the Lord. We will consider the table of the bread of God's presence first.

The table of the bread of God's presence was made of acacia wood and covered with pure gold. All of the elements on the inside of the Tabernacle were of pure gold or covered with pure gold. As mentioned earlier, the gold represents the shine of the presence of God, and so it is fitting that the inside furniture should be of gold. The table measured three feet by one and a half feet on top and was two feet three inches above the ground. It had a border of about a handbreadth (about 4 to 5 inches) around the top to hold it together and to hold the four legs. There were two ornamental wreaths, one under the top of the table and one under the rim below it.

On the table were twelve dishes in two rows of six with a loaf of bread on each one. The number twelve represents the number of tribes of Israel, and the bread represents fellowship. Also, the Hebrew word for bread, *léchem* (Heb. לֶחֶם), comes from the same word root as battle *milchamáh* (מִלְחָמָה). When we break bread with the Lord, we are not only nourished, but we are also pledged to fight on the same side with Him in His battles against the enemy, and He will also fight on our side in our battles.

Along with the bread and its dishes on the table are spoons, covers, and bowls. The bowls, according to Olford, "were the flagons such as were used for the rite of the drink offering, which appears to have regularly accompanied every drink offering."[23] It is especially interesting that these are called *menaquiyyothav* (מְנַקִּיֹּתָיו, Exodus 25:29) from the causative stem of the verb "to be empty" or "to be clean." a good etymological translation would be "its emptiers." It is probable that an "emptier" would be related to a drink offering because it is emptied as it is poured out before the Lord. We need to be emptied of ourselves—especially our own ideas and desires—in order to receive the Lord's words as nourishment and His Spirit, as well.

In addition to the cleansing of the believer, the Word of God also nourishes him. In John 6 Jesus teaches us that he is the bread of life (v.33, NASV mg.): "For the bread of God is He who comes down from heaven and gives life to the world." It is interesting to note along with this teaching that Jesus is born in Bethlehem, which means "House of Bread." Later, after scandalizing many people with this teaching by saying that people needed to eat His flesh and drink His blood to have life in them, Jesus states plainly to his disciples (v. 63), "It is the Spirit who gives life, the flesh profits nothing; the words that I have spoken to you are spirit and are life." We may rightfully consider that all Scriptures are the words that Jesus speaks unto us, and therefore all of Scriptures are spirit and they are life.

As a part of the Christian's daily devotional time, the Bible *study* portion represents the bread of the presence. As one studies the Bible, he not only learns more about God, but also his spirit is nourished with the words of Jesus, which are both spirit and life. It is good to follow some regular plan, such as reading the Bible through in a year. A good idea for a new Christian is to use a regular devotional guide with a reading and brief meditation for each day of the year. The most important thing is to be studying and meditating regularly on the Word of God in order to grow spiritually.

After the time of Bible study, there is another prayer in three parts, corresponding to the remaining three items of furniture in the Tabernacle: the golden lampstand, the altar of incense, and the Ark of the Covenant (especially the mercy seat on top of it). As we shall see, these three correspond to our prayer for the anointing of the Holy Spirit, our praise of God, and our petitions, in the same order. Let us consider them in the same order.

5. The Golden Lampstand. Opposite the table of bread of the Presence of God is the golden lampstand, known by its Hebrew name *menoráh.*(מְנֹרָה) Its size is not given, as that of the laver, probably to call attention to the fact that the oil and light have no limits in themselves. They fill whatever size and shape container they are put in. The menorah is made in one piece of beaten pure gold, and it is described as having seven branches—three branches out of each side and one in the middle. In Exodus 27:20 the Lord orders that the menorah is to "burn continually," and it is to be fueled by pure beaten olive oil. The tongs and snuffers in Exodus 25:38 are for the priests to trim the wicks and remove the trimmings so that the seven lights will continue to burn. "Tongs and snuffdishes" (AV) is a better translation than the NASV "snuffers and their trays" because the first word, *malqacheha* (Heb. מַלְקָחֶיהָ) is from the verb "to take" and means "takers," or tongs. The other item is *machtotecha* (Heb. מַחְתֹּתֶיהָ) from the verb "to snatch up" fire or coals, the etymological meaning is given by Gesenius as censer or snuff dish.[24]

It would appear that the menorah corresponds to the Holy Spirit's anointing of the believer, which should result in a radical difference in his life. We are called Christians for this step in our relation to

God, as Christian means "anointed one." This design, a single one followed by three pairs, is especially appropriate to the naming of the seven spirits of God in Isaiah 11:2: "And the Spirit of the LORD (Jehovah) (1) will rest on him, the spirit of wisdom (2) and understanding (3), the spirit of counsel (4) and strength (5), the spirit of knowledge (6) and the fear of the Lord (Jehovah) (7)."

I have added the numbers and the material in parentheses to illustrate how the menorah reflects the seven Spirits of God or the sevenfold fullness of the Holy Spirit. This scheme fits the form of the menorah, in that there is first the one in the middle, and then (as we go down the main trunk) the internal pair next to the trunk, next the middle pair (the middle lamp of the three on each side), and finally, the outer pair.

When praying for the anointing of the Holy Spirit, the present author has found it useful to concentrate on each of the Seven Spirits at a time and ask for the anointing with each Spirit consecutively until all seven are named. We all need the sevenfold anointing of the Holy Spirit in order to shine in every area of our lives. On days when fasting is involved and more time is set aside, it has proven helpful to go through these seven areas of life for the confession of sins and the application of the blood, as well as the washing at the laver. Here the focus is on each of these topics and areas of life in the same order. Thus all seven areas of life pass through the stages of washing, purification from contamination, and anointing.

The anointing has three major blessings in our lives, corresponding to the almond like bowls, the knoblike decorations, and the flowers. According to Olford, "It is generally accepted that the bowls were almonds, while the knops represented pomegranates, and the flowers were lilies."[16] The word "almonds" in Hebrew (*shekedím*, שְׁקֵדִים) is from the same root as *shoqed* (שֹׁקֵד) the verb meaning "to watch" or "to wake."[25] We also need to heed the warning that Jesus gave to His disciples in the Garden of Gethsemane (Matthew 26:41), "Keep watching and praying that you may not enter into temptation; the spirit is willing, but the flesh is weak." The almonds remind us that the anointing should be accompanied by watchfulness and alertness spiritually—when we think things are at their best we are most vulnerable to attacks of the enemy.

The second blessing of the anointing is represented by the pomegranates, which are a symbol of fruitfulness. Jesus says in John 15:5, "I am the vine, you are the branches; he who abides in Me, and I in him, he bears much fruit, for apart from Me you can do nothing." The anointing makes us fruitful, as it comes from our abiding in Christ.

The lilies represent the third blessing of the anointing. Olford says concerning them, "The lilies speak of Christ in His life of purity. The Song of Solomon speaks of our Lord as the 'lily of the valleys' (2:1) and, as such, He was 'holy, harmless, undefiled, separated from sinners' (Hebrews 7:26)".[25] The anointing makes us more and more like Jesus in this respect, as well. It gives us His holy hatred for sin of any kind, especially our own, and a desire to separate from it.

6. The Altar of Incense. As one went beyond the menorah and the table of the bread of the Presence toward the Most Holy Place, he arrived at the altar of incense, just in front of the curtain that separates between the Holy Place and the Most Holy Place. The altar of incense was also made of acacia wood overlaid with pure gold. It was to have a golden wreath around the outer edge and four horns—one on each corner. The top was square, measuring one and a half feet on a side, and it was three feet high.

It may seem strange to us that an altar where incense is burned should have horns, but our praise to God can be a sacrifice of praise. In Psalm 50:14-15 we have some insight on praise as a sacrifice: "Offer to God a sacrifice of thanksgiving and pay your vows to the Most High; Call upon Me in the day of trouble; I shall rescue you, and you will honor Me."

The first phrase is literally, "Sacrifice unto God praise." How can praise be a sacrifice? When we are in a difficult situation, a crisis develops, and we must choose between our love for God, Who put us in this situation, and our desire to escape to improve our circumstances. By accepting the difficult situation as from God and waiting on Him for the answer, we are affirming God's sovereignty over us. We are also affirming that our love for God is stronger than our desire for better circumstances.

By sacrificing praise we win the battle over our own selfish desires of the flesh to make things comfortable again or to complain that our rights are violated. Remember, Job's problem was that he justified himself, rather than God. Our continuous sacrifice of praise in all situations leads us into a closer relation with God while it tears our flesh with the horns of this altar of incense.

As was explained earlier, the verb that is translated "to praise" God actually has three meanings. The first one, to confess sin, has already been carried out at the bronze altar. The second one means to confess God's character by means of confessing God's names, and this is part of the praise here. As we confess that God is omniscient, we affirm His wisdom over ours. As we affirm His omnipotence, we trust His power over ours and give Him the glory at the end, etc. This type of confession praises God and sets up the worshipper to act in accordance with what he is affirming. The third meaning of this verb is "to praise" God. This includes showing gratitude for all He has done.

In Revelation 5:8 we see that our prayers can fill heaven with incense: "When he had taken the book, the four living creatures and the twenty-four elders fell down before the Lamb, each one holding a harp and golden bowls full of incense, which are the prayers of the saints." It is exciting to think that our prayers can fill up heaven with a pleasing aroma. In Exodus 30:34 the four elements that make up the incense in equal parts are listed, and each one reminds the Christian of something about his praise to the Lord. Before the list begins the Lord mentions that they are sweet spices. They are to give a pleasing aroma before the Lord. Our praise is to be focused on pleasing God, not ourselves. We need to get our attention off of ourselves and what we want or think is good for us, and focus it on God and what will be pleasing to Him.

The first ingredient of the incense is *natáph*, (נָטָף) translated stacte in the AV and NASV. It comes from the verb "to drop" or "to drip," and refers to the need for our praise to be continuous, as the dripping of this plant. In Job 29:21-23 this verb illustrates how human speech can drip down blessings on others. Here Job says about those whom he rescued from oppressors, "To me they listened and waited, And kept silent for my counsel. After my words they did not speak again,

And my speech dropped on them. They waited for me as for the rain, And opened their mouth as for the spring rain."

Here the word *nataph* shows the continual dripping or dropping down of blessings through speech. In I Thessalonians 5:18 Paul exhorts us: "In everything give thanks; for this is God's will for you in Christ Jesus." Giving thanks is a part of praise, and the word "thank you" in Modern Hebrew, *todáh*, is from the same root. God wants the incense of our praise to be continuous, not sporadic.

The second ingredient of the incense is *shehélet* (שְׁחֵלֶת), translated onycha in the AV and NASV. Gesenius says that this is "the operculum, or closing-flap, of certain mollusks, with pungent odor when burnt."[26] This root is not common in Hebrew, but it does have an uncommon word for lion from it. Cognate Semitic languages yield the idea of calling or proclaiming. Our praise must be proclaimed in an audible voice in order to glorify God. As the pungent odor is sent out strong, so our praise should be sent out strong.

The third ingredient of the incense is *chelbenáh* (חֶלְבְּנָה) translated galbanum in the AV and the NASV. This word comes from the Hebrew root for milk and fat. This refers to our prosperity. All Christians have varying degrees of prosperity, but as we thank the Lord for His bountiful provisions and focus on the many blessings we have, we will overflow with praise for God. This is the attitude of thankfulness that we are to have when we come with petitions, which will be the next step at the Mercy Seat. Paul reminds us of this in Philippians 4:6: "Be anxious for nothing, but in everything by prayer and supplication *with thanksgiving* let your requests be made known to God." This is the step where the thanksgiving is picked up before the requests are even made.

The final ingredient of the incense is *lebonáh* (לְבֹנָה) translated frankincense in the AV and NASV. The word *lebonáh* is from the Hebrew root referring to whiteness. This incense gives forth a white smoke and reminds us of Jesus' holiness. We are to be covered in Jesus' holiness and be holy ourselves when we are praising the Lord. That is why Paul instructs us in I Timothy 2:8: "Therefore I want the men in every place to pray, *lifting up holy hands*, without wrath and dissension." As was said earlier, our hands are symbol of our praise, and holy hands can only come from a holy life, which only Jesus can live through us, but we have to give Him full control. Exodus 30:34 concludes, "there shall be an equal part of each." All of these ingredients are equally important in our praise as worship of God.

7. The Ark of the Covenant and the Mercy Seat. The altar of incense stood in front of a curtain, which separated the Holy Place from the Holy of Holies. The only person allowed beyond this point was the High Priest, and he was allowed beyond this point only once each year on *Yom Kippur*, the Day of Atonement. On that day he had to come with the blood of a sacrificial bullock for his own sins and the sins of his family, as well as the blood of a sacrificial goat for the sins of the people. Even then, there was a cord tied around his ankle so that he could be pulled out if the Lord struck him dead because something was not right in him or his procedure. This was the only access to God at that time, but it was extremely limited. It was good, but what we have in Christ is better.

In Hebrews 9:6-8 we read the reason for this limitation of access: "Now when these things have been so prepared, the priests are continually entering the outer tabernacle performing the divine worship, but into the second, only the high priest enters once a year, not without taking blood, which he offers for himself and for the sins of the people committed in ignorance. The Holy Spirit is signifying this, that the way into the holy place has not yet been disclosed while the outer tabernacle is still standing."

Thus, "the way into the holy place (Holy of Holies) has not yet been disclosed" during the time of the Old Testament because the access was limited. With Jesus' death on the cross, as the supreme and efficacious sacrifice, we read in Matthew 27:50-51: "And Jesus cried out again with a loud voice, and yielded up His spirit. And behold, the veil of the temple was torn in two from top to bottom; and the earth shook and the rocks were split."

Though this was in the Temple, rather than in the Tabernacle, it was essentially the same veil that separated between the Holy Place and the Holy of Holies, where the access was limited. After Jesus' death, burial, and resurrection from the dead, there were three changes made: the first is that the access was made into the Heavenly Sanctuary, which is superior to the earthly one. As the author to the

Hebrews continues (Hebrews 9:11-12): “But when Christ appeared as a high priest of the good things to come, He entered through *the greater and more perfect tabernacle*, not made with hands, that is to say, not of this creation; and not through the blood of goats and calves, but through His own blood, He entered the holy place once for all, having obtained eternal redemption.”

It is interesting that the name for the ask of the covenant *aron-habbrith* (אָרוֹן־הַבְּרִית) is the same as the word for a coffin. In Genesis 50:26 we read about Joseph: “he was embalmed and placed in a coffin (*aron*) in Egypt.” During the Old Testament period, access to God’s presence in the Tabernacle and later Temple was limited to the High Priest once per year because he was alive. The New Testament believer comes to God as dead, buried, and risen with Jesus, and therefore there is continuous access to God’s presence. We are coming as dead to ourselves so we can have fellowship with God.

The second change was that the resulting access was continual and open to all believers in Jesus, as we read in Hebrews 4:16: “Therefore let us (i.e. all believers) draw near (keep on drawing near) with confidence to the throne of grace, so that we may receive mercy and find grace to help in time of need.” There are no longer any limits on the believer’s approach to God or on how often or according to any schedule. There is a standing invitation to all believers to approach God in the holiest place in the universe, His throne of grace in heaven, and receive immediate audience for forgiveness of sins and help in any difficulties. It is to a better sanctuary with continuous access for all believers.

Let us now consider what the earthly Ark of the Covenant was in order to under to understand the heavenly one better. The ark measured three feet nine inches long by two feet three inches wide by two feet three inches high. It was made of acacia wood, covered with gold on the inside and outside. This was the only item that had gold on the inside as well as the outside, showing the greatest value and the final stage of God’s presence. Around it was a crown of gold also. Since gold represents the shine of the presence of God, then this was the place where there was the most gold. Like other objects, it had gold rings and wooden boards to put through them to carry the ark without touching it.

On the top of the ark was the mercy seat (*kapporet*, כַּפֹּרֶת). The Hebrew suggests that it was known for being the place where the blood of the atonement (*kapparah*,כַּפָּרָה) was placed and where the forgiveness was granted. There were two golden cherubim on the mercy seat facing one another, one on each side. The word cherub means, "neared one," and the High Priest, upon seeing the cherubim was reminded that he was "neared," or brought near to God as he approached the mercy seat.

In Exodus 25:22 God tells Moses why the mercy seat is there: "There I will meet with you; and from above the mercy seat, from between the two cherubim which are upon the ark of the testimony, I will speak to you about all things that I will give you in commandment for the sons of Israel."

The third change is that we do not need a cord around our ankle in case we are not received. We are always accepted in Jesus. What Moses needed we also need and have: a place to go to meet with Jesus and to commune with him. However, we may go directly into the Heavenly Sanctuary before the mercy seat there. We receive mercy and help at the heavenly mercy seat, and God also gives His leading through the Holy Spirit. This is a place to ask for mercy and grace to help in time of need, and it is also a place to just rest and enjoy God's presence. Communing with God is very special. As we contemplate Christ, we are being changed more and more to be like him, as Paul says in II Corinthians 3:18: "But we all, with unveiled face, beholding as in a mirror the glory of the Lord, are being transformed into the same image from glory to glory, just as from the Lord, the Spirit."

The Second Prayer: the Candelabra, the Altar of Incense, and the Mercy Seat.

We see then, that the last three steps to approaching God are by another prayer in three parts: the prayer for the anointing, the prayer of praise and affirmation of God's names and character, and the prayer of petition, along with enjoyment of the Presence of the Lord.

These correspond to the anointing with oil, the incense of praise, and the mercy seat for petitions and presence of God.

Conclusion: The Importance of Each of the Seven Steps.

The mercy seat, with the presence of the Lord, is the most special place in the universe, and all believers in Jesus have continual access to it. Only we must remember to pass through all of the preceding steps before we arrive. As we have observed the seven steps to approaching God in the earthly tabernacle, we have also found a corresponding seven steps for approaching God in the Heavenly Tabernacle.

It is important to follow each one of these seven steps in approaching God or we may not receive the answer to our petitions at the end when we approach the mercy seat with them. Let us see now a Biblical reason that each of the steps is important in receiving our petition from God.

The Door. We must come through the door by receiving Jesus as our Savior in the first place, as Jesus is the Door. If we are unsaved, the only petition God is ready to grant is the petition to be saved through Jesus' blood in the first place. In John 10:1 we read: "He who does not enter by the door into the fold of the sheep, but climbs up some other way, he is a thief and a robber." We know that God will not reward thieves and robbers. Even if someone could sneak into God's presence without Jesus, as in the wedding guest without a wedding garment (i.e. without being clothed in Jesus' righteousness, see Matthew 22:12-13), we would be bound and cast into outer darkness. All may come, but they must use the door.

The Altar of Bronze. We must confess any known sins at the altar of bronze and put them beneath the blood. In Psalm 66:18 the psalmist acknowledges: "If I regard wickedness in my heart, the Lord will not hear." The application of blood for salvation establishes our permanent relation with God, but the continual application of that blood deals with the daily sins that hinder the fellowship. If we are to commune with the Lord where the help is given, we must not have any unconfessed sin hindering the fellowship.

Also, at the altar of bronze we claim the crucifixion of the flesh. If we are walking in the flesh, we are filled with all types of desires that are contrary to God's will, as explained in Galatians 5:19-21. That being the case, we are bound to make petitions that are incorrect. James warns us (James 4:3): Ye ask, and do not receive, because you ask with wrong motives, so that you may spend it on your pleasures." If the flesh is crucified at the bronze altar, then it will not rise up and make the wrong petitions later at the mercy seat.

The Laver of Bronze. We must wash our hands and feet in the bronze laver. Our hands are our "praisers" and our feet are our "evangelizers." Jesus showed the importance of this step when He said to Peter (John 13:8): "If I do not wash you, you have no part with Me." This is only the feet (and probably the hands also for us), not the whole body. The bath of the whole body corresponds to our washing at conversion and the foot washings are the daily cleansings from contact with the world. About the whole body Jesus says (v. 10): "He who has bathed needs only to wash his feet, but is completely clean." We do not want to come before the mercy seat with petitions and hear the Lord Jesus say, "You have no part with me because you have not washed your hands and feet." We won't get our petitions that way until we return for the daily washing.

The Table of the Bread of God's Presence. This table had the Bread of the Presence, which corresponds to our devouring the Word of God. We need to study and meditate regularly on the Scriptures. Jesus says (John 15:7): "If you abide in Me, *and My words abide in you*, ask whatever you wish, and it will be done for you." There is a condition to be met here before we can expect God to answer our petitions. We need to commit ourselves to God and memorize and meditate on His Word. As His Word becomes a part of us, we will be more and more like Jesus and the Father will grant the requests, which will be coming from a dedicated believer filled with Scriptures.

The Menorah of the Anointing. In order to make petitions in line with the will of God, the believer needs the anointing of the

Holy Spirit, Who makes petitions that are right even when we do not know how or what to pray. Paul tells us in Romans 8:26-27: “In the same way the Spirit also helps our weakness; for we do not know how to pray as we should, but the Spirit Himself intercedes for us with groanings too deep for words; and He who searches the hearts knows what the mind of the Spirit is, because He intercedes for the saints according to the will of God.”

Without the anointing of the Spirit, we will not know what to pray. However, as the Holy Spirit guides us in our prayers, the petitions are brought into line with God’s perfect will for us and they are then granted.

The Altar of Incense. The altar of incense represents our praise of God. Praise is not just some low priority option in our approach of God. In Psalm 100:4 we are ordered: “Enter His gates with thanksgiving, And His courts with praise. Give thanks to Him, bless His name.” Since the next step is to enter into God’s very presence, we need to pick up the praise here. Also, Paul repeats this order to praise the Lord as we bring our petitions in Philippians 4:6: “Be anxious for nothing; but in everything by prayer and supplication *with thanksgiving* let your requests be made known to God.” If we pass over this step, we are giving our petitions in an incorrect manner—i.e. without praise and thanksgiving—and God may not grant them.

The Ark of the Covenant and the Mercy Seat. There are two things to remember as we bring our petitions to the throne of grace. First of all, we are to bring them there, and to no other place in the universe. We can tell others about our problems, but they can usually only sympathize without helping. There is no excuse for bringing our petitions before idols or the evil spirits that inhabit them. That would even anger the Lord. As Hebrews 4:16 says, we must “draw near with confidence to the throne of grace” to present our petitions, not some other place.

The second thing to remember about the petitions is to bring them. If we suffer and complain to others about our problems but we don’t bring our petition to the Lord, He will not answer. James says (James 4:2): “You do not have because you do not ask.” Asking God for things is a way of confessing our need and inability to meet that need, as well as setting up the situation for the Lord Jesus to get the glory when the answer comes. This is pleasing to the Father because He has desired to give Jesus all of the glory.

As we commune with God at the mercy seat, we may enjoy His presence, as well as answers to our petitions. However, we need to come to Him His way. The earthly tabernacle shows us the outward form of the heavenly tabernacle, into which we go as believers in Jesus. As we follow similar steps in the heavenly tabernacle, we find our blessings in the New Covenant. As the Epistle to the Hebrews claims, the old is good, but the new is better. One way in which it is better is in our daily devotional time. This practice of spending devotional time with God every day should be established early in our Christian walk, just as the earthly tabernacle was constructed at Mt. Sinai, shortly after the Exodus from Egypt.

Chapter 9

Mt. Sinai III: Old Testament Laws: The Working of the Potter— The Christian and the Old Testament Law— "If You Love Me, Keep My Commandments"

The Israelites spent about two years at Mt. Sinai, and they learned many things there. In the last three chapters we have seen the first three elements of their time there: covenant establishment (chapter 6), the sacrificial system (chapter 7), and the making of the tabernacle (chapter 8). Now we need to consider the laws given as part of that covenant. In the last three chapters we have seen that the recently converted Christian needs to understand everything that already happened to him when he received Jesus as his Savior. These things correspond with the three steps above. However they are already his by virtue of having received Jesus in the first place. They are not future or in the process of being implemented, as are the benefits of the Old Testament believer at this point.

The covenant establishment in chapter six corresponds with an understanding of what the new covenant is for the New Testament believer. The sacrificial system in chapter seven corresponds with an understanding of the many different applications of Jesus' sacrifice, which was once for all applied to the New Testament believer's life.

The tabernacle in chapter eight corresponds to the New Testament believer's permanent and continuous access to God's presence in the Heavenly Tabernacle. At this point he should begin to have a devotional time each day to enjoy the benefits of this total access to the God of the Universe and to get to know Him better.

In this chapter we will consider first the relation of the New Testament believer to the Old Testament law. Is a Jewish person still to keep the laws of Moses if he believes in Jesus? Second, what is the difference of the concept of law itself, according to the Old Testament and the New Testament? This discussion includes how the Old Testament laws are different than the New Testament laws in their nature. We will also summarize the similarities and differences as they affect the Christian walk of the New Testament believer. Our goal will be to see both continuity and discontinuity. How is law in general, as well as particular commandments different under the two covenants, and how are they the same?

I. The relation of the New Testament believer to the Old Testament law.

Is a Jewish person still to keep the laws of Moses if he believes in Jesus?

What is the relation of the believer in Jesus to the Old Testament Law? Are we bound to keep it? Is it today a cultural shtick given for the enrichment of modern Jewish believers? Is it to be avoided at all cost and shunned as "sub-Christian?" Is the Old Testament Law to be kept as a witness to unbelieving Israel? Are there elements of the religious customs and Old Testament laws of the religious Jews that are to be observed by us and others to be avoided? What light can dispensationalism shed on this issue?

In this section we will take a look at the relation of the Old Testament Law as it affects the issue of the Christian life. Our first task will be to answer the question: What is the relation of the Jewish believer in Jesus to the Old Testament Law? Then, in the light of the answer we establish, we will look at the various perspectives and practices of modern Jewish believers in Jesus and evaluate these in the light of the Scriptures. Through this analysis, we hope to develop a perspective on the Old Testament that will allow us to be guided in some way by it, without being under it. Our purpose here is not to limit ourselves to one philosophy as the only Biblically consistent practice, but we will try to evaluate the different practices in the light of the Bible.

In order to understand the relationship of the believer in Jesus to the Old Testament Law, We need to clear up the following 3 questions: Can one be a Jew and a Christian at the same time? How do Jews enter and leave the laws of Moses? And, are Jews still under the laws of Moses if they believe in Jesus?

A. Can one be a Jew and a Christian at the same time?

There is a great deal of confusion today over the question as to whether a person can be a Jew and a Christian at the same time. I believe that this confusion is due chiefly to the definition of a Jew recognized by modern Jewry: "A Jew is one born of a Jewish mother and not converted to another religion." This definition recognizes modern Judaism, a religious movement founded by the Pharisees, as the only legitimate expression of Judaism and continuation of the faith of the Old Testament. The definition begins as a sociological definition, in which the matriarchal descent is counted as definitive. Then the definition switches to a religious and ideological definition when it excludes those converted to another religion, mainly those who believe in Jesus.

After using the doctrinal definition to exclude Jewish believers in Jesus from Israel, the Jewish community then tosses away their doctrinal definition and welcomes in all Jewish people, regardless of belief. Thus, there are, among Jews in good standing, New-Agers, atheists, agnostics, and a host of others—even Buddhists—that do not have the faith of the Pharisees, who are accepted as Jewish by this definition. If Christianity differs from modern Rabbinical Judaism over the question of whether or not Jesus is the Messiah of Israel, the atheist, agnostic, and New-Ager, among others, differ by far more in that they do not even recognize the God of Israel even remotely like He is presented in the Old Testament.

An Historical Perspective.

In the first century there were many different groups among Jews: the Sadducees (Acts 5:17), the Pharisees (Acts 15:5), Herodians (Matthew 22:16), Zealots (Luke 6:15), Essenes (associated with the Dead Sea scrolls), and the Christians, among others. In Acts 24:5, Paul is called a ringleader of the Sect of the Nazarenes, and Christians are still called "Nazarenes" (*notzriym*, נוֹצְרִים) in Modern Hebrew. Nobody in the first century doubted that anyone in any of these groups was Jewish, though they often did not get along well among themselves.

By the Final Jewish Revolt against the Romans (132-135 AD), there were only three groups left among the Jews: The Pharisees, the Zealots, and the Christians. The Sadducees had ceased to be a factor when the Second Temple was destroyed in 70 AD because they were the priests. The Essenes were isolated from the rest of the Jews and became absorbed back into the Jewish community when their long-awaited Messiah, or Teacher of Righteousness, did not come. The Herodians were pragmatists, who collaborated with the Romans, hoping to lighten the conquerors' yolk. When the last revolt came, they threw in their lot with the rest of the Jews as patriots, and no longer could collaborate with Rome.

Up to this point, the followers of Jesus were fighting the Romans as Jewish patriots in a war against a foreign enemy. However, at the height of fighting, Rabbi Akiba, a leader of the Pharisees, declared Simeon Bar-Kochba the Messiah (equivalent to the Christian understanding of the Second Coming of Jesus) thinking to unite the Jews further. Instead, this act divided the Jews. The followers of Jesus quit the war because it was now for the promotion of a false messianic movement. When the Jews lost the war, the Jewish Christians were blamed in part; and from that point on it was not considered "kosher" for a Jew to be a follower of Jesus. This attitude toward the Jewish believers in Jesus continues even today.

Upon losing the last revolt against the Romans, the Jewish people went into their worldwide Diaspora, or dispersion. Of the two remaining groups, the Zealots were destroyed. The Romans filled the countryside with crosses and succeeded in killing off the Zealots. Those Zealots who survived disappeared in the Jewish population with their hopes for a Jewish state permanently dashed for the time being.

The Pharisees alone were left of all the groups among the Jews of the Diaspora. Although Rabbi Akiba suffered a horrible death at the hands of the Romans, many of the Pharisees were left to carry on the labor of preserving Israel in the Diaspora. Their work was carried on by a few in Israel, and then a great many in Babylon, which became the main center to which the Jews could look for leadership. Though the Pharisees had never represented but a small percentage of the Jews, they now took over as undisputed leaders of the scattered Jewish population, as they prepared their Jerusalem Talmud and Babylonian Talmud.

After being isolated from the rest of the Jewish people, the Jewish followers of Jesus were largely absorbed into the church, which by now had a largely Gentile character, and were able to avoid the dispersion. This explains the small number of references to Christianity in the Talmud. In the formative centuries of modern Talmudic Judaism, Christians were not around—neither in the Jewish community nor among the surrounding Gentiles. Modern Judaism was formed as an expression of the religious thought of the Pharisees, who had gained a monopoly over the thinking of the Jewish people through the historic circumstances mentioned above.

The Pharisees used their monopoly of influence to keep others from accepting Jesus, though they remained very flexible about other beliefs that people had. Jesus' indictment of those of his time remains true for Jewish leaders today: "But woe unto you, scribes and Pharisees, hypocrites, because you shut off the kingdom of heaven from people; for you do not enter in yourselves, nor do you allow those who are entering to go in" (Matthew 23:13).

Having explained that the Pharisees only gained the undisputed leadership over an otherwise very diverse group through historical circumstances, we may reopen the issue as to whether they have a right to maintain this monopoly over the religious thought of all Jews in the presence of other groups again today in the twenty-first century. While it is true that the Jewish believers in Jesus quit the revolt and contributed in part to its failure, it is also true that the Pharisees backed a false Messianic movement.

When Peter and John were arrested and brought before the Jewish Sanhedrin for preaching in the name of Jesus, Rabbi Gamaliel, a leading Pharisee and the teacher of Saul of Tarsus, said: "So in the present case, I say to you, stay away from these men and let them alone, for if this plan or action is of men, it will be overthrown; but if it is of God, you will not be able to overthrow them; or else you may even be found fighting against God" (Acts 5:38-39). If we were to apply Rabbi Gamaliel's advice to the two Messianic movements of Bar-Kochba and Jesus, we can see that Jesus' movement survived, indicating that it should be recognized as from God, while the other movement failed. Israel as a nation was guaranteed survival, whether or not they followed God, and so their survival does not prove that God approves of the Pharisees. It was only messianic movements that would fail if they were not of God.

Should the followers of Jesus continue to be rejected by other Jews for not following this Messianic movement that was obviously not of God? If Bar-Kochba had really been the Messiah, the movement would have succeeded without the help of Jesus' followers, anyway. Since it was not of God, they were right in not following it. Should they be rejected for being right? The Jewish followers of Jesus were the only Jews who did not suffer the Diaspora, which was threatened as a punishment for not obeying God, according to Deuteronomy 28:49-68. The Pharisees themselves were no exception to this judgment. They also suffered the dispersion. Only the followers of Jesus avoided it. We may conclude from this fact that the followers of Jesus were doing what the God of Israel wanted, since they alone avoided the Diaspora judgment, while the Pharisees were among those that were not doing the will of the God of Israel.

Also, the Pharisees continue to have only a minor following today, and have had to relinquish their monopoly among Jews. The Zionist movement was largely secular and has resembled the Zealot group more than the Pharisees. There are the people who seek peace at any cost, who resemble the Herodians more than any other group. There are again a large number of groups found among modern Jews, and the Pharisees are hard-pressed to continue to claim their monopoly on religious thought. Why should they succeed in continuing to exclude the Jewish followers of Jesus from the People of Israel?

Also, it must be noted that both the church and the Pharisees (modern Rabbinical Judaism) historically have sought Gentile proselytes to follow the God of Israel as they believe is right. In constituency, Rabbinical Judaism is not different from Christianity: both include a remnant of the Gentiles and a remnant of Jews and follow the God of Israel. Of course, the percentages are overwhelmingly Gentile for Christianity and overwhelmingly Jewish for Rabbinical Judaism, but both groups contain a remnant of Jews and Gentiles..

We must also define the church, or Christianity, in order to answer the question of whether or not a person can be Jewish and Christian at the same time. The Church is the remnant of all nations, including Israel, that worships the God of Abraham, Isaac, and Jacob through the New Covenant, which He cut with Israel (Jeremiah 31:31-34), and then opened up to all Gentiles, as well. The church recognizes Jesus of Nazareth as having fulfilled the prophecies of the Suffering Messiah and believes that He will return to fulfill the prophecies of the Glorious Messiah. In Isaiah 49:6 (49:5 in the Masoretic text) The God of Israel tells the Messiah, "It is too small a thing that You should be My Servant to raise up the tribes of Jacob and to restore the preserved ones of Israel; I will also make You a light of the nations so that My Salvation may reach to the end of the earth." Jesus is accepted by a remnant of Israel, as well as a remnant of the Gentiles. This is the make-up of the church, and it is presented about seven centuries before Jesus came.

Solution to the Confusion:

I propose for the sake of honesty that the Jewish people leave the Rabbinical Jews (Pharisees, or Modern Judaism) over the synagogues, but reserve the synagogues only for them. If they exclude Jewish believers in Jesus from the synagogues for doctrinal differences, it would only be reasonable for them to exclude others who are in even greater disagreement with them. It would be appropriate for them to throw out the atheists, agnostics, New-Agers, Buddhists, and others who also do not agree with them. This, however, they do not do.

Concerning the State of Israel, Jewish community centers, *Magen David Adom* (their equivalent of the Red Cross), and all other ethnic, non-religious relations, it would be reasonable to accept all Jews, including those who believe in Jesus. If there are no religious criteria used for screening people, don't invent one to eliminate the Jews who believe in Jesus. It is not reasonable to listen to the Rabbinical Judaism's objections here if they aren't giving opinions to exclude anyone else on the basis of religious belief.

Therefore, we must conclude that a Jewish person who believes in Jesus remains a Jew ethnically, but cannot be a Jew religiously, since this would include following Rabbinical Judaism, which is a religious viewpoint inconsistent with following Jesus. Jesus states clearly (Matthew 5:20) "Unless your righteousness surpasses that of the scribes and Pharisees, you will not enter the kingdom of heaven," (see also Matthew, chapter 23). It is only honest to require that Jewish people be either Rabbinical Jew, follower of Jesus, or neither; but no one can honestly be a follower of Rabbinical Judaism and Jesus at the same time. They are mutually exclusive. Either one offers to the God of Israel his own righteousness, as the Rabbinic Jews do, or he offers the God of Israel Jesus' righteousness, which Jesus claims is the only perfect righteousness. He cannot offer both, however. This should not bother the Jewish followers of Jesus, though, as the other Jews who do not practice the Talmud in all honesty should not claim to be Rabbinical Jews, either.

B. How Do Jews Enter and Leave the Authority of the Laws of Moses?

Having established that a Jew that believes in Jesus can be an ethnic Jew, but not a Rabbinical Jew, we now need to focus on answering the question: How do Jews enter and leave the authority of the Laws of Moses?

Deuteronomy 12:1 provides the explanation for the applicability of the Law to Jewish people: "These are the statutes and judgments which ye shall carefully observe in the land which the LORD, the God of your fathers, has given you to possess, **as long as you live on the earth.**" Before birth and after death the Jewish person is not under the Laws of Moses.

When a religious Jewish man is buried in his prayer shawl (*talit*, תָּלִית), the 613 knots in the fringes (representing the 613 commandments of the Old Testament, or Tenach) are removed or defaced, representing the fact that, as he is dead, he is no longer under the responsibility to observe these laws.

Thus, we see that a Jewish person enters under the authority of the Laws of Moses by birth to Jewish parents, and that the Jewish person passes out from under the authority of the Laws of Moses by death.

The time one is here on the earth, one is said to be in "This Age" or "This World" (*ha-olam hazzeh*, הָעוֹלָם הַזֶּה). When one dies, he passes into "the Age to Come" or "the World to Come (*ha-olam habba*, הָעוֹלָם הַבָּא)." We can say age or world for either because time and world are combined in the Hebrew term, and there is no English equivalent. Thus, we see that This Age and the Age to Come are both simultaneously present. Between birth and death, one is said to be in This World, or Age, and after death one passes into the World, or Age to Come.

In the Biblical situation, however, the change of location is irreversible. One cannot go back and forth between This World and the World to Come, as one can travel back and forth between the United States and Canada—each time changing the law to which he is subject. One changes once from This World to the World to Come through death (whether by physical death or by dying and rising with Christ), and may never return.

The Hebrew language of the Old Testament reflects this understanding, and I would like to show the problem that comes in through the translation of the Hebrew word *olam*. Taking into account that Moses has said that the laws given through him are for a person after birth and before death, we see what he means when he gives the commands. For example, in Exodus 29:9, we read concerning Aaron and his sons, "they shall have the priesthood *by a perpetual statute*. So you shall ordain Aaron and his sons."

Here the phrase translated "by a perpetual statute" is "*le-hukkat-olam*" (לְחֻקַּת־עוֹלָם). This should be rendered "by a statute of the age." This means that Aaron and his descendants will exercise this priesthood while they are alive, and while This World (or This Age) exists. This expression even includes the Millennial Kingdom, as the last millennium of This World's existence. That is why the priesthood is revived in the Millennial Kingdom, even though Jesus' redemptive work is already finished (Ezekiel 40-48). However, whenever a descendant of Aaron dies, he passes into the World to Come, and no longer is to be allowed to exercise the priesthood.

There are many other examples of this usage in the Old Testament, some of which are as follows: observe Passover (Exodus 12:14), the priesthood is for Aaron's family (Exodus 29:9), observe the Sabbath (Exodus 31:16), celebrate the Day of Atonement (Leviticus 16:29), observe all prescribed holidays (Leviticus 23), keep the menorah lit perpetually (Leviticus 24:3), same treatment for stranger and native-born (Numbers 15:15), no landholdings for Levites (Numbers 18:23), etc.

There are many more references with this expression *le-olam* (לְעוֹלָם) in the Hebrew Old Testament, but they are translated in different ways, and almost all of the translations miss the two-fold meaning: this is for you if you qualify during y our lifetime here on earth, but not after you die. However, it is still in effect for others who are alive. Also, the other limit is for as long as this world exists. Let us list a few of the different translations of this expression: permanent (Ex. 12:14), forever (Ex. 12:24 & 31:17), perpetual (Ex: 27:21), and everlasting (Lev. 24:8).

It would appear that the length of time in these translations has been converted into eternity by the translators because the dual notions of time and world have not both been kept, and partly, perhaps, by the limitations of English. The notion of this world has been passed-over. For example, the expression in Modern Hebrew for the First World War is *milchemet ha-olam harishon* (מִלְחֶמֶת הָעוֹלָם הָרִאשׁוֹן). It is obvious here that the expression *ha-olam* here does not refer to eternity, as then there would not have been a Second World War. The First World War lasted only about four years and three months. In this example the length of time is less important and the fact that the whole world was involved was the main expression.

The combined idea for the expression *le-olam* is "while this world exists and while you are in it" (i.e. between your birth and death). The assumption is also made that the particular person qualifies as being an Israelite, or even further, is of the family of Aaron. If we understand this use of the term "for the age" and the scope and limitations of the Old Testament Law, we will be ready to answer the next question.

C. Are Jews still under the Laws of Moses if they believe in Jesus?

As we have seen up to this point, the Jewish person comes under the Laws of Moses by birth, and passes out from under them by death. Based upon this, we shall now answer the question as to whether or not Jews who believe in Jesus are still obligated to observe the Laws of Moses. At this point we need to know what actually happens to one who believes in Jesus. Romans 6:1-4 says: "What shall we say then? Are we to continue in sin so that grace may increase? May it never be! How shall we who died to sin still live in it? Or do you not know that all of us who have been baptized into Christ Jesus have been baptized into His death? Therefore we have been buried with Him through baptism into death, so that as Christ was raised from the dead through the glory of the Father, so we too might walk in newness of life."

What is Paul saying here? —that the act of receiving Jesus Christ as our own savior passes us through a type of death and resurrection. This would mean for a Jewish person who believes in Jesus that he is no longer under the Laws of Moses. As we have already seen, it is death that passes a Jewish person outside of the sphere of obligation to keep the Law of Moses. That is what Paul shows us in the next chapter, Romans 7:1-4: "Or do you not know, brethren (for I am speaking to those who know the law), that the law has jurisdiction over a person as long as he lives? For the married woman is bound by law to her husband while he is living; but if her husband dies, she is released from the law concerning the husband. So then, if while her husband is living she is joined to another man, she shall be called an adulteress; but if her husband dies, she is free from the law, so that she is not an adulteress though she is joined to another man. Therefore, my brethren, you also were made to die to the Law through the body of Christ, so that you might be joined to another, to Him who was raised from the dead, in order that we might bear fruit for God."

Paul here takes the example of a Jewish married couple in which the man dies. In this case, the widow would be free to remarry, as death cuts the effect of the Law over her conduct in the area of marriage, leaving her free to marry another. Paul then reverses his argument and places the believer in the position of the dead husband, since the surviving wife would still be under the Jewish law in all other matters. In the same way the widow would be free to remarry, the dead husband would also be free to remarry. Then he states that believers, indeed, have remarried—to Jesus who conquered death and rose again.

His statement, "you also were made to die to the Law through the body of Christ, so that you might be joined to another," shows the discontinuity of leaving one Law to be under another. This is the case because a person that receives Jesus dies to this world and enters the world to come. The Law of Moses only has jurisdiction over this world—not the world to come. As one dies, he leaves the jurisdiction of the Law of Moses, and enters the World to Come, under the jurisdiction of a different law. What is the new Law the believer is under? In Romans 8:2 Paul states, "For the Law of the Spirit of life in Christ Jesus has set you free from the law of sin and of death." By receiving Jesus, a Jewish believer leaves the location of jurisdiction of the Law of Moses, as well as its sphere of influence, which is This World, and enters into the World to Come. Here, the believer comes under a new Law and is released from obligation to the old Law.

Let us use a modern example. Let us suppose that a man robs a bank in Miami, Florida. He is in violation of the laws of Miami-Dade County, the State of Florida, and the United States Federal Government. But what if he flees to Toronto, Ontario in Canada and robs another bank there. Is this second robbery in violation of the laws of Miami-Dade County, the State of Florida, and the United States? No! The second robbery is in violation of the laws of the City of Toronto, the Province of Ontario, and the nation of Canada. Why? Because this person traveled beyond the limits where the laws of the United States were in effect, those laws held no jurisdiction over him and he could not break any of the laws of the United States. However, he entered another nation and could break its laws. Even if the Canadian law were to say the same thing about bank robberies as the United States law, the bank robber could only break the laws of the governing body in the place where he was at the time of the crime.

In Jeremiah 31:31-34, the Lord promises to Israel a New Covenant (New Testament), which will not be like the other He cut with them at the time of Moses. Since the covenant with Moses is "for This World and Age," it is necessary that all those who enter into the New Covenant leave This Age and enter the Age to Come. We read: "Behold, days are coming," declares the LORD, "when I will make (Heb. "cut") a new covenant with the house of Israel and with the house of Judah, not like the covenant which I made with their fathers in the day I took them by the hand to bring them out of the land of Egypt, My covenant which they broke, although I was a husband to them," declares the LORD. "But this is the covenant which I will make ("cut") with the house of Israel after those days," declares the LORD, "I will put My law within them and on their heart I will write it; and I will be their God, and they shall be My people. They will not teach again, each man his neighbor and each man his brother, saying, 'Know the LORD,' for they will all know Me, from the least of them to the greatest of them," declares the LORD, "for I will forgive their iniquity, and their sin I will remember no more."

Here we note that there is promised a New Testament, or New Covenant, and we will note that the Scriptures of Christianity claim to be this New Testament. In Hebrews 8:7-13 this passage is used to refer to the New Testament that Christians have. We have thus far established that the Laws of Moses are binding on a Jewish person as long as he is alive in This World. The receiving of Jesus terminates his actions as a part of This World and under the Law of Moses, place him in the World to Come and under the Law of the Spirit of life in Messiah Jesus, which is also the New Law of the New Testament. This is on the heart, rather than on tablets or scrolls.

II. What is the difference of the concept of law itself, according to the Old Testament and the New Testament? How are the Old Testament laws different than the New Testament laws in their nature?

This drastic change upon receiving Jesus necessitates a sharp break with the past. Since one is dying to This World and passing through the resurrection to become a new creature, the relation to the things in the old sphere change.

A. The New Testament believer's guidance (*torah*) is internal and on the heart.

First of all, the New Testament believer's guidance (*torah*) is internal and on the heart. The laws of the books of Moses dealt with external matters (with the exception of the commandment not to covet), which are readily visible and relatively easy to enforce. The emphasis is on the outside of the person. However, with the coming of the New Testament, the guidance is directly by the Holy Spirit internally. Only the Holy Spirit knows if the person is following the guidance or not, most of the time. We are told not to judge one another, except in extreme cases. The believer must be freed from the preoccupation with commandments about things of This World in order to focus on things of the World to Come.

In Colossians, chapters 2 and 3, Paul makes this case. Because the believer has died and risen with Christ, he is in a new sphere of operation (2:13), "When you were dead in your transgressions and the uncircumcision of your flesh, He made you alive together with Him, having forgiven us all our transgressions." The result of this new life is stated in verses 16 & 17, "Therefore no one is to act as your judge in regard to food or drink or in respect to a festival or a new moon or a Sabbath day—things which are a mere shadow of what is to come; but the substance belongs to Christ."

We must notice that the things of this world, including Sabbath days, new moons, and meat and drink are all items addressed by the Mosaic Law. If these things are no longer items to be reckoned with, then the New Testament believer is not to occupy himself with them. Paul continues to make this point in chapter 3:1-3: "Therefore if you have been raised up with Christ, keep seeking the things above, where Christ is, seated at the right hand of God. Set your mind on the things above, not on the things that are on earth. For you have died and your life is hidden with Christ in God."

It is impossible to keep the Old Testament law without setting your mind on the things that are on earth, for it deals almost entirely with things of the earth. A later example that Paul gives is in verse 9: "Do not lie to one another, since you laid aside the old self with its evil practices." Paul could have referred to the commandment not to lie in the Ten Commandments if he had been so inclined, but he chose to avoid it, referring to our new life in Christ as the reason not to lie. The Old Testament Law is not treated in parts, some of which are still in effect while some have been canceled. On the contrary, it is treated as a single unit, applicable to one sphere of existence, vacated by the believer in Jesus, and replaced by the New Law, which is effective in the new place—the World to Come. This means that the "law (*Torah*) of the Spirit of life in Christ Jesus" (Romans 8:2) replaces the previous Law of Moses for the new Testament believer, though the Jewish person who has not accepted Jesus is still under the Mosaic Law.

B. The Change of Priesthood.

In Hebrews the author emphasizes the replacement of the Old *Torah* by the New *Torah*. In chapter 7 he shows that there is a change in the priesthood for the New Law and draws the conclusion (v. 12): "For when the priesthood is changed, of necessity their takes place a change of law also." Because there is a new priesthood in the New Covenant, there must also be a new law. Since Jesus is of the Tribe of Judah, he couldn't sacrifice in the Temple because the priesthood is reserved for Aaron and his sons "for the age," as we have seen above.

No man of any tribe but Levi could go beyond the court of the men into the Holy Place or Holy of Holies under the Mosaic Law; and so Jesus, being from the Tribe of Judah, could do nothing under the Old Law for people's sins. Because Jesus was a "priest forever according to the order of Melchizedek" (Ps. 110:4), and not the order of Aaron, His priesthood is not of This World, but rather is of the World to Come. Finally, in Hebrews chapter 10, the author shows the superiority of Jesus' priesthood, in contrast to the sacrifices of the Old Law. He quotes Psalm 40:6-8, in which God expresses displeasure in the sacrifices of the Old Law and is answered by the Messiah who vows to do the will of God fully (Hebrews 10:5-9): "See, Therefore when He comes into the world, He says, 'Sacrifice and offering You have not desired, But a body You have prepared for Me; In whole burnt offerings and sacrifices for sin You have taken no pleasure. Then I said, 'Behold, I have come (In the scroll of the Book it is written of Me) To do Your will, o God.'" After saying above, 'Sacrifices and offerings and whole burnt offerings and sacrifices for sin You have not desired, nor have You taken pleasure in them' (which are offered according to the Law), then He said, 'Behold I have come to do Your will.' **He takes away the first in order to establish the second."**

It is clearly stated that God "takes away the first" (i.e. the Old Law, including its sacrificial system) "in order to establish the second" (i.e. the New Law, including Jesus' perfect, once-and-for-all sacrifice, victory over death, and perfect obedience). To treat the Mosaic Law as anything other than something "taken away" for the New Testament believer, would be to treat it different than God treats it now, and thus to treat it in a erroneous way.

C. The Relationship of Obedience to the Blessings of the Covenant.

The third way in which the Old Law may be shown to be incompatible with the New Law is that the Old Law gave the commandments first, and then made the blessings conditional upon obedience to the commandments. This order is clear throughout the Old Testament, and is most clearly presented in Deuteronomy, chapter 28. Here Israel is presented with blessings and curses. The first 14 verses are blessings that are only given if they will obey the Lord. From verse 15 through verse 68 is a series of threatened curses if the Jewish people do not obey their God. These verses form the sad history of Israel in advance, and include general curses (vv. 15-35), the Assyrian and Babylonian captivities (vv. 36-48), and the Roman occupation and worldwide dispersion (vv. 49-68).

On the other hand, in the New Testament, all of the blessings of the New Covenant come with the sole condition of receiving Jesus in the first place. On the basis of the gifts received through the grace of God, the Christian is exhorted to submit to the Holy Spirit in order to be transformed by the power of God. This is the basic order of several of the New Testament epistles. For example, Ephesians, chapters 1-3, tells us of the riches of Christ that already belong to every believer, by virtue of having received Jesus once and for all. Some of these blessings are: election (1:4), predestination (1:5), adoption (1:5), grace in Jesus (1.6), forgiveness of our trespasses through the grace of God (1:7), inheritance (1:11), sealing with the Holy Spirit (1:13-14), resurrection and seating in heavenly places in Christ (2:5-7), and unity between Jewish and Gentile believers (2:13-18).

Having received these blessings, conditional only upon receiving Jesus as Savior in the first place, the New Testament believer is exhorted to act accordingly in Ephesians 4:1: "Therefore I, the prisoner of the Lord, implore you to walk in a manner worthy of the calling with which you have been called." In 4:1 through 6:9 there is a series of instructions given as exhortations for us to follow *in the light of the blessings we already have, not with the view of earning our blessings.*

Paul's view in Ephesians is best summed up in chapter 2, verses 8-10: "For by grace you have been saved through faith; and that not of yourselves, it is the gift of God; not as a result of works, so that no one may boast. For we are His workmanship, created in Christ Jesus for good works, which God prepared beforehand so that we would walk in them." Thus, our obedience is to be the result of our blessings, not the reason for them.

This difference is well illustrated by the fairy tale of Cinderella. In the kingdom where she lived, all of the people were trying to get ahead by keeping the laws and working hard for merit. Perhaps the King would notice their efforts and give them a government job or reward them some other way. This is equivalent of the mentality in the Old Testament believer. The New Testament believer is like Cinderella after she marries the Prince. She has to say yes to his marriage proposal, but after that all of the blessings of being married to the Prince come from that acceptance. However, now that she is elevated from her status of commoner and she lives in the palace, she is exhorted to live worthy of her new position and learn palace etiquette. Her relation to the rules is after her relation to the Prince. For the New Testament believer, his obligation is to say yes to Jesus' proposal of eternal life. After that he has a new position, status, and privileges. Then, in the light of this new position, he is exhorted to walk worthy of all of the blessings which he now has since he believed in Jesus.

D. The Nature of the Actual Laws.

This is the fourth mutually exclusive difference between the Old Law and the New Law: the actual nature of the laws is different. In the Old Testament the believer was to read and understand the Law on the tablets and to keep it as best he could through his own understanding and effort. He was not to count on the enlightening and empowering of the Holy Spirit of God. However, in the New Law, the same Spirit, Who is our Guide, is also our Enabler. In addition, He even brings about the circumstances for us to do good works (Ephesians 2:10). This is the difference between the dead works of the Old Law and the living works of the New Law. The dead works were done under one's own intelligence and strength, and insight as to how to obey the law, separate from the leading of the Holy Spirit of God. Living works are "prepared beforehand that we should walk in them" by the Holy Spirit, and that same Spirit "who is at work in you, both to will and to work for His good pleasure" (Philippians 2:13). This is another reason why we cannot be under both laws at once and why reception of the New Law removes one from being under the Old Law—we cannot be under our own direction and energy, and under the guidance, inspiration, and empowering of the Holy Spirit at the same time.

The New Testament commands are usually different from the Old Testament commands. For example, Phillip was conducting an evangelistic campaign in Samaria in Acts 8: 26-27, and the Holy Spirit commanded him to leave and head down the desert road towards Gaza. Does this command to Phillip mean that every Christian must make a pilgrimage to Gaza at least once in his lifetime? No. This command was specific just for Phillip. The Christian is to listen for the voice of the Holy Spirit to guide him with specific commands that are not for others—just for him. This is a new type of command than those on the stones. The individual received the commandment just for him, and it was very specific. He did not have to figure out how to apply it to his life, nor did anyone else have to keep it. It was specific and just for him.

It is important to note here that God does not anticipate our treating any of His Laws by picking part and rejecting another part. Either we are debtors to do the Old Law or debtors to do the New Law. Paul says in Galatians 5:3: "And I testify again to every man who receives circumcision, that he is under obligation to keep the whole Law." If one is in Israel and in This World, he is a debtor to do the whole of the Old Law. If he is in the church and in the World to Come, he has the riches of Christ and is exhorted to turn control of his life to the Holy Spirit, as fulfillment of the New Law.

The author was in a meeting of Jews in a community center one time, and they were planning for the education of Jewish children in the Chicago land area. The consensus opinion was that the best thing to do was to give them a taste of everything in Judaism—both secular and religious—like a cafeteria line, and let them pick and choose the things that they would want to observe as Jews to make themselves feel more Jewish. Nothing could be farther from the view of God, concerning His Law. He expects obedience to everything, or there are consequences. The sacrifices are provided to take the death that every Israelite deserved for even one sin, but the expectation was that each Israelite was under obligation to keep the whole law.

E. Applications for Today

For all of the above reasons, we must conclude that the New Testament believer, whether Jewish or Gentile by background, is not under the Laws of Moses from the moment he accepts Jesus. Since we have shown that the Jewish person is no longer under the Laws of Moses from the moment he believes in Jesus, it follows that the Gentile passes directly from being under his conscience to being under the New Law of the "Spirit of life in Christ Jesus" without ever having been under the Law of Moses. But how does this affect his practice? What are the implications for our actions in the local churches? There are some considerations that we need to take into account as we approach the subject of Jewish practices in local Christian groups.

The first consideration is that we are far happier to have the problem of what Jewish practices can continue in the church among Jewish believers than to have no Jewish believers at all. We need to remember that a true understanding of the atonement is the real doctrine necessary for salvation, and that those who have really trusted in Jesus' substitutionary atonement are saved and brothers and sisters in the Lord. Some may be immature and have excess baggage inconsistent with deeper doctrine; but we need to trust that, as their knowledge grows, the Lord will lead them to drop things that are inconsistent with the faith. This chapter should be considered such an exposition of the doctrine on a deeper level that should shed light on individual practices.

The second consideration is our liberty in Christ. Since we are dead to this world, our actions in the world, as such, do not directly affect our relation to the Lord. However, there are two additional matters that deal indirectly with our actions. First of all is our attitude toward the Lord. Our acts in this world should proceed from the proper motivation to the Lord reflecting the fruit of the Spirit and the empowering of the Spirit. Also, our acts in this world should reflect a concern for how others will understand the acts, and should neither be a stumbling block to unsaved people to hinder them from receiving Jesus as Messiah, nor a stumbling block to believers to hinder them in the faith. As Paul says in I Corinthians 10:32: "Give no offense either to Jews or to Greeks or to the church of God."

With this attitude of remembering our freedom in Christ, yet not wanting to offend nor be misinterpreted, we would like to evaluate our practices in the light of Scripture, as well as the point of view of others.

Synagogue or Church?

The first practice we want to consider is whether to use the term church, synagogue, or congregation to describe our group. *When all of His disciples were Jewish*, Jesus said in Matthew 16:18: "...upon this rock I will build My church." Also, Jesus gave His expectation that "They will make you outcasts from the synagogue, but an hour is coming for everyone who kills you to think that he is offering service to God" (John 16:2). Jesus does not give any hope that his followers will be accepted into mainstream Judaism, especially among religious Jews, and that they should not expect to be.

In the book of Isaiah we are told several things about the Jews who will believe in the coming Messiah: In chapter 66, verse 5, we read God's message to the remnant of believing Jews: "Hear the word of the Lord, ye that tremble at His word; your brethren that hated you, that cast you out for my name's sake, said, Let the Lord be glorified: but he shall appear to your joy, and they shall be ashamed" (AV).

The expectation was that the majority of Jews, who reject God, would expel the remnant of believing Jews in the future after Isaiah's day. These were indeed expelled from the rest of Israel over the Lordship of Jesus in the late first and early second centuries. Did this catch God by surprise? No! Not even in the Old Testament period, for in Isaiah 65:13-15 God says that He will split the remnant from the unbelieving majority so that He can give the believers blessings and the unbelievers curses: "'Therefore, thus says the LORD God, Behold, My servants will eat, but you will be hungry. Behold, My servants will drink, but you will be thirsty. Behold, My servants will rejoice, but you will be put to shame. Behold, My servants will shout joyfully with a glad heart, but you will cry out with a heavy heart, and you will wail with a broken spirit. You will leave your name as a curse to My chosen ones, and the LORD God will slay you. But My servants will be called by another name.

In Isaiah's day, the name Israel was used for the 10 northern tribes until they went into captivity, and Judah was used for the Southern two tribes. Thus, these people were already referred to as either Israelites or Jews. Neither of these can be the "other name" to which God's servants were to be referred. Now we must remember that it is the believing remnant that were to receive the new name— not the majority, who retain the name of Israelites or Jews.

In the time of Acts, as the followers of Jesus were becoming more and more marginalized from the unbelieving majority of Israel, they were referred to as those "belonging to the way" (Acts 9:2), then later at Antioch Christians (Acts 11:26, Greek meaning "Messianic people"), and finally by the opposition in Acts 24:5, Paul is called "a ringleader of the sect of the Nazarenes." This latter name has survived with all of its pejorative connotations in Modern Hebrew, where the followers of Jesus are called Nazarenes (*notzriym*, נוֹצְרִים). This name was because Nazareth was considered a secular and undesirable part of the country where Jesus was from. It is a bit like calling someone a "hillbilly" in the U.S. today.

Whether the name given was favorable or unfavorable, the followers of Jesus got the new name, indicating that the believing remnant of Israel went with Jesus, not the unbelieving majority. Having a new name means 2 things: having a separate group (since the remnant was expelled from Israel), and having a different character, according to the name. We are called Christians, or "people of the Messiah." The Hebrew equivalent would be "*beney-Mashiach*" (בְּנֵי־מָשִׁיחַ). This is an accurate term, as our salvation, position before God, and function in the world is to be described as "in Christ," or "in the Messiah."

Seeing that God's intention was that the remnant of Jewish believers was to be separated from the unbelieving majority of Israel and joined to the remnant of the Gentiles (Isaiah 49:6, 49:5 in the Masoretic text), and that Jesus said he would build his church at the time all his followers were Jews, one wonders what could be the problem in Jewish followers accepting the name church. The term synagogue means a "gathering together." Jews are "gathered together" in this world to wait for the world to come. On the other hand, word church is *ekklesía_(ἐκκλησία)*, meaning "called out assembly" because we are "called out" from This World to enjoy the World to Come. There is an important significance in the meanings of the terms, and we need to follow Jesus, who said that his followers would be kicked out of synagogues and that He was founding the church.

There are three reasons then to prefer the term church over synagogue: first, because Jesus labeled it church and warned that His followers would be expelled from the synagogues, secondly, because the term is closely identified with the reality of our translation into the world to come and Christian doctrine, and thirdly, in order not to confuse unbelieving Jews. We are not trying to trick people into our meetings, and in a number of cases unbelieving Jews have attended a Messianic Synagogue because of the word synagogue in the name, and then left feeling that they had been deceived.

Kippahs or no Kippahs?

Another question that arises is whether to use the *kippah*, or *yamulke*. The first is the Hebrew name and the latter the Yiddish name for the skullcap that Jewish men wear in synagogues, and some Jewish men wear all of the time. Some Jewish believers opt to continue wearing them after receiving Jesus as Savior. What can we say about their use in meetings? We must note that in I Corinthians 11:4 the Apostle Paul says, "Every man who has something on his head while praying or prophesying disgraces his head."

The intention of the passage is to show that it is inappropriate for a man to be in a worship meeting with his head covered. On the other hand, the Jewish tradition leads the Rabbinical Jews to cover their heads at all times, and to require it of all men in their synagogue meetings. The question here is "What are the Jewish believers following?" For them to follow something ordered by the tradition where it goes directly against the New Testament is to send the message to other Jews symbolically that they are following the tradition over the New Testament, while their words say the opposite. The result is confusion and an unclear testimony.

Prayer Shawls or no Prayer Shawls?

Consider the *talit* (תָּלִית), or prayer shawl, worn by Jewish men, as well. The *tsitsit* (צִיצִית), or fringes found on both ends, contain knots carefully tied to remind the wearer that he is under obligation to obey the 613 laws in the Old Testament. This number represents a counting of every law for every purpose. If a Jewish believer in Jesus wears this shawl with the 613 knots, he is saying to other Jews that he is still under the Laws of Moses, and not the New Testament, or that he is trying to be under both laws at once. We have seen above that, in fact, the Jewish believer in Jesus can only be under the

New Law, and cannot be under the Old Law anymore. Since that is the case, why would he want to give that impression to other Jews?

I would like to give an illustration about a Jewish man who dies being buried in his *talit*. The fringes with the knots are cut off before he is buried, representing the fact that he is no longer under these commandments after death. Let us say that his brother accepts Jesus as the Messiah of Israel and joins a church. At his baptism, it would best represent the New Testament truth for him to walk down to the front of the church, wearing his prayer shawl over his baptismal robe. As he enters the tank for baptism, he should hand the *talit* over to an elder standing by with a pair of scissors. As he goes down into the water and comes up, that elder should take a pair of scissors and cut off the fringes from the shawl. As he leaves the tank, he should wear the shawl as much as he wants from then on, but without the fringes. This would be a symbolic way of testifying to all that he is no longer under the 613 laws of Moses, but rather under the Law of the Spirit of Life in the Messiah Jesus. However, to wear the shawl with the fringes on is to create confusion after one becomes a believer in Jesus.

Saturday or Sunday Worship?

The issue of Sunday worship versus Saturday worship is worth a separate chapter in itself. The arguments are lengthy for the change to Sunday worship. Suffice it to say that the change was made during the New Testament period, as indicated by 3 passages. In I Corinthians 16:2 the Apostle Paul gives instructions for the gathering of the offering for the believers in Jerusalem: "On the first day of every week each one of you is to put aside and save, as he may prosper, so that no collections be made when I come." Paul was asking for a weekly offering on the first day of the week because that was the day that they met for worship.

The second reference to Sunday as the meeting day in the New Testament is Acts 20:7 (AV): "And upon the first day of the week, when the disciples came together to break bread, Paul preached unto them." This shows that the custom was to meet the first day of the week. R.J. Knowling says about this verse, "We must remember that I Corinthians had been previously written, and that the reference in I

Cor. xvi. 2 to 'the first day of the week' for the collection of the alms naturally connects itself with the statement here in proof that this day had been marked out by the Christian Church as a special day for public worship, and for 'the breaking of the bread.'"[1]

The third reference to Sunday worship in the New Testament is in Revelation 1:10, where the Apostle John says: "I was in the Spirit on the Lord's day, and I heard behind me a loud voice like the sound of a trumpet." By the time this last book in the New Testament was written, Sunday was so fully established that it was already called "the Lord's Day." This expression has never been used of the seventh day of the week, nor of any worship associated with it. It is clearly a reference to the first day of the week, the Lord's Day, for the Christians. So we see that Sunday worship was clearly established within the New Testament's formative period, and receives clear apostolic support.

There are also other reasons why modern Christians should worship the Lord on Sunday, instead of Saturday. Another reason is because the church was founded on a Jewish Feast of Pentecost, which should always fall on a Sunday. In Leviticus 23:15, we read that the counting of days for the feast of Pentecost was to begin "from the day after the Sabbath." There are two possibilities of meaning for the word Sabbath: the seventh day in the week, or the feast day, since both were days of rest. The Pharisees and modern Judaism, which comes from them, interpret this Sabbath to be the first day of unleavened bread, the feast day. The result would be that Pentecost would always fall on the 6th of the month of *Sivan*, and could be on any day of the week. The Christians, Sadducees, and all others among Jews interpret Sabbath to refer to the seventh day of the week that falls within the eight days of unleavened bread.

The latter should be seen as the correct because verse 16 says, "You shall count 50 days to the day after the seventh Sabbath." The name Pentecost means 50 in Greek, and so for this reason the feast is called Pentecost. It is called *shavuot* (weeks) in Hebrew because seven weeks are counted. If we begin on a Sunday, the first day of the week, and count seven complete Sabbaths, we have 49 days, and the day after the seventh Sabbath would be the 50th day. This is the only way we can get exactly fifty days. If we counted seven

Sabbaths of holidays, we could go all the way around the year before we counted 7 of them, and the number of days would be well over 50. If we began on any other day to count, the 49th day would not be a Sabbath (so that the 50th day would be the day after the seventh Sabbath). Therefore the day Sabbath must refer to the 7th day of the week, and Pentecost must always fall on a Sunday.

Of course, every Christian considers Sunday special because Jesus rose from the dead on a Sunday. Jesus did not rise from the dead on Sabbath. There were four watches in the night, and each one lasted 3 hours. If Jesus had risen at any time other than the fourth watch (from 3-6 AM on Sunday morning), the soldiers on the next watch would have discovered Jesus' resurrection, not some women of his followers. For the Jewish people, Sunday had already begun at about 6 PM on the previous Saturday evening, and so there is no doubt that Jesus rose from the dead on Sunday.

What about Sabbath worship then? In Exodus 31:16 we read: "So the sons of Israel shall observe the Sabbath, to celebrate the Sabbath throughout their generations as a perpetual covenant." Here again the expression translated "as a perpetual covenant" is *berit olam*. As was shown earlier, this means that the command to observe the Sabbath was "for the age," not forever. As shown above, when a Jewish person accepts Jesus, he leaves "This Age" (or "This World") and enters "the Age to Come" (or "the World to Come"), and therefore is no longer under rules that are "of the age."

Rabbi or Pastor?

Many Jewish believers who are zealous to live the Gospel in the context of the modern Jewish culture have chosen to call their leaders Rabbis. Is this a good idea? What does the Bible say that Christians should call their leaders, and what titles are forbidden? In Matthew 23:8-11 Jesus forbids three titles for Christian leaders: "But do not be called Rabbi; for One is your Teacher, and you are all brothers. Do not call anyone on earth your father; for One is your Father, He who is in heaven. Do not be called leaders; for One is your Leader, that is, Christ. But the greatest among you shall be your servant."

There are three titles that are forbidden for followers of Jesus to have: Rabbi, father, and leader (here the Greek καθηγητής means master). Rabbi means "my great one" in Hebrew and implies a hierarchy of importance among people with the Rabbi at the top. Jesus condemned the Pharisees for seeking the uppermost places of importance among the people, along with this title in verses 6-7. It is not our purpose in this paper to criticize the motives of contemporary Rabbis at this present time, and I find no objection to calling Jewish Rabbis who do not believe in Jesus "rabbi." However, Christians must be true to Jesus, Who says in John, 14:15: "If you love me, you will keep my commandments." Since Jesus gives us as a commandment in Matthew 23 not to receive the title of Rabbi, it is not a fitting title for a Christian leader. There are quite a few Jewish customs that are not out of place for a believer in Jesus, but the title rabbi is not acceptable, according to Jesus.

The second title that Jesus forbids is father. We are to recognize only God as our Father in any religious sense at all. I don't think that Jesus is actually forbidding us to address our earthly father as father, but it is not appropriate for any religious use. Roman Catholics and Eastern Orthodox have failed to follow this Scripture, and we often criticize them for this. If we use the title rabbi, though, we also fall under our own criticism, because that title is also forbidden.

The third title that Jesus forbids is leader (NASV), or master (AV). The Greek for this word is kathegetés (*καθηγητής*), which means teacher in the sense of being a master. We do not have authority because of our studies, but rather the Scriptures themselves have the authority. If we teach the Bible, our teaching is the truth because it is the Word of God we are teaching. The teaching is not true because the teacher is a master of the subject. The authority is in the Scriptures—not in us.

If we are forbidden to call our leaders rabbi, father, or master, what should we call them? In Ephesians 4:11-12 we have five specialized ministries with their respective titles: apostles, prophets, evangelists, pastors and teachers. Of these, the last two are especially appropriate for our congregations. The word pastor should be used for the maximum human leader of a congregation, and there may be one or more assistant pastors. The word teacher is *didáscalos* (*διδάσκαλος*), and emphasizes the person's ministry of teaching, rather than any superior position over others, such as *kathegetés* does. These are the two designations that are most appropriate for our leaders, according to the New Testament.

What are we communicating if we claim to follow Jesus, and then we follow Jewish custom where it contradicts Him directly? The result is just confusion if our claims are to follow Jesus, and our titles and practices contradict our claims. Let's do what we can to live the Gospel message within the Jewish context, if God calls us there, but make sure that we are not outside of the limits of the New Testament on any point. Let's not promote confusion.

What about Jewish Holidays?

Of course, almost every Jewish believer will want to celebrate the holidays that he has grown up with from the Old Testament. What should be our approach to the celebration of the Old Testament holidays? First of all, we have to recognize that Rabbinical Judaism has no monopoly on these holidays. Also, we do not want to copy its practices and confuse everyone. With regard to taking these things from the Old Testament, a Christian, whether he is a Jew or Gentile by birth, believes that both OT and NT are true, but that he is only under the New. At the same time, he realizes that the Jews really are under the Old Testament. **Therefore, to avoid confusion, we need to follow these two rules whenever we observe anything from the Old Testament, or even Rabbinical traditions about it:**

1. **We may feel free to observe anything in the Old Testament—and even in Rabbinical Judaism as long as we select material as it points to Jesus and we emphasize that fulfillment in Jesus.**
2. **We must at all times make clear to all present that we ourselves are not under the OT Law. We are just observing it for teaching purposes.**

F. The Christian's Application of Old Testament Laws

Application of Principles behind OT Laws

Just as one living in the United States may learn by studying Canadian laws without being subject to them, so the New Testament believer can learn from the Old Testament laws. One way is by applying principles found in the Old Testament to situations in which one finds himself today. In I Corinthians 9:9, Paul quotes the commandment not to put a muzzle on the ox that is treading the grain (Deuteronomy 25:4) and applies it to giving financial support to Bible teachers. It is not applied to Christian farmers as instructions for their harvest, but rather the principle is found that the laborer participates in the fruits of the harvest, and then applied to our situation in the church.

Understanding OT Historical Narratives

Another blessing of studying the Old Testament has been to see the whole history of Israel as forming a perceptual model of the life of the Christian in the World to Come. For the most part, this entire book is a depiction of the life of the Christian in the World to Come as it is in parallel with the history of Israel. In this case the individual Christian is like the entire nation of Israel. The Patriarchal Period corresponds to the Infancy of the Christian. As Paul says in Romans 7:9: "I was once alive apart from the Law; but when the commandment came, sin became alive and I died." Dying here is the equivalent of going down to Egypt and becoming the Natural Man. The Passover (salvation by the blood of the lamb) and Exodus correspond to the conversion of one, leading him to be a Carnal Believer, as Israel in the Desert, as we have seen in chapters five and six.

Crossing the Jordan is another crisis leading him to enter Canaan, which corresponds to the Spiritual Man. Even after becoming a Spiritual Man, one needs to be careful of being taken captive by Assyria (success spoiling one), or Babylon ("mixing in" with the world again). From either captivity, one would have to rebuild his life, following the guidance by Ezra, Nehemiah, Haggai, and Zechariah.

The names of the enemies of Israel have spiritual problems in the roots of their names in Hebrew. For example, Amorites (bad talking), Hittites (the bad kind of fear), Perizzites (greed), Philistines (depression), and Egypt ("the 2 oppressors"—the world and the flesh), are only some of the references. This author is excited about the Old Testament and its applications to the Christian's life, but is not directly under it. The Old Testament is for This World, and the author is in the World to Come.

Of course, there are direct historical lessons to be learned from the study of the Old Testament, such as the five major sins of Israel in the wilderness, which we are also to avoid in the Christian life. These are explained in I Corinthians, chapter 10. By and large, if we remember that we are not in This World, and the Old Testament is writing to This World, we will be careful how to apply the text to our lives in the World to Come.

Thus, we see that the believer in Jesus is not under the Laws of Moses, and we need to take this into consideration in many ways in our efforts to reach and disciple Jewish people in the way of the God of Israel after the New Covenant. This is also true of the Gentile believer in Jesus. These few comments are not an exhaustive treatment of the topic. However, we need to see by this study how the erroneous translation of the expression *Le-olam* or just *olam* in combinations meaning "of the age" can lead to the false idea that the Laws of Moses are forever. As we meditate on this theme, let us remember to follow always the voice of the LORD through the Holy Spirit. Remember, our law is the Law of the Spirit of life in Messiah Jesus. This law has made us free from the other law, but it has not freed us from law in general. We who believe in Christ have crossed into the World to Come, and we are to follow the Holy Spirit Who is the Law there. At this stage in the pilgrimage, the new believer in Jesus should learn that he is under the Holy Spirit as his law, and he is to follow that Spirit.

Chapter 10

From Sinai Northward: The First Approach to the Land: Early Zeal for the Lord with Many Mistakes

After a little more than a year at Mt. Sinai, the Israelites headed northward toward the Promised Land. In Numbers 10:11-12 we read, "Now in the second year, in the second month, on the twentieth of the month, the cloud was lifted from over the tabernacle of the testimony; and the sons of Israel set out on their journeys from the wilderness of Sinai. Then the cloud settled down in the wilderness of Paran." The Israelites had been freed a little over a year from Egypt, and they had learned the lessons that God wanted to teach them at Sinai.

As mentioned here, the first place they arrived at after leaving Sinai is the wilderness of Paran, which means beauty.[1] It is still a wilderness, or desert, but the Israelites have some beauty now because the Divine Potter has been working on them in Mt. Sinai, which means "Mountain of My Clays." At this point God considers that they are ready to go on for Him, so He lifts the cloud from off of the Tabernacle as a sign that they are to move on.

For the believer in Jesus, after the time learning the basic lessons, he needs to set forth to possess what the LORD has for him. We need to remember at this time that there are three types of people: the natural man, the carnal man, and the spiritual man. These correspond to the unsaved man, the immature believer, and the mature believer, respectively. As the Land of Canaan is the goal of the Israelites, and becoming the spiritual man is the goal of the believer in Jesus at this point. Here the believer in Jesus is still a carnal believer. Paul contrasts the spiritual and natural man in I Corinthians 2:12-16: "Now we have received, not the spirit of the world, but the Spirit who is from God, so that we may know the things freely given to us by God, which things we also speak, not in words taught by human wisdom, but in those taught by the Spirit, combining spiritual thoughts with spiritual words. But a natural man does not accept the things of the Spirit of God, for they are foolishness to him; and he cannot understand them, because they are spiritually appraised. But he who is spiritual appraises all things, yet he himself is appraised by no one. For who has known the mind of the LORD that he will instruct Him? But we have the mind of Christ."

Paul explains that the mature believer knows the Holy Spirit and can commune with Him. He therefore understands what that Spirit is revealing to him. On the other hand the natural man, who is not born again, does not understand things that are spiritual. As we considered in the last chapter, the person who believes in Jesus passes through a sort of death to This World and resurrection to the World to Come, where he is under "the Law of the Spirit of Life in Christ Jesus" (Romans 8:2). Therefore he can understand and communicate with the Holy Spirit of God. The natural man is living in This World, and thus cannot ever understand spiritual things, because they are part of the World to Come. Then Paul introduces a third type of person—not in This World anymore, but not exactly acting according to the World to Come, either. He is the carnal man (I Corinthians 3:1-3): "Now And I, brethren, could not speak to you as to spiritual men, but as to men of flesh (carnal men), as to infants in Christ. I gave you milk to drink, not solid food; for you were not yet able to receive it. Indeed, even now you are not yet able, for you are still fleshly. For since there is jealousy and strife among you, are you not yet fleshly, and are you not walking like mere men?"

Here the Apostle Paul introduces a third type of person. He is already out of Egypt, but he is not yet in the land. The Christian at this stage is the extreme type of misfit. He can no longer fit in the world, but he is not ready yet to live as one of the mature believers. As we have seen before, Israel living in Egypt represents the natural man, living in the desert represents the carnal man (or immature believer), and living in the Land of Canaan represents the spiritual man (or mature believer).

The believer needs a certain amount of time to mature, just as Israel needed a certain amount of time to reach the Promised Land. We cannot just jump right into our spiritual blessings right after conversion. We have to prepare ourselves for them. God could have led them directly along the coast, but decided not to (Exodus 13:17-18) because "the people might change their minds when they see war, and return to Egypt. Hence God led the people around by the way of the wilderness to the Reed Sea." The people were not ready yet for a full-scale war, such as they would have had to fight against the Philistines, so God took them the long way around. In the same way, no recently converted Christian is ready to fight spiritual battles, so the Holy Spirit leads him the long way around so that he can learn the necessary lessons for the later warfare. That is why the Apostle Paul urges us not to invest recent converts with positions of authority in the church (I Timothy 5:22): "Do not lay hands upon anyone too hastily and thereby share responsibility for the sins of others…" The understanding is that new believers will make many mistakes, and we should not place them in a position of authority where their errors can hurt others.

The author of the letter to the Hebrews in the New Testament explains first the problem of Israel in the desert (3:16-19): "For who provoked Him when they had heard? Indeed, did not all those who came out of Egypt led by Moses? And with whom was He angry for forty years? Was it not with those who sinned, whose bodies fell in the wilderness? And to whom did He swear that they would not enter His rest, but to those who were disobedient? So we see that they were not able to enter because of unbelief."

There is a certain amount of time that the believer will be a carnal believer, just as Israel had a certain minimum amount of time that they needed to prepare themselves in the desert. However, they spent many more years there than were actually necessary because of their lack of faith in God. Often believers take an extra long time to get beyond the carnal state, as well. In the letter to the Hebrews, the author warns believers that they can spend their entire life here on earth as carnal believers and not become spiritual believers.

Setting out from the Camp: God's order

I. Judah, Issachar, and Zebulun

In Numbers 10: 13-14; we read that the Tribe of Judah went first in the order. The word Judah indicates 3 meanings by its root in Hebrew: to confess God's attributes (by confessing His names), to confess one's sins to God, and to praise God.[2] It is easy to see why the Tribe of Judah would lead the nation. In many places we are exhorted to praise the Lord, be thankful to Him, and to confess our sins to Him. This verb puts man in his rightful place before God. For example, In Psalm 100:4 we are to "Enter His gates with thanksgiving." In Philippians 4:6 Paul exhorts us, "Be anxious for nothing, but in everything by prayer and supplication with thanksgiving (lit. "*after* thanksgiving") let your requests be made known to God."

In Psalm 8: 2 we read, "From the mouths of infants and nursing babes You have established strength." It is interesting that when Jesus quotes this passage in Mat. 21:16 he says, "Out of the mouth of infants and nursing babes You have prepared praise for Yourself." Here Jesus related praise and strength. In the same way Judah, representing praise, was the strongest tribe of Israel. We need to remember to enter into our world for the day being prepared with confessed sin, praise and thanks to God, and confidence in God's attributes. Then we will be able to face any enemy we have.

Leading Judah's army was Nahshon, the son of Amminadab. Nahshon comes from the root meaning serpent, to practice divination, enchantment, and copper or bronze.[3] Amminidab means, "my kinsman is noble," according to Gesenius.[4] At this stage the New Testament believer is still in the flesh, and thus resembling more "the Serpent," or Satan in his mentality, but he is in the company of other believers, and they are noble in their intentions. If we are in the flesh at any time we will not be pleasing to God, but God overlooks it at this stage because Israel is heading the right direction.

The second tribe was Issachar, which means, "recompense" (Gen. 30:17-18). One thing that leads and motivates believers is that there is really a recompense for the sufferings that we go through. Paul finishes I Corinthians 15, that great chapter on the resurrection with verse 58: "Therefore, my beloved brethren, be steadfast, immovable, always abounding in the work of the Lord, knowing that your toil is not in vain in the Lord." All Christians can appreciate that God will reward our labor for Him, but this is especially important for the new believer, as he still thinks, "What's in it for me?" more than the others.

Leading the army of Issachar is Nathaniel, the son of Zuar. Nathaniel means "God gives," and Zuar (tsuar, צוּעָר), means "insignificant." We need to realize that the recompense is a gift from God. We are not really earning it. Jesus says (Luke 17:10), "So you too, when you do all the things that are commanded you, say, 'We are unworthy slaves; we have done only that which we ought to have done." Along with this attitude, we need to realize that it is all about Jesus, not us. We are insignificant. As John the Baptist said about Jesus (John 3:30), "He must increase, but I must decrease."

This third tribe in the national caravan was Zebulun. Zebulun means "elevation, height, or lofty abode," according to Gesenius.[5] Many people say that if we are too heavenly-minded, we will be no earthly good. The opposite seems to be true. As we think more and more on heavenly things, we are more likely to act on the high level of God Himself. Thus, Paul exhorts us in Colossians 3:2, "Set your mind on the things above, not on the things that are on earth." Paul asserts that this is the way to be more like God and less like the world. The result, however, will be of great benefit to those in the world, since forgiveness, unity, peace, love and good works will follow. The idea is to be heavenly-minded in order to be an agent of earthly good.

Leading Zebulun's army was Eliab, son of Helon. Eliab means, "My God is Father", and Helon probably means fortress.[6] This root can refer to dancing or writhing, as well as strength, or army. We need to remember that My God is Father, that God will be there as a father to provide and lead us as we go forth. As the Israelites could see the column of fire by night and cloud by day, so the Christian should look for the leading of God in his daily life. Helon refers to our writhing, or agonizing in prayer. This is where our strength comes from. Jesus won the victory for the battle of the cross in the Garden of Gethsemane. The disciples, however, slept then and scattered later. We need to go forth with total seriousness, trusting in God to be as a Father for us, because there will be many attacks of the enemy.

After the tribe of Zebulun comes the first part of the Tribe of Levi. In verse 17 we read that the Tabernacle was taken down and the sons of Gershon and Merari carried all of the elements of it. We have already seen that the Tabernacle was the "Tent of Meeting," where God met with Moses and Aaron as representatives of the people. Though we sometimes feel abandoned by God, we are in contact with God at all times in our lives. Levi means, "joined," as they were specially joined to God for ministry. The believer is joined to God for ministry in everything God wants from us.

The sons of Levi that carried the Tabernacle were Gershon (variant reading Gershom) and Merari. In Exodus 2:22 Moses gives the meaning of Gershon as "a sojourner there," remembering that this son was born while he was a sojourner in Midian. By believing in Jesus, the believer is automatically a stranger here on the earth. We are exhorted to apply this truth in Hebrews 11:13 where the author talks about the heroes of the faith, and says, "All these died in faith, without receiving the promises, but having seen them and having welcomed them from a distance, and having confessed that they were strangers and exiles on the earth. For those who say such things make it clear that they are seeking a country of their own." Just as Israel had rejected Egypt and was seeking a country for their own as they wandered through the wilderness, so we believers are on this earth living as strangers here and looking forward to heaven.

The other ancestor of those who carried the Tabernacle was Merari. Gesenius places this name under the root meaning bitterness.[7] This root refers to bitterness and includes the bitter myrrh plant. However, when the plant was crushed it gave forth a sweet perfume, which was used in the sacred oil of the priesthood, as well as incense. At this stage the Israelites exhibit more bitterness than perfume or incense, but later, after going through the trials of God, some of them develop the right fragrance for God under trials. The Christian at this point has this potential for God, but God has not developed it yet.

II. Reuben, Simeon, and Gad.

After the Tabernacle, carried by some of the Levites, there were three more tribes: Reuben, Simeon, and Gad. Reuben was the firstborn of Jacob, and his name means, "behold, a son." We, as believers, should continue to be excited about our salvation and always keep before us the glorious fact that we are born again and we are sons and daughters of God. However, this fact should not be our main focus, as there is a long process leading to our maturity. The captain of this tribe's army (v. 18) is Elizur the son of Shedeur, and both names remind us of blessings that come with the new birth. Elizur means, "My God is a Rock," and reminds us to trust in the Lord as our defense in every tough situation. Shedeur, according to Gesenius, means, "the almighty is a flame,"[8] and reminds us that God is the light and power, and we are not to trust in ourselves. The new birth is a great beginning, and we need to remember these blessings we have just because we were born again. However, we must press on without resting on these blessings.

The next tribe is Simeon, the second born son of Jacob. Simeon means hearing, and reminds us of the importance of Listening to God. Jesus says in John 10:27: "My sheep hear my voice, and I know them, and they follow Me." When we were unsaved, we were dead in our trespasses and sins. That means that there was no connection between our human spirit and God. When we were born again, that connection was re-established, and we have had spiritual contact with God since that time. Our potential to hear Jesus is there, but we have to cultivate sensitivity to His voice spiritually. The Christian life is about doing God's will, and this requires hearing His voice.

Commanding the army of Simeon was Shelumiel, the son of Zurishaddai. Shelumiel means, "God is my peace," or "God is my completeness." One motive of listening for God's voice regularly is that we are aware that we are incomplete without God. The word *shalom* in Hebrew means peace, but also gives the idea of completeness or wholeness. God gives us peace by paying the price for our sins, and He gives wholeness by meeting everything necessary that we are lacking in our lives. Zurishaddai means, "the Almighty is my rock." This speaks of the trust that we need to have for God in order to seek His voice and obey Him, instead of setting out in our own strength and our best efforts. Yes, hearing God's voice is also important for our pilgrimage.

There is, however, quite a gap in most of us—especially at this stage—between hearing the will of God and doing the will of God. In James 1:22-24, James warns us that hearing the Word of God is not enough: "But prove yourselves doers of the word, and not merely hearers who delude themselves. For if anyone is a hearer of the word and not a doer, he is like a man who looks at his natural face in a mirror; for once he has looked at himself and gone away, he has immediately forgotten what kind of person he was." When we are recent believers, we need to learn more about hearing God's voice; but as we mature, God expects us to put more and more into practice in our lives. At this stage, the believer has all he can do to learn to hear the voice of God.

Next in Israel's caravan comes the troop, or Gad. The Hebrew root behind this word has two basic meanings that are difficult to combine into one: good luck or good fortune, and to penetrate, or cut. The meaning troop fits in as a band of marauders that penetrates into another territory. The idea of good luck is also included here. The New Testament believer at this stage needs to think of himself as powerful in battle, as long as he is under the power of God. He needs to learn that he is powerful as a boxing glove in God's hand, but powerless by himself.

Luck is another matter. We know that God is working all things together for our good, according to Romans 8:28, but too often we want to supply the criteria by which things are judged as good or bad. In the very next verse, Romans 8:29, God defines the criteria by which He judges all things to be good or bad for us: "For those whom He foreknew, He also predestined to become conformed to the image of His Son, so that He would the be the firstborn among many brethren." God defines something as good in our lives if it makes us more like Jesus, and bad if it makes us less like Him. From this viewpoint, we can look back on different problems in our lives and see them as good in they resulted in our being more like Jesus.

In verse 21 we find that another group of Levites follows. The Koathites carried the holy objects, and the other Levitical party already set up the Tabernacle before they arrived. This was so that they could bring the holy objects directly into the finished Tabernacle. Thus every night that the Tabernacle moved, it was pitched that night and the holy objects were placed in it. Thus, the Tabernacle is a picture of God's presence going everywhere with His people.

In the same way, Jesus' body was a fulfillment of the Tabernacle. John says about Jesus' arrival (John 1:14): "And the Word became flesh, and dwelt (lit. "tabernacled," ἐσκήνωσεν) among us, and we saw His glory, glory as of the only begotten from the Father, full of grace and truth." Here John makes a verb in Greek out of the name of the "Feast of Tabernacles" (skenai, σκῆναι,). The teaching here is that Jesus' body was like the Old Testament Tabernacle walking around with the presence of God inside. The same is true about the New Testament believer. The fact that the Tabernacle was set up every night that Israel moved indicates that God's provisions were always ready for them. We can count on God to be with us and for His grace and mercy to be active in us wherever we are and at all times, once we have accepted Jesus as our Savior.

III. Ephraim, Manasseh, and Benjamin.

The next three tribes to travel are Ephraim, Manasseh, and Benjamin. It is appropriate that here God put together Joseph (from whom are Ephraim and Manasseh) and Benjamin, the two children of Jacob by Rachel. Ephraim is important for the New Testament believer because it means "two fruitfulnesses." This refers to fruitfulness in the material sphere of existence, as well as fruitfulness in the spiritual sphere of existence. The believer in Jesus is alive spiritually, and so he can be fruitful in the spiritual dimension of life, in addition to the material, in which believer and unbeliever alike can operate. The young believer at this stage needs to remember that God is with him during his workweek, as well as on the weekends in church. God is with him in both places to bless and to see that his behavior does not differ from place to the other.

Leading the army of Ephraim is Elishama Ben-Ammihud. Elishama means My God has heard, and refers to the fact the God has heard us, and has been hearing us all along. That is the reason for the double fruitfulness. Ammihud means, "My kinsman is majesty. This represents the ability to see the glory of God on other believers, to see our kinsman in the body of Christ as having the majesty of Christ on them. This optimism is good to motivate the believer at this stage, but things can get very difficult later on. We need to develop a true appreciation of other believers in Christ while still remembering that they are capable of anything bad while in this life.

The next tribe in order is Manasseh, which means forgetfulness. The young believer in Jesus needs to forget all of the difficulties, wrongs done by others, and sins of the past so that he can go on in the Lord. Near the end of his life, the Apostle Paul gives advice that is good for believers at any stage. Referring to the prize of God's highest approval, Paul says (Philippians 3:13-14): "Brethren, I do not regard myself as having laid hold of it yet; but one thing I do: forgetting what lies behind and reaching forward to what lies ahead, I press on toward the goal for the prize of the upward call of God in Christ Jesus." There are certain things that we need to remember, and many of them are mentioned here. However, we also need to forget many things, leaving them at Jesus' feet so that they do not hinder. We must often leave emotional baggage, bitterness, anger, resentment, addictions, and many other things behind so that we can go on unimpeded.

Leading the army of Manasseh was Gamaliel, the son of Pedahzur. Gamaliel means "reward of God."[9] When Manasseh was born, Joseph decided to leave all of his resentment and bitterness toward his brothers behind so that he could go on. He said when his oldest son was born (Genesis 41:51), "God has made me forget all my trouble and all my father's household." God helped him to do that so well that after their father died and his brothers feared his retaliation, he said (Genesis 50:20-21): "As for you, you meant evil against me, but God meant it for good in order to bring about this present result, to preserve many people alive." After much unjust suffering, Joseph was promoted to second in command in Egypt and became rich. From that perspective, he could see God working in his previous suffering, and could leave everything behind in God's control. God then humbled Joseph's brothers and reunited the family. But Joseph had to forget the injustices and hand them over to God or they would have ruined his life in spite of his newfound prosperity. In the same way, we need to hand over to God the injustices we suffer so that we can forget them and go on for God. This leaves God to deal with the guilty and to reward us.

Similarly, Padahzur means, "the rock has ransomed." As we focus on the fact that God the Rock has ransomed us, we are made aware of our own sins and forgiveness, and can more easily forgive others that have hurt us, and leave the hurts behind us. In its rightful place and exercised properly, forgetfulness can be a real blessing to us and to others around us, as long as we forget the right things.

After Manasseh came Benjamin, "the son of my right hand." As Christians, we need to be aware of our position in Jesus as we go out. Our victory over the enemy is due to our position in Jesus, not our own strength. The whole epistle of Paul to the Ephesians reflects this truth. In the first three chapters, Paul explains our position in Jesus. This is probably best summed in 2:4-6: "But God, being rich in mercy, because of His great love with which He loved us, even when we were dead in our transgressions, made us alive together with Christ (by grace you have been saved), and raised us up with Him, and seated us with Him in the heavenly places in Christ Jesus." Our position is at the right hand of the throne of God in heavenly places, which is the highest authority in the universe. We have this authority in Jesus, the Messiah

The next two chapters in Ephesians outline what should be our daily conduct because of that position. The New Testament believer is like Cinderella in the famous fairy tale. Cinderella does not make it into the palace because of her merits, or because she has kept the law of the land. She made it because she said yes to the marriage proposal of the prince. However, because of her new position, she now lives in the palace, and she needs to learn the palace etiquette. She is not learning it to get into the palace, nor did she learn it to stay there, but rather as a loving response to the prince, whom she loves. In a similar way, our position in Jesus should affect our daily conduct as we march along.

Finally, chapter six of Ephesians deals with the warfare of the believer. The believer is to put on the armor of God and fight against the enemies of God as they attack him. Often in military campaigns the position of the army in the terrain gives them the advantage. If they are defending the high ground, they can win with fewer soldiers because of the advantage of their position. The New Testament believer's position is at the right hand of God in heavenly places, even though we are fighting the battle here on the earth. This position gives us the authority to win the battle against every spirit of the enemy. As we go forth, we must remember that we are sons of the God's right hand, and that we represent Him, and not ourselves.

In our warfare, based on our position in Messiah Jesus, we need to remember that God is the final authority and judge, and over the army of Benjamin is Abidan the son of Gideoni. Here Abidan means, "Mi Father judges," and Gideoni means "my cutting down."[10] As God's representatives in Jesus, we can cut down the enemy with the Sword of the Spirit, the Word of God. We must remember, though, that we are representing the Father in judgment. We are acting on His behalf.

IV. Dan, Asher, and Naphtali.

The next three tribes come directly after Benjamin. There is no group from the Tribe of Levi between. The first of these is the Tribe of Dan, which means judgment. This is in a way a continuation of the meaning of Abidan above. The believer who goes forth in the world needs to have sound judgment as to right and wrong—not just following his conscience. Often the popular culture has conditioned his conscience to favor things that God does not approve of. At this point, God is guiding the believer through the Holy Spirit so that he can have the true discernment as to what is right and wrong.

Over the army of Dan was Ahiezer, the son of Ammishaddai. Ahiezer means, "my brother is a help,"[11] and Ammishaddai means, "my kinsman is almighty."[12] As we are near the beginning of our walk as believers here, we still need the help and counsel of other believers.

Also, we need to remember that the Lord is our kinsman. No matter how hard things get for us, we need to keep reminding ourselves that we are on the Lord's side. We are adopted into His family. An attack against us is really an attack against God.

In Romans 8:15-18 the Apostle Paul describes how this fact of being adopted into the family of God should help our mindset for our spiritual battles: "For you have not received a spirit of slavery leading to fear again, but you have received a spirit of adoption as sons by which we cry out, "Abba! Father!" The Spirit Himself testifies with our spirit that we are children of God, and if children, heirs also, heirs of God and fellow heirs with Christ, if indeed we suffer with Him so that we may also be glorified with Him. For I consider that the sufferings of this present time are not worthy to be compared with the glory that is to be revealed to us."

As we focus on our position and privileges as members of the family of God and our future glory, we are to consider the things of this world and our sufferings in this world as nothing by comparison.

After the tribe of Dan came Asher, which means happy one.[13] As we go forth for the Lord, we are to consider that we are already blessed in Jesus. Even when we are in a difficult situation, we are to see our sure entrance into heaven and the blessings that we have in Jesus, and we should already count them as ours in the Messiah. Every blessing we have, we received at the same time we received Jesus as our Savior, and they are 100% certain for us for all eternity. No one can take them away from us. We are to walk by faith in the Christian life, but our faith is in the definite promise of God. In Ephesians 1:3 the Apostle Paul writes to the believers: "Blessed be the God and Father of our Lord Jesus Christ, who has blessed us with every spiritual blessing in the heavenly places in Christ." He then goes on to name many of them: being chosen, holy, blameless, predestined to adoption as sons, being accepted in Jesus, redemption, forgiveness, the grace of God, knowing the will of God, an inheritance, sealing with the Holy Spirit, and the Holy Spirit as a pledge of our inheritance in heaven.

Even though every believer has all of these spiritual blessings, he cannot take them into account or benefit from them until he realizes that they are his. The story is told about a sheep rancher who was about to lose his ranch during the Great Depression in the United States. He did not know that under the ranch there was a vast petroleum deposit. It was not until one day an oil company representative came and received from him permission to drill that he found out about the wealth that was there. The ranch was saved, and the man became very wealthy. In the same way the believer in Jesus has to learn about the great riches that are his in Christ. After Paul has told the believers in Ephesus about the blessings that are theirs in Christ, he then goes on to pray for them (Ephesians 1:17-19): "that the God of our Lord Jesus Christ, the Father of glory, may give to you a spirit of wisdom and of revelation in the knowledge of Him. I pray that the eyes of your heart may be enlightened, so that you will know what is the hope of His calling, what are the riches of the glory of His inheritance in the saints, and what is the surpassing greatness of His power toward us who believe."

As God opens up our eyes to the blessings we already have in Jesus, we can claim them and put them to work for us in order to receive the benefit. Remember, though, what we are seeing as coming in gradually through the narrative of the history of Israel represents blessings that the believer receives instantly at conversion as he is born again. It is the discovery and appropriation of these benefits that takes place gradually over time for him. However, being blessed is just as surely a part of the Christian's position in Jesus as the Tribe of Asher is a part of Israel.

Commanding the army of Asher was Pagiel, the son of Ochran. Pagiel means "God encountered me".[14] For the believer in Jesus to be blessed, he needs a visitation by the Lord Jesus in his life. Ochran means "disturbance" or "trouble".[15] When the Lord meets a believer to prosper him, the Devil is not far behind to cause disturbances or trouble in his life. That is why the believer cannot achieve wealth on his own. The enemy is always opposing him. However, the Lord can intervene and bless him by blocking the Devil's attacks and prospering his endeavors. These two names remind the believer that his prosperity is only because of the Lord's favor, and that it will not be without opposition and trouble from the enemy.

It is this opposition and trouble from the enemy that reminds the believer that we are in for a fight, and the final tribe, Naphtali, means "wrestling." In the Hebrew root, wrestling has as its base meaning, "to twist" in the simple stem. Here in the reflexive stem (niph-al) it gives the idea of people all twisted up together as they struggle and fight, hence our word "to wrestle."[16] Though the image behind the verb is physical, the wrestling can be mental or emotional, as Rachel struggled with Leah. As this the second son was born to her handmaid Bilhah (Genesis 30:8), she said, "'with mighty wrestlings I have wrestled with my sister, and I have indeed prevailed.' And she named him Naphtali." The struggle between Rachel and Leah was a battle of the wills and emotions. Their bodies were not tied up in knots in a physical struggle, but their conflict was real. Our spiritual conflicts with the enemy are also real. Though we do not get physically "tied up" with him, we can sometimes feel him as we grapple with him spiritually.

Naphtali was the last tribe in the column (Numbers 10:27), and the one that would have to protect the rearguard, as well as any stragglers that couldn't keep up with their tribe ahead of them. In our wrestlings for the Lord, we may have to fight to protect other believers who are weaker from the attacks of the enemy. To defend this rearguard of Israel, this tribe's army was led by Ahira, the son of Enan. Ahira means, "my brother is evil,"[17] and can explain how a number of our wrestlings can be with other believers, and why we need to be alert among church people, as well as those in the world.

In order to wrestle, we need to be alert. Enan refers to an eye or wellspring.[18] One of my first insights gained from the study of Biblical Hebrew while still in seminary was to connect these two meanings with the continuous exhortations of my homiletics (Biblical preaching) professor that it was most important to maintain eye contact with the congregation while preaching. I realized that, according to Biblical Hebrew, the eye was the wellspring of the soul. In order to communicate what is in one's soul, he should maintain eye contact, as well as speaking.

Enan reminds the Christian to keep an eye out for attacks of spiritual enemies, as well as human enemies. We may have to wrestle at any time to protect others and ourselves. The flesh and the old nature are evil and can flare up in us, as well as in others—both believers and unbelievers—and we must be watching and ready to wrestle against it. When He was praying in the Garden of Gethsemane, Jesus warned His disciples to be ready (Matthew 26:41): "Keep watching and praying that you may not enter into temptation; the spirit is willing, but the flesh is weak."

Thus the column of Israel begins with Judah and ends with Naphtali. So also the Christian moves out with praise, thanks, and confession to relate right with God, and ends up with watchfulness and wrestlings with spiritual attacks and with human attacks.

V. Let your Conscience be your guide?

As the Israelites are about to set out, Moses invited his brother-in-law, Hobab to accompany them as a guide (Numbers 10: 29-32). He declined the offer to be a guide, and Moses insisted further that Israel needed him as a guide. The Scripture does not indicate if he went with them or if he returned to his people. What we do know and what was stated in earlier chapters is that the Midianites became enemies of Israel from around this time onward.

In Romans 2 Paul mentions that the Gentiles will be judged by their own conscience, as it shows itself in their own affirmations of what is right and wrong. In a child the conscience is very important to bear witness of right and wrong. However, the conscience is often distorted in its content by the norms of the society in which we were raised. Also, we can alter our conscience by repeatedly going against it in a particular area until it no longer bothers us about something we are doing. So we see that the human conscience has its limitations.

There is another problem with the natural conscience. Though it inspires guilt feelings when there is real guilt, and it moves us to want to get forgiveness, it has difficulty accepting forgiveness and going on. Our natural conscience convicts us of sin and moves us to receive Jesus' Gospel of forgiveness, and then it leads us to know the Law of God in order to avoid more guilt. However, once we want to go on for the Lord and trust in the efficacy of His shed blood, the conscience opposes us, saying such things as these: "It can't be that easy! You are guilty! Look at the things that you have done! How could God love you?" The natural conscience then can keep us from entering into a rest in the sufficiency of Jesus' plan of salvation and maturity (the Land of Canaan). At some point the believer has to reject his natural conscience and trust by faith that his sins are atoned-for. Then he has to go on by faith, trusting that God has taken over and accepts him just as he is. If he cannot overcome the accusations of his natural conscience, he will never mature.

At this stage, the believer has to let go of his natural conscience and let the Holy Spirit take over. In Romans 8:2 Paul tells that the believer has a new guide to replace his natural conscience: "For the law of the Spirit of life in Christ Jesus has set you free from the law of sin and of death." The believer needs to listen to the voice of the Holy Spirit instead of his natural conscience. The Holy Spirit will tell him when he is wrong in a more reliable way, and He will also confirm to him that he is permanently forgiven of the penalty of his sins, as far as his standing as a son of God goes. However, he will always have to confess the sins to restore the fellowship with God after the sins, and he may still suffer some consequences of sins here on earth.

For example, if a person was an alcoholic before accepting Jesus, he may still have a problem with cravings for alcohol. If the person fails to listen to the voice of the Holy Spirit to resist these cravings and becomes drunk, he has sinned. The Holy Spirit still confirms that he is a believer, but he must now confess this sin in order to reestablish the fellowship with God, even though the relationship was never affected. After he confesses the drunken binge as sin, the fellowship between him and God is restored. However, over the long range, this person may still be affected by cirrhosis of the liver and die at a younger age than he would have had he not given himself over to alcohol for a great part of his life. God could heal him, but He could simply leave the consequences, as He decides. No matter what God does with the consequences, the person is forgiven and restored to fellowship.

At this point the natural conscience comes and tries to persuade the person that he is so bad that God could not love him because he is an alcoholic. It keeps on accusing him to the point that he will become depressed if he listens to it. Instead, he needs to reject it and trust in the Word of God by faith and overcome these accusations that speak against the efficacy of the atoning work of Jesus. He needs to defeat the natural conscience to go on for the Lord. In the same way, the Midianites that helped Israel up to Mt. Sinai become enemies for the rest of their history. They have to defeat the Midianites to go on for the Lord.

VI. Speaking upon leaving and speaking upon settling down.

In the last four verses of chapter 10 of Numbers, Moses and the Israelites followed the Ark of the Covenant as they set out from Mt. Sinai. When the ark set out and moved forward, Moses said (Numbers 10:35): "Rise up, O Lord! And let Your enemies be scattered, and let those who hate You flee before You." Here Moses showed his dedication to seek the Lord's glory. He was not concerned that the enemies of Israel be put to death because they were enemies of Israel. He wanted them put to death because they were enemies of God and were opposing Israel because they opposed God.

When the ark stopped so that the Israelites stopped and set up camp, he said (v. 36), "Return, O Lord, to the myriad thousands of Israel." Here his emphasis was on God's presence with His people. Here Moses invoked the presence of God to rest on His people as they were camped. He used the word Israel rather than Jacob here because Israel means "Prince of God," and was the name of the patriarch that God gave him after his conversion. Moses wanted God to look on Israel according to their descent from the converted patriarch, not his pre-conversion self-seeking schemes.

In the same way, we come to God in Jesus' name, not Adam's. This presents us as we are in Christ, as acceptable to God because of the perfection of Jesus on our account. If we invoke Him any other way, we will not have His help along the way because He only seeks to glorify and respond to Jesus, not Adam, nor us, nor angels, nor anything else.

VII. The Bread of Heaven or the Food of Egypt?

In chapter 11 of Numbers the Israelites crave meat as they move along on their trip. They do not want to slaughter their herd animals The food of Egypt also has many attractions for the believer to draw him back, as they complained here in Numbers 11: 4-6: "The rabble who were among them had greedy desires; and also the sons of Israel wept again and said, 'Who will give us meat to eat? We remember the fish which we used to eat free in Egypt, the cucumbers and the melons and the leeks and the onions and the garlic, but now our appetite is gone. There is nothing at all to look at except this manna.'" What were the Israelites craving? —the things of Egypt. What do they represent for the Christian? The flesh is always considered a major enemy for the believer in Jesus, but what specifically does the flesh represent? The word flesh in Hebrew is from the same root as the word Gospel. What is the flesh, then? It appears best to represent the false gospel (good news) of our self-promotion. It is the promotion of our interests in the world above the interests of others, and often at the expense of others.[19]

The list of things of Egypt that the people craved includes six other items, as well: fish, cucumbers, melons, leeks, onions, and garlic. We have discussed these items in chapter 6, as well, as this problem arises several times during the wilderness wanderings. The word fish in Hebrew comes from the root that means "to multiply" or "to increase."[20] I believe that fish represent the idea of the worldly people that one must always be striving at increasing his portion in life. In the extreme they do this because they are perpetually fearful of lacking what they need. The opposite of this fearful activity to increase one's portion is the Sabbath, in which one "ceases" from his activity by resting. One can rest one day per week because he trusts in God for his portion in life, instead of fearfully and feverishly working to increase it constantly without rest. In I Timothy 6:6-10 Paul explains this truth to Timothy: "But godliness actually is a means of great gain when accompanied by contentment. For we have brought nothing into the world, so we cannot take anything out of it either. If we have food and covering, with these we shall be content. But those who want to get rich fall into temptation and a snare and many foolish and harmful desires which plunge men into ruin and destruction. For the love of money is a root of all sorts of evil, and some by longing for it have wandered away from the faith and pierced themselves with many griefs."

The second of the additional foods of Egypt was cucumbers. The original root indicates nothing more than cucumbers; but there are two cognate roots that refer to more. One refers to being hard or severe, and the other old or dried up.[21] There are many people in this world that pride themselves on being hard people to deal with, and they always trust themselves, and do not rely on any spirit to help them. This is really a front that people put up to look self-made to others, but it is really hiding a miserable person. As a new believer, we may actually crave the front that we put on before we knew the Lord because it was comfortable. It is easy to forget the misery and fear that go with "self-sufficiency."

The third food was melons. The Hebrew root behind this food is the word trust.[22] Many people in this world have a trust in a false object that gives them a sense of security. The current idea that everyone is right for himself further adds to this mentality. There is therefore no reason to check if the object of the trust is valid, or trustworthy. The current idea is that the trust of the person makes the experience valid. It is easy to live with the careless idea that your belief makes anything valid; but after learning the truth and being converted, one can no longer look to the inadequate objects of faith that the world has in preference to the Omnipotent Creator God. However, in the dry desert of early Christian experience, some of us may be tempted to look nostalgically at our earlier naïve trust in a worthless object when life was much simpler.

The fourth food was leeks. The Hebrew root behind this food refers to the idea of an enclosure and protection, as well as grass, leeks, and other herbage that grows abundantly.[23] Protection and prosperity are not so important to one in the world who eventually sees through them and their fleeting nature. This root also refers to grass as a type of what is quickly perishing in Psalm 90:6: "In the morning it flourishes and sprouts anew; toward evening it fades and withers away." During trying times in our early development as Christians, we are tempted to crave the unsure earthly riches that we sought before without thinking on the fact that they will not last.

The fifth food that the Israelites craved from Egypt while in the desert was onions. The basic meaning of the root is "to strip off,"[24] as onions have many layers to peel off. This refers to the various layers of false front that we may put on so that others do not see us as we really are. It is scary to reveal what we are really like to others so that they can see us with all of our flaws and weaknesses. Very few people want to be that vulnerable. It may seem frustrating to follow a God that knows everything because we cannot hide anything from Him; but if we learn to be open with Him and let Him change us, then we can be transparent with others. At this stage, though, the believer may wish that he could cover up himself so others-and even God-cannot see him. We should resist the urge to cover up our sins, faults, and other problems before God especially. Watch out for the craving for onions!

The sixth food that the Israelites craved from Egypt was garlic. Garlic in Hebrew comes from the root for the word *name*, which is from the root that Gesenius says refers to being high or lofty.[25] The word *heaven* comes from this root. Garlic refers to our making a name for ourselves. This can refer to being popular with friends or being famous in general. There is a real desire to be "someone" among people of this world, and it is sad that people think that popularity will solve all their ills. One has only to look at the currently popular television show *American Idol* to see how desperately some people crave acceptance by others. We Christians at this stage must learn to give up on popularity and seek to please Jesus—the opposite of pleasing others. This is repulsive to the unsaved people, as the Apostle Paul comments in II Corinthians 2:14-17: "But thanks be to God, who always leads us in triumph in Christ, and manifests through us the sweet aroma of the knowledge of him in every place. For we are a fragrance of Christ to God among those who are being saved and among those who are perishing; to the one an aroma from death to death, to the other an aroma from life to life. And who is adequate for these things? For we are not like many, peddling the word of God, but as from sincerity, but as from God, we speak in Christ in the sight of God."

For the unsaved person, our dedication to God is like pouring ourselves out for nothing, and so it has a spiritual fragrance like death to him. To the believers, our sacrifices for Christ are a fragrance of life, because they perceive that they have eternal rewards. Now from God's point of view, all of the effort of people to build up a name for themselves stinks, even as garlic gives our breath a bad odor. From the time of the Tower of Babel (Genesis 11:4), mankind has said, "let us make for ourselves a name," and all of our efforts to do that are a stench to God—like breathing in someone's breath filled with garlic smell. Our entire craving for "fame" in this world is an offence to God. Let's give up the spiritual garlic!

The meat, bread, fish, cucumbers, melons, leeks, onions, and garlic of Egypt could not satisfy the Israelites even if they did get them in abundance. In the same way, our "false gospel" of self glorification, our false battle to promote our own interests, our seeking material abundance in this world, our hardness to get ahead, our false confidence, our temporary prosperity, our many layers of facades that protect us from being known, and our craving for popularity or fame cannot satisfy us New Testament believers in our lives now. God has something better for us!

The Israelites were beginning to adapt to God at this stage after about two years outside of Egypt. They had been brought up under the evil spirits that the Egyptians worshipped, and there is ample evidence that they had been, and still were idolaters (to some extent) like their former masters. However, for two years the Israelites had been traveling outside of Egypt at this point. After being outside of the influence of these evil spirits, having escaped the territory where they have their power, they can now feel the influence of their God and can remember the gods of Egypt, as well.

God, however, had not taken away the provision of the Nile, the pots of meat, the bread of Egypt, and the other various cravings without substituting something else, that was according to His plan for the Israelites. The same is true for the believer in Jesus. After the Lord removes his worldly things, he begins to fill us up with His good provisions. The major provisions for food immediately were quail for meat, just like in Exodus 16, and the bread of heaven.

The Lord promised meat, and so the Israelites had meat: God sent quails. As we read in Numbers 11:31: Now there went forth a wind from the Lord and it brought quail from the sea, and let them fall beside the camp, about a day's journey on this side and a day's journey on the other side, all around the camp and about two cubits *deep* on the surface of the ground." The word deep is not in the original Hebrew, and the reading "two cubits above the surface of the ground" is to be preferred. The quail were not piled

3 feet deep on the ground, but rather were brought down to fly at three feet above the ground. All the Israelites had to do was to club them, clean them, and cook them. Here in the middle of the desert a nation of about 2 million people had all the meat they could eat without slaughtering their precious herd animals. What a blessing and miracle! According to Koehler and Baumgartner he word *quail* refers to fatness, according to the only cognate root available from Arabic.[26] This is probably correct, as they mention that the residents of Egypt often club these quail today in the same way, as they are fat, clumsy, and awkward.

In Exodus 13, the Lord tolerated the complaining of the Israelites because they had just left Egypt, but now after two years of teaching at Mt. Sinai in Numbers 11, He judges them twice in this chapter. At the beginning in response to complaints He sends fire to burn some of the outskirts of the camp until the people repent, and at the end of the chapter He strikes the people with a plague (vv. 33-34): "While the meat was still between their teeth, before it was chewed, the anger of the Lord was kindled against the people, and Lord struck the people with a very severe plague. So the name of that place was called Kibroth-hattaavah, because there they buried the people who had been greedy."

The question here is not whether the Israelites will eat meat, but rather which meat they will eat—the pots of meat from Egypt or the quail. In the same way, the believer will evangelize a message (i.e. "flesh out" a message). We have to choose whether it is the message of our own exaltation or the message of the exaltation of Jesus. The Lord can give us the miracle of showing the Gospel through us to encourage us along the way! We just have to seek Him and stop seeking the fulfillment of the gospel of our own self-fulfillment. This is the lesson for us, since the root for flesh is also that of gospel and the verb *to evangelize.*[19] The Israelites sought the flesh and bread of Egypt, and God gave them flesh and bread—but not of Egypt.

God had been giving them the bread of heaven all along since they left Egypt. In Numbers 11:7-9 we read, "Now the manna was like coriander seed, and its appearance was like bdellium. The people would go about and gather it and grind it between two millstones or beat it in the mortar, and boil it in the pot and make cakes with it;

and its taste was as the taste of cakes baked with oil. When the dew fell on the camp at night the manna would fall with it."

Manna means "Whatchamacallit," and is not exactly a flattering expression for God's gracious provision of bread in the desert. Jesus prefers to call it the "bread out of Heaven" in John 6:32. Moses describes this "bread out of Heaven." We are told here that its appearance was like bdellium, and that "its taste was as the taste of cakes baked with oil." Here Gesenius prefers "a dainty item" over "cakes" of the NASV.[27] Also, it is different than *ugoth*, translated "cakes" in the Exodus passage, and the word "baked" is not in the Hebrew. This description of "manna" serves to show us the difference between the diet of Egypt and the diet of the Lord.

As we consider that God's bread is also from the Hebrew root for battle, we see by the ingredients that the battle is different. The Egyptian bread was leavened. Leaven makes the dough ferment and rise up. People who are in sin are continually fermenting, or boiling up in their spirit and prone to bitterness and rebellion. Also, they do not submit to self-abasement, but rather are trying to exalt themselves and rise up against God. In I Corinthians 5:6-7 the Apostle Paul compares the leaven in bread to sin and exhorts believers to purge it out: "Do you not know that a little leaven leavens the whole lump of dough? Clean out the old leaven so that you may be a new lump, just as you are in fact unleavened, for Christ our Passover also has been sacrificed."

The bread of Heaven, on the other hand is made differently. The word coriander (gad, in Hebrew) comes from the root that means, "to penetrate or cut."[28] God first penetrates and cuts us as His best provision for us. To be penetrated by God is our best way of being strengthened, as He is beginning to replace the old Adam, who died and was raised with God in baptism, symbolized by the crossing of the Reed Sea. As we feed upon God's presence every day, more and more of Him penetrates us and we become more and more like Him. How is this done? John says at the beginning of his Gospel (1:14): "The word became flesh and dwelt among us." This was in the person of Jesus of Nazareth. As we read, memorize, and meditate on the word of God, the Lord is becoming more and more a part of us. The Hebrew word for meditation comes from the root meaning, "to chew the cud."[29] We need to think over what we read and memorize of the Scriptures in order for them to penetrate, or they do not become "like coriander seed" for us.

The second description of manna is that it was white. We need to realize that the Word of God is white, i.e. totally truthful and without error. We must have the highest view of the truth and inerrancy of Scripture or we will begin to judge the Scriptures by some other criteria that we put above it. We will then fall into all types of error. Let's remember that "Every word of God is tested: He is a shield to those who take refuge in Him. Do not add to His words, or He will reprove you, and you will be proved a liar (Proverbs 30:5-6)." We must judge everything else by the Scriptures, but never judge the Scriptures by anything else. If we feed on the truth, we will be able to distinguish error because it is different; but if we study a mixture of truth and error, as is in the world, we will never be able to separate the truth from the error.

The third description of the manna is that of wafers. The word in Hebrew comes from a root that means, "to make wide or broad."[30] The name Jesus comes from a different root meaning to make wide or broad, as well. In the sense of Jesus' name, it means, "to make wide or broad" for someone bound up by sickness, evil spirits, or one's own sins. Here, the sense can refer to spreading us out in preparation to work on us as a Divine Potter. From this root comes the word for a flat, or broad jug—one that was literally "spread out" by the potter into its shape. Here in the Desert of Beauty it is necessary to be spread out by the Divine Potter so He can continue to work on getting out all of the ugly spots in us. We need to expose ourselves to the Word of God for it to affect us.

The fourth ingredient of Manna was "honey." Though the Scripture says it was "like wafers made with honey (16:31)," we need to know about honey to know why manna is like honey in some way. According to Gesenius, honey comes from the root referring to its color of reddish brown.[31] It is interesting to think that pottery jars are this color. This is symbolic of the fact that at this stage, God, as the Divine Potter, is preparing Israel for His labor of love to transform them in the future. While the whiteness describes the purity, the honey describes the clay-colored material. The human being is made of the same elements as clay and is formed from the clay, but God breathed into him the breath of life. In that we differ from clay. This fact reminds us that all of the glory must go to God. As Paul writes in II Corinthians 4:7: "But we have this treasure in earthen vessels, so that the surpassing greatness of the power will be of God, and not from ourselves."

The "dainty item of the oil" also reminds us of several truths. First of all, God always gives the best. A dainty item would be something special on the menu, and anything from God should have top priority and approval. The oil reminds us that we are special, and God's anointing is on us and on His provision for us. We are holy, meaning, "set aside" for God.

So we see that the "battle" related to the bread of heaven is different from the "battle" related to the bread of Egypt. The "battle" of the bread of heaven is to fight against those things in us that rise up against the Lord, and the "battle" of the bread of Egypt is to fight for our self-exaltation in a world where everyone is doing the same thing. God's bread brings us into submission to Him and peace, and the world's bread brings us into a war where everyone is trampling all over one another.

VIII. The Beginning of the Sanhedrin.

The Sanhedrin was the political governing body of Israel in the days of Jesus, and it consisted of 70 men who met in a council. The Sanhedrin was just beginning here in the wilderness in the time of Moses. Here after complaining that leading Israel was too much for him, Moses receives instructions to bring in seventy leaders of Israel to the Tent of Meeting (Numbers 11:17): "Then I will come down and speak with you there, and I will take of the Spirit who is upon you, and will put Him upon them; and they shall bear the burden of the people with you, so that you will not bear it all alone."

When God came down to the Tent of Meeting in a cloud, He put the Holy Spirit on the 68 men there and they prophesied. However they only did it once, not regularly as Moses did. There were two men Eldad and Medad who were among the seventy, but had not yet arrived at the Tent of Meeting. These two men's names show how the Holy Spirit changes people. Eldad means, God has loved," according to Gesenius.[32] I prefer the equally possible reading "God loves." The reason that God sent the Holy Spirit was to show His love to the person receiving the Holy Spirit, and through that person to others. The other person was Medad. Gesenius takes this to be from a root meaning "to love."[33] This would then be from a causative stem and mean, "he who causes love." The emphasis would be on that person, as a result of the Holy Spirit's work, would inspire others to love. It would appear better to split it into two words, meaning "waters of love." Here the emphasis would be on the love flowing from this person because of the Holy Spirit within him. When the Holy Spirit was put on these two, they also began to prophesy in the camp in front of the people as the others in the Tent of Meeting were doing. When a young man told Moses about these two, Joshua suggested that they be stopped. Moses rebuked Joshua and said he wished that all the people were prophets.

The outpouring of the Holy Spirit for every believer was to wait for over 1400 years until the Day of Pentecost after Jesus' resurrection from the dead. However, Moses sees the importance of it, even in his time. For the New Testament believer there is one time in which he receives the Holy Spirit at conversion, which would correspond to the Exodus from Egypt. However, there are many fillings of the Holy Spirit along the way. The water from the Rock in the desert, the Bread of Heaven each morning, the theophanies at Mt. Sinai, the wells at *Elim* (Exodus 17), and this outpouring of the Holy Spirit on the leadership of Israel all symbolize the special presence of the Holy Spirit coming on the believer to fill him. This filling is to meet a need of his, to prepare him for service, or to bring him closer to God in some way. The carnal believer, still in the desert, cannot hold much of the anointing of the Holy Spirit, and quickly loses the benefit. He needs to enter into the land of Canaan in order to receive the benefits of the rains of God's outpourings in his life and produce a harvest of good fruit of the Spirit for God. Meanwhile, this outpouring of the Spirit should have unified the leadership.

Did it unify the leadership? No. At this point some racism appears. In Numbers 12 Miriam and Aaron grumbled against Moses' leadership position in their resentment against him because he had married an Ethiopian woman. The Hebrew reads "a Cushite woman." Cush was a son of Ham who fathered the Black race. Moses had already married a Midianite woman Zipporah, and so we must conclude that either he took this Black woman as an additional wife or Zipporah had died and left him a widower. Either way, God showed His displeasure by smiting Miriam with leprosy. After healing her at Moses' request, He ordered her to be purified from the leprosy for one week, according to the rites already ordered in the Torah.

Was Moses wrong to marry a foreigner, in violation of the Biblical injunction? It appears not. The Biblical commandment not to marry a foreigner was given so that the family was not religiously mixed. Here the Ethiopian woman, in addition to the Midianite first wife of Moses, had obviously converted to following the God of Israel so no foreign deity was recognized at all within the family. This passage, however, shows us how much God hates racism. If a New Testament believer wants to get beyond the stage of carnality—no matter which race he comes from—he had better learn to love all human beings, no matter how different they are from him.

From here, Israel moved on toward the land of Canaan. They were now ready to face the Canaanites, and they camped in position near the border, ready to move in. In the next chapter, we will see their first attempt to enter the Promised Land.

Chapter 11

The 38 Extra Years in the Wilderness: Unbelief Brings About An Unnecessary Detour

At the end of Numbers 12 the Israelites were camped in the Wilderness of Paran, which means beauty,[1] because the Lord, as the Divine Potter, had been working on them for two years at Mt. Sinai, which means "Mount of My Clays." They had set out in the wilderness according to God's orders and they had arrived at the edge of the Promised Land, Canaan. In spite of several failures in their faith, they were ready at this point to enter in and conquer the pagan inhabitants so they could take over their land. The fact that they were not in the land after 11 days, even though it was an 11-day trip from Egypt to Canaan, was not to be held against them. To some extent the Israelites had to be wanderers between Egypt and Canaan. The city they were in at this point was called Kadesh Barnea, which means "holy one, son of wandering."[2] At this point, God considers Israel set apart for Him (holy), even though they are not settled in the land. They are still sons of wandering. The word son is even in Aramaic, as Israel is more foreign than followers of God so far.

In the same way the new believer in Jesus has to go through a period of time as a carnal, or immature believer while he is in preparation to cross over to become a spiritual believer. In spite of this fact, God still has him set aside, or sacred to Him. There is a crisis through he must pass, as well as an important lesson: the lusts of the eyes, the lusts of the flesh, and the pride of life that he feels are not really his any more. These are of the world, symbolized by Egypt, and he must now see that world as the enemy of God, as well as his enemy. As God says in I John 2: 15-17: "Do not love the world nor the things in the world. If anyone loves the world, the love of the Father is not in him. For all that is in the world, the lust of the flesh, the lust of the eyes, and the boastful pride of life, is not from the Father, but is from the world. The world is passing away, and also its lusts; but the one who does the will of God lives forever."

When these desires come up, he must want to fight against them, instead of pampering them and complaining to God that they are not being met, as he had been doing as an immature, carnal believer. Just as the Israelites learned the danger of cravings for the things of Egypt, so the New Testament believer must to stop lusting after the things of this world, and see them as his enemies.

All new believers must go through a time in this condition of immature, or carnal believer. Even the Apostle Paul, who was brought up under the teaching of the Law at the feet of Gamaliel the Elder, passed three years in the desert learning the Scriptures under the teaching of the Holy Spirit before he appeared to any congregation. He also passed another fourteen years before he went into full-time ministry (see Galatians 1:15-18, 2:1). Paul also says concerning believers that we should not lay hands (to install in a church office) on anyone too soon after their conversion. In I Timothy 3:6 Paul says a bishop should be "not a new convert, so that he will not become conceited and fall into the condemnation incurred by the devil." In chapter 5, verse 22, he says further about installing people in church offices, "Do not lay hands upon anyone too hastily and thereby share responsibility for the sins of others."

On the other hand, some people lag behind, and spend their whole lives in the desert. They can testify that God saved them, but they have no new testimony of His blessings in their lives. There come critical tests and times that a person may pass into maturity. If he flunks this test and rebels at that time, he must wander in the desert of carnality for a time before the opportunity presents itself again.

I. The Test: Where is Your Trust?

In Numbers 13 this is what happened to Israel. They had the opportunity to enter into the land of Canaan, but they first had to pass the test of showing their faith in the Lord, rather than in their own abilities. The Lord told Moses to choose one leader from each tribe in Israel to go and spy out the Land of Canaan. In chapter 10 the tribes and leaders of the armies were in the order that they camped around the Tabernacle. Here, however the order is scrambled. There was no person on the list of the 12 spies that was on the list of the military leaders in chapter 10. All were different, since the highest military leader of a tribe was not chosen as a spy. These spies, however, were very much respected by their tribe, as God had told Moses in verse two to pick a leader from each tribe.

The instructions for the spies come in verses 17-20. Moses tells them to go to the Negev (southern desert) and the hill country, covering the whole land. They were also (v.18) to "see what the land is like, and whether the people who live in it are strong or weak, whether they are few or many." Finally (vv.19-20) they were to find out if the land was good or bad, the cities were fortified or not, whether there were trees or not, and they were to bring a sample of the fruit of the land, which was at the beginning of the grape harvest.

With this in mind, the 12 spies set out from Kadesh Barnea for forty days to spy out the land. They went the whole length of it from the desert of Zin, which is in the south, all the way up to "the going down to Hamath." According to Norman and Millard, "The going down to Hamath" is "probably modern Lebweh, NNE of Baalbeck, at the watershed of the Beqa valley, near one source of the Orontes, so at the head of the road N to Hamath."[3] This latter city is about 30 miles north of Damascus, and was considered the northern limit of Canaan, though the Israelites did not occupy that far up under Joshua later on.

On their way back, they passed through Hebron in the Negev desert, where Ahiman, Sheshai, and Talmai, the sons of Anak were. These men were significant, as Anak means neck.[4] It would appear that this problem refers to our stiff-neck, or stubbornness as resistance to God's leading in our lives. Anak's three sons (v.22) represent three different dimensions of our stiff-neckedness, or stubbornness: owning others, owning myself and my abilities, and owning my actions and plans. All three of these dimensions leave the person in control running things and represent his stubbornness against submitting to God and His plan.

The first son was Ahiman, which means, "my brother is a gift."[5] There are two cognate Hebrew roots from which the latter part of the word could come, and the combination of the two roots leaves us with the idea "my brother is a gift and a portion." This fits the stiff-necked person's idea of others. God gave them to him, but they are his portion, or possession, to direct. If we think we own others, as though they were our portion in life, we will try to run others' lives as though we owned them, instead of submitting to God's sovereignty and plan over the lives of all people and just following His lead in our lives. Other people are His gifts to us to enjoy, but not as a portion, as though we owned them.

The second son was Sheshai, which means "my sixes."[6] Since six is the number of man, it would appear best to represent owning myself and my abilities (my humanity). This is the opposite of what the Christian is to remember from I Corinthians 6:19, "Or do you not know that your body is a temple of the Holy Spirit who is in you, whom you have from God, and that you are not your own?" The stiff-necked person refuses to follow the leading of the Holy Spirit because he still thinks that he belongs to himself to act as he wants to act. He has forgotten or has never learned that he has been bought by God to be a dwelling place for His Spirit, and is the property of God. In addition to thinking he owns others, he thinks he owns himself. Therefore, he rebels against God's leading in his life.

The third son is Talmai, which means "my furrows."[7] The idea here is that the stiff-necked person is making his own plans and using his own efforts to carry it out, instead of waiting on God for His plan and trusting in God to carry it out while one obeys God's leading. He thinks he owns his own actions and plans. Thus the stiff-necked person is stubborn because he thinks he owns others, he thinks he owns himself and his abilities, and he thinks he owns his plans, his goals, and his actions to achieve them. When one is so bound-up in himself, there is no room for God, and he is stubborn in refusing to follow God's leading because he is running things for himself. As Anak and his sons were formidable foes for the Israelites, so our stiff-neckedness is a formidable foe to overcome in order to serve the Lord.

Afterwards in Numbers 13:23-24 they came to the Valley of Eshcol, which means, "the Valley of the Cluster." This was because they found a cluster of grapes so large that two men carried it between them on a pole. That enormous cluster of grapes was a symbol of the fruitfulness of the land. It was greatly to be desired. This valley was in the south of Canaan, which today would be just south of Hebron. This area today is very dry, and would not be able to grow large clusters of grapes without the special irrigation that Israel has today. In the time of these spies, the annual rainfall must have been much higher than it is now. In fact, during most of the Old Testament time, the climate seems to have had much more rainfall than now.

For those who doubt that this is possible, God threatened to withhold rain as a punishment for sin in many places of the Scriptures (e.g. Deuteronomy 28: 23-24). It is a fact that the rainfall during the Jewish Diaspora was extremely small, and Palestine was seen as largely a desert, and at best a steppe land. It is also true that in many cities of Israel rainfall has tripled since the Jewish people started returning at the end of the nineteenth century.

Our modern experience of this is to see that climates exist in bands around the world. During the time Israel was scattered all over the world, the band of Mediterranean climate that brought them sufficient rain was moved north of them, and the desert band, in which the Egyptian and Sinai deserts were, was moved north over the land. In the second half of the twentieth century, especially, the Mediterranean band of climate has moved south again and covered most of the land of Israel, while the desert band has also moved south, devastating the lands on its southern fringe from Mali across to Ethiopia with desert drought, turning many steppe lands into a full desert.

After forty days of spying out the land, the twelve returned to Moses and gave their report. They said (Numbers 13:27): "We went in to the land where you sent us; and it certainly does flow with milk and honey, and this is its fruit." At first they showed the people the fruit of the land. They even showed two of them carrying a bunch of grapes on a pole, because it was too large for one man to carry. The rest of the fruit of the land was very good, as well. They were very positive about the goodness of the land, but they were divided about their ability to conquer it.

At first the men gave their report about the inhabitants of the land. They showed their fear about how strong the people were (vv. 28-29): "Nevertheless, the people who live in the land are strong, and the cities are fortified and very large; and moreover, we saw the descendants of Anak there. Amalek is living in the land of the Negev and the Hittites, and the Jebusites, and the Amorites are living in the hill country, and the Canaanites are living by the sea and by the side of the Jordan."

They all had an accurate understanding of the people who lived there, and the strength of their cities. However, ten of them looked only at the strength of the enemies, and only two looked at the greater strength of their God. In the next verse Caleb, accompanied by Joshua, said, "We should by all means go up and take possession of it, for we will surely overcome it." They both realized that God had promised this land to them, and therefore He would give them the victory.

The other ten spies saw only the enemy, and could only respond (vv. 31-33): "We are not able to go up against the people for they are too strong for us… The land, through which we have gone in spying it out, is a land that devours its inhabitants; and all the people that we saw in it were people of great size. There also we saw the Nephilim (the sons of Anak are part of the Nephilim); and we became like grasshoppers in our own sight, and so we were in their sight."

The ten only compared themselves to the enemy. They noted that the enemies were descendants of the *Nephilim*. The Septuagint translates this word *gigantas* (γίγαντας), which is the same as our word giants. This translation is no doubt due to the fact that the men mention apart from this name that they felt small as grasshoppers by comparison. The word *Nephilim* really means "fallen ones," and may refer to the offspring of fallen angels with human women, as in Genesis 6:1-2. In Genesis 6:4 the Septuagint also calls the offspring of the fallen angels and human women *gigantes* (γιγάντες).[8] No matter what they really were, they looked like very large and formidable enemies to fight in hand-to-hand combat, and the ten terrified spies even thought that the inhabitants of Canaan thought the same about them, even though fear had paralyzed them and fueled their imaginations.

It is interesting to see what the inhabitants of Canaan really thought about the Israelites from their own point of view. In Joshua 2:9-11 the harlot Rahab told the Israelite spies (two this time) what the inhabitants of Canaan really thought about them even thirty-eight years later: "I know that the LORD has given you the land, and that the terror of you has fallen on us, and that all the inhabitants of the land have melted away before you. For we have heard how the LORD dried up the water of the Red Sea before you when you came out of Egypt… When we heard it, our hearts melted and no courage remained in any man any longer because of you." It seems that both sides were afraid of each other. Even the sons of Anak were quivering in their boots because of the Israelites, and ten of the Israelite spies were quivering in their boots over the Canaanites.

Only Joshua and Caleb chose to see the conflict from God's point of view. Caleb took action (v.30), "Then Caleb quieted the people before Moses and said, 'We should by all means go up and take possession of it, for we will surely overcome it.'" Caleb was sure that Israel would win against all of the inhabitants of the land because he looked to God to fulfill His promise. Their names give us a clue as to what is needed to carry on for God. First of all, Caleb is from the same root as dog in Hebrew.[9] Dogs were looked down on in Israel, and were often used as an example of what is worthless. If we see ourselves as worthless for the battle to take the Promised Land, then we will not be frustrated at our inabilities to achieve great things. We need to remember that, in our own strength, we are hopeless. We do not trust in our abilities, attractiveness, or strength to overcome the enemy. We depend on the Lord. His father was Jephunneh, which means "made to face," or "made to turn toward (God)." If we can be made to face God, our own feelings of worthlessness will be converted to confidence in God, rather than in ourselves.

The other good spy's name was Joshua. This name means "Jehovah saves." This name is different from the name Jesus, which is Yeshua, or Savior, in that Joshua refers to someone else, Jehovah, doing the saving. However the name Jesus means Savior because He is the Savior. This means that He is Jehovah, the one doing the saving. We need to remember that the salvation will be through Jehovah, not ourselves. Thus Caleb reminds us of our inability and Joshua reminds us of God's ability. As long as we keep these two facts in place, we can overcome because it will be God overcoming through us, and it will be God Who gets the glory. Joshua was the son of Nun, which means, "propagate," or "increase."[10] When we trust the Salvation of Jehovah, we can expect to have an increase in our portion on the earth.

What about the other ten spies? Some of them have great names, but they don't live up to them. In verses 4-15 of Numbers 13 we find the spies named. Shammua, the son of Zaccur, means "Hearing, the son of remembering." He failed to trust God because he did not listen to and remember God. Shaphat, the son of Hori, means "judging, the son of my whiteness, or my paleness."[11] This man judged the situation and became pale with fear.

The third spy was Caleb, who is described above. The fourth spy was Igal the son of Joseph, which means "He redeems," the son of "he adds." He failed in that he though of himself as the one who redeems and the one who adds. If he had thought of God as doing the redeeming and adding, he would have been ready to enter and fight for the land. The fifth spy was Joshua, the son of Nun, and he trusted the Lord, as described above.

The sixth spy was Palti, the son of Raphu, which means "my fugitive," son of the healed one." This person represents one who runs from a fight as a fugitive and seeks healing from any injuries he might have. If we are most concerned with our own safety, we will make preparations to run away, in case we lose. With that mindset, we will not be ready for the battle. We need to trust in God for our safety and healing. The seventh spy was Gaddiel, the son of Sodi, which means, "God is my fortune" son of "my secret." He should have trusted God for his fortune, or lot in life, and sought to be in God's deepest secret counsel. Instead he ran for fear. The eighth spy was Gaddi, the son of Susi, which means, "My fortune," the son of my horse." This name represents seeking our own fortune and our own speed and effort, as horse comes from the root meaning swift. If we are self-centered like this, we will not trust the Lord.

The ninth spy was Ammiel, the son of Gemalli, which means, "my people of God," the son of "my benefit" or "my reward." If a person is emphasizing that he is a member of the people of God only to look for the reward or benefit of belonging (in this case dividing the plunder after conquering the land), rather than the glory of God, he will not be ready to stand before an enemy. The tenth spy was Sethur, the son of Michael, which means, "hidden one," the son of "Who is like God?" We may be convinced that there is none like God, but we will not conquer the Promised Land while we wish to remain hidden from the battle.

The eleventh spy was Nahbi, the son of Vophsi, which means, "my hiding," son of Vophsi. The origin of the word Vophsi is unknown. However, hiding will not inspire one to conquer the land. The twelfth spy was Geuel, the son of Machi, which means, "Majesty of God," son of "Machi." The origin of the word Machi is unknown, but if one is preoccupied with the majesty of God, he should not run from his enemies. This last spy did not live up to his name either, like so many of them.

God's response to the grumbling of the people is extreme and direct. In Numbers 14: 11-12 he tells Moses, "How long will this people spurn Me? And how long will they not believe in Me, despite all the signs which I have performed in their midst? I will smite them with pestilence and dispossess them, and I will make you into a nation greater and mightier than they." God declares His intent to wipe out Israel and start over with Moses. Moses' response was to intercede for Israel on the basis of God's own glory, not anything good in Israel. Moses makes the point that the nations already know about the 10 plagues and God's mighty power. If God were to kill the people at this point, the nations would conclude that He killed them because He could not bring them in to the land. Moses reminds God that He is just and punishes the guilty (v.18). The indication here is that Moses understands that the guilty should be judged, but that the sin should not be considered a national sin.

God seems to change His mind here by not killing everyone in the nation. Instead, He condemns the nation to wander 38 more years in the desert, He kills the ten spies who brought a bad report by a plague right away, and He orders that all males twenty years and older would die in the desert without entering into the land of Canaan, with the exception of Joshua and Caleb.

Did God really change His mind? If so, is He really immutable (unchangeable, as a characteristic)? What really happened? God is unchangeable in His characteristics, in and of Himself. However, His relations with His creatures may change, depending on their changing attitudes toward Him. Our changes can change the relationship, not God's character.

We Christians must pass through a crisis in order to go on from the carnal state of an immature believer to become a mature, or spiritual believer. If we pass the test like Joshua and Caleb did, we can pass on to the stage of maturity sooner. However, if we flunk the test, as did the ten other spies, God must spend more time preparing us before we can enter the land, or go on to maturity. Remember our keys to victory in this test are to remember the names of the two spies: Caleb tells us we are but as dogs, and cannot win the fight in our own strength and have no worth apart from God living in us. Joshua's name reminds us that we are dependent on Jehovah to save us, and the victory is through His power, which is appropriated on our behalf through His grace and our faith.

In I Corinthians 10, the Apostle Paul warns us believers to learn from the five sins of Israel in the desert, lest we also remain in the wilderness. In verse 10 Paul mentions grumbling, which was the last of the five sins. This is what the people did instead of believing in God to bring them into Canaan. The result for Israel was 38 more years of wandering, and for us believers it means more time wandering around in our immaturity and carnality.

In verse 11 Paul then emphasizes a major point that is behind the perspective of this book. He says about the history of Israel in the desert, "Now these things happened to them as an example, and they were written for our instruction, upon whom the ends of the ages have come." The Christian is outwardly still a member of This Age (also called This World, or the *olam hazzeh*), but inwardly he is already in the Age to Come (also called the World to Come, of the *olam habba*). That is why the lessons of Israel are applicable to us, but not just repeated. We have died and been resurrected with Jesus and are in the Age to Come, and therefore things have a slightly different application for us, than for Israel. Israel's stages are Patriarchal, Egypt, the Desert, and Canaan, with detours through Assyria or Babylon and a worldwide dispersion, and finally, the Millennial Kingdom. The Christian's stages are infancy, the natural man, the carnal man, the spiritual man, possible detours through spiritual captivities, and a final glorious state of reigning with Jesus in the New Heavens and the New Earth. As we learn the lessons of Israel in This World, we can apply them to our walk in the World to Come, where our pilgrimage is.

In Hebrews, chapters 3 and 4, the author also mentions this lesson from Israel's history. The Christian must learn this lesson also, though it is applied on a different dimension. Just as Israel could not enter the land of Canaan because of unbelief at this stage, so the Christian cannot enter into God's rest unless he believes in God to back him up in all of his conflicts. So he concludes about the Israelites (3:19): "So we see that they were not able to enter because of unbelief." At this point the author of Hebrews turns the lesson on the reader (4:1): "Therefore, let us fear if, while a promise remains of entering His rest, any of you may seem to have come short of it."

In our dimension of reality there is a similar objective that needs to be conquered, and it requires the same faith in the goodness and power of God to back us up to reach it. He concludes chapter 4, verse 16: "Therefore, let us draw near with confidence to the throne of grace, so that we may receive mercy and find grace to help in time of need." We need the same lessons Israel had. We need the lesson of Caleb, that we are as dogs and unable to win the battle in our own strength. We also need the lesson of Joshua, that "Jehovah is salvation." We need to remember that the battle is the Lord's and He will give us the victory.

In Numbers 14: 25 God orders Israel to turn around and head back into the wilderness toward the Reed Sea. This was the way they had come, and would involve 38 more years of walking through the wilderness. After Moses tells the people about this judgment of the Lord in verse 39, "the people mourned greatly." This was not repentance from the heart, but rather a remorse and self-pity over the long wasted years ahead of them. For those over 20, it meant that they would wander for the rest of their life in the desert and die there.

The Long Delay (Numbers 15:1-21:3).

In Numbers 14:40-45, after Moses announced that all those who murmured against the Lord would spend 38 more years in the desert and would die there, the people decided presumptuously to go in and conquer the land. Here they were warned by Moses not to go in, but they disobeyed again. In verses 44 and 45 we find the place where the Israelites left the timetable of the Lord. "But they went up heedlessly to the ridge of the hill country; neither the ark of the covenant of the Lord nor Moses left the camp. Then the Amalekites and the Canaanites that lived in that hill country came down, and struck them, and beat them down, as far as Hormah."

Hormah is the place where the Israelites began their detour of 38 additional years of wanderings. The Israelites began their extra wanderings because they talked bad about the Lord. In Deuteronomy 1:44, Moses mentions that the Canaanites that joined the Amalekites to defeat Israel were Amorites. In Hebrew the verb from which the name Amorites comes is "to talk." Thus Amorites represent sins of the tongue.[12] The Israelites were first defeated by the sin of talking bad about the Lord when they received the report of the 10 spies and rejected the good report of Joshua and Caleb. Then they were defeated by the "talkers", the Amorites. We New Testament believers need to learn to keep our mouth shut when tempted to speak bad things about God because of our depressing circumstances. We need to speak only the positive truths about God and trust in Him to give us the victory, as Joshua and Caleb did.

The enemies defeated them up to Hormah. Hormah comes from the root in Hebrew that can mean dedicate, consecrate, or exterminate.[13] This odd combination of meanings can be explained by the fact that the basic meaning is to dedicate. If we dedicate something to God that He accepts and can use, then it is positive dedication. However, if we dedicate something to God that He cannot use (such as Canaanite peoples), they must be exterminated, as dedicated to God's judgment. Thus we see that the Israelites were slaughtered until they made a rededication to the Lord at Hormah. When we dedicate ourselves to the Lord, what He cannot use, such as the flesh, must be crucified, and what He can use must be placed completely under His direction under the Holy Spirit.

It is interesting to note that in Numbers 33, which lists the different places that the Israelites camped in the 40 years, there are 11 places mentioned between Raamses in Egypt and Mt. Sinai (vv. 3-15), 21 places between Mt. Sinai and Kadesh Barnea (vv. 16-36), then only four places that we know of for the thirty-eight years of wandering (Hormah, Mt. Hor, Kadesh Barnea, and Hormah again), and finally, eight places between Hormah and the Plains of Moab opposite Jericho. Imagine! Only four places were mentioned for the thirty-eight years of wanderings! As God mentioned that this time was wasted, there is little indication of anything that was of value during that time. God still sustained them with Manna and water, but they did not go anywhere. If they did go anywhere else, it was not worth mentioning, as far as God was concerned.

Chapter 15 contained diverse laws that the Israelites were to keep when they arrived in the land of Canaan. Why would God give laws that would not become effective for another 38 years? These laws were probably for those under twenty to repeat for them God's desires and to give them something to look forward to while they wait for that time. This would help them, even as they were to watch the older generation dying off. They themselves would have something better to look forward to. It can be encouraging also for carnal Christians to actually see older mature believers enjoying the leading of the Holy Spirit and the blessings of being filled with the Spirit. This way they are encouraged to continue in the faith onward to maturity.

Here in verses 32-36 a man is stoned by God's orders for breaking the Sabbath by gathering sticks. This is indicative of the many judgments under which Israelites fall in this period of their journey. God is merciful, but in these thirty-eight years, He has a short temper, and judges every sin promptly. Since this whole generation of adults was condemned to die in the wilderness, God saw fit to make examples of them by judging their sin quickly.

In a similar way, a believer in Jesus who has hardened himself against God and is going through the "thirty-eight year judgment" is likely to suffer consequences more quickly for sins because God wants to get this out of him so He can take the believer to the border of Canaan to try again soon to enter the land of Canaan (meaning "humility"), which corresponds to the spiritual stage of his development.

In verses 37-41 God commands the Israelites to put visible signs on their clothing: tassels, with a blue thread in the ones on the corner. The design for the modern Israeli flag follows this design. It has a white background, as most clothing was white, and a blue stripe along the top and bottom borders. The Star of David in the middle is extra. God says that the purpose for these tassels and cord of blue are "to look at and remember all the commandments of the Lord so as to do them and not follow after your own heart and your own eyes, after which you played the harlot." Every time an Israelite saw the tassels on the fringes of his garment and the blue thread in the corner ones, he was to remember to obey the Lord and not follow his own ideas, thus wandering away from the Lord.

It would also be a good idea for believers in Jesus in these circumstances also to put up something physical to remind us to follow God. It may seem sad to us, but at this stage it seems that God is scaring the carnal believers all over again to instill in them the fear of the Lord so that they will follow Him later. Also, God's fierce justice and holiness is the only clear background upon which we can see His mercy and grace, so it is important to instill it in the next generation for Israel, as well as in the carnal wandering Christian for later memory.

Chapter 16 is about Korah's rebellion. Korah was a Koathite from the tribe of Levi, who led a rebellion against Moses and Aaron. He assembled 250 of the top leaders of Israel, and he claimed Moses and Aaron were exalting themselves over Israel, even though all Israel was as holy as they were (v.3). Upon hearing this accusation, Moses fell on his face. It appears that he did this in order to intercede for Israel so that God would not kill everybody, but only the rebels. This is indicated by verse 5 in which he sets up a lineup, in which the Lord would show who is holy.

Even the names of the three top conspirators show their haughty self-exaltation. Korah Ben-Yitzhar is the leader's full name. Korah means "bald one" or "ice," according to the root,[14] and Yitzhar means freshly pressed oil, or light.[15] If we combine these ideas, we see that Korah was cold towards God and trusted in his own light, even though he was a Levite, which means, "joined (to God)." Being joined to God in Salvation does not make us special in ourselves. We are special because it is God we are joined to.

The other two main rebels were Dathan and Abiram. Dathan comes from the same root as the word law.[16] The immature, or carnal believer may resort to trying to follow the law in his own efforts as a substitute for being filled with the Spirit of God. The word law means religion in Modern Hebrew. Following law or religious practices only leads to our being like God on the outside, while we are far from Him on the inside. This is futile and leaves us empty and unsatisfied. However, while one is emphasizing external things, there is a tendency to compare oneself with others and look down upon others who are not keeping the external form of religion as well as one.

Abiram means, "my father is high" or "my father is exalted." This name could refer to the idea that this person's Heavenly Father is high, or his earthly father is high. The former would fit better the context of their claim that all of the people of God are holy on the same level (v. 2). This person was not claiming that he was above the others; but that all were on the same level and the Moses and Aaron were exalting themselves over the others.

While it is true that all believers are on the same level before God and all have equal access to God, some believers have gifts of leadership and administration, and God has chosen to lead the people of God through them. The Apostle Paul writes to the saints (holy ones) in different cities in his letters, but recognizes that some are to be leaders and others are not to be leaders. He mentions apostles, prophets, pastors and teachers (Eph. 4:11), as well as bishops (I Tim. 3:1-7), and leaders (Rom. 12:8). All of these positions place some believers in authority over other believers. This leadership position does not mean that the leader is more holy, important, or close to God than the followers. He is just exercising a spiritual gift to serve the others. It is a sad truth, however, that immature believers often see the pastor as exalting himself over the church because he is exercising leadership. This is usually a problem that requires God's intervention in the church, as it occurred at this point in Israel's history.

Moses responded by setting up an opportunity for God to reveal those whom He has chosen to lead Israel. He ordered them to appear with Aaron before the Lord on the next day with censers with incense in them. The Lord would then pick whomever He wanted to lead Israel. The rebels answered that Moses had brought them out of a land flowing with milk and honey to have them die in the wilderness, and that he was just lording himself over them. Both accusations were false. In reality they had called Egypt the land flowing with milk and honey, instead of Canaan. This was equivalent to calling God a liar and reversing things.

Also, Moses was not exalting himself over them. Moses tried to avoid God's call in Exodus 3, and Moses complained to God about the difficulty of leading Israel and asked God to kill him and replace him with someone else (see Num. 11:11-15). Moses saw his position of leadership as a service to God by serving the nation of Israel as a leader. What Korah and his people said about Moses was a lie against God's established authority in the nation and had to be dealt with publicly.

The next day Moses, Aaron, and the rebels, led by Korah, Dathan, and Abiram, appeared before the Lord at the tent of meeting and the glory of the Lord appeared before them. The first thing God said was that Moses and Aaron should step back from the whole congregation so that He could burn up the whole nation instantly (vv.20-21). After Moses intercedes, asking God to judge the guilty only, the Lord instructed him to separate the other Israelites from the rebels (vv. 22-24).

After the others moved away from the rebels, Moses announced that the Lord would show who was accepted as a priest because the ground would open up and swallow all of the rebels. After the earth swallowed up the rebels' tents and fire came down from heaven and burned up the rebels, the people ran terrified, afraid that the innocent would be swallowed up, as well. The censers were used to cover the altar because they had been offered to the Lord. It is probable that they were used to cover the altar of sacrifice in the courtyard of the Tabernacle. This is because that altar was of bronze and was where any Israelite man could go, and this plating was to be a warning to others that only the priests could offer incense in the holy place. On the other hand, the actual altar of incense was in the holy place, accessible to the priests only, and it was made of gold, not bronze. It would hardly be fitting to cover gold with bronze, and it would not be a visible reminder hidden away out of sight of those that needed the reminder.

After the rebellion of Korah was ended with God's judgment, there was a worse problem: there was a general grumbling of the people against Moses and Aaron, blaming them for "the death of the Lord's people" (v.41). Instead of seeing that the Lord killed the rebels and fearing the Lord, these people blamed Moses and Aaron, God's visible agents. As a result, there was a plague with 14,700 more dead people. This time God did not want the people to miss Who was doing the killing, and so He killed people directly with a plague until Aaron stood between the dead and the living. Then the people saw again that Moses and Aaron were on their side and were not exalting themselves in leading Israel.

What can Christians say about the application to our lives of these two rebellions? First of all, we must remember that the individual Christian believer is like all of Israel. God cut off individuals in Israel, but never cut off the whole nation. In the same way, God cuts off parts of us, but never cuts us completely off.

For this reason, we can look for the equivalent of Korah in us. We experience coldness and trust in our own light, even though we are joined to God in salvation. This false self-confidence must die, just as Korah and his group had to die before Israel could go on. We also need to get over our false religiosity made up of external rules and comparisons with others (Dathan). We also have to quit appealing to our position in Christ (Abiram) to defame Christian leadership in our local church or the Holy Spirit's leading within us, saying we are all on the same level. We will never be on the same level of authority with the Holy Spirit in us. When the Lord judges us and cuts of these problems from us, we should rejoice that we are one step closer to the Promised Land of Canaan (humility), rather than complaining that an important part of us was taken away. God's judgment for the latter problem was greater than the rebellion of Korah.

In chapter 17 of Numbers, God took the initiative to show the Israelites that Aaron was the only authorized High Priest in Israel, and only the tribe of Levi was authorized to do lesser priestly duties in the Tabernacle. God told Moses to have one leader from each tribe bring his staff to the meeting place. He took the 12 staffs and locked them up overnight. In the morning (17: 8, MT 17:23) "the rod of Aaron for the House of Levi had sprouted and put forth buds and produced blossoms, and it bore ripe almonds." In contrast, nothing happened to the other staffs.

For us Christians, the lesson is clear. We need to submit to the Holy Spirit in order to have real fruit. Any other leadership will leave us fruitless. Just as Moses and Aaron were the only legitimate leaders of Israel, so the Holy Spirit is the only legitimate leader for us in our lives, as He leads through the leaders of the local church where we are. As the other Israelites who were not from the Tribe of Levi were finally afraid to approach God on their own (vv. 12-13), so we Christians need to arrive at the place where we are afraid to try to lead ourselves, instead of following God's leading.

The almonds are *shekedim* (שְׁקֵדִים) in Hebrew, meaning "watchers."[17] The real leaders are the ones who are watching and praying over the people of God. Jesus rebuked His disciples for not being vigilant while He was agonizing in prayer in the Garden of Gethsemane in Matthew 26: 40-41: "And He came to the disciples and found them sleeping, and said to Peter, 'So you men could not keep watch with Me one hour? Keep watching and praying that you may not enter into temptation; the spirit is willing, but the flesh is weak.'" Those who have the real calling are the ones that are watching and praying over the people of God. The others are only exalting themselves.

Having established the authority of the Tribe of Levi, the Lord takes chapter 18 to explain that Aaron's family would have the high priesthood in Israel. Then He tells Aaron (v. 2), "But bring with you also your brothers, the tribe of Levi, the tribe of your father, that they may be joined with you (*veyillavuw aleycha*) and serve you, while you and your sons with you are before the tent of the testimony." Here God uses the verb from the word Levi, translated "will be joined," to show the relationship. Thus the Levites were to show their position of "being joined" to God by "being joined" to Aaron's family.[18] They were authorized to carry out labor in the courtyard (v. 3), but not "the furnishings of the sanctuary and the altar."

For their economic sustenance, the family of Aaron was to receive various parts of offerings, as well as every devoted thing (v. 14), the firstborn of all clean animals, the redemption money for all unclean animals, and 5 shekels redemption money for all firstborn of people (vv. 15-19). Then the Lord tells Aaron that his family may have no land at all (v. 20). The Lord Himself would be their portion and inheritance.

This last promise is a blessing for the Christian, as well. We need to realize that, whether we have lands and inheritances or not, the Lord is our portion. We are to trust that God will meet all our needs, though probably not all of our wants. It is hard to see this as the greatest security there is, rather than counting on lands, farms, and other financial security. We have Jesus, the High Priest after the Order of Melchizedek, in us, so we can count on God's provision. Christian leaders are also to live off of the offerings of the believers, whether pastoral staff of a church, missionaries, etc.

The rest of the tribe of Levi was promised the tithes of the other tribes of Israel. Ten percent of 11 tribes' income should be enough for them, as long as the other tribes paid their tithes. Like the family of Aaron, they were not to receive agricultural land. In addition to tithes, they received cities, along with their nearby pasture lands (Joshua 20-21). After they received the tithes, they were ordered to give a tithe, as well (Num. 18: 26), "When you take from the sons of Israel the tithe which I have given you from them for your inheritance, then you shall present an offering from it to the Lord, a tithe of the tithe."

We believers in Jesus should tithe, not because it is a requirement, as it was in the Old Testament, but because it was considered the minimum back then. A person was not giving an offering until it surpassed the tithe. Since we are under grace, rather than the Law, we are exhorted to give as the Lord leads, but we should consider the tithe as a minimum starting point. As the Apostle Paul teaches about giving offerings to the Lord in II Corinthians 9:7, "Each one must do just as he has purposed in his heart, not grudgingly or under compulsion, for God loves a cheerful giver." Even Christian leaders, such as pastors, ought to consider the importance of giving. As the Levites received tithes and were expected to tithe, so pastors and other Christian leaders that live off of offerings of God's people should give offerings to the Lord, as well.

Because God made distinctions of callings and labors in Israel, some people were closer to God than others. For the Christian it is not so. However, in the church, every believer has the same access to God, no matter what his job or position. This fact is because each Christian corresponds to the whole nation of Israel. We all have One greater than Moses and Aaron in us, and His name is Jesus. There is always a remnant of us that still believes in God, no matter how much of us the Lord cuts off and removes. In Ephesians 2:18 Paul mentions our position in Messiah Jesus and declares, "for through Him we both (Jew and Gentile believers) have our access in one Spirit to the Father."

Chapter 19 of Numbers tells us of a special sacrifice to purify someone that had touched a dead body. It seems out of place here in the Book of Numbers, but the Israelites in this stage of their history were walking around for 38 extra years burying all of the generation that came out of Egypt. If we were to average approximately two million Israelites by the approximately 13,879 days in 38 years, then almost 150 people died every day, on the average. Their relatives that handled and buried the body would need purification. This ritual taught the next generation something about the holiness of God as they buried their parents while wandering in the desert.

In Galatians 6:14, the Apostle Paul mentions that by the cross of Christ, "the world has been crucified to me, and I to the world." This truth, of course, extends to all Christians. Therefore, whenever we touch the world, we touch something dead. We also need a similar purification. This material was considered under the topic of the laver in the Tabernacle. This would be at the third step in approaching God in the Tabernacle, mentioned in Chapter 8.

The Lord instructed Aaron's family, through Moses, to take a red heifer. The animal had to be female and completely red (Numbers

19:2). The word red is *adummah* (אֲדֻמָּה) in Hebrew, and is from the same root as Adam. This sacrifice depicts for us how Jesus took on our humanity and was completely submissive to the Father. As the priest filled a bowl of blood and sprinkled it on the Tabernacle seven times (v.4), Jesus was full of the seven spirits of God, the fullness of the Holy Spirit. This animal was completely burned up with fire—all of it (v.5). In the same way Jesus was completely given over to the fire of the Holy Spirit.

As the animal was burning, the priest was to throw into the fire cedar wood, hyssop, and scarlet material (v.6). These three things show different elements of Jesus that were totally turned over to the Father and placed under the control of the Holy Spirit. The cedar wood refers to Jesus' counsel, or plans. Wood (*etz*, עֵץ) in Hebrew comes from a cognate root as the word counsel (*etzah*, עֵצָה).[19] While Gesenius does not connect them, it would appear better to combine those roots into one larger one with variant spellings. As the wood was thrown into the fire, Jesus' independent plans (counsel) were considered burned up, and he followed the counsel wholly from the Father. Jesus said in John 5: 19: "Truly, truly, I say to you, the Son can do nothing of Himself, unless it is something He sees the Father doing; for whatever the Father does, these things the Son also does in like manner." In this complete surrender to the Father, Jesus expressed the perfect life that God the Father approved of.

The second thing thrown into the burning red heifer was hyssop (v.6). Hyssop was an herb with purging qualities. The hyssop in the mix was to represent the need for purging from the contact with death. Hyssop was also used to apply the purified waters mixed with the ashes and other added items (v.18). Hyssop is used to apply the purification, as well. While Jesus did not need hyssop to purify Himself, being perfect, it is needed to apply the purification to us to purify us from contact with the world, which is dead for us. Also, it imparts to our will the effects of Jesus' pure will completely surrendered to the Father in place of the evil desires in the world.

The third material thrown into the burning red heifer is scarlet material, according to verse 6. The Hebrew is *sheni tolaath*, (תּוֹלַעַת שָׁנִי). Koehler and Baumgartner consider *tolaath* the feminine form of the word worm.[20] This is consistent with the previous word *sheni* in that sheni is, according to Gesenius, a worm that yields a red color when dried.[21] Jesus personified this in that He did not exalt himself. As in Psalms 22:6, prophesying about Jesus' crucifixion, He says, "But I am a worm (Heb. *tolaath,* תּוֹלַעַת) and not a man, a reproach of men and despised by the people." Jesus humbled Himself as a worm and received the reproach of the people in order to follow the Father's will.

Thus we see that the red heifer purification was a model of the way that God purifies the Christian from contact with the world—something dead for us—by washing away the effects of touching the world on us and imparting the obedient counsel, the purity, and the humility of Jesus, all through the "Living Water" of the Holy Spirit. Verse 17 says that "flowing water" (Heb. *mayim hayyim,* מַיִם חַיִּים) is to be added to these three things and the ashes of the red heifer in order to apply them.

In the New Testament "Living Water" is another reference to the Holy Spirit in John 8: 37-39: "Now on the last day, the great day of the feast (of Tabernacles), Jesus stood and cried out, saying, 'If anyone is thirsty, let him come to Me and drink. He who believes in Me, as the Scripture said, From his innermost being will flow rivers of living water.' But this He spoke of the Spirit Whom those who believed on Him were to receive..."

In Numbers 20:1 we read that Moses' sister Miriam died and was buried in the wilderness of Zin. Zin (*tsin,* in Hebrew) comes from the same root as *tsinnah,* a large shield that would cover the whole body.[22] While God was shielding them from enemies, hunger, and other dangers, they were back at *Kadesh Barnea,* which means "holy one, son of the wandering." They were still holy, or "set apart" for the Lord and they were still wandering. They also happened to be back at the very same place from where the 12 spies went out. In chapter 21, verses 1-3 the Israelites actually had a battle with the Canaanites and defeated them all the way to the city of Hormah, where they had been defeated years earlier; after they sided with the 10 doubtful spies, and God had announced the extra years of wandering. This time it was not a battle of presumption and failure, but rather of obedience and victory.

We read also in chapter 20, verse 1 that it was the first month. This is the first month of the 40th year in the wilderness, their last year in the desert. After wandering 37 unnecessary years in the desert, the Israelites were back at the place where they were judged, and were locked back into God's program for them again right at the place where they had failed and had been judged.

Here they rebelled again because there was no water. This time, however, Moses got in trouble with God because he took some of the credit for the miracle of water from the rock. Because of his sin of presumption with his lips, he was disqualified from entering into the land of Canaan. A number of commentators have said that the reason Moses was judged was because he struck the rock twice (v.11), rather than speaking to it (v.8), as God had ordered. On the surface this looks good, but nobody of Israel knew what instructions he had received from the Lord, and so this would not appear to be a disobedience that the people would have noticed that he was not treating God as holy in their sight (v.12).

The sin of Moses appears to have been taking some of the credit for the water that came out of the rock. In Psalm 106:33 we read that Moses' sin was that "he spoke rashly with his lips." Moses and Aaron gathered the people together before the rock and said (Numbers 20:10): "Listen now, you rebels; shall we bring forth water for you out of this rock?" Here Moses was taking some of the credit for the miracle of water from the rock, and sharing it with either Aaron or God, rather than giving all the credit and glory to the Lord. Because of this sin of speaking rashly with his lips, Moses was not able to enter into the Promised Land. He would die just on the edge before Israel entered. Later in this chapter Aaron died and was replaced by his son Eleazer. And so all of the generation that left Egypt died in the wilderness without entering into the land of Canaan, except Joshua and Caleb.

It is interesting to note that Moses means "the drawn out one." While Israel was under Moses, they were just "drawn out" from Egypt. They were not good for much except complaining. They continually lusted after things of Egypt, they engaged in idolatry, and they did other things that God hated. It was finally when they were under Joshua that they were good for fighting for the Lord and furthering His program. Joshua means "Jehovah saves," and through Joshua's leadership, Jehovah did save Israel and bring them into the Promised Land.

For the Christian it is similar. We start out our time as carnal (immature) believers just "drawn out" of the world. We complain when anything goes wrong, and we rebel against God's leadership regularly whenever we feel that we are not getting our way. We have to go through the critical process of voluntary identification with Christ before we are ready to be spiritual. Then we will recognize those desires contrary to God's will that are arising in us as something foreign to us—something that is trying to take over, rather than our own desires that must be pampered or we will explode with anger again. When we have the victory, we are under Jesus. Jesus means "savior," and is a bit different than Joshua. Joshua means "Jehovah saves," meaning Someone else will do the saving. Jesus, however, means "Savior" because He is the one doing the saving. That is because He is also Jehovah.

In the next chapter we will deal with this process of identification, by which we become the spiritual believer. We will see this in the light of Israel's history as they finish their desert wanderings and cross the Jordan River.

Chapter 12

The Law of Identification: From Hormah to Jericho: Finishing the Desert Journey Well—Learning the Lessons at Last!

As the Israelites entered into their fortieth year of wandering in the desert, they returned to Kadesh Barnea, where they were camped when they listened to the bad report of the ten spies. God had judged them 38 years ago by sentencing them to wander the desert until they completed forty years there. In Numbers 14: 39-45 many Israelites decided that they would repent and try to take the land in their own strength. Moses warned them not to try, but they went, anyway, and (v.45), "Then the Amalekites and the Canaanites who lived in that hill country came down and struck them and beat them down as far as Hormah."

Hormah means devotion to God. If something was *h̲erem* (חֵרֶם) and was usable in a positive way, it was brought into the Lord's service and used by the priests, but if was not usable by God— especially the pagan Canaanites—then they were all to be put to death. Either way, they were dedicated to God.[1] In Leviticus 27:28-29 we read, "Nevertheless, anything which a man sets apart (*h̲erem*) to the Lord out of all that he has, of man or animal or of the fields of his own property, shall not be sold or redeemed. Anything devoted to destruction (*h̲erem*) is most holy to the Lord. No one (*h̲erem*) who may have been set apart (*yahoram*) among men shall be ransomed; he shall surely be put to death."

So we see that in this case the Israelites were slaughtered until they arrived at a rededication of themselves to the Lord. After 37 more years of wandering in the wilderness, the next generation has taken over. In Numbers, chapter 20, both Miriam and Aaron died, and Moses sinned in a matter that resulted in his exclusion from the Promised Land. He would continue to lead Israel up to the Jordan River, but could not cross over.

Right here at the beginning of the fortieth year, the King of Arad attacked the Israelites, but the situation was different from their defeat at Hormah. Whereas, before they were slaughtered first and then they rededicated themselves to the Lord, now they rededicated themselves to the Lord, consulted the Lord, and promised to devote (same verb—*ve-haharamti*) their cities to utter destruction. The Lord gave Israel the victory (v. 3), "then they utterly destroyed (*vayyaharem*) them and their cities. Thus the name of the place was called Hormah." After the Israelites dedicate themselves first, this time the enemies are slaughtered. In the same place where the Israelites were defeated before, they were now victorious.

What was the difference between victory and defeat? In Deuteronomy 1:44 Moses says, "The Amorites who lived in that hill country came out against you and chased you as bees do, and crushed you from Seir to Hormah." The word Amorites comes from the same root as the word "to say," and these people represent sins of speaking.[2] The first time, when Israel spoke badly about God, following the ten bad spies (Numbers 14:1-4), Israel lost to these "talkers." By the beginning of the fortieth year, however, they consulted the Lord and showed their faith in Him (Numbers 21: 2). This showed that they were talking rightly, and the Lord gave them the victory over the "talkers" (Amorites).

There is no way that a carnal, or immature Christian can pass on to the next stage of being spiritual until he can control his tongue when under pressure. Later on, these same Israelites have to defeat other Amorites on the east side of the Jordan River before they can cross the Jordan River and enter into the Promised Land. Whether they had followed the two good spies and entered without the extra years in the wilderness or they followed the ten bad spies and wandered another 38 years, they still had to fight Amorites before entering into the Promised Land. In the same way, the Christian must learn to defeat the urge to speak badly about God when under pressure and learn to speak only positive things about God and His goodness before he can pass on to be a spiritual believer. Whether it is sooner or later, the believer must still learn this lesson first.

The Christian's identification with Christ is an application of the various aspects of Christ's suffering, death, burial, and resurrection, and what they make available to the Christian today. The aim of this chapter, however, will be to focus on Identification as a crisis through which the believer needs to pass to become a spiritual believer. As Israel had to pass through the Jordan River to reach the Promised Land, so the Christian needs to pass through a crisis of identification to enter into the spiritual stage of his development.

The crossing of the Jordan River is the point of crisis that is the transition between the carnal man and the spiritual man (I Cor. 2:15-16). If there is a place in the history of Israel that would correspond with a second crisis and "second blessing" in the life of a believer, this is it. While our conversion, corresponding to our crossing the Reed Sea, places us under all of the blessings of Jesus' high priestly work legally, the crossing of the Jordan corresponds to our entering in vitally to the appropriation of these riches in our experience.

Passing the Jordan leads to Canaan for Israel, and entering into our identification with Christ (through appropriation of his blessings in our lives now) leads us to the position to be able to battle for our humility, our Canaan. Before the crossing of the Jordan, the Israelites were under Moses (the "drawn out" one), though they always won their battles under Joshua, even in the Desert. However, during the crossing and the conquest of Canaan, they are under Joshua ("Jehovah is salvation"), and they are able to win battles and accomplish things for the Lord. In the same way, as we pass through the crisis of identification with Christ, we become able to win battles with the enemies of God, as we are under Jesus' leadership.

The name Jesus is similar to the name Joshua, but there is one difference. Joshua means "Jehovah saves," and Jesus means "Savior," because he is also Jehovah. Joshua refers to someone else doing the saving, but Jesus is the agent of salvation, because He is also Jehovah. As we are "in Christ" we are victorious in our battles. It is hoped that this brief summary of the major correspondences between the history of Israel and the life of the believer in Christ will serve as background for our discussion of the transition period of identification crisis, which corresponds to Israel's crossing of the Jordan River.

As we seek to guide a believer through the steps to his crisis of identification with Christ in his experience of that which he already has legally attributed to him, we will seek to set up the steps by following the steps of Israel in crossing from the desert to Canaan, and then making application to appropriate New Testament passages. At all times we are to remember that we are New Testament believers, and we are not under the Old Testament. We are just using it for teaching purposes.

On page 68 of his book, Handbook to Happiness, Dr. Charles Solomon draws the same 5 stages for Israel, as for Christian development. These are the same as we have been using in this book. He compares Egypt to the natural man as in slavery to the world; the wilderness to the time a believer is a carnal man and battling against the flesh; and Canaan to the Spiritual man, who is a slave of Christ and a mature believer.

What is interesting is his focus on the crossing of the Red Sea as the crisis of salvation and the crossing of the Jordan River as the crisis of identification with Christ. About these two crises, he writes: "The Red Sea is a picture of salvation; the Jordan River is a picture of identification with the Lord Jesus Christ. The children of Israel did not enter in because of unbelief (Heb. 3:19), and many Christians follow their example. They feel that God ran fresh out of miracles the day they were saved. It certainly took a miracle to open the Red Sea, and it takes a miracle of grace to change the human heart at salvation. It also took a miracle to open the Jordan River, and it is a miracle of illumination when we see that we are crucified with Christ and are set free from our "Wilderness Wanderings" to enjoy freedom and victory in the Lord—the victorious life is not a flowery bed of ease, but the battles are the Lord's, if we let Him fight them."[3]

In this chapter we are covering the journey of Israel from where they returned to the Lord at the beginning of the fortieth year of the wanderings through the stages leading up to the crossing of the Jordan, the actual crossing of the Jordan, and the experiences of Gilgal and Jericho on the other side of the river. Dr. Charles Solomon, Dr. Neal Anderson, Major Ian W. Thomas as well as the Old Testament narrative bolstered by New Testament commentary, combine for a step-by-step procedure for entering into the identification experience.

There are seven steps that we shall consider in the Israelites' crossing of the Jordan River; and we shall attempt to show 7 steps for Christians to our identification with Christ as a transition from carnal to spiritual believers, making reference to the New Testament and other Christian literature on the subject.

I. Preparations to move on for the Lord (Numbers 20:1-3).

As we begin the story about Israel, finally the time of God's judgment has passed, the Israelites are again back at the place where they left the will of God a generation earlier, and the time is right for them to move on to reach the land when God said so. The 38 years of wanderings were not necessary, and a long time in the desert is not necessary for a Christian. Two years was the amount of time that God considered sufficient for Israel, had they obeyed. If one is at this point of time, and dedicates himself to the Lord and believes the promise, he may enter into the spiritual stage of his development fully dedicated to the Lord. However, those who have been wandering in the desert for a long time must return to the place that they departed from the Lord and rededicate themselves to His loving process of development before they may continue onward to the land. That is the lesson of Hormah, as we have seen above.

II. Passing Edom: The Long Way Around (Numbers 20:4-20).

In conjunction with the victory at Hormah is the account of the first contact with Edom in Numbers 20:14-21. Here Moses entreated Edom, the people descended from Esau, as a brother and asked for safe passage through his territory. They promised that they would stick to the main route and even pay for any water that they drank from there. Edom rejected this request and arrayed for battle against them. The Israelites then turned away and prepared for a long journey around Edom.

To understand why Esau (Edom) and Jacob (Israel) are so much at odds, we need to understand how they were different. The name *Esau* (Heb. עֵשָׂו) comes from the Hebrew verb meaning "to do" (*asah*, עָשָׂה).[4] Esau trusted in his works to be accepted by his father and his father's God, and was not interested in his birthright. He sold his birthright to Jacob for a pottage of lentils because he did not value it. Since good works were the important thing for him, God rejected him, and God also allowed Jacob to trick Esau out of the blessing of the firstborn.

In Malachi 1:2-4, The Lord says, "I have loved Jacob; but I have hated Esau." The Lord also calls Esau's descendants "the people toward whom the Lord is indignant forever." Why did the Lord love Jacob more than Esau, the one who trusted in his own works and despised his birthright? In the first place, the birthright represented the messianic blessing of the line of the one Redeemer of mankind promised from the Garden of Eden in Genesis 3:15. The birthright also involved the special blessing of having the True God as your God and the blessings given to Abraham and Isaac. Esau despised these things and preferred a pottage of lentils.

Jacob, on the other hand, was a conniver and schemer, as his name indicates in the Hebrew.[5] In fact, the name for "heel" in the Hebrew comes from the same root as his name. When God said that Satan would bruise the Seed of the Woman on the heel (Gen. 3:15), that indicated how he would be attacking deceitfully and cleverly throughout every generation to try to prevent that Seed of the Woman from coming. It is not a pleasing term. "Following at the heel" was the lowest form of being an enemy. From the time of his birth, Jacob lied and tricked people to obtain what he wanted. Finally, at his conversion, he trusted God and inherited things as a "Prince of God," which is what Israel means.

God loved Israel more than Esau, but He still gave Esau territory. In Deuteronomy 2:5, God said at this point to treat the Edomites well because "I have given Mt. Seir to Esau as a possession." It is interesting to note here that Seir is from the same Hebrew that a word for demon is from.[6] Also, Edom is from the same root as Adam, the first human and a generic reference to humanity in general as descended from him.

To put this connection in the setting of the Christian life, we would say that the old Adam is given over to demons and there is no way that we can please the Lord while walking in the flesh. We are immediately reminded of Galatians 5 at this point, where we read (v. 17): "For the flesh sets its desire against the Spirit, and the Spirit against the flesh; for these are in opposition to one another, so that ye may not do the things that you please." There are two lists that follow: the first vv. 19-21) is a list of all the worst sins, and the second (vv.22-23) is the fruit of the Spirit. The key to the difference in our life is verse 16: "Walk in the Spirit and ye shall not fulfill the lust of the flesh."

The Christian at this stage of his pilgrimage must learn the lesson that the old nature is not his friend. As a child, he learned to respect and appreciate the nature he received from Adam, as he learns to assert himself—even as Esau and Jacob were reconciled after Jacob's return from Laban's house. However, as an adult, he needs to realize that he died to this world as he was converted, and now he has another nature. What is left of the old man he was before is but an illusion of the enemy to trick him, as well as indwelling sin. He is no longer what he was, and so the old nature is no longer his friend.

Let us consider an analogy here. It is as though we were all born as pigs in Adam. We grew up with the nature of a pig and act like pigs. When we did things that are wrong, we were acting according to our nature and could not be expected to do anything else (Ephesians 2:2-3). When, however, we received Jesus as our Savior, we were immediately changed into lambs. As II Corinthians 5:17 says: "Therefore if anyone is in Christ, he is a new creature."

False religion tries to educate the pig to act like a lamb; and no matter what he does, he remains a pig. Immature lambs may still wallow in the mud through habit, but a true change of nature took place at conversion. Though they act like pigs, they are no longer pigs. In one of the lectures of his course on Identification, taught at Jacksonville Theology Seminary, Dr. Bob Dean stated that Jesus not only took on Himself our sins, but also our sin nature when He died on the cross.[7] Therefore, the old sin nature is actually dead, and all believers have the new nature of Christ at conversion. We still have to battle against the habits of the pig in us, though.

The experience with Edom taught Israel that Edom could no longer be trusted, but must be treated as an enemy. This experience for the Christian means that he needs to reject the desires that come from his own flesh because they are no longer for his good. In Romans 7:19-20, the Apostle Paul finds himself in this battle: "For the good that I want, I do not do, but I practice the very evil that I do not want. But if I am doing the very thing I do not want, I am no longer the one doing it, but sin which dwells in me." The evil desires arising from his flesh are bad habits from the time he was in the old pig nature that came from Adam, and these desires are now part of "Demon Mountain" that is given to Edom. He needs to go around Edom, but he cannot go through to have fellowship, nor can he eradicate Edom. Indwelling sin will be a problem until we die, and behind it lie evil spirits that are trying to seduce us into sin.

When we are tempted to sin, we need to recognize that that desire is not our own, nor does it arise from the nature of Christ in us, but rather it is from the enemy. There are 3 dimensions of the spiritual battle that the Christian faces: the external, the internal, and unseen. The external corresponds to Egypt, the actual slave driver of the unsaved and the torturing memories and alluring temptations from the outside to the saved person. The internal is primarily the flesh, the habit patterns, former desires, and self-gratifying principle of the old life that the believer once had. The word "flesh" is from the same root in Hebrew and the word "gospel." The flesh is the false "gospel" of self-glorification, which is the essence of the nature of Satan that we originally inherited from Adam, but was crucified in our conversion. It exists now as a collection of lying ideas, lusts, and habits of the "old pig" that is dead, and is stirred up and energized by the unseen: Satan and his hosts, who are the demons of Demon Mountain.

As Israel began to pass around Edom, Israel passed Mt. Hor and Aaron died (Numbers 20:22-29). While the Hebrew lexicon is not clear about the root of the name Aaron, I believe that it is only a slight modification of the word meaning a hollow box. It is used to refer to an offering box (2 Kn. 12:10-11), the mummy case in which Joseph was buried (Gen. 50:26), and the Ark of the Covenant in the Holy of Holies in the Tabernacle and later Temple. This describes him as an empty container to hold God's presence.[8] Israel is not ready for God to be present in every man at this stage, but one man has been set aside to be an empty container for the Lord's service. In the same way, the Christian believer at this stage is more of an empty place for God's dwelling than a Spirit—filled blessing to the world. His son Eleazer, "God helps", succeeds Aaron here. It is progress here to see the Old Adam as one's enemy run by demons and also progress from being an empty container for the Lord to seeking God's help and getting it.

In Numbers 21:4-9 the Israelites were traveling the long way around Edom and had become discouraged. They complained about the length of the journey, the food, and the lack of water. The Lord sent fiery serpents among the people and they bit them and many died. When they repented, the Lord had Moses make an image of a serpent and place it on a pole. Everyone that was bitten was healed by looking at the snake on the pole.

Jesus stated in John 3:14-15: "As Moses lifted up the serpent in the wilderness, even so must the Son of Man be lifted up; so that whoever believes will in Him have eternal life." Why did God have them look at a serpent on a pole to be saved? It was because when Jesus died on the cross for our sins, it was the Devil, the Old Serpent that was defeated. The Israelites needed to be reminded again that God had the provision for the defeat of the enemy. To Israel it may only have meant that God was greater than those serpents that were biting them. According to Jesus, the serpent on a pole in Numbers 21shows us that our victory is in the cross, and this is to be appropriated through our identification with Jesus in His death. Either way, the believer needs a new focus on his helplessness and God's provision at this stage to encourage him to press onward.

There is another lesson to be learned here in preparation for entering into the Promised Land. The people needed to learn to stop complaining about everything and trust God to meet their needs. Numbers 21:4 says literally (my translation), "the soul of the people was short because of the way." The opposite of a "short soul" is found in the New Testament. In Galatians 5:22 the word for "long-suffering" is *makrothumía* ($\mu\alpha\kappa\rho o\theta\upsilon\mu\acute{\iota}\alpha$), makros meaning "long" and thumos meaning "passion" or "anger." God wants us to have a long soul, not a short soul. Then there will be a long time before we react with anger or complaints to adverse circumstances. We need to share our problems with the Lord and then wait on the Lord for His help and answer.

There is a final lesson for the Israelites, as well as for the Christian believers passing through this period. The healing came from looking at a snake on a pole. This remedy required the Israelite to trust God simply. For the Christian this is the equivalent of seeing that Satan was defeated in Jesus' crucifixion. To the whole world, Jesus was crucified on the cross, but in reality, the devil was defeated at the cross. We need to see that Jesus defeated Satan at the cross and claim the victory when we are "bitten" by the enemy. As Jesus took on himself our sin and shame on the cross, he also took all the venom of the Serpent in Himself. As we look to Jesus during times of temptation, we realize that he overcame the enemy, and we find strength to resist the venom of the constant temptations to do evil and overcome with his help. At this stage we need his help; but later in the land, He will repel the enemy while seated on the throne of our heart.

There is also a progression in the movement of Israel, as indicated by the names of the places that they stop as they continue. We read in Numbers 21:10 that the Israelites set up tents at Oboth. Oboth can mean skins, as in water skins, or necromancers, meaning those who contact the dead.[9] As a water skin is full of water, so a necromancer is full of a spirit. The believer in Jesus just needs to avoid the temptation to seek out special knowledge and move on. Those who have been dabbling in the occult need to confess this sin before moving on. Sometimes it could appear tedious to deal with every small place like Oboth, but I believe that the sum total of all of these places provides a checklist, for which one person will need one insight and another will need another insight. For some people one place will have special importance, while for another person a different place will have special meaning.

From Oboth they moved on to Iye-Abarim in the wilderness that is before Moab. Iye Abarim means "coastlands of those who crossed over," and describes the next step well. In the first place the Israelites are also called Hebrews (from the same root), which means "those who cross over." It is only used on the lips of Gentiles to describe Jewish people, and, I believe, is a reference to their crossing over away from the Gentiles to being a special people of the Creator God. The coastlands are here because the Israelites are entering the boundary where the desert ends and sedentary civilization begins. From here on, the enemies are mostly sedentary and established, rather than nomadic.

The last step in the trip around Edom was to pass between Moab and Ammon. The word Ammon survives in Amman, the capital of Jordan, and there is a good possibility that many of the Jordanians are descended from the Ammonites. As Esau was friendly formerly, and then later turned against Israel, so also do the Moabites and the Ammonites. Both of these people are descendants of Lot, the nephew of Abraham. They, like Edom, betrayed Israel after all of the help Abraham gave Lot. If we see from the Hebrew roots of their names, we can get some reason why Moab and Ammon are opposed to the Israelites. Moab refers to carnal desires.[10] Shortly, we will find out how these enemies attacked Israel with carnal sexual desires to join them in an ecumenical sexual orgy to get God angry at Israel. Later, Ehud the judge slays a King of Moab so fat that his sword doesn't come out the other side. Whether it is gluttony or fornication, the Moabites represent carnal desires in their name and in their actions.

The Ammonites represent our relatives, as the root indicates.[11] As Israel cannot conquer Edom, Moab, or Ammon at this stage in their development, so the believer can never reach sinless perfection while on this earth. We cannot eradicate the old Adam in us, our carnal desires, or our relatives, as they have to make their own decision. In the Millennial Kingdom these three do not exist; and when we are in heaven, our battles with the old nature, carnal desires, and relatives will be over.

The next stop was the Wadi Zared, the boundary between Edom and Moab. After leaving the Valley of Zared (unknown root), they cross the brook Arnon, the boundary between the Moabites and the Amorites. The name indicates that the brook is rushing and roaring.[12] We need to watch out that our carnal desires are not rushing like a river. The Amorites (speakers) represent sins of the tongue, and we also need to make sure that our tongue is not rushing like a river.

From here the Israelites make a few stops to get ready to fight for the land. The next place is Beer (Numbers 21:16-18). *Beer* means "well," for here the Israelites dug the first well that they would have in the land. North of Arnon is the actual area that the two and a half tribes would have on the east side of the Jordan River, once they took it from the Amorites. This is in the area that Reuben was to have later. Here there is the first permanent work of the hands of the Israelites under God's direction. God told Moses to have the people dig the well, "that I may give them water." We also read in verse 18 about "the well which the leaders sank, which the nobles of the people dug, with the scepter and with their staffs."

From Beer, they continued to Mattanah, which means "gift," in Hebrew. The Israelites needed to see that the Lord was rewarding their efforts, made at His instructions and according to the directions of the lawgiver. God had been cursing their self-efforts for so long, that they needed to understand that the Lord is not some "Divine Killjoy," but rather that He wants His followers to trust Him, follow Him, and rely upon Him so that He will receive the glory. We believers also need some positive experiences of trusting the Lord, seeing good results, and receiving a "gift" to encourage us in the proper mindset for the coming fight for the Land of Canaan.

After Mattanah, the Israelites arrive at Nahaliel (v. 19), which means, "God is my River." They were learning to trust more and more in God's provision through these lessons. We believers in Jesus also need to learn the lesson that "God is my River," in preparation for renouncing our own self-efforts to "do the best we can." We need to learn the lesson that "God is my river" of provision, but only as I follow His leading and stay in the plan He has for my life.

Finally, the Israelites reach Bamoth. These were probably a few "High Places" that were still near the country of Moab. Here Israel is in a precarious position representing the height of their improving condition, in an overall valley, showing that they are not yet arrived at their goal, and near the territory of Moab, relating to carnal desires, from which area they are soon to be tempted.

III. Heshbon: From Nomads to Landowners.

Next (Num. 21:21), the Israelites ask for safe passage through the territory of the Amorites living on the east side of the Jordan River. The Amorites respond with the same refusal that the Edomites did and came out to war against Israel. However, this time the Lord told them to go and fight and He would give them the victory.

It is interesting to note that the problems related to peoples that Israel is supposed to conquer have in their roots the references to problems that the Christian can and should overcome in this life. However, those peoples outside of the boundaries that God gave to Israel and that Israel cannot conquer and must learn to live with have in their names problems that the Christian cannot eradicate in this life.

Egypt (the World), Edom (the habits of the Old Adam), Moab (carnal desires), the Ammonites (our relatives), Assyria (success), and Babylon ("mixing in" with the world) will always be a threat to Israel until they are in the Millennial Kingdom (corresponding to the believer's time in heaven). At that time, Egypt and Assyria will be blessed with Israel (Is. 19:23-25—the world will be organized in favor of God, and success will no longer spoil them), and the others will be annihilated and their land given to Israel. The believers in heaven will no longer battle with the habits of the Old Adam (Edom), carnal desires (Moab), our relatives (Ammonites), or "mixing in" with the world (Babylon), even as Israel no longer finds them in the time of the Millennial Kingdom. Also, success (Assyria) will be always present but will not spoil us as it can now.

The Amorites, unlike the Edomites, needed to be conquered by Israel to enter into the land. There were Amorites on the South side of the Land of Canaan who defeated the Israelites when the 10 spies gave a bad report and they "talked bad" about God, and there were Amorites on the east side of the Jordan ready to fight them 38 years later. What were these Amorites like?

The king who came against Israel with his army is named Sihon, King of Heshbon. Sihon is from the root meaning "complaint,"[13] and Heshbon is the word meaning "accounting."[14] Here the first root meaning includes musing and anxiety, as well as complaint. If we are anxious and thinking about our situation for a while, it will motivate us to start making comparisons with other people. We believers will never enter into the place of God's blessing for us until we stop keeping accounts of how much God gives to other believers and how much He gives to us and complaining about it. It seems that we always pick someone that has more of something than we do and complain about it. Instead, we ought to pick someone who has much less than we do and show gratitude to God and share with them, as God leads. The best thing of all is to stop comparisons altogether and just worship and follow God.

The second root means accounting. The Modern Hebrew word for an accountant is Baal-Heshbon. It is for God to take into account what He has called us to do and provide for us. Our duty is to praise and thank Him for His provision for our needs. If we cast our burden on God, and trust Him to sustain us, we won't go around making comparisons with others.

Israel conquers Sihon, King of Heshbon, and so should we. We need to praise God continually and accept His will for us in the things that we have. If we want something we don't have, we should ask God for it with thanksgiving (Philippians 4:6), and trust that God knows best whether or not we should have it. In II Timothy 6:6-11 Paul warns Timothy about the deceitfulness of riches, and calls the love of money "the root of all evil."

This territory would eventually be given over to Reuben and Gad. Reuben means, "Behold, a son." This refers to our conversion experience in the first place. We can be sure that God will supply all of our needs just because we belong to Him, and His reputation is at stake in our lives. The word Gad means, "a troop." This refers to the fact that we are mighty in the Lord, and we need to concentrate on God's power in us, rather than our own power. We believers need to declare ourselves dead to anything on the "accounting" sheet so that God can be powerful through us.

The last people that the Israelites conquer on the east of the Jordan are the Amorites under Og, King of Bashan. Through their roots, Og refers to cake, or cookie,[15] and Bashan refers to smooth and fertile.[16] Here we see the Israelites beginning to become sedentary and obtain the capacity to produce their own food, though the manna does not cease just yet. In parallel with Israel here, it is good to see Christians that can "feed themselves" in the Christian life by studying the Bible and other Christian literature, thinking about it, applying it to their lives, and growing during the week between Sundays without depending on the pastor alone to carry them along and feed them. Also, being fertile refers to reproduction, and we need to remember that healthy sheep reproduce. When believers are feeding themselves and taking the initiative in their development, they can also follow God directly and reproduce themselves in leading others to faith in Jesus.

This land was given to half of the Tribe of Manasseh. Manasseh means, "causing to forget," according to Joseph in Genesis 41:51. Joseph had great joy at the birth of his firstborn son, and through it, God made him forget the sufferings that he went through. In addition to leaving behind comparisons with other people, we need to forget the past troubles and heartaches and press onward. The Apostle Paul reminds us of this in Philippians 3: 13-14: "Brethren, I do not regard myself as having laid hold of it yet; but one thing I do, forgetting what lies behind, and reaching forward to what lies ahead, I press on toward the goal for the prize of the upward call of God in Christ Jesus." A major part of the identification experience is letting go of the past hurts and troubles so that we can press on without a lot of emotional baggage bogging us down.

IV. Baal-Peor—Learn to Be Faithful to the Lord in Temptations.

After the Israelites conquered the Amorites east of the Jordan, they camped on the plains of Moab on the east side of the Jordan River opposite Jericho. This was newly conquered territory that would later belong to Reuben. It is interesting to note that Reuben was the son who committed incest with Bilhah, his father's concubine. Where is Reuben located in the land? On the east side of the Jordan near the Moabites, who represent carnal desires. Reuben lost his firstborn blessing and double portion, which passed over to Joseph, the firstborn of Rachael, the other wife of Jacob, because of incest with a concubine of his father (Gen. 35:22). He had a portion in the land, but it was not what it could have been because he could not keep his sexual desires in check.

There are believers that are similar to Reuben. They have a portion from God, but the glory and the portion that they could have had goes to someone else because they would not surrender their carnal appetites to be crucified with Christ. Later, in the period of the judges (Judges 3:12-30), the Moabites have a glutton King. King Eglon is so fat that Ehud sticks his sword into him and it does not come out the other side. We believers also need to reign in our physical appetites to avoid gluttony, bad health, and a poor testimony through that, as well.

The name of the last place that the Israelites camp in east of the Jordan was called Baal—Peor, or "Lord of the Pit." Through King Balak of Moab and the Midianites, the Devil, as Lord of the Pit, did his best to stop the Israelites here. King Balak, the Devastator or Destroyer, according to the Hebrew root,[17] was terrified of Israel after he saw what they did to the Amorites, and hired against them Balaam, the Son of Beor, from Mesopotamia. Our carnal desires can be devastating if they get control over us, and we must avoid mixing with them and burning.

There are a number of carnal appetite addictions that the believer may have to overcome to get the victory here: gluttony, bulimia, heterosexual addiction, pornography, homosexuality, etc. Balaam tried to curse Israel and found that God physically prevented the words of his curses from leaving his mouth. Instead a blessing came forth for Israel each time.

In order to collect on the money that Balak promised him, Balaam, the "Mixer of the Peoples," as his name means,[18] the son of Beor, counseled Balak to have an ecumenical sex orgy with Israel so that God would curse them (Num. 31:16). Some Israelites at this point succumbed to a temptation of a religious sexual orgy, thus mixing with the Midianites and Moabites and burning with lust, and the Lord became angry against Israel. God ordered through Moses that the judges kill every man below them that had been joined to Baal—Peor.

As they were about to begin the judgment, they saw Zimri, from the tribe of Simeon, take Cozbi, the daughter of Zur, a leader in Midian, into a tent for the purpose of fornication, right in the sight of the people who were weeping and repenting of this sin (Num. 25:6). Then Phineas, the son of Eleazer, the High Priest, was filled with zeal for the Lord and entered the tent with a spear and speared them both through, killing them in the act of fornication. The Lord commends this, and promises him a covenant of peace. This act turned away the wrath of God from the Israelites, though 24,000 die in a plague that the Lord sends (v. 9).

What does it mean for us at this stage? We need to watch out for any careless idea that we can take sin lightly and "mix" with it. Balaam means "mixer of the peoples," and his counsel was to do just that. Just as God hates all mixing of Israel with other peoples, so also He hates our mixing with the sins that their names represent. Balaam was the son of Beor, meaning "burning" and "dull-heartedness,"[19] His counsel was in favor of burning with lust, and he was so dull-hearted to God's leading, that it did not even get his attention when God spoke to rebuke him through his own donkey. The believer at this stage needs to watch his reactions to the world and keep himself separate from it, as well as cultivating receptivity to the Lord—the exact opposite of Balaam Ben Beor.

In plain view of everyone (Numbers 25:6) Zimri ("my pruning") took a Midianite woman Cozbi ("my lie") for fornication, Phineas, which to me means "turn and seek refuge," according to the 2 roots which the name comes from,[20] initiates the victory by stabbing the two of them through with a spear. When the believer is tempted to wallow in his lies and continue with sensual behavior which displeases the Lord, the first step in victory is to "turn and seek refuge" in the Lord. In conjunction with these sins of the desert, the Apostle Paul tells us in I Corinthians 10:13: "No temptation has overtaken you but such as is common to man; and God is faithful, who will not allow you to be tempted beyond what ye are able, but with the temptation will provide the way of escape also, so that you will be able to endure it."

The Devil will make many temptations available to believers with his last shot attempt to keep them from "crossing the Jordan" and passing from carnal to spiritual Christians. We need to be on guard for these temptations and "turn and seek refuge" in God during the temptation. That is the way of escape and the way of victory over "my lie (Cozbi)," and the means of "my pruning (Zimri)." As Israel is weakened through the loss of 24,000 people because of the sin (Numbers 25:9), the believer is also weakened every time he gives in to a temptation to sin. As God cuts off individuals from Israel because of sin, so God cuts off parts of us New Testament believers because of sin, but He never cuts us off completely once we are saved. Just as He always leaves a remnant in Israel, He also always leaves a remnant of us.

The Moabites are not alone in their opposition to Israel here. They are accompanied by Midianites. According to the root of their name, the Midianites correspond to the natural conscience of the believer. The Midianites are friends of Israel through the time when they arrive at Mt. Sinai. Moses even marries a daughter of the High Priest of Midian, and He helped Moses and his people initially. However, from the time Israel set out northward from Mt. Sinai to go to Canaan, the Midianites became their enemies.

In a similar way, when a believer wants to go on for the Lord, and trust in His finished work, the natural conscience turns on him and says, "Look at the bad things you have done! How can you believe that God just forgave you so easily?" The Midianite lady Cozbi, meaning, "my lie," refers to these lies that one's conscience might invent to make him feel guilty and unworthy of God's help. As we struggle on without God's help, we become easy prey for temptations. These failures bring about guilt feelings of unworthiness, and the cycle gets worse and worse. Thus, the believer needs to avoid all lies that may be from his natural conscience. The Apostle John encourages us (I John 3:19-20), "We will know by this that we are of the truth. And we will assure our heart before Him in whatever our heart condemns us; for God is greater than our heart and knows all things."

As long as the believer lingers around doubting the efficacy of the shed blood and the cross in his daily life, he will be unfit and unable to be a spiritual believer. We need to watch out for the Midianites in our experience. When the thought occurs to us that we are too wicked to be used of God, this is the sin of doubting God, and "Whatever is not from faith is sin (Romans 14:23)." We are not saved by our merits, nor do we continue in salvation because of our merits. The basis of our relation with God is the blood of Jesus. When our conscience condemns us we should turn to the cross and take refuge in Jesus. First confess any known sin and claim forgiveness (I John 1:9), and then rebuke the conscience for doubting the efficacy of the blood of Jesus and continuing in feelings of guilt. Then trust God for the victory.

Without faith, we begin working to do our best in the energy of the flesh, and we fall worse in whatever temptation we meet. Instead of "turning to the refuge," we condemn ourselves for our failures. The resulting vicious circle cannot be broken until we trust our Lord to work through us, reveal sin in us, and bring continued assurance of our acceptance and sonship in Christ. When we do, we will realize that our "natural conscience" is an illusion of Satan. The word Satan means "accuser," and we need to learn to turn a deaf ear to him, remembering that we are dead to sin and the natural conscience, as well. We only need to listen to the Holy Spirit, Who mentions sins that we need to confess; and then does not bring them up again once we have repented and confessed them. If we are continuously tortured by the thoughts of sins we have committed and confessed, then we need to rebuke the spirit of unbelief, praise the Lord for the forgiveness through His blood, and go on.

After Israel has repented and judged those who were involved in the wickedness, God orders Moses to attack the Midianites. So they pick 1000 from each of the 12 tribes for a total of 12,000, and then add Phineas to accompany them with trumpets. They succeeded in killing all of the Midianites that were there at the time, except for the virgin females, whom they took into their families. The plunder from the Midianites was considerable for Israel, and they also killed Balaam the Son of Beor. They had finally learned not to mix with the Midianites and Moabites.

Like Israel, the believer at this point needs to repent of his self-will and fleshly activities, and to confess his sins. Also, he needs to take the battle against Satan and his own self-condemnation. He needs to set his face to "turn to seek refuge" whenever he is tempted, and memorize Bible passages that confirm the truth about God's grace. We need to enjoy the "plunder of the Midianites" for ourselves in the form of the peace and joy of forgiveness, and the release from a lying, negative natural conscience that doubts the blood of Jesus, as well as avoiding temptations and more real sin.

V. Pisgah—Preparation for Warfare Against the Flesh.

Before the war against the Midianites, the Lord told Moses that he was to climb Mount Abarim, a nearby mountain, and view the Land of Canaan before he died (Numbers 27:12). He was also to install Joshua as his successor before the people. Moses means the "drawn out one." Pharaoh's daughter gave him this name as she drew him out of the Nile River as a baby. Israel, while under Moses, was also just "drawn out of Egypt," but not good for anything positive.

Now Israel was to go forth under Joshua, which means "Jehovah saves." They were to conquer the land under Joshua because Jehovah would be giving them the victory. Even in the desert, when Israel fought against their enemies, Joshua led them in victory, not Moses. As Israel leaves the desert and prepares to enter into the Land of Canaan, they need new leadership. They are no longer under Moses, as they are no longer just "drawn out" from the world. They are under Joshua, just as they are dependent on Jehovah to save them in their battles.

It is the same for the believer. At this critical transition stage between operating in the flesh in the desert and being spiritual in the land, there must also be a change in mentality. We need to realize that we are no longer just "drawn out" from the world and not good for anything, but rather we are directly under, not Joshua, but Jesus, who is the Savior.

The names Joshua and Jesus are similar in Hebrew, but there is a major difference. The name Joshua means, "Jehovah saves." It is a different One other than Joshua Who is doing the saving. The name Jesus means Savior, because He is Jehovah doing the saving. When his name was announced to Joseph in Matthew 1:21, the angel said, "She (Mary) will bear a son; and you shall call His name Jesus, for He wall save his people from their sins." The name Jesus means Savior because he is Jehovah and he is doing the saving, while the name Joshua was a reminder that Jehovah was doing the saving, not Joshua himself.

As we enter into the experience of identification with Christ, we realize that Jesus is the source of the blood that cleanses us continually from all sin. We also realize that it is his cross which cancels out our false striving and dead works and allows Him to live through us, and his life is our salvation from the sin of self-effort, compromise with sin, burning in lustful passions, and all other things that hinder us from following the Lord. He really is Jehovah Savior in us, and all we have to do is surrender to His will to take over and set things straight in us.

At the creation of this world in Genesis 1:2, we see that the world was without form and void, and that the Spirit of God was hovering over the surface of the deep. In the creation He was bringing order out of existing chaos. In Jeremiah 4:23, the prophet sees the people morally in the same position as the world before God's Spirit hovered over it. He says, "I looked on the earth, and behold, it was formless and void" (the same words as in Genesis 1:2). The people of Israel in Jeremiah's time were so far gone in rebellion that they were as chaotic as this world before God began to work in the creation. That is the way we normally are because of the sin that came upon the earth. We need the Creator to be constantly living His life through us. That is salvation from being "formless and void," from God's perspective. It was only the Spirit of God Who was moving over the surface of the waters to bring order in the first place, and He is the only one who can move in us to bring order out of our chaos.

The change of leadership takes place on Mount Abarim, which is also called Mount Pisgah. Mount Abarim means, "mount of Hebrews" or "Mount of those who crossed over." Here Israel needs a renewal of the experience of "crossing over" to God from Egypt, and they are preparing to "cross over" from their desert state of rebellion to become real followers of the Lord in the land. This is where Moses is given a chance to view the Land of Canaan promised to Israel, though he is forbidden to enter there.

We need to renew our experience of "crossing over" to God in our salvation as we prepare for the step of identification with Christ. As we meditate on our crossing of the "Reed Sea" (the Sea which makes an End), we remember that we really died and were resurrected in our conversion and baptism, seen as a single event. We are really already in our newness of life, as mentioned in Romans 6:1-6, and we prepare to live constantly in that reality. We need to remember that we have already "crossed over" to God and that we are no longer our own.

The other name of the mountain is Pisgah, which means cleft. There were probably twin peaks at the top of the mountain. The lesson here for us is that we need to perceive the difference between the new man and the flesh and delineate clearly the battle lines. We need to learn that all of those cravings for Egypt that we had in the desert were not really our cravings, but rather sin that dwells in us. The battle occurring in the Apostle Paul in the next chapter of Romans is between himself as a new creature and indwelling sin, which he calls "the flesh."

What is the flesh? The word "flesh" comes from the same root in Hebrew as the word "Gospel." I believe that the flesh, as presented in Paul's works, is not his physical flesh, but rather the lies of Satan that he is still in Adam and still to operate that way in self-exaltation. It is the false gospel of self-exaltation in things of this world. The real Gospel, on the other hand, is the Good News of Jesus' crucifixion, death, burial, resurrection, and life in the believer right now. We are to "flesh out" the Gospel, to use an expression of a former Seminary Professor of mine, Clark Pinnock.

At this point the believer in Jesus is setting up the mindset that the desires for things of this world are not really coming from him, but from indwelling sin. This prepares him to reject the desires as foreign to the new nature that he now has. To resume our analogy of the pig and the lamb, he realizes that all of the cravings for things of this world are really habits and desires of the pig he was born as (in Adam). They no longer represent him because he has been born again and is now a real lamb with nature of a lamb (Jesus, the second Adam). The Apostle Paul explains this in Romans 7. He still finds that he often does things that are the opposite of what he wants to do. He concludes (vv. 16-17), "But if I do the very thing I do not want to do, I agree with the Law, confessing that the Law is good. So now, no longer am I the one doing it, but sin which dwells in me." Human responsibility lies in deciding whether to walk in the flesh or to walk in the spirit. The key is now to focus on Jesus and let the indwelling sin fade away, as Jesus lives through the believer.

Our mindset is important in preparing for the experience of identification with Christ. In Psalm 16 King David has a problem of worrying about all of the wicked people that are after him, as he represents God before the world. He sets forth a few steps to solidify his commitment to the Lord and to upright judgment and he asks the Lord to intervene on His behalf. In verse 5 he affirms: "The Lord is the portion of my inheritance and my cup; You support my lot (portion in life)." He recognizes that the Lord Himself is the greatest part of his portion in life, and the source of his life itself. That the Lord should be David's cup indicates the source of his life. He recognizes that the Lord is sustaining his portion in life, and therefore renews his dedication to obey and submit to God as the way to get ahead, instead of the way of the wicked men who work against him, thinking that they can get ahead by their own efforts.

After repeating his satisfaction in his inheritance and portion in the next verse, David surprises us with his understanding of the Lord's instruction in verse 7: "I will bless the Lord who has counseled me: indeed, my mind (kidneys) also instructs me in the night." The word rendered mind is really *kidneys* in the Hebrew. How could David's kidneys instruct him at night? I believe that it is because the adrenalin glands were considered part of the kidneys in ancient Israel. As David lay awake at night thinking about the events of the day, the emotions of fear and anger triggered a response of adrenaline in the blood from the adrenaline glands. As a result he lost sleep and suffered the debilitating effects of excess adrenaline.

As David realized that he was losing sleep over the adrenaline, he decided to take a course of action to overcome the problem. This included a major change of focus of his thinking, which he explains as he continues. Through an act of the will in verse 8, he has decided to change what he is thinking about. Instead of thinking about all of the wicked men who are making his life miserable in verses 1-4, he changes his focus to think about his overall lot in verses 5-7. The real change, however, comes in verse 8-9: "I have set the Lord continually before me; because He is at my right hand, I will not be shaken. Therefore my heart is glad, and my glory (liver) rejoices: my flesh also will dwell securely." There is a textual variant that reads *liver*, which appears better in the light of the mention of the kidneys before it. It is a very slight variant that leaves out the Hebrew letter *waw*. The liver is the organ that spews out bile when we are angry. David believed firmly in the goodness of the Lord. Therefore, he changed all of his focus to the Lord and abandoned himself into the Lord's care. As he did, his liver rested from its continuous stress from anger. This is the essence of the identification experience, as far as it could go before Jesus' resurrection from the dead.

It is also important to note here that David says that his flesh also shall rest in hope. While the ensuing verses indicate that he is thinking about losing his fear of physical death, the verse takes on a greater meaning for the believer in Jesus. The key to entering into the Land of Canaan as it relates to a believer in Jesus is our ceasing from our works, as God ceased from His (Hebrews 4:9-11). As we saw above, Moab refers to carnal desires, and the war against them is a battle that the believer might have against certain addictions of the flesh, such as gluttony, sexual lust, etc.

In his book The Saving Life of Christ, Major Ian Thomas describes the cycle of habitual sin the following way (p.50): "Where suggestion becomes desire, desire becomes intent, and the intent becomes an act—the act becomes a memory and that memory is hung like a picture upon the wall of your imagination, in the picture gallery of your mind. When later in your thoughts you wander through the picture gallery, you see the memory on the wall, and this memory becomes a suggestion, and this suggestion becomes desire, and this desire may become intent; and if this intent becomes an act, you will then have hanging on the wall *two* memories, and the process can begin all over again with double force!"[21]

It is easy to see how a few repetitions of this process can develop eventually into an addiction. There is an adrenaline connection here. The adrenaline is released with the excitement of the gratification of the flesh in the memory of the first sin in the chain. The act of thinking on the behavior triggers the same adrenaline response from the glands, which, in turn, pushes us beyond the control point. As we lose control, we engage in the sin with no restraint. The activity produces another memory and the double strength of these two memories triggers a larger adrenaline response later. In this case the addiction is to the adrenaline itself.

David proposes only one way to break the chain once his kidneys have instructed (rebuked) him at night: he refocuses his thoughts so that they are centered only on the Lord personally, his personal resurrection beyond his death, the resurrection of his descendant, God's Holy One, who is to come from David's descendants, and the true pleasures from God both in this life and in the life after death. As David thinks about God and becomes excited about God, his kidneys begin to pump the adrenaline to reinforce his focus on God, and the cycles are built up for good, not bad. There is a strong probability that this is the reason that God sent so many scary signs to Mt. Sinai with the giving of the Law—so that the people will associate the emotion of fear with the giving of the Law and obey it and focus on it.

David mentions that his flesh (including his liver) will rest in hope, but our flesh needs to rest in hope in another way. When we accepted Jesus as our Savior, in a very real sense, we Christians died with Him in our conversion and baptism seen as a single event. In the identification experience, we reckon our flesh to be dead and start acting that way, trusting in Jesus to live his life through us. We have to let our flesh rest in hope—not just the hope of a future resurrection, but also the hope of Jesus' continuous resurrection life in our life through our death. Jesus' resurrection life is the only power that can defeat sin. As we refocus our thinking on Jesus in every way and let the Holy Spirit have control of our kidneys to excite us over the things of the Lord only, the memories of our sinful addictive behavior will fade and affect us less and less, while Jesus affects us more and more through His life in us.

The New Testament teaching on this point is found in 2 Cor. 3:18, where Paul says, referring to believers, "But we all, with unveiled face, beholding as in a mirror the glory of the Lord, are bring transformed into the same image, just as from the Lord, the Spirit." Instead of battling against worldly desires and disorderly lusts in us, we are to replace them by focusing on the glory of the Lord. This act of focusing on the glory of the Lord releases the power of the Holy Spirit to transform us as we are doing it.

That is the message of Pisgah—that the desires to sin are not really our desires, and we need to fight against them. Also, we do this by the refocusing of our mind and the surrender of our body and mind to the Lord.

VI. Crossing the Jordan River: the Lowest Place on Earth.

After the Israelites mourn for Moses for 30 days (Deuteronomy 34:8), Joshua receives orders from God direct to take the people Israel into the land that He had promised to their fathers. He says (Joshua 1:3): "Every place on which the sole of your foot treads, I have given it to you, just as I spoke to Moses." The Lord had given the entire Land of Canaan to the Israelites when He gave it to Abraham in Genesis 15:18. He still promised the land to them, and was ready to deliver it to them—all of it. However, they had several requirements to get it: to be brave and courageous, to be obedient to the Scriptures, as well as to the personal leading of the Lord, and to go out and actually tread upon the land, including fighting for it.

As the believer contemplates being no longer "drawn up" from the world, the prospect of fighting in an army under the command of Jesus himself is a bit frightening. Now he is responsible for submitting to the cross continually and denying himself daily. As Jesus says (Matthew 16:24): "If anyone wishes to come after Me, he must deny himself, and take up his cross and follow Me." We are frightened when we think of confronting the enemy with our own strength and resources. We should, instead, rejoice that it is impossible to confront the enemy at all in our own strength. It is a miracle that we are even on the same battlefield with the enemy. We should rejoice in the hopelessness of our strength and glory in the fact that the battle will be the Lord's and not ours. Thus, He will provide the power through us, and He will get the glory from the victory.

Thirty-eight years earlier the Israelites were poised at the edge of the land and drew back because they looked from a human standpoint, and not through the eyes of faith. Now they were again in the position of looking at human resources or trusting in the Lord and they chose to trust in the Lord.

Having prepared themselves with this mindset, they were ready to descend to the lowest point on earth: where the Jordan River empties into the Dead Sea. The main purpose of all of the travels of the Israelites in the desert period was to bring them to the end of the desert—either to enter the land at Kadesh Barnea ("Holy One, Son of the Wanderer") after 2 years or at the Plains of Moab at the Jordan opposite Jericho after 40 years. The whole of the trials and difficulties of the Christian's desert experience also have one purpose: to prepare in us the mindset to want to humble ourselves. The very name Jordan River means "The River that Descends." The Apostle Peter captures this truth well when he says (I Peter 5:6): "Therefore humble yourselves under the mighty hand of God, that He may exalt you at the proper time."

There is mountain range on the east side of the Jordan called the Anti-Liban Range. It is higher than anything else there, but it is much lower than the Lebanon range that is west of the Jordan. Between them is a valley where the Jordan River flows down to the lowest spot on earth—the Dead Sea, called the Salt Sea (*yam hamelach*,יַם־הַמֶּלַח) in Hebrew. The Israelites had to descend to the lowest spot on the face of the earth in order to be able to climb to the highest mountains in the area. In their book, *The Wycliffe Historical Geography of Bible Lands*, Pfeiffer and Vos describe the two mountain ranges with the Jordan River between in this way: "The Jordan River is part of a great rift in the earth produced by two parallel geological faults. North of Palestine the rift separates the Lebanon Mountains from the Anti-Liban Range. The Orontes and the Leontes rivers flow through the northern rift. South of the Jordan the rift continues and forms the Dead Sea and the Arabah (*Wadi el'Araba*), the Red Sea, and southwestward, where it becomes the Great African Rift."[22]

The Jordan divides these two mountain ranges in the middle. It is the most remarkable river, in that it descends to the lowest point on earth. As Pfeiffer and Vos continue: "From its principal source at the foot of snowcapped Mt. Hermon, which rises 9,232 feet above sea level, to its mouth at the northern tip of the Dead Sea, the Jordan flows only eighty air miles. Its tortuous, winding course, however, gives it a total length of about two hundred miles. The Jordan Valley is marked by a rapid descent. By the time it reaches the Sea of Galilee, it is 695 feet below sea level, and it continues to descend until it is 1285 feet below sea level when it enters the Dead Sea. No spot on earth, uncovered by water, sinks to such depths. The floor of the Dead Sea itself is 1300 feet deep."[22]

God made the Israelites descend to the lowest point on the surface of the earth, where the Jordan River empties into the Dead Sea, and then passed them along the bottom of the River Jordan, before He let them begin to ascend on the other side. In a similar way, the Lord humbles the believer to the lowest he can get, and the believer is to accept this humbling, before the Lord raises him up on the other side.

One of the best New Testament passages about this truth is Philippians 2:5-11. It would even be a good idea to memorize this passage. It stands in stark contrast to the attitude and judgment of Satan, as recorded in Isaiah 14:12-15. In Philippians 2 Jesus humbles himself in 7 ways, and the Father exalts him in 7 ways. In Isaiah 14:13-15 Satan exalts himself in 5 ways and God humbles him in 2 ways. It is interesting to note that that mindset of exalting oneself and being humbled is the whole pattern of behavior that we inherited by birth from Adam. All sin is a type of self-exaltation above God and His just reign on earth as Creator of the universe.

Let us consider first the pattern of Satan, consisting of fivefold self-exaltation (Isaish 14:13-15): "I will ascend into heaven;" "I will raise my throne above the stars of God;" "I will sit on the mount of assembly in the recesses of the north;" "I will ascend above the heights of the clouds;" and "I will make myself like the Most High." In each of these expressions Satan (called *heyleyl ben-shachar*, or "Shining One, Son of the Dawn" here in v. 12) exalts himself in some way. He is not content with his portion, and he does not wait for promotion from the Lord, even though he was probably one of the three top created beings, if we take into account what is said about him in Ezekiel 28:11-19. Here we read God's sentence upon him. God's two judgments upon him are as follows: "You will be thrust down to Sheol," "To the recesses of the pit." Instead of: "the recesses of the north," Satan goes to the "recesses of the pit." This is the pattern of behavior and judgment of the nature of Adam, which lies behind all sin, and this behavior receives the same condemnation from God, whether Satan does it of we humans do it.

The other pattern is the attitude of Jesus and His nature. This is the nature that was born in us at our conversion. In Philippians 2:5-11 Jesus humbled Himself in a sevenfold way and the Father exalted Him in a sevenfold way. We read that Jesus "Did not regard equality with God to be grasped," "Emptied Himself," "Taking the form of a bondservant," "Being made in the likeness of men," "Humbled Himself by becoming obedient," "Obedient unto death," "Death on a cross." These are the seven steps downward in self-humbling that Jesus took. Notice that Jesus really took these humiliations, and that they were the will of the Father. Following are the seven glorifications that the Father gave Jesus in response. This is what the Father did to Jesus: "God Highly exalted Him," "Bestowed on Him the name," "Name, which is above every other name," "At the name of Jesus, every knee will bow," "Of those in heaven, on earth, & under the earth," "Every tongue will confess Jesus is Lord," "To the glory of the Father."

The nature of Adam is to exalt ourselves, as Satan did, with the result that we are humbled by God. However, the nature of Jesus, which we received at the time we were born again, leads us to humble ourselves and wait on the Lord. Then God will raise us up at the time He sees fit. We need to get to the lowest place on earth first. For Israel that place is literally the river bottom of the Jordan River where it empties into the Dead Sea. For us it is whatever God wants to put us through. Then, as Israel crossed the Jordan River to possess even higher mountains than they left, so the New Testament believer will have heights with the Lord that he didn't know even existed after he has crossed through the low places where the Lord has sent him first. We have to follow the pattern of Jesus—not that of Satan.

As the Israelites are crossing the Jordan River on the dry river bottom, Joshua relates an interesting occurrence (3:16): "the waters which were flowing down from above stood and rose up in one heap, a great distance away at Adam, the city that is beside Zarethan: and those that were flowing down toward the sea of the Arabah, the Salt

Sea (Dead Sea), were completely cut off. So the people crossed opposite Jericho."

The first thing we should note here is that the waters backed up to a city named Adam, as the Lord held them back. The Lord's holding back the waters as far as Adam is significant because it shows how the Lord can supernaturally block all of the attitudes and activities of the Old Adam in us in order to bring us the victory of His rule in us. Remember the Old Adam is to be treated as dead by this time, having been "ended" in the Reed Sea ("the sea that makes an end"). This represents the behavioral holdovers of the dead old Adamic nature, which the Apostle Paul refers to as indwelling sin.

The city Adam is beside Zarethan, which means, "the lamenting (or howling) of oppression."[23] I believe that the actual crisis of the identification experience is a supernatural experience of awareness of the death of the Old Adam (the city), the howling of its oppression (Zarethan), and the power of the enemy to work through it (the waters of the Jordan), through which the Lord imparts a special faith in the death of the Old Adam and the reality of Christ's living through us. It is a faith that recognizes the odious nature of sin and the sin nature, seeks the filling of the Holy Spirit so that Jesus lives through the believer, and provides a willingness to cooperate 100% by getting out of the way of God's working. It is a faith that backs up the functioning of the old pattern to Adam and replaces it with Jesus Himself. It is the lowest place on earth for man, but the place of the Lord's highest blessing. It is not an emotional high (often called the Baptism of the Holy Spirit, or Second Blessing), such as many Pentecostal brothers claim, but rather a supernatural awareness of the presence of Jesus in us that was there since conversion, but has been covered over by a veil of uncrucified flesh. The emotional high which may follow this experience, and which is called by many the baptism in the Holy Spirit, would appear to correspond rather with the conquest of Jericho, which followed soon after.

Accompanying this awareness is another awareness: that the old Adam is really not who we are—an awareness that every desire for lust of the flesh, lust of the eyes, and pride of life is an attempt of indwelling sin to take over us and make us something we are not. What we really are is Jesus Christ living through us. The great revelation in the crisis of identification is that we are now to fight against these false desires, instead of pampering them, obeying them, and complaining to God whenever their gratification is restricted. That is what Israel did in the wilderness, and that is what the carnal Christian does.

At conversion we received everything necessary for a victorious Christian life, but we didn't understand what had taken place right away. The crisis of identification, corresponding to the crossing of the Jordan River, brings us into a supernatural awareness and understanding of the potential of living in the Spirit, as well as a Spirit-led desire to surrender to that life on the higher level.

In the Greek of the New Testament, there are 3 types of action of the verbs. The first type of action in Greek verbs is the aorist. This refers to action at one point of time. Our experience of accepting Jesus as our personal Savior and being born again is an example of this action. Acts 16:31 is an example of this type of verb: "Believe in the Lord Jesus, and you will be saved, you and your household." The Apostle is seeking a decision on the spot that will accomplish all of the action necessary for their eternal salvation. This is the simple action of the aorist.

It is noteworthy that Romans 12:1 also uses this same simple action for the experience of identification as was for the original conversion experience. When Paul exhorts us to present our bodies as a living sacrifice, the verb is this simple one-time action. I had originally thought that this was something that had to be done daily, as it is mentioned in Romans 6:16, but it is a one-time decision. The Christian life is a battle to learn the new truths and walk in the light of them. The Israelites crossed the Reed Sea only once, and they crossed the Jordan only once. In the same way, we are only saved once, and only pass the crisis of identification in one point of time. After the crisis decision, the battle revolves around Satan's lies that we are not saved or that we are still the boss in our lives after this surrender. We need to reaffirm these decisions, not make them all over again.

In Greek verbs there is also the perfect tense, which emphasizes the enduring results of a past action. It is a one-time event with enduring results. An example of this is Galatians 2:20: "I have been crucified with Christ." This tense describes positional truth—truth available to be put into action from the conversion experience onward. The new truth is there, and the Christian is to deal with anything that has become a lie in the light of it. We are born pigs, and at the new birth we become new creatures: lambs. The entire Christian walk is affected by the fact that we are now lambs, and the sanctification process is the uprooting and removing of everything related to our "pigness," which has now become a lie in the light of the new birth.

The third tense is the progressive, sometimes called the present. These verbs denote continuous action. I John 1:7 says, "If we are walking in the light, as He is in the light, we are having fellowship one with another, and the blood of Jesus His Son keeps on cleansing us from all sin." I have translated these verbs direct to show their verbal action better in this verse. All of these verbs are in continuous action. They describe the Christian's daily walk. Our battles with sin as a lying action and false beliefs as lies of the Devil are a matter of continuous action. Jesus says, "Keep watching and praying that you may not come into temptation (Mark 14:38)." Watching for lies and temptations is a continuous activity, and is therefore in this tense.

In his book, Handbook to Happiness, Dr. Charles Solomon describes the relation to the conversion and identification experiences this way, "Total surrender is essential to total usefulness. Occasionally, a person accepts the Lord Jesus Christ as Savior and makes him Lord of his life at the beginning. That is what should happen in all conversions. One should not accept Jesus Christ as Savior and then wait ten or fifteen years to yield completely to him. This should take place the day a person accepts Christ. When it doesn't, a person has to see the futility of running his own life—or ruining it, as is frequently the case—and come to the place where he is ready to say, "Lord, I want to take my hands off my life. I want you to run it."[24]

The Jordan experience of identification is for the believer that has wandered the 38 extra years in the desert, and it is important that we understand these steps to pass through the process, as illuminated by the history of Israel, so that we can get as many believers as possible out of the desert of carnality and into the land of spiritual blessing. The Israelite's crossing of the Jordan corresponds to that one-time total surrender, which is mentioned in Romans 12:1, and which is called the believer's identification experience.

This experience is entered into by faith, just like the Israelites' crossing of the Jordan River. Just as the Israelite Priests carrying the Ark of the Covenant had to step into the water before the river was held back (Joshua 3:15-16), so the believer has to affirm the truth of identification with Christ and surrender totally to him by faith and believe that it is a done deal. It is an aorist one-time event, and doubting it can ruin your effectiveness as much as doubting your salvation.

VII. Gilgal: Circumcision and Restoration.

When the Israelites came up out of the dry river bottom of the Jordan, the Lord ordered them to select 12 men, one from each tribe, and for each to take a large stone from the dry river bottom. The purpose was to build a memorial on the other side so that this crossing would be remembered forever (Joshua 4:1-7). We are also reminded that this was the new lowest point on the earth's surface. Before the surface of the river was the lowest point, but now they were even on the river bottom below that!

We Christians also need to remember that our decision of identification with Jesus in His death is also a once and for all decision, and we need to remember it very clearly. It would be appropriate to set up our own memorial to commemorate the day when we surrendered totally to the sovereignty of the Lord Jesus in our lives, or, perhaps, to write an inscription in the flyleaf of our Bible. In later days when things get difficult for us, we can go back and see a tangible testimony of our commitment to the Lord. Also, we can fix it better in our minds by doing something about the decision.

This memorial was set up at Gilgal, the first place that the Israelites camped on the west of the Jordan. Here the Lord ordered the circumcision of every male in Israel. The people that came out of Egypt had been circumcised, but those born in the wilderness had not been circumcised. After they were circumcised, the Lord said to Joshua (5:9), "'Today I have rolled away the reproach of Egypt from you.' So the name of that place is called Gilgal to this day."

Gilgal means "rolling away" according to its Hebrew root,[25] the same root as a familiar place: Golgotha. Should we be surprised? Of course not! Every believer learns early in his Christian life the importance of the blood of Christ. The blood of Christ cleanses us from sin. What is harder to learn, however, is that it is the cross of Christ that gives us power. The blood brings us up to zero, erasing the negative sin. But we don't want to stay at zero. The cross, or Golgotha, "rolls away" the burden of self-life, making it possible for the Holy Spirit to channel His power through us. It puts us above zero in our walk with God.

In his excellent book, *Beyond Identity*, Dick Keyes explains how our relationship with God is healed at this point. He shows the difference between guilt and shame, and how the Lord deals with both in order to bring us into close communion with Him. It is relatively easy to understand guilt and forgiveness. Both are relatively straightforward and the atonement deals with sin and provides forgiveness. But what is shame? Mr. Keyes writes: "The problem of shame, a violation of our models, is not so clearly resolved. In fact, many conclude that the problem is irresolvable. Some existentialists have said that shame is just there and nothing can be done about it. It is part of the sickness of being a human being."[26]

Mr. Keyes goes on to distinguish between false shame and objective, or true shame. True shame is doing something dishonorable in the sight of God. He gives the example of Isaiah standing before the presence of God in the Temple in Isaiah 6:1-5, and comments about the shame Isaiah felt, and we would have felt: "God sees through all our sham, deceit, pretense, and respectability. Our whole sense of self would be threatened. Any sense of being heroic would be exposed as pretension. What then does God do about our shame? He does not forgive it because so many of the things for which we feel shame are not moral problems which would need to be forgiven. God's answer is acceptance. God accepts us personally in our shame."[27]

Acceptance goes beyond forgiveness. Forgiveness is for an act, but acceptance is for the person that committed the act. Forgiveness is for sin, but acceptance is for the identity of the sinner. In Hebrews 2:11 God says that He is not ashamed to call us brothers—to be identified with us. Acceptance is there from God, but how can we appropriate it to deal with our own shame? Keyes continues, "This then is the first step to resolve shame—to realize that God, through Jesus Christ, accepts you. Your adopting Father joyfully receives you with all your vanity, sin and contradictions. God accepts the Christian whether the Christian accepts himself or not. Then one day He will replace our shame with its opposite—true glory and honor. The hope of the Christian is that he will pass through death and its shame (there is nothing less heroic than being dead) and to go into the presence of God, to share something of the very glory of God Himself."[28]

At this point Keyes has hit on the first step to our overcoming shame—to realize that God, through Jesus Christ, accepts us. However, like most believers, he focuses on the future glory that we have in Christ.

In the Old Testament the Lord did not want Israel to wait until the Millennial Kingdom to receive glory. He wanted to glorify Israel so that other nations would know the He is the True God. In the same way, God does not want to wait for our entrance in heaven to give glory to us. He wants to do it during our lifetime so that others will turn to Him. However, He will not glorify someone who is not totally dedicated to Him, as that would glorify the person instead of glorifying God.

As we contemplate Gilgal (Golgotha) as "rolling back" the reproach of Egypt, we need to realize that God sees as being already dead to the indwelling problem of sin that we have. An alcoholic that accepts Jesus is no longer an alcoholic, but a redeemed son of God with a drinking problem that he is in the process of overcoming. The same is true of other addictions. In the book *Freedom from Addiction*, Mike Quarles tells of continual battle with alcohol. In the alcoholics anonymous group, he was taught to stand up at every meeting and confess, "I am an alcoholic." He thought of himself as an alcoholic even when he was dry for a period of time. His identity was that of an alcoholic. His role model was a non-drinker, and his shame was continuous—whether he drank or not—because he believed he was an alcoholic and his role model was "non-drinker." There was no way that he could ever experience anything but shame. It was guaranteed to be permanent and continuous.

However, he was listening to some tapes of a Bible teacher, and he realized that he had a mistaken identity. He says, "All Christians died with Christ so all Christians have been freed from sin. If they don't believe they're free from sin, they'll probably not live like it. We act according to our beliefs. The central issue is always identity. If you don't know the central truth about your identity 'in Christ,' it doesn't make any difference what programs you are involved in or what spiritual exercises you are doing."[29]

Since we have died with Christ already, we have passed through the total extreme degree of the experience of shame. We have given up on our performance for earning salvation and have declared ourselves unfit for the Kingdom of Heaven, and worthy of death and eternal damnation. That is the bad news. But there is also good news: in Christ we have conquered hell risen again and been seated in Heavenly places. Now Jesus is living in us.

Our identity is explained by the phrase "in Christ." In Christ we already died to our sins, went to hell, rose again, and are seated at the right hand of the Father in Heavenly places (Eph. 2:6). With such a high identity, our role model should only be Jesus himself. That role model makes the living out of our identity impossible, and should condemn us to the same hopeless shame as Mr. Quarles before his deliverance. It doesn't, however, as he says, "Besides understanding my identity "in Christ" I had another life-changing insight. If I am a new creation "in Christ" (2 Cor. 5:17), then I am no longer a sinner and I don't have to sin. For many years I had been taught, believed, and also preached that everyone, including Christians, had a sin nature."[30]

Quarles had believed that he had a sin nature and therefore sinned. When he realized the truth of 2 Cor. 5:17, that we are new creatures in Christ, he became free to act differently according to this new truth. He concludes: "The key to knowing Christ is understanding that we died with Him. Paul says, 'For you have died and your life is hidden with Christ in God' (Col. 3:3). <u>Without this understanding we try to become someone we already are.</u> We try to do for ourselves what Christ has already done for us. This is an exercise in futility."[31]

We have all failed, according to our own efforts for salvation. It is the same as far as living the Christian life is concerned. Quarles was set free as he realized, "For 18 years of my Christian life I tried to act like a Christian in my own strength. Then one day it is as if God said, 'Mike, your act is no good. This is what I think of your act—I have crucified it and you. I've taken care of it and you.' God has no interest in improving our old nature or our natural life. He desires that we exchange our old life in Adam for a new life in Christ."[32]

Isn't this just living in perpetual shame, devoid of any chance of living up to our role model? Not at all! The truth of the matter is that in Christ we actually died when He died, and we entered into that death at conversion. We have just been living a lie—Satan's lie that we are still in Adam. As long as we see ourselves as still in Adam, we will continue to sin like Adam, in one or more of the many varieties available to us.

How then is victory achieved so that we can live up to our role model? The liberals and other existentialists have made each man the measure of himself and thus have excluded shame at the cost of morality. They seem happy when they are declaring that their particular sin is just an "alternative lifestyle." However, they still don't want to accept the fact that, if someone were to hold a gun to their head and demand a transcendent reason beyond pragmatism and social contract why they should not blow their brains out and take their wallet, they could not give one. Under the influence of this mentality, all of social order has been breaking down, though people feel better about themselves, having overcome shame. It is interesting to note that in Spanish, the most common way to say that someone is evil and has no conscience is to say, "He has no shame"[33]

The Biblical solution to shame is that the Role Model is actually living His life out through us. This is true potentially from the moment we are saved, but only becomes reality through the identification experience. Once we cross the Jordan of identification with Christ, we can experience Gilgal (or, for us, Golgotha). Here the burden of self-effort drops off of us like an old cocoon, and we are "metamorphosized" through the indwelling Spirit (no longer grieved at our self-efforts or quenched with our pride). In Romans 12:1 we are urged to turn over our body as a living sacrifice in a once-and-for-all decision, which corresponds to the identification experience with Christ. The next verse gives us the results of such a decision: "and do not be conformed to this world, but be transformed (literally "metamorphosized") by the renewing of your mind."[34]

Because through the identification commitment Jesus is living unlimited through us, there will be a perfect correlation between our actions and the role. There will be no shame. The Old Adam with all his shame is dead, and the Second Adam is perfect, living up to all expectations. In Christ we can claim the acceptance of the Father at Jesus' baptism, as well as the Transfiguration: "This is My Beloved Son, with whom I am well-pleased." If we sin because we begin to try with our effort, we have only to confess it and go on. It was not really us in the first place, but indwelling sin. We were responsible for failing to get out of the way and to let the Spirit live Christ's life through us, but the failure was not a functional failure: dead people don't malfunction.

VIII. Conquering Jericho: The Empowering of the Holy Spirit.

After their rededication to the Lord at Gilgal, the Israelites were ready to conquer Jericho. In Joshua 5:10-12, the Israelites celebrated the Passover that they hadn't celebrated since the first month of the second year in the desert, mentioned in Numbers 9:1-5. Now they were in the land, and they had something to celebrate. When they were in the wilderness, they had nothing to celebrate, since the wilderness was worse than Egypt. Now, however, they were eating from the food of the Promised Land, and they could celebrate God's blessings.

Ian Thomas makes this point well in the case of the Christian that we need to be in the land to really celebrate the redemption that we have. For a carnal believer, the state he is in is worse than that of those in the world, and so he does not appreciate the celebration of the Lord's Supper. To him it is just an additional 10-15 minutes tacked onto the end of an already boring church service once a month. When, however, he enters into all of the fullness of the blessing that God has for him in Christ, passing through the identification experience of dying to self and enjoying Jesus' life in him, he is most excited in the celebration of such deliverance, for now he has entered into the blessings for which he was delivered from the world in his conversion in the first place. "There is only one place where you can intelligently celebrate your redemption through the death of Jesus Christ, and that is in the fullness of his resurrection life! This is a spiritual principle!"[35]

Even after our rededication to the Lord at Gilgal, everything is incomplete in the identification experience as a transition to our being spiritual men and women without the initial experience of the filling of the Spirit. This is what many Pentecostal brethren refer to when they talk of a second blessing experience. As far as can be determined, there is no special spiritual gift associated with this experience, though one or more gifts might be manifest for the first time at this point in some cases. After the crossing of the Jordan and encampment at Gilgal, corresponding to our Identification with Christ and our rededication, Jericho is Israel's first fight for the land west of the Jordan.

What does Jericho represent for the Christian? The word Jericho is from the Hebrew root referring to three things: the first is spirit, the second is fragrance, or aroma, and the third is wide open spaces.[36] Conquering Jericho for Israel corresponds with the believer's initial filling with the Holy Spirit in power as a spiritual believer after a full surrender and rededication to the Lord as the transition into the spiritual phase of his experience with the Lord. It also gives him a new fragrance before the world. Paul talks about this new fragrance, which he calls an aroma in 2 Cor. 2:14-16: "But thanks be to God, who always leads us in triumph in Christ, and manifests through us the sweet aroma of the knowledge of Him in every place. For we are a fragrance of Christ to God among those who are being saved and among those who are perishing; to the one an aroma of death to death, to the other an aroma of life to life. And who is adequate for these things?"

The world can detect our death to things of the world and perceives it only as death because they are unable to perceive the better spiritual things that we enjoy. The believers, on the other hand, sense that our deathlike reaction to things of this world is evidence of our higher life in the things of our Lord Jesus and the World to Come. As we are filled with the Holy Spirit, all people around us will be able to sense that something is different about us.

The fragrance is only a small part of our conquest of Jericho. It is the power of the Holy Spirit being channeled through us that is the key difference between a spiritual and a carnal believer. The behavioral change should be the most noteworthy. In his book, *Christ Esteem: Where the Search for Self-Esteem Ends*, Don Matzat explains well how the behavior is a part of the life that we have. "All forms of life possess attributes. For example, a robin flies south in the wintertime because such an ingredient is a part of robin-life. Obviously, the action is not motivated by a conscious decision to be a 'good robin' (obeying the external code for being a responsible robin), but is simply a spontaneous result of life. It's a law of life. The robin is not doing the law. Instead, the law is 'doing the robin.'"[37]

This illustration makes clear much of the confusion between the life of Adam, which we received in our physical birth, and the life of Jesus, which we received when we were born again with the second birth. There is a quality of self-exaltation we received in our birth from Adam, which is like Satan's self-exaltation in his rebellion against God. This leads men to try to exalt themselves with the 3 items with which Satan tempted Eve in the Garden of Eden: the lust of the flesh ("the woman saw that the tree was good for food"), the lust of the eyes ("and that it was a delight to the eyes"), and the pride of life ("and that the tree was desirable to make one wise"—Gen. 3:6). Matzat continues describing Adam's life: "Natural human life, gained from Adam, possesses various attributes. Death, sickness, emotional and mental problems, pain, worry, fear, and frustration are built in to Adam's life. Adam's life is by nature selfish, rebellious, proud, and disobedient. … Paul speaks of this reality as the 'law of sin and death.' Adam's life does not contain within itself the spiritual standards expressed in the Divine Law any more than the life of my dog contains within itself human standards, or than a petunia bears apples. If you leave Adam-life alone and allow it to 'do what comes naturally,' you will have moral chaos."[38]

God knows this already, and wants us to choose what is right—not at the level of the actual occasion—but rather at the level of choosing our master. We can choose to submit to the new nature that God has placed in us, or we can choose to operate under the lie that the old nature is still there and allow indwelling sin to rob us of the blessings that God has for us. We choose at the level of master, not at the level of each individual choice, as many believe.

To understand the power and blessings of the life that the believer experiences in the first special filling of the Spirit after the experience of identification, Matzat describes the life that is in Jesus Christ in similar terms as the other descriptions: "The life that is in Christ Jesus also contains numerous attributes. The life in Christ is eternal. The concept of "eternal life" is not a future existence, but is the quality of the life received in Christ. Paul speaks of Jesus as being our wisdom, righteousness, sanctification, and redemption (1 Cor. 1:30). Love, joy, peace, and contentment are all a part of the ingredients of Christ-life. Christ-life spontaneously fulfills the will of the Father in heaven. It contains the desire for good works. Whereas rebellion, sin, and death are built into Adam-life, obedience, righteousness, and eternal life are built into Christ-life."[39]

At this time in Israel's history, the manna had ceased and they were about to take Jericho. In Joshua 5:13-15 Joshua had a vision of a man who described himself as the Captain of the Host of the Lord. Joshua fell down and worshipped Him, and the Captain tells him to take his sandals off, as Moses had to do before the burning bush in Exodus 3. If this were just any angel, he would have rejected worship, as the angel in Revelation 22:8-9. Instead, he even tells Joshua to remove his sandals because he was on holy ground, as God said to Moses from the burning bush in Exodus 3:4-5. This shows that He is God Himself. It appears that this is a preincarnate appearance of the Messiah in the Old Testament.

As the believer is committing himself to follow the Lord 100%, it is to be expected that Jesus will make a personal intervention in the person's life. The manifestation will be different for each person, but they will have a heightened awareness of the presence of the Lord in their life as a result. For the believer at this point, Jesus will not be in the distance going before him, but rather Jesus will be going forth through him.

Finally, Jericho was conquered by the action of the Lord, not the Israelites. After circling the city once per day for 6 days, they circled it 7 times on the last day and shouted. God knocked the walls down, and all they had to do was attack straightforward and take the city. The victory was given to them by the power of the Lord on the day they were tired after walking around 20-25 miles apiece so that they could not have gotten the victory by their own strength or cleverness. God got all of the glory.

For the believer, it is the same. When we enter into the experience of identification, it is to begin by recognizing that we are unworthy and have an unworthy life in Adam—both to get salvation and to walk the Christian life. We are to hand over the Old Adam for crucifixion at conversion, and cease to recognize him for identification. The initial filling of the Spirit as part of identification has to be entirely an act of God, as are all subsequent fillings. We have to get our focus off of ourselves and onto Jesus only. He is our life, righteousness, power, wisdom, and everything else.

It is clear that there are many benefits from Jesus' Christ's identification with us, but they are only available to us as we identify with Him. It is hoped that an exposition of the relevant history of Israel and the Hebrew background have helped the New Testament believer pass through that critical transition between the carnal and the spiritual man.

One final note:

The scope of this book has been to start with the nature of God, then revelation, then to identify who we are as human beings. After that we have considered our story as human beings from our birth onward. We have meditated on the meaning of our birth and our composition of body, soul, and spirit. We have also seen how we become involved in sin and go through the equivalent of being kicked out of the Garden of Eden. As the Israelites became slaves in Egypt, so we became the natural man and became slaves in the world. Israel's deliverance from Egypt through the plagues and the Passover corresponded to our salvation experience of being converted and covered with the blood of the Lamb Jesus (John 1:29) "Who takes away the sin of the world."

As Israel crossed the Reed Sea, they met their "end" as Gentiles and just one of the nations, and became the people of God. In the same way, the New Testament believer in his conversion and baptism, seen as one event, died to This World and entered the World to Come. He died to Adam and was born again to Jesus living in him.

Then as Israel was set free in the wilderness, the believer in Jesus became a carnal, or immature believer. The purpose of this period was to bring the believer to see that the false desires of the old life were not really his any more, and to bring him to wage war against them, rather than continuing to pamper them and complain whenever they were not gratified.

Finally, we have seen the crisis of identification with Jesus, which corresponds with Israel's crossing of the Jordan River. As we noted above, "the actual crisis of the identification experience is a supernatural experience of awareness of the death of the Old Adam, the howling of its oppression, and the power of the enemy to work through it, through which experience the Lord imparts a special faith in the death of the Old Adam and the reality of Christ's living through us. It is a faith that recognizes the odious nature of sin and the sin nature, seeks the filling of the Holy Spirit so that Jesus lives through the believer, and provides a willingness to cooperate 100% by getting out of the way of God's working. This experience ends the believer's carnal (immature) period and begins the spiritual period, in the same way that the crossing of the Jordan River ended Israel's stay in the desert and began their presence in the Land of Canaan.

This first volume of the two leaves the Israelites across the Jordan River and ready for their conquest of the land. It also leaves the Christian believer through the identification experience and ready to conquer his humility (as Canaan means humility, in Hebrew). This crossing of the Jordan River is not our entrance into heaven, as many Christian hymns would suggest, but rather the beginning of a long fight, as Israel fought under Joshua and his successors.

At each stage there are people that lag behind and stay there permanently. Those that stay behind in Canaan are children that die at an early age or those whose mental development does not pass beyond that of a child. They stay in Canaan and are not lost in the first place. The vast majority remains in Egypt. They never believe in Jesus, and do not accept His shed blood for them. Jesus' death, burial, and resurrection for them were just that—Jesus' death burial and resurrection. They did not receive it. They chose their sin and did not repent of it and receive what Jesus did for them so they will pay the penalty for their own sin forever in the Lake of Fire. Jesus says about this majority of humanity (Matthew 7:13-14): "For the gate is wide and the way is broad that leads to destruction, and there are many who enter through it. For the gate is small and the way is narrow that leads to life, and there are few who find it." Most of humanity stays behind in Egypt, the "Two Oppressors", where Satan, as Pharaoh, sets them free from the law to do their own thing. They drink in continually from the false "Light-giver" Nile and die in their sins.

Others of us continue on for God and receive Jesus Savior. But also many of these spend their entire lives in the Wilderness as carnal, or immature believers. They are saved by the blood of Jesus, but they never live for Him. They never get beyond thinking that the indwelling sin and its false desires are really their own. They believe in Jesus for salvation, but not for daily living. They have the eternal life from Jesus as a pass into heaven, but it is not their daily life. God's harsh criticism of them from Hebrews 3:19 is not that they did not try hard enough in their own strength, but rather, "they were not able to enter because of unbelief." They had enough faith to get out of Egypt, the two oppressors, but not enough to get into Canaan, or humility."

It has been the purpose of this first volume to show Israel's history from the call of Abraham until the crossing of the Jordan River and its fulfillment for the Christian from birth through the identification experience. The remaining volume will tell the story of Israel in the Biblical periods from the conquest of the land under Joshua until the Millennial Kingdom. This story corresponds to the spiritual period of the believer, with a possible exile and return if he falls into rebellion against God again, and final glory in heaven. As in all stages, a person can just stay there forever in unbelief or defective belief or he can through a real growing faith press onward to maturity, becoming more and more like Jesus every day.

It is the hope of the author that this story is put forth in such a way that the reader may discover where in the Christian pilgrimage he is, to learn the appropriate lessons, and to take steps to go on for the Lord. Let's plan to pay whatever price is necessary to go as far as possible in this life to be like Jesus because we let Jesus take over and live His life through us.

Endnotes

Chapter 1: Come to the Waters: An Inquiry into God's Characteristics As They Satisfy Man's Greatest Longings and Needs

1. Crabbe, Dr. Larry, *Inside Out*, (Colorado Springs: Navpress, 1988), pp. 57-58.
2. Ibid., p. 58.
3. From *Meditation II*, by René Descartes, in *The European Philosophers from Descartes to Nietzsche* by Monroe C. Beardsley (ed.), (New york: The Modern Library, 1992), pp. 82-83.
4. Grof, Christina, *The Thirst for Wholeness*, (San Francisco: Harper Collins Publishers, 1993), p.264.
5. Ibid., p.267.
6. Delitzsch, Franz, *Commentary on the Old Testament, Vol. VI: Proverbs, Ecclestiastes, Song of Solomon*, (Grand Rapids, Michigan: Eerdmans, Originally published 1872), p.261.
7. Mahler, Gustav, *Symphony No. 2 in C Minor, 'Resurrection"*, (New York: Vanguard Recording Society, Inc., 1967. This translation appears on the record jacket.
8. Brooke, Tal, *When the World Will Be As One*, (Eugene, Oregon: Harvest House, 1994), p. 154.
9. Ibid., pp. 155-156.
10. Ibid., p. 156.
11. Ibid., P. 160.

12. Cherry, Matt & Mollen Matsumura, "Ten Myths About Secular Humanism," article from *Free Inquiry Magazine*, Volume 18, Number 1, found on the internet at p. 2 at this address: http://www.SecularHumanism.org/library/fi/
13. Nietzsche, Friedrich, "The Superman," in *The European Philosophers from Descartes to Nietzsche* by Monroe C. Beardsley (ed.), (New york: The Modern Library, 1992), p. 857.
14. Ibid., p. 856.
15. Ibid., p. 857.
16. Cherry, p. 2.
17. Berkhof, L., *Systematic Theology*, (Grand Rapids, Michigan: Eerdmans, 1977), p. 59.
18. Nietzsche, p. 857.

Chapter 2: God's Revelations to Mankind: How Can We Get to Know God?

1. Descartes, René, "Meditation V: That God Necessarily Exists," in *Metaphysics: Readings and Reappraisals*, ed. by W. E. Kennick and Morris Lazerowitz, (Englewood Cliffs, New Jersey: Prentiss-Hall, 1966), p. 158.
2. Berkouwer, C. G., *Studies in Dogmatics: Man: The Image of God*, (Grand Rapids, Michigan: Eerdmans, 1972), p. 307.
3. This discussion is largely a summary of teaching from chapter 3, pp. 16-19.
4. Gesenius, William, Edward Robinson tr., with Francis Brown, S. R. Driver, and Charles A. Briggs, *A Hebrew and English Lexicon of the Old Testament*, (Oxford: Clarendon Press, 1968), pp. 695-696.
5. Bauer, Walter, translated and adapted by William F. Arndt and F. Wilbur Gingrich, A *Greek-English Lexicon of the New Testament and Other Early Christian Literature*, (Chicago: The University of Chicago Press, 1971), p. 448.
6. Ibid., p.437.

7. Baillie, John, *The Idea of Revelation in Recent Thought*, (London: Geoffrey Cumberlege, Oxford University Press, 1956), p. 109.
8. Ibid., p.119.
9. Barth, Karl, *Die Kirchliche Dogmatik*, p. 115, quoted and translated in Baillie, p. 35.
10. Baillie, p. 119.
11. Ibid., p. 120.
12. Brooke, Tal, *When the World Will Be As One*, (Eugene, Oregon: Harvest House, 1994), p. 154.

Chapter 3: Just Who Are We, Anyway? What is a Human Being?

1. Gesenius, William, Edward Robinson tr., with Francis Brown, S. R. Driver, and Charles A. Briggs, *A Hebrew and English Lexicon of the Old Testament*, (Oxford: Clarendon Press, 1968), pp. 793-796.
2. Ibid., P. 135.
3. Ibid., pp. 427-428.
4. Ibid., pp. 35-36 for the root איש, and pp. 60-61 for the root אנש. In the light of the controversy between placing the word *ishah* (אִשָּׁה) under the one root of the other, it would be possible to merge the two roots, treating them as cognate roots. There are also many other examples of the feminine form of a noun formed by the addition of *qamats he* at the end, as well.
5. Ibid., pp. 853-854.
6. Berkouwer, C. G., *Studies in Dogmatics: Man: The Image of God*, (Grand Rapids, Michigan: Eerdmans, 1972), p. 29.
7. Ibid., pp. 28-29, footnote 35.
8. Gesenius., 119-125. Gesenius lists *ben* and *bath* separately, but there is no other root to place *bath*, and the sense is plain. This author has read of this connection made by contemporary Jewish Rabbis, as well.
9. Ibid., pp. 820-821.
10. Ibid., pp. 650-651.

11. Berkhof, L. *Systematic Theology*, (Grand Rapids, Michigan: Eerdmans, 1977), pp. 202-203.
12. Ibid., p. 203.
13. Gesenius, pp. 196-198.
14. Ibid., pp. 198-199.
15. Hatch, Edwin, and Henry A. Redpath, *A Concordance to the Septuagint*, (Graz, Austria: Akademische Druck-u Verlagsanstalt, 1975), pp. 1486-1490.
16. Berkouwer, p. 307.
17. Crabb, Dr. Larry, *Men and Women: Enjoying the Difference*, (Grand Rapids, Michigan: Zondervan Publishing House, 1991), p.160.
18. Gesenius, p. 666.
19. Crabb, p. 163.
20. Ibid., pp. 162-163.
21. Gesenius, pp. 9-10.
22. Ibid., pp. 972-973.
23. Ibid., pp 863-864.
24. See note 4 above.

Chapter 4: The Problem of Sin: Seen in the Light of Israel's Bondage in Egypt

1. Gesenius, William, Edward Robinson tr., with Francis Brown, S. R. Driver, and Charles A. Briggs, *A Hebrew and English Lexicon of the Old Testament*, (Oxford: Clarendon Press, 1968), p. 488.
2. Ibid., pp. 21-22.
3. Ibid., p. 505.
4. Ibid., pp. 357.
5. Ibid., pp. 716-721.
6. Ibid., 784-785.
7. Ibid., 793-796.
8. Ibid., pp. 247-248.
9. Ibid., pp. 864-866.

10. Thiessen, Henry Clarence, *Introductory Lectures in Systematic Theology*, (Grand Rapids, Michigan: Eerdmans, 1963), p. 196.
11. Gesenius, p. 940.
12. Berkouwer, C. G., *Studies in Dogmatics: Man: The Image of God*, (Grand Rapids, Michigan: Eerdmans, 1972), p. 123.
13. Ibid., p. 136-137.
14. Gesenius, p. 1014.
15. Thiessen, p. 244.
16. Gesenius, pp. 192-193.
17. Thiessen, p. 240.
18. Gesenius, p. 177. Gesenius does not suggest an etymology here, but it would appear to be a shortened form of the Hebrew root (נגשׁ), which is explained on pp. 620-621.
19. Ibid., pp. 864-866.
20. "Egypt," from *The New Bible Dictionary*, J. D. Douglas, Ed., (Grand Rapids, Michigan: Eerdmans, 1965), p. 338.
21. Gesenius, pp. 828-829.
22. Gerber, Charles R., *Christ-Centered Self-Esteem: Seeing Ourselves Through God's Eyes*, (Joplin, Missouri: College Press Publishing Co., 1996), p. 33.
23. Bauer, Walter, translated and adapted by William F. Arndt and F. Wilbur Gingrich, *A Greek-English Lexicon of the New Testament and Other Early Christian Literature*, (Chicago: The University of Chicago Press, 1971), pp. 697-698.
24. Gesenius, p. 947.
25. Ibid., p. 692.
26. Ibid., p. 837.
27. Ibid., p. 853.
28. Keyes, Dick, *Beyond Identity: Finding Your Self in the Image and Character of God*, (Ann Arbor: Servant Books, 1984), p. 27.
29. Ibid., p. 30.
30. Ibid., p. 26.
31. Wheelis, Allen, *The Quest for Identity*, (W. W. Norton and Co., 1958), p. 87.

32. Colson, Charles, *Kingdoms in Conflict*, (Zondervan Publishing House, 1987), p. 214.

Chapter 5: Doctrine of Salvation—Egypt and the Exodus: Our New Birth Into Spiritual Life

1. Gesenius, William, Edward Robinson tr., with Francis Brown, S. R. Driver, and Charles A. Briggs, *A Hebrew and English Lexicon of the Old Testament*, (Oxford: Clarendon Press, 1968), pp. 136-137.
2. Ibid., p. 1014.
3. Ibid., p. 806.
4. See chapter 2 for a fuller discussion on this topic.
5. Bauer, Walter, translated and adapted by William F. Arndt and F. Wilbur Gingrich, *A Greek-English Lexicon of the New Testament and Other Early Christian Literature*, (Chicago: The University of Chicago Press, 1971), p.55.
6. Gesenius, p. 698.
7. Ibid., p. 821. This means "One who is made to groan" if we take the Hebrew word as a pual passive participle of the root *pe-ayin-he* (פעה). Gesenius does not list a root from which this name could be derived on p. 806, where *Puah* (פּוּעָה) appears.
8. Ibid., p. 837.
9. Hart, Dr. Archibald D., *Adrenaline and Stress*, (Dallas: Word Publishing, 1995), p. 36.
10. Gesenius, pp. 828-829.
11. Thiessen, Henry Clarence, *Introductory Lectures in Systematic Theology*, (Grand Rapids, Michigan: Eerdmans, 1963), p. 244.
12. Gesenius, p. 602. It is always best to follow an explicit explanation in the Bible. Moses was so named because he was "drawn out" of the river.
13. Berkhof, L. *Systematic Theology*, (Grand Rapids, Michigan: Eerdmans, 1977), p. 116.
14. Bauer, p. 902.
15. Gesenius, 861-862.

16. Ibid., pp. 761-763.
17. Ibid., p. 786.
18. Ibid., p. 1006.
19. Ibid., p. 806.
20. Ibid., p. 87.
21. Ibid., p.508.
22. Ibid., pp. 692-693.
23. Ibid., pp. 180-185.

Chapter 6: From the Reed Sea to Mt. Sinai And Covenant Enactment: Entering into a Covenant with the Creator God

1. Gesenius, William, Edward Robinson tr., with Francis Brown, S. R. Driver, and Charles A. Briggs, *A Hebrew and English Lexicon of the Old Testament*, (Oxford: Clarendon Press, 1968), pp. 694-695.
2. Ibid., pp. 180-185. *Midbar*, is from the root *dbr* (דבר), meaning word.
3. Ibid., pp. 1003-1004.
4. Hart, Dr. Archibald D., *Adrenaline and Stress*, (Dallas: Word Publishing, 1995), p. 22.
5. Ibid., p.36.
6. Gesenius, pp.695-696.
7. Ibid., pp. 142-143.
8. Ibid., pp. 535-537.
9. Ibid., pp. 185-186.
10. Ibid., pp. 903-905.
11. Ibid., p. 105.
12. Ibid., pp. 346-348.
13. Ibid.. p. 130.
14 Ibid., pp. 1027 & 1029.
15 Koehler, Ludwig and Walter Baumgartner, Revised by Walter Baumgartner and Johann Jacob Stamm, with assistance from Benedikt Hartmann, Zeev Ben-Hayyim, Eduard Yechezkel Kutscher, and Philippe Reymond, Tr. & Ed. Under the supervision of M. E. J. Richardson, *The Hebrew and Aramaic Lexicon*

of the Old Testament, CD-ROM Edition, (Konniklijke Brill NV, Leiden, The Netherlands, 1994-2000). #9146, שְׁלָו, selav.

16. Gesenius, P. 545.
17. Ibid., p.151.
18. Ibid., pp. 211-212.
19. Ibid., p. 860.
20. Ibid., p. 185.
21. Ibid., p. 771.
22. Ibid., p. 951.
23. Ibid., 351-352.
24. Thomas, Major Ian W., *The Saving Life of Christ*, (Grand Rapids: Zondervan Publishing House, 1961), p. 78.
25. Ibid., p. 80.
26. Koehler / Baumgartner 5769 & 5770 and Gesenius, p. 602 cite the Bible as connecting the name Moses with the verb *mashah* (מָשָׁה), as in II Samuel 22:17 and Psalm 18:17 (18:16 in Christian Bible), though they also cite a possible etymology from the word *child* in the Egyptian language. It would appear best to trust Moses under Divine inspiration to understand his own name.
27. Gesenius, p. 221, 447-448. Gesenius sees Joshua as a combination of *yeho* (short for Jehovah) and *shua* (short for *yeshuah*), meaning salvation. Therefore meaning "Jehovah is Salvation."
28. Here the Hebrew in Exodus 17:13 the expression "with the edge of the sword" appears in the original Hebrew as *lepiy-hareb* (לְפִי-חָרֶב), meaning, "with the mouth of the sword".

29 Here in the Greek of Hebrews 4:12 we read "than any two-edged sword." In the Greek we read *huper pasan machairan distomon* (ὑπὲρ πᾶσαν μάχαιραν δίστομον). *Stoma* is "mouth," and *distomon* means, "double mouthed."

30. Gesenius, p. 651. The root is *nss* (נסס). Here the Hebrew is *yhwh nissiy* (יהוה נִסִּי), meaning, "Jehovah is my standard" or "Jehovah is my miracle."
31. Ibid., pp. 192-193.
32. Ibid., pp. 695-696. Here Gesenius suggests an Egyptian root, meaning *clay*. The "ay" ending is for the masculine plural

with possessive "my." Therefore Sinay would mean "my clays."

33. Bauer, Walter, translated and adapted by William F. Arndt and F. Wilbur Gingrich, *A Greek-English Lexicon of the New Testament and Other Early Christian Literature*, (Chicago: The University of Chicago Press, 1971), p. 155.
34. Friberg Greek Lexicon in Bibleworks, version 6.0. #21619 *περιούσιος* on strictly, of property owned as a rich and distinctive possession; metaphorically in the NT, of God's redeemed people as his costly possession and a distinctive treasure *special, choice, chosen* (TI 2.14) Friberg Greek Lexicon
35. Gesenius, pp. 384-385.
36. Ibid., p. 1051.
37. Ibid., p. 461.
38. Bauer, p. 418. See also *argéo* (*ἀργέω*) on p. 104.
39. Gesenius, pp. 1047-1049.
40. Ibid., p. 136.
41. McNeil, John T., ed., *Calvin: Institutes of the Christian Religion*, (Philadelphia: The Westminster Press, 1960), Book II, Chapter 10, p. 428.
42. Ibid., pp. 429-430.
43. Chafer, Lewis Sperry, *Grace: The Glorious Theme*, (Grand Rapids, Michigan: Zondervan Publishing House, 1975), p. 153.
44. Ibid., pp. 232-233.

Chapter 7: Mt. Sinai I: The Believer's Riches in Jesus' Sacrifice: God's Provision for Continuous Cleansing and Fellowship with Him

1. Gesenius, William, Edward Robinson tr., with Francis Brown, S. R. Driver, and Charles A. Briggs, *A Hebrew and English Lexicon of the Old Testament*, (Oxford: Clarendon Press, 1968), p. 695.
2. Ibid., p. 461

3. Brooke, Tal, *When the World Will Be As One*, (Eugene, Oregon: Harvest House, 1994), pp. 80-81.
4. Ibid., p. 83.
5. Ibid., p. 87.
6. Keyes, Dick, *Beyond Identity: Finding Your Self in the Image and Character of God*, (Ann Arbor: Servant Books, 1984), p. 92.
7. Ibid., p. 114.
8. Matzat, Don, *Christ Esteem: Where the Search for Self-Esteem Ends*, (Eugene, Oregon: Harvest House, 1990), p.72.
9. BDB, p. 526 *levonah* is from the Hebrew root (לבן), which refers to whiteness, symbol of purity. Our service for others must be pure.
10. BDB, pp. 571-572. *melach*—salt comes from the root (מלח), whose verb means, "to tear away" or "to dissipate." Our service for others is often dissipated, or without any real benefit in order to test our motives. If we can do our best for others even when no good results that we could claim for our pride, then we are doing it for the right motives.
11. BDB, pp. 1023-1025. *shalom* comes from the Hebrew root (שׁלם). The reader would do well to explore all of the meanings under this root on these pages. It is great to have *shalom* with God. God gives us much more than the absence of war with this sacrifice!
12. BDB, p. 136.
13. Ibid., pp. 196-198.
14. Ibid., pp. 477-480.
15. BDB, pp. 415-416. yasar
16. Ibid., pp. 480-483.
17. Hart, Dr. Archibald D., *Adrenaline and Stress*, (Dallas: Word Publishing, 1995), p. 67 ff.
18. Ibid., p. 7.
19. Ibid., pp. 81-82.
20. Ibid., p. 203.
21. Ibid., p. 205.
22. Ibid., p. 208.
23. Matzat, pp. 77-78.

Chapter 8: Mt. Sinai II: Approaching God Regularly: The Tabernacle And Our Daily Time Of Personal Fellowship with God

1. Koehler / Baumgartner 5769 & 5770 and Gesenius, p. 602 cite the Bible as connecting the name Moses with the verb *mashah* (מָשָׁה), as in II Samuel 22:17 and Psalm 18:17 (18:16 in Christian Bible), though they also cite a possible etymology from the word *child* in the Egyptian language. It would appear best to trust Moses under Divine inspiration to understand his own name.
2. Gesenius, pp. 180-185.
3. Ibid., pp. 488-489.
4. Ibid., pp. 13-14.
5. Koehler / Baumgartner, #203.
6. Gesenius, pp. 247-248.
7. Ibid., p. 75.
8. Caldecott, W. Shaw and James Orr, "Tabernacle," in *The International Standard Bible Encyclopedia*, Volume V, (Grand Rapids, Michigan: Eerdmans, 1952), p. 2889.
9. Olford, Stephen F., *The Tabernacle: Camping with God*, (Neptune, New Jersey: Loixeaux Bros., 1973), p.59.
10. Ibid., p. 60.
11. Gesenius, pp. 493-494.
12. Olford, p. 64.
13. Gesenius, p. 1067.
14. BDB, pp. 17-19.
15. Olford, p. 85.
16. Bruce, F. F., *The Epistle to the Hebrews*, (Grand Rapids, Michigan: Eerdmans, 1970), pp. 189-190.
17. Olford, p. 67.
18. Keil, C. F., *The Pentateuch, Volume II*, (Grand Rapids, Michigan: Eerdmans, no year given), p. 186.
19. Ibid., p. 212.
20. Ibid., p. 213.
21. Gesenius, p. 392.
22. Ibid., pp. 142-143.

23. Olford, p. 119.
24. Gesenius, p. 367.
25. Olford, p. 112.
25. Gesenius, p. 1006.

Chapter 9: Mt. Sinai III: Old Testament Laws: The Working of the Potter—The Christian and the Old Testament Law—"If You Love Me, Keep My Commandments"

1. Knowling, R. J., *The Acts of the Apostles,* in *The Expositor's Greek Testament* by W. Robertsom Nicoll (ed.), (Grand Rapids, Michigan: Eerdmans, 1970), Vol. II, p. 424.

Chapter 10: From Sinai Northward: The First Approach to the Land: Early Zeal for the Lord with Many Mistakes

1. Gesenius, William, Edward Robinson tr., with Francis Brown, S. R. Driver, and Charles A. Briggs, *A Hebrew and English Lexicon of the Old Testament*, (Oxford: Clarendon Press, 1968), pp. 802-803. Here Gesenius shows that the verb *Pa-ar* (פָּאַר) in a causative stem means "to beautify" or "to glorify." The noun *paran* is in the simple stem, which would mean "beauty."
2. Ibid., p. 392. Examples of the three meanings are 1. to praise the Lord (Psalm 111:1-AV): "I will praise the Lord with my whole heart." This is better than the NASV "I will give thanks to the Lord." 2. to confess the name, or names of God (I Kn. 8:35, paralleled in II Chron. 6: 26): "When the heavens are shut up and there is no rain, because they have sinned against You, and they pray toward this place, and confess Your name and turn from their sin when You afflict them..." This involves recognizing God's character, as represented by His different names. 3. to confess our sins to God (Prov. 28:13): "He who conceals his transgressions will not prosper, but he who confesses and forsakes them will find compassion."

3. Ibid., pp. 638-639. Here Gesenius splits these meanings into 4 roots, but it appears better to place all under one root and look for a common idea. The root IV would appear to be best explained as a variant of root II.
4. Ibid., p. 770.
5. Ibid., p. 259.
6. Ibid., p. 298. Here Gesenius places the name under the Hebrew root חול or חיל.
7. Ibid., pp. 600-601.
8. Ibid., p. 994.
9. Ibid., p. 168.
10. Ibid., p. 154.
11. Ibid., p. 27.
12. Ibid., p. 994.
13. Ibid., pp. 80-81.
14. Ibid., p. 803.
15. Ibid., p. 747.
16. Ibid., p. 836-837. Here the root is (פתל), and the initial *nun* forms the *niph-al*, or simple reflexive stem of the verb.
17. Ibid., p. 27.
18. Ibid., pp. 744-745.
19. Ibid., pp. 142-143, Basar—Flesh, Gospel, and Evangelize. Let's "flesh out" the good news.
20. Ibid., pp. 185-186, fish—multiply.
21. Ibid., pp. 903-905—cucumbers.
22. Ibid., p. 105—melons—false trust.
23. Ibid., pp. 346-348—leeks—unsure earthly riches.
24. Ibid., p. 130—onions—layers of false fronts we put on so others don't know us as we really are.
25. Ibid., pp. 1027 & 1029 Shem—be high or lofty—fame. Our self-promotion stinks to God and others.
26. Koehler / Baumgartner #9146 selav—quail
27. Gesenius, p. 545.
28. Ibid., p.151.
29. Ibid., pp. 211-212, *hagah*—chew the cud.
30. Ibid., p. 860.
31. Ibid., p. 185.

32. Ibid., p.32. The past tense and the participle can be equally taken. The participle appears to be better for a name, as it is ongoing.
33. Ibid., pp. 391-392. Here Gesenius places the name under the Hebrew root (ידד), which means “to love.” The *mem* would make it from the hiphil, or causative stem of the verb. This would mean that the person caused other people to love. If we split the word into two words (Heb. מֵי־דֹד), it reads, “Waters of love.” This would refer to love flowing out of the person like waters flow.

Chapter 11: The 38 Extra Years in the Wilderness: Unbelief Brings About An Unnecessary Detour

1. Gesenius, William, Edward Robinson tr., with Francis Brown, S. R. Driver, and Charles A. Briggs, *A Hebrew and English Lexicon of the Old Testament*, (Oxford: Clarendon Press, 1968), pp. 802-803. For a discussion of this, see footnote 1 of chapter 10.
2. Ibid., pp871-874. *Kadesh* (קָדֵשׁ) is from the same root as the word holy, and means “holy one.” *Bar* (בַּר) is Aramaic for son. *Nea* (נַע) in the Qal participle means vagabond, p. 631. The composite meaning of this name would thus best be interpreted as “holy one, son of wandering.”
3. Norman, J. G. G. and A. R. Millard, “Hamath,” in *New Bible Dictionary*, (Downers Grove, Illinois: Intervarsity Press, 1996), pp. 450-451.
4. Gesenius, p. 778. In the Old Testament the expression “stiff-necked” appears in the AV, and “stubborn” appears in the NASV, and it is rendered by the Hebrew *qeshe-oref* (קְשֵׁי־עֹרֶף). However, the reference to the neck in this context suggests this meaning, as the enemies of Israel represent spiritual problems. Our stiff-neck can be a formidable obstacle to overcome.
5. Ibid., pp. 584-585. The roots are *manah* (מָנָה) and *manan* (מָנַן). The former (p. 584) has as its base meaning, “to count, reckon, apportion, etc.,” and as a noun “portion.” The latter means

"portion," without verbs. Gesenius takes this name to be "my brother is a gift" from a cognate root. It would appear best in this context to see the brother both as a gift and a portion.

6. Ibid., p. 995. Gesenius places this word under the Hebrew root (שׁדשׁ) because of cognate Semitic roots that spell their words under this root both with and without the "d." Under this root is the number 6, the number of man. It would seem best to translate this name "my sixes," because of the pointing of the ending.
7. Ibid., p. 1068. The Hebrew root here is *tlm* (תלם). The base meaning behind the root is not clear, but the word *furrow* represents our forging a plan with our own direction and efforts.
8. These words are the same in Greek. *Gigantas* (*γιγάντας*) is in the accusative case as the direct object of the sentence, and *gigantes* (*γιγάντες*) is in the nominative case.
9. Gesenius., pp. 476-477. In II Samuel 9:8, Mephibosheth humbles himself before King David.by saying, "What is your servant, that you should regard a dead dog like me?" Byreferring to himself as a dog, and a dead one at that, Mephibosheth was humbling himself to the limit possible. Hear a dog was considered a disgusting and low animal.
10. Ibid., p. 630.
11. Ibid., pp. 301, 359-360. Gesenius is not sure whether to place the name under the root חרר or the root חור. He lists it under the former, but suggests it might be under the latter. As we see the meaning in the context, the latter seems the more probable rendering,meaning "paleness."
12. Ibid., pp. 55-57.
13. Ibid., pp. 355-357.
14. Ibid., p. 901. Gesenius enters two roots with the same spelling. Our approach is to combine everything from a root with the same spelling. Perhaps, baldness is connected with the head being cold.
15. Ibid., pp. 843-844, see also the cognate root זכר on pp. 263-264. The combination of freshly pressed oil and light is that the oil gives off light when burned.

16. Ibid., p. 206. Nun is often a suffix on nouns, and is not always a part of the root.
17. Ibid., p. 1052.
18. Ibid., pp. 530-533. Gesenius admits (p. 532) that the Bible claims that *Levi* (לֵוִי) is under the root *lvh* (לוה) but suggests other possibilities. It would appear best to follow the Biblical affirmation of the etymology of the word, as *lvh* is mentioned at the patriarch's name at birth (Genesis 29:34), as well as this tribe "being joined" to the priests (Numbers 18:2). Thus, the name at birth was both descriptive of Leah's desire to "be joined" to her husband, and was also prophetic, in that this tribe "became joined" to the priests.
19. Ibid., pp. 419-420. The word *etzah* (עֵצָה, counsel) is listed under the root יעץ and the word עֵץ (*etz*, tree) under the root עצה, on pp. 781-782. It would be better to combine the two roots with all their meanings under one root.
20. Koehler, Ludwig and Walter Baumgartner, Revised by Walter Baumgartner and Johann Jacob Stamm, with assistance from Benedikt Hartmann, Zeev Ben-Hayyim, Eduard Yechezkel Kutscher, and Philippe Reymond, Tr. & Ed. Under the supervision of M. E. J. Richardson, *The Hebrew and Aramaic Lexicon of the Old Testament*, CD-ROM Edition, (Konniklijke Brill NV, Leiden, The Netherlands, 1994-2000). #10087 *tolea* (תּוֹלֵעָה), see also #9813 *shani* (שָׁנִי).
21. Gesenius, p. 1040. He says that the word refers to scarlet "prop. *coccis ilicis*, which attaches itself to leaves and twigs of *quercus coccifera*; the dried body of female yields colouring matter."
22. Ibid., pp. 856-857.

Chapter 12: The Law of Identification: From Hormah to Jericho: Finishing the Desert Journey Well—Learning the Lessons at Last!

1. Gesenius, William, Edward Robinson tr., with Francis Brown, S. R. Driver, and Charles A. Briggs, *A Hebrew and English Lexicon of the Old Testament*, (Oxford: Clarendon Press,

1968), pp. 355-356. Here *Hormah* (חָרְמָה), meaning "dedication," <u>*herem*</u>, meaning "dedicated," and <u>*haram*</u>, meaning "to devote" are all from the same root (חרם).

2. <u>Ibid</u>., pp. 55-57. Gesenius places the Amorites under the root אמר, but misses the connection and suggests that it could mean "mountain-dwellers." Our procedure has been to favor the meaning of the root, which makes a better connection between the material and spiritual spheres of existence, rather than their dwelling place.
3. Solomon, Charles R., *Handbook to Happiness*, (Wheaton: Tyndale Publishers, 1989), p. 68.
4. <u>Gesenius</u>, pp. 793-796.
5. Ibid., pp. 784-785.
6. <u>Ibid</u>., pp. 972-973.
7. *The Law of Identification*, a course taught by Dr. Bob Dean at Jacksonville Theological Seminary, Jacksonville, Florida.
8. <u>Gesenius</u>, p.14. Here Gesenius lists Aaron without a Hebrew root. It would appear best to locate this name under the root *,rn* (ארן). Under this root on pp. 74-75 is *aron* (אָרוֹן), which means coffin, as the coffin in which Joseph was buried (Genesis 50:26), and the Ark of the Covenant (Exodus 25:16). Aaron thus symbolizes man as useful for bringing God's presence because he is empty of everything else.
9. <u>Ibid</u>., p.15. Here the Hebrew root is *,wb* (אוב). Through this root a medium for a false spirit is compared to a leather skin bottle that carried water. He is a body covered by skin and he has a spirit (symbolized by water) inside.
10. <u>Ibid</u>., pp. 555 and 383. On page 555 Gesenius lists Moab apart from a root and says that its etymology is uncertain. On page 383 there is a root (יאב), of which Moab could be a participle of the Hiphil stem. In this case the meaning would be "one who lusts after (things)." This is appropriate in the light of the later seduction by the Moabite women (Numbers 15:1) and Eglon, the extremely fat King of Moab in Judges 3:17. It would appear best to consider that the Moabites represent carnal desires.

11. Ibid., pp. 766-770. The root (עמם) has as its basic idea proximity, and refers to common people, kinsman, the preposition with, and Ammonites. It appears best to view Ammonites as representing opposition that comes from our relatives.
12. Ibid., p.75. Here Gesenius lists Arnon alphabetically without being under a root. He does suggest right there that it be considered to mean "the rushing, roaring stream," following the Hebrew root *rnn* (רנן) on p. 943.
13. Ibid., pp. 966-967.
14. Ibid., pp. 362-364. The Modern Hebrew word for an accountant is Baal-Heshbon.
15. Ibid., p. 728.
16 Ibid., p. 143.
17. Ibid., pp. 118-119.
18 The name Balaam has four major consonants in it. Therefore it needs to be broken down into two roots with the same second and third consonants. Thus, it appears best to take as the first root *bll* (בלל) and the second root ʿ *mm* (עמם). The first root is found in Gesenius on page 117, and means to mingle, mix, or confuse. According to Genesis 11:9, Babel (Babylon) is from this root. The other root, found on pages 766-770, means the people. Thus we have as the full meaning, "the mixer of the peoples." This is just what Balaam did to bring judgment on Israel.
19. Ibid., pp. 128-129. There are two major meanings behind this root: to burn, and to be dull-hearted, or brutish. These ideas can combine in that those that are always burning with anger; lust, etc. are usually unreceptive to correction from others or from God.
20. Ibid., p. 810. Gesenius follows the Egyptian and renders this name as "the Negro." However, following our principle of splitting up long roots into smaller ones, we can form the roots *pnh* (פנה, pp. 815-819) and *ḫsh* (חסה, p. 340). The first root means "to turn" and the second means "refuge." The idea here is "to turn for refuge" in God away from our temptations, see also pp. 118-119

21. Thomas, Major Ian W., *The Saving Life of Christ*, (Grand Rapids: Zondervan Publishing House, 1961), pp. 50-51.
22. Pfeiffer, Charles F., and Howard F. Vos, *The Wycliffe Historical Geography of Bible Land*, Chicago: Moody Press, 1970, p. 166.
23. Gesenius, pp. 864-866, 1072. Here, following our normal procedure, we divide Zarethan, (*tzarethan*, צָרְתָן) into two Hebrew roots: *tzrr* (צרר) and *tnn* (תנן). The latter root on page 1072 refers to lamenting or howling, as a jackal, since the jackal, or *tan* (תַּן), is from this root. The other root, combining all five different listings, has as its main idea oppression. Thus, our understanding of this city would be "the howling of oppression."
24. *Handbook to Happiness*, p. 34.
25. Gesenius, pp. 164-166.
26. Keyes, Dick, *Beyond Identity: Finding Your Self in the Image and Character of God*, (Ann Arbor: Servant Books, 1984), p.80.
27. Ibid., p.81.
28. Ibid., pp. 83-84.
29. Anderson, Neil T., and Mike and Julia Quarles, *Freedom from Addiction*, (Ventura, California: Regal Books, 1996), p.126.
30. Ibid., p. 127.
31. Ibid., p. 129.
32. Ibid., p. 129.
33. In Spanish the expression which means that a person has no scruples, whatsoever is the following: "El no tiene vergüenza." This means literally, "He has no shame."
34. The Greek here is *metamorphousthe* (*μεταμορφοῦσθε*), from which the English word metamorphosis comes, and it has the same meaning.
35. Thomas. p. 44.
36. Gesenius, pp. 924-926. Gesenius combines words from the root *rvh* (רוח) and *ryh* (ריח). These cognate roots are really one. There is a third root that may be added here, and that is *ravah* (רָוָח), in which the same consonants are pointes in

the normal way, instead of forming a hollow verb. The root idea here is that things are spacious, and one is not confined. Adding this root to the other two to form one root adds the extra truth that when we are filled with the Holy Spirit, there is no law against anything we want (Gal. 5:22-23). Although Gesenius lists Jericho apart on page 437 and claims the root and meaning are dubious, he still mentions that some scholars locate this city name under this root referring to the good fragrance of the area.

37. Matzat, Don, *Christ Esteem: Where the Search for Self-Esteem Ends*, (Eugene, Oregon: Harvest House, 1990), p. 168.
38. Ibid, pp. 168-169.
39. Ibid., p. 169.

BIBLIOGRAPHY

Anderson, Neil T., and Mike and Julia Quarles, *Freedom from Addiction*. Ventura, CaliforniaRegal Books, 1996.

Anderson, Neil T., *The Bondage Breaker*. Eugene, Oregon: Harvest House, 1993.

Baillie, John, *The Idea of Revelation in Recent Thought*, London: Geoffrey Cumberlege, Oxford University Press, 1956.

Bauer, Walter, translated and adapted by William F. Arndt and F. Wilbur Gingrich. *A Greek-English Lexicon of the New Testament and Other Early Christian Literature*. Chicago: The University of Chicago Press, 1971.

Barth, Karl, *Die Kirchliche Dogmatik, München*: 1932.

Beardsley, Monroe C. (ed.), *The European Philosophers from Descartes to Nietzsche*, New York:The Modern Library, 1992.

Berkhof, L., *Systematic Theology*, Grand Rapids, Michigan: Eerdmans, 1977.

Berkouwer, C. G., *Studies in Dogmatics: Man: The Image of God*. Grand Rapids, Michigan: Eerdmans, 1972.

Brooke, Tal, *When the World Will Be As One*. Eugene, Oregon: Harvest House, 1994.

Bruce, F. F., *The Epistle to the Hebrews*. Grand Rapids, Michigan: Eerdmans, 1970.

Caldecott, W. Shaw and James Orr, "Tabernacle," in *The International Standard Bible Encyclopedia*, Volume V. Grand Rapids, Michigan: Eerdmans, 1952.

Chafer, Lewis Sperry. *Grace: The Glorious Theme*. Grand Rapids, Michigan: Zondervan Publishing House, 1975.

Cherry, Matt & Mollen Matsumura, "Ten Myths About Secular Humanism," article from *Free Inquiry Magazine*, Volume 18, Number 1, found on the Internet at p. 2 at the following address: http://www.SecularHumanism.org/library/fi/

Colson, Charles. *Kingdoms in Conflict*. Zondervan Publishing House, 1987.

Crabbe, Dr. Larry. *Inside Out*, Colorado Springs: Navpress, 1988.

Crabb, Dr. Larry. *Men and Women: Enjoying the Difference*. Grand Rapids, Michigan: Zondervan Publishing House, 1991.

Dean, Dr. Bob, *The Law of Identification*, a course taught at the Jacksonville Theological Seminary, Jacksonville, Florida.

Dearman, J. Andrew, *Religion and Culture in Ancient Israel.* Peabody, Massachusetts: Hendrickson Publishers, 1992.

Delitzsch, Franz, *Commentary on the Old Testament, Vol. VI: Proverbs, Ecclestiastes, Song of Solomon*, Grand Rapids, Michigan: Eerdmans, Originally published 1872.

Descartes, René, "Meditation V: That God Necessarily Exists," in *Metaphysics: Readings and Reappraisals*, ed. by W. E. Kennick and Morris Lazerowitz, Englewood Cliffs, New Jersey: Prentiss-Hall, 1966), pp. 156-158.

Douglas, J.D. ed. "Egypt," from *The New Bible Dictionary*. Grand Rapids, Michigan: Eerdmans, 1965, pp. 337-353.

Dunteman, Paul L., "The Biblical Doctrine of Man," unpublished paper, submitted to Jacksonville Theological Seminary for the course entitled, The Doctrine of Man.

Dunteman, Paul L., "God's Revelations to Man: An Analysis and Discussion of God's Natural Revelation, Written Revelation, and Personal Revelation in Jesus of Nazareth," Unpublished paper submitted to Jacksonville Theological Seminary for the course entitled, The Doctrine of Scriptures.

Elliger, K. and W. Rudolph, *et al.*, *Biblia Hebraica Stuttgartensia*, Stuttgart: Deutsche Bibelstiftung, 1977.

Friberg, Barbara, Timothy Friberg, and Neva F. Miller. *Analytical Lexicon of the Greek New Testament*. Grand Rapids: Baker Books, 2000 (Electronic edition in Bibleworks 6.0).

Gerber, Charles, R. *Christ-Centered Self-Esteem: Seeing Ourselves Through God's Eyes.* Joplin, Missouri: College Press Publishing Company, 1996.

Gesenius, William, Edward Robinson tr., with Francis Brown, S. R. Driver, and Charles A. Briggs, *A Hebrew and English Lexicon of the Old Testament*. Oxford, Clarendon Press, 1968.

Grof, Christina, *The Thirst for Wholeness*, San Francisco: Harper Collins Publishers, 1993.

Hart, Dr. Archibald D., *Adrenaline and Stress*. Dallas: Word Publishing, 1995.

Hatch, Edwin, and Henry A. Redpath. *A Concordance to the Septuagint*, Graz, Austria: Akademische Druck-u Verlagsanstalt, 1975.

Hession, Roy, *The Calvary Road*. Ft. Washington, Pennsylvania: Christian Literature Crusade, 1955.

Hughes, Philip Edgcumbe, *The True Image: The Origin and Destiny of Man in Christ*. Grand Rapids, Michigan: Eerdmans, 1989.

Keil, C. F., *The Pentateuch, Volume II*. Grand Rapids, Michigan: Eerdmans, no year given.

Keyes, Dick. *Beyond Identity: Finding Your Self in the Image and Character of God*. Ann Arbor, Michigan: Servant Books, 1984.

Knowling, R. J., *The Acts of the Apostles*, in *The Expositor's Greek Testament* by W. Robertsom Nicoll (ed.), Grand Rapids, Michigan: Eerdmans, 1970, Vol. II.

Koehler, Ludwig and Walter Baumgartner, Revised by Walter Baumgartner and Johann Jacob Stamm, with assistance from Benedikt Hartmann, Zeev Ben-Hayyim, Eduard Yechezkel Kutscher, and Philippe Reymond, Tr. & Ed. Under the supervision of M. E. J. Richardson, *The Hebrew and Aramaic Lexicon of the Old Testament*, CD-ROM Edition in Bibleworks 6.0, (Konniklijke Brill NV, Leiden, The Netherlands, 1994-2000).

Kurtz, J. H., *Sacrificial Worship of the Old Testament*. Minneapolis: Klock & Klock, 1980.

Lisowsky, Gerhard, *Konkordanz Zum Hebraischen Alten Testament* (2nd edition), Stuttgart: Württembergische Bibelanstalt, 1958.

Matzat, Don, *Christ Esteem: Where the Search for Self-Esteem Ends.* Eugene, Oregon: Harvest House, 1990.

McClain, Alva J., and Herman Hoyt, ed. *Romans: The Gospel of Grace.* Chicago: Moody Press, 1973.

McDowell, Josh, *His Image My Image.* San Bernardino, California: Here's Life Publishers (Campus Crusade for Christ): 1988.

McNeil, John T., ed. *Calvin: Institutes of the Christian Religion.* Philadelphia: The Westminster Press, 1960.

Moulton, Rev. W. F., and Rev. A. S. Geden, *A Concordance to the Greek Testament*, Edinburgh, T. & T. Clark, 1974.

Nee, Watchman, *Love Not the World.* Ft. Washington, Pennsylvania: Christian Literature Crusade, 1972.

Nicoll, W. Robertson. *The Expositor's Greek Testament.* Grand Rapids, Michigan: Eerdmans, 1970.

Norman, J. G. G. and A. R. Millard, "Hamath," in *New Bible Dictionary*, Downers Grove, Illinois: Intervarsity Press, 1996.

Olford, Stephen F., *The Tabernacle: Camping with God.* Neptune, New Jersey: Loixeaux Bros., 1973.

Rahlfs, Alfred, *Septuaginta* (8th edition), Stuttgart: Württembergische Bibelanstalt, 1935.

Solomon, Charles R., *Handbook to Happiness.* Wheaton, Illinois: Tyndale House Publishers, 1989.

Thomas, Major W. Ian, *The Saving Life of Christ.* Grand Rapids, Michigan: Zondervan Publishing House, 1961.

Thiessen, Henry Clarence. *Introductory Lectures in Systematic Theology.* Grand Rapids, Michigan: Eerdmans, 1963.

Whiteley, D. E. H. *The Theology of St. Paul.* Philadelphia: Fortress Press, 1971.

Wiesner, Rabbi Naphtali, *In his Own Image.* Brooklyn, New York: Mesorah Publications, 1992.

Breinigsville, PA USA
18 September 2009

224329BV00001B/5/P